SOUTH AMERICA

Arthur S. Morris

BARNES & NOBLE BOOKS
TOTOWA, NEW JERSEY

SOUTH

AMERICA

The photograph reproduced on the title-page is of Lake Calima, the reservoir created by the Alto Anchicaya dam, which provides a source of power for Cali industries. It also serves to control flooding on the Cauca river.

Library of Congress Cataloging in Publication Data

Morris, Arthur Stephen
   South America.
   Bibliography: p.
   Includes index.
   1. South America.   1. Title.
   F2208.M65   980   79-13729
   ISBN 0-389-20243-6

First published 1979 by Hodder and Stoughton Educational
Second edition 1981
Second impression 1985

Copyright © 1981 Arthur S. Morris

Published in the U.S.A. 1982 by
BARNES & NOBLE BOOKS
81 ADAMS DRIVE
TOTOWA, NEW JERSEY, 07512

Printed and bound in Great Britain.

Preface

It is common for Northern Hemisphere readers to think of all South America as a fairly homogeneous unit, all of it belonging to the Iberian languages and civilization, all in the Third World category, nearly all of it characterized by simple economies, including subsistence agriculture and the production of one or a few items for export. The present text is intended to correct such views, by demonstrating the diversity of landscapes, societies and economies in the continent. In addition to presenting the physical, economic and other patterns, some attempt is made at analysis, based on the author's firmly held view that the best mnemonic for a geographical pattern is understanding of the underlying processes.

As the book is intended for readers not familiar with Spanish or Portuguese, only a limited number of foreign terms is used, with italics and accent marks except where an English form is well known. A glossary is included in the appendixes.

Any regional text in geography is inevitably, to a considerable extent, indebted to a wide variety of authors and to practical help from many sides. I cannot list here all those Latin Americans who have aided me while in the regions or my colleagues who have helped in many ways over the years. They must accept this non-specific note of my gratitude. I must particularly thank Mr I. Tilbrook of Chipping Campden and Dr R.P. Beckinsale of Oxford who taught me geography, and the latter especially for suggesting this book. My wife also deserves credit for forbearance, and for designing the maps.

Preface to the Second Edition

Three years is perhaps a short time for important changes in the geography of a region, even for countries such as Brazil whose cities are growing at an explosive 4.3% per annum. My own ideas have matured with respect to some themes since the First Edition of this book however, and I have been able to glean some more information on others. The systematic chapters have all been modified, by introducing for example a section on ecology in the physical geography chapter, re-interpreting urban growth patterns in Chapter 5, and reforming the discussion of socio-economic development in regions and nations in Part III. In regional chapters, the statistics and some other details have been updated and the chapters on Ecuador and Venezuela re-written. The general level of discussion and thus the intended readership remain however the same.

Acknowledgments

The author and publisher wish to thank the following for permission to reproduce the illustrations in this book:

Booker McConnell Ltd, plates 35 and 36; the Brazilian Embassy, plates 5, 6, 7, 30, 31 and 34; Dr Myron Frankman, plates 37 and 39; Spectrum Colour Library, plates 3 and 22 (photographs by C.E.C. Gannon); John Topham Picture Library, cover photograph, plates 1, 14, 21, 41 and 43 (photographs by Nicholas Sapieha); David Wickers, plates 8, 9, 12, 13, 17, 23, 25, 38 and 40.

The remaining photographs were taken by the author.

Contents

Plates

Maps and Diagrams

Introduction

The weight of South America in world affairs is relatively slight. It is a continent of substantial size, with area comparable to that of North America, but its *oecumene*, the inhabitable area at the present stage of technological progress, is quite restricted. Areas of very slight population include the cold deserts of the mountain tops and middle-latitude Patagonia; hot deserts, especially along the west coast; and the upland parts of the hot and humid Amazon Basin, where alluvium is not provided by rivers and soils are infertile. Collectively these areas cover more than half the continent, and have defied man's attempts at permanent settlement to date. Thus the impression of the continent as a region of wide open spaces awaiting the settler is not accurate. Population figures of 219 million in 1975, compared to a resident population of nearly 213 million in the United States alone, should not lead us to suppose enormous possibilities for growth.

Nevertheless, the importance of the continent is growing. It is a part of the Third World, which also includes most of Africa, the Middle East and South-East Asia. As such, it is a region which attracts increasingly the attention of the developed countries, for a variety of reasons. First, there is competition amongst the major powers for political influence among these countries, which can give their support to big-power policies in international assemblies and litigation as well as in war.

Second, there is an economic interest in these countries of Latin America, on the part of industrial powers which need their contribution of raw materials and foods in order to supply their manufacturing and processing enterprises. Japan, North America and Western Europe all rely on South American contributions of food and materials. On the other hand, these same industrial countries plus the Soviet bloc all seek to promote their own industrial products as exports to the continent, wherever possible exporting directly from home to a South American market, and if not permitted to do so, penetrating it by setting up subsidiaries on the continent.

Finally, much of the renewed interest in the region must derive from its evidence of internal change. There are all signs, social, economic and political, of a people in the process of development, a process more all-embracing than economic development, involving a challenge to old ideals and attitudes on class, religion and the State.

The violent political revolutions which have affected Bolivia (1952) and Cuba (1959) are indices of the forces for change, which are currently repressed to some extent in almost every country by military governments. Chile, with something of a democratic tradition, and Uruguay, where democracy had brought some aspects of the welfare state into being early in this century, have both had their floodtide of change abruptly stopped in recent years by military take-overs. To the pessimist this might seem merely a continuation of the secular situation of governmental disorder and impermanence, but there is evidence that dictatorial governments are having greater tasks because of the spread of political consciousness, and cannot continue indefinitely without popular support.

This political consciousness is itself a function of the rise in education, health and other welfare standards over the continent, which stimulates interest in a better life, the so-called revolution of rising expectations. It is also a function of urbanization, a universal phenomenon but one which has particular force in Latin America because of the rapidity of its occurrence. Within a generation, many families have pulled up their roots and moved from completely rural to urban communities; the factory, or unemployment, has replaced work on a farm; the radio and newspaper replace illiteracy; concern for personal status replaces an unthinking acceptance of humble positions in a strongly stratified rural society.

To systematize the interrelated phenomena of this society in motion, and the physical and human factors involved in its varied face from one country and from one region to another, is the intent of the following chapters.

1. Physical Geography

The continent of South America occupies 17.85 million sq km, making it slightly smaller than North America but still a great land mass, far larger than Europe west of the Urals, which covers 10 million sq km.

STRUCTURE

In tectonic and structural terms this is an important continental block, and one exhibiting considerable activity, for its nearest relative, as predicted long ago by Wegener and recently substantiated by a variety of lines of evidence, is the shield block of Africa, from which it was separated in the Mesozoic era. The central unit of the South American continent is the Brazil—Guiana shield, occupying half the continent and most of Brazil and the Guianas, covered often with thin sediments or volcanic sheets, but not undergoing any kind of folding after the Assynt orogeny of late pre-Cambrian and early Cambrian time.

This shield is relatively young compared with the African and North American ones, and radioactive decay dating places most of its rocks as less than 1000 million years old. It seems to have grown from an ancient core in the Bolivian frontier region of Chiquitos, and to have added mountains in the pre-Cambrian, including the Espinhaço and original (now re-uplifted) Serra da Mantiqueira mountains, in the southeast of Brazil. To the south of Brazil there is another great shield unit, no doubt related to it, the Patagonian block, also locally covered with sediments and volcanics. In the north, the Guiana

section of the shield is separated by the rift valley of the lower Amazon, opened out in Tertiary time.

The Andes

Flanking the shield to west and north are high mountains. The Andes are the world's greatest range of continuously high (over 3000 m) mountains, along a line which extends from Tierra del Fuego, to Venezuela and through Colombia into Central America, linking to the North American systems. These mountains are of varying age, ancient remnants dating back to the early Palaeozoic, but the present height of the range and its latest immense fold—fault system are of recent origin. Fold movements producing mountains in the location of the present ranges have their beginnings in late Mesozoic time, probably related to the initial separation of America and Africa, and they continue well into the Tertiary, pushing up high mountains to the west of the roots of older Palaeozoic ones. At this same time, the strains on the earth's crust of continental drift were relieved by basalt outpourings over $2\frac{1}{2}$ million sq km of the Paraná Plateau, in Brazil and neighbouring parts of Paraguay and Uruguay.

In late Tertiary time, after a period of relative quiescence, the mountain system was subject to massive uplift without much folding, to produce finally the present high mountains, fault-flanked horst blocks rather than fold mountains. Some of the recent uplift is shown in the high level marine terraces, now lying more than a thousand metres above present sea levels though only recently cut by the sea, along thousands of kilometres of the Pacific coast.

Pleistocene glaciation was highly localized and did not produce ice sheets as in the Northern Hemisphere, but valley glaciers over most of the Andes. In the far south a fairly large glacier system in the Patagonian Andes was able to expand and form broad piedmont glaciers occupying the southernmost Patagonian plateau and reaching the Pacific to the west. Morainic material is abundant in central and southern Chile, from the several glaciations, and terminal moraines hold back the glacial lakes of the Argentine Patagonia, lakes Viedma, Argentino, Buenos Aires and San Martín. To the present day, a combination of low temperature and heavy precipitation in the southernmost Andes permits a discontinuous icecap of more than 10000 sq km, between 46°S and 51°S latitude, on the Chilean side of the mountains. The fact that there are moraine dams west of the main line of mountains means that there is a difference between the peak line and the drainage divide, creating room for problems between the two frontier countries, Argentina and Chile.

Tectonic activity has not come to an end in the continent. All along the Andean line, from the Chile icefields north into Venezuela, there is volcanic activity, occasionally causing damage through hot ash deposits on farmlands. More important by far are the earthquakes which have devastated many Andean towns more than once, either by direct shock waves, or as in the dramatic Peruvian quake of 1970, through dislodging pieces of ice and rock which then form landslides.

Topographically, the Andes do not form a single line of mountains. Three or more lines, subparallel to one another, are common. Between them are high basins, filled in with masses of detritus from the surrounding slopes, and forming flat land areas which can be of great human significance. The altiplano of Bolivia and Peru is the largest of these upland basins, but there are many others on a smaller scale, and the advanced civilization of eastern Colombia, the Chibchas, occupied as centre, a series of small altiplanos formed in similar fashion on the eastern Cordillera of that country. In Colombia too, where the cordilleras open out more and present access to the Caribbean, major rivers occupy the intermontane valleys, the Cauca and Magdalena.

The plains

Between the Andes and the Shield there are broad expanses of plains country where the surface is of loose sediments of Tertiary or Recent origin, swept into the depression of the Shield adjacent to the mountains. Stream action and sheet floods form here an enormous flat surface, where there are indeed regional slopes to the east, though invisible to the human eye and creating the impression of a completely level plain. The Paraná—Paraguay system belongs to this region, as well as the Orinoco and Upper and Middle Amazon basin. The lower Amazon is of somewhat different nature, formed essentially as a rift valley, fault-lined, between the shield blocks.

In some places, the plains are broken by islands of old rock, either of the Shield or related to Andean structures. In the central part of the Bolivian Oriente, the thinness of the sedimentary fill allows low projections of ancient rocks in the Chiquitos uplands, and in northwest Argentina a series of fault blocks produces a basin and range topography something like that of the United States Southwest in the Sierras Pampeanas — literally the 'hills of the plains' — the mountain blocks parallel to but older than the Andes to the west of them; in the driest areas the basins have salt lakes and no drainage to the exterior.

Geomorphic processes

Landscapes in a largely tropical continent are often distinct from those of temperate lands. The rivers, for example, flood relatively easily over their floodplains, for the ultimate product of tropical weathering is clay particles, not silt or sand size particles in any quantity, so that levees are not built up in the same way as in middle latitudes for want of a heavy fraction, and the rivers soon swell beyond their beds. It has been claimed that meanders are less frequent on this account, though no proof of this can be adduced. Tropical weathering is also probably responsible for the frequency of falls and rapids on the rivers, as opposed to the more usual middle-latitude graded courses of streams.

The processes of tropical weathering down to clay account for the typical tropical sugar-loaf mountains, rounded or chunky mounds standing above a general level. These are the result of very deep weathering, penetrating up to a hundred metres, of a chemical nature, followed by erosion which eats out in selective fashion the mass of rock waste, penetrating deep where joints have allowed water to penetrate and act chemically, and leaving behind hills which are giant joint blocks into which the ground water has not been able to run. Mass movement in landslides is the main form of wearing down of the rounded bosses themselves, and occurs frequently with devastating results in such areas as the Rio de Janeiro district of Brazil, where the sugar-loaf hills, the *morros*, have been colonized by shanty-town populations.

CLIMATE

South American climate is everywhere dominated by the oceanic circulation cells, giving no room for separate continental cells; although the continent is large, it has no great width in middle latitudes where continental air masses might be generated by the greater cooling of land during winter seasons.

On the other hand, lack of a forceful continental circulation in summer or winter allows the middle-latitude dynamic forces produced by the encounter of tropical and arctic air to have considerable penetration into the tropics, so that depressions originating in the South Pacific may curl round Cape Horn or over the lower Southern Andes to move far north and form the Argentine *pamperos* which sometimes reach into the Chaco and cause cold waves as far north as the Amazon. The depression eye usually moves along the coast, causing year-round but particularly spring and autumn rainfall in the Pampas, and into southern Brazil as far as the Sao Paulo—Rio region, though also at times on to the shoulder of Brazil and Cape São Roque.

Some further special factors may be noted here. First, climatic types are all closer to the Equator than their Northern Hemisphere equivalents, partly because the world's heat equator is in the north, forming the base line for climatic zonation. Second, with only a small mass of subtropical land, there is nothing comparable to the Indian monsoon or even that of the Southeast United States.

Another important climatic factor is the strong northward-setting ocean currents, operating on both sides of the continent, and contributing to the northward displacement of climatic regions. The Humboldt current, a veritable river in the sea which moves millions of tonne/kilometres of water daily, is a determinant of the coastal desert which occupies the west coast from 30°S to near the Equator. Its cold water is due to both its origin and to upwelling of water along the coast, due to offshore winds and to a differential Coriolis effect on heavier, colder water.

This cold water cools the base of an already stable South Pacific anticyclonic airmass, forming ultrastable air all along a coast which curves round to the west, following the average anticyclone shape itself and helping in its prolongation northwards. On the other side, the Falklands current is equally cold, but can have less effect since it lies downwind of the continent. It is however true that the driest part of the Patagonian desert is adjacent to this coast.

The mountains themselves have their own climatic effects; forming such a high wall, they separate in good measure the circulation patterns on either side, allowing in particular little transfer of moisture from one side to the other. From the human utility point of view, the mountains are of the highest importance, for they penetrate into cool zones where moisture may be preserved as snow for the lowlands irrigation, and in the tropics they provide the oecumene for all man's activity.

REGIONAL CLIMATES

Amazon Basin

A continuous inflow of warm and humid air from the Atlantic in the easterly trades maintains an equatorial climate typified by thunderstorms at frequent intervals and little seasonality. However, there are dry spells everywhere of different length, and probably only the eastern Peru—westernmost Brazil zone has a year-round high level of rainfall. Cold waves from the south also serve to provide occasional variety in temperature. Georgetown, Guyana, provides an example of the coastal, central phase of this climate, while Belem, near the Equator, shows a Southern Hemisphere seasonality reflecting the fact that heat equator and intertropical front remain north of the geographical equator for most of the year.

On the western edge of the Amazon Basin, rainforest continues under a slightly less equatorial temperature regime, in the eastern mountain fringe of Peru and Bolivia. Rainforest of a similar nature occupies the coast of Brazil in Ilheus, Rio and Sao Paulo, fed by constant rains and having equable maritime temperatures.

Pacific Coast equatorial climes are similar to those of the Amazon Basin, though the main source of moisture is now no longer the easterlies, but winds blowing in from the Pacific, which give enormous annual totals of rainfall, over 3000 mm, to the coast and mountains which face them directly in Colombia and Ecuador.

Equatorial highlands

Rimming the Amazon Basin to north and west are high mountains with a complete set of climatic zones, equatorial to subarctic, though with special features because of their tropical location. The climatic differences are recognized in local usage, in most places denominated as *tierra caliente, tierra templada, tierra fría* (with European temperatures averaging around 15°C),

2 In the páramos, *from Bolivia to Venezuela, unusual plant types are found. Espeletias, woolly-leaved and with bright yellow flowers, shown here in the Andes of Mérida, Venezuela, are common in the Northern Andes*

and *páramos*, lying above the treeline and thus generally over 3500 m in altitude. *Tierra fría* and *tierra templada* are often considered to be optimal climatic locations, having the reputation of lands of eternal spring, because their seasonal variation, as in the neighbouring lowlands, is very slight, and the average temperatures very pleasant. This lack of seasonal variation is true even up into the *páramos*, as the figures for Cruz Loma, only three kilometres from Quito but 1000 m higher, indicate.

In fact one month is quite similar to any other in temperature, but diurnal temperature variation is great, with the rapid outward radiation of heat permitted by a thin cap of atmosphere, and comparatively little water vapour in this cap. Indians of the Ecuadorian altiplano wear woollen shawls and with good reason, for their nights are cold, regularly reaching freezing point at 3000 m altitude.

Tropical woodlands climates

Away from the permanent proximity of the inter-tropical convergence there are lower totals of precipitation and definite dry seasons, thus producing a less luxuriant forest cover or even grass and parkland landscapes. There are also larger seasonal variations in temperature, excluding some of the plant life of the equatorial belt which is not cold-tolerant. Cuiabá (see table) is typical of this climate, though it covers a large part of central Brazil and has many local variations on the central theme of seasonality.

The dry lands

A large dry zone occupies the whole northeast shoulder of Brazil; it has no single name, for it merges gradually with other zones and to the Brazilians is merely part of the backcountry, the *sertao*, of interior Brazil. Nor is it always very dry, receiving an irregular amount of rainfall of perhaps 500-700 mm per annum, though rain usually comes in the form of brief heavy showers which are of little benefit to plants, for they are soon dissipated, lost by runoff and evaporation from open soil surfaces.

For six months of the year the region is under the South Atlantic anticyclone, which retreats away in summer to allow the inter-tropical convergence zone disturbances to move in, but anticyclonic departure may be delayed thus provoking droughts of an extremely damaging

CLIMATIC DATA FOR REPRESENTATIVE STATIONS

Type and Station Lat. and elevation		Jan	Feb	Mar	Apr	May	Jun	Jul	Aug	Sep	Oct	Nov	Dec	Year
Equatorial Rainforest														
Belém, Brazil	T	25.2	25.0	25.1	25.5	25.8	25.8	25.8	25.9	25.8	26.1	26.3	25.9	25.7
1° 28′ S, 24 m	P	339	408	436	343	288	175	145	127	118	92	86	175	2732
Georgetown, Guyana	T	26.3	26.4	26.8	27.1	27.0	26.7	26.7	27.2	27.7	27.7	27.4	26.7	27.0
6° 48′ N, 2 m	P	251	122	113	178	296	346	281	185	88	98	147	313	2419
Tropical Forest and Campo Cerrado														
Cuiabá, Brazil	T	26.4	26.2	26.2	25.9	24.3	23.0	22.5	24.8	26.6	27.0	26.8	26.5	25.5
15° 35′ S, 171 m	P	213	200	222	106	46	14	9	27	48	124	161	208	1378
Equatorial Highlands														
Quito Ecuador	T	13.0	13.0	12.9	13.0	13.1	13.0	12.9	13.1	13.2	12.9	12.8	13.0	13.0
0° 13′ S, 2818 m	P	124	135	159	180	130	49	18	22	83	133	110	107	1250
Cruz Loma, Ecuador	T	6.1	6.5	6.7	6.8	6.4	6.2	6.1	6.0	6.1	6.4	6.7	6.4	6.4
0° 13′ S, 3950 m	P	198	185	241	236	221	122	36	23	86	147	124	160	1780
West Coast Desert														
Lima, Peru	T	21.5	22.3	21.9	20.1	17.8	16.0	15.3	15.1	15.4	16.3	17.7	19.4	18.2
12° 30′ S, 11 m	P	1.2	0.4	0.6	0.1	0.5	0.8	2.0	2.3	1.2	0.4	0.1	0.4	10.0
La Serena, Chile	T	18.2	18.4	16.9	14.9	13.4	12.1	11.7	12.0	12.7	14.0	15.5	17.0	14.7
29° 54′ S, 35 m	P	0.1	0.8	0.6	2.6	21.9	43.7	29.7	23.2	6.0	3.7	0.7	0.3	133
Argentine Deserts														
Trelew, Argentina	T	20.6	20.0	17.3	13.2	9.6	6.1	6.0	7.6	10.2	14.0	17.3	19.3	13.5
43° 14′ S, 39 m	P	6	14	17	11	19	11	15	13	14	17	13	14	165
Mendoza, Argentina	T	23.6	22.5	20.2	15.6	11.5	8.1	7.6	10.2	13.9	16.7	20.4	22.7	16.1
32° 53′ S, 769 m	P	28	21	22	10	11	8	7	10	14	23	20	23	197
Humid Pampas														
Bahía Blanca, Arg.	T	20.6	20.5	17.8	15.0	11.1	8.3	7.8	7.7	11.2	13.9	17.0	17.7	14.3
30° 00′ S, 10 m	P	40	67	80	65	52	25	30	31	77	45	66	43	621
Córdoba, Arg.	T	24.2	23.2	20.7	16.8	13.8	11.0	10.6	12.3	15.1	17.9	20.8	23.1	17.4
31° 24′ S, 425 m	P	101	88	93	39	24	10	8	15	29	77	88	108	680
Artigas, Uruguay	T	26.6	26.1	23.6	19.1	16.2	13.9	13.6	15.4	17.0	19.2	22.6	25.2	19.9
30° 24′ S, 117 m	P	115	102	122	139	103	127	81	64	123	149	81	118	1325
Middle Latitude West Coast														
Valdivia, Chile	T	17.0	16.4	14.5	11.8	9.7	8.2	7.7	8.0	9.3	11.5	13.3	15.3	11.9
39° 48′ S, 9 m	P	65	69	115	212	376	414	374	301	214	119	122	107	2489
Subtropical Uplands														
Curitiba, Brazil	T	20.1	20.1	19.2	17.1	14.3	12.9	12.1	13.4	14.5	15.9	17.7	19.3	16.3
25° 26′ S, 949 m	P	183	149	106	75	88	104	69	85	124	122	120	138	1363

NOTES: *Temperature in degrees Centigrade, precipitation in millimetres.*
Both temperature and precipitation are in the form of monthly means.

3 Arid landscape. Desert scrub on the Bolivian altiplano, with bunch-grass cover on the hills behind

kind, because this is a region of dense agricultural population, as it has been since the time of colonial plantations.

The West Coast subtropical desert is of somewhat different type. Here the anticyclone is stronger, reinforced in the east Pacific by the flanking action of the Andes and by cold water alongshore. The result is complete desert, with no recorded rainfall at some points in the Atacama, and brief storms accounting for most of the record further north and south. At either end, the desert has its transition, rapidly to the north in Ecuador, more gradually in Chile in the Mediterranean and subtropical steppe zones of that country. Lima, Peru, is an example of the climate of the central desert; La Serena, at 30°S, of the transition through steppe to the Mediterranean climate north of Santiago.

East of the Andes there are other desert or semi-desert zones in the west of Argentina, with 200-500 mm of rainfall. Here the Pacific anticyclone is not active but the mountains themselves provide a substantial rainshadow, not from the immediate west but from the southwest where South Pacific depressions might otherwise enter. The region also holds an interior position with respect to the Atlantic depressions. A lee effect from the Andes continues on into Patagonia, which is also largely desert, from the Andean foot to the Atlantic. Foehn winds are present all along the mid-latitude Andes, most noticeably in central western Argentina, where the sucking in of small quantities of hot and dry air in the Zonda to form a shrivelling northern wind may cause complete crop loss in the agricultural oases of Mendoza and San Juan.

Examples of the Patagonian and interior desert climates are given in the figures for Trelew and Mendoza.

A last dry zone is that along the north coast, starting in Venezuela with the region of Cumaná, and continuing along the northward-projecting pieces of Venezuelan coast and the offshore islands of Curaçao and Bonaire, into the Guajira peninsula of Colombia. The cause of drought here seems to lie in the divergent nature of the tradewinds along this coast, aided by differential friction of land and sea on winds which are sub-parallel to the coast.

Pampas climates

The Argentine Pampas, Uruguay and to some extent Paraguay and Southeast Brazil, are all affected by similar airmass systems. Through most of the year, the predominant influence is that of depressions moving along the ocean front, into Brazil's coastal region and as far north as Rio de Janeiro and Bahia. These give rainfall throughout the winter half of the year, and are balanced by summer thunderstorm rainfall. Bahia Blanca and Córdoba are examples of the fringes of the Pampas to the south and west, where the winter depressions carry little moisture, and Artigas in Uruguay, an example of the northern edge, where the depressions are dominant and cause equinoctial maxima, unusual in this latitude where the world pattern would suggest a simple summer maximum of rainfall.

Typical middle-latitude depression features are well known from this region. The *pampero* is a wind resulting from the passage of a cold front northwards at the rear of a depression, and causing dust storms when strong and when the soil is dry and loose. During the summer, the region may be more influenced by tropical air from the South Atlantic or even from the Amazon basin, since a general low pressure cell develops within the Chaco of northern Argentina.

Middle-latitude forest climates

An important area of southern Chile has climate similar to that of British Columbia or coastal Northwestern Europe, with a high frequency of depressions throughout the year, and high rainfall with constant cloud cover and moderate temperatures. This incidence of Polar front

depressions is responsible for precipitation of around 2500 mm annually at such stations as Valdivia, providing for rapid forest growth. Further south, the climate continues wet, but deteriorates in temperature and increases in wind force to give one of the world's most inhospitable climates to the Chilean section of Tierra del Fuego.

Another midlatitude forest climate is found in southern Brazil, where the Paraná Plateau basalts lie at levels around 1000 m and support a coniferous vegetation dominated by the Paraná pine, *Araucaria angustifolia,* related to the Chilean pine, *Araucaria araucana,* a member of the Chilean forest assemblage. This forest is best developed in the provinces of Paraná and Santa Catarina; the plateau receives regular winter frost and snowfall is often possible in the southern parts, precipitation totalling from 1200 to 1700 mm. Curitiba, for example, has 1360 mm annually. The source of the through-year regular precipitation is the South Atlantic, though the rainfall mechanism may be thunderstorm or depression in type.

SOILS AND VEGETATION (fig. 1)

Soil types exhibit variations in correspondence with vegetation, climate and topography—geology, forming with these elements a unified physical system. In South America there are large areas where this system has been left to act with little modification by man. Over the most favourable agricultural land however, and in an increasingly large number of tropical forest locations where only temporary agricultural use is made of the soil, man has destroyed the cycle of soil and vegetation, taking out important consituents such as potash, phosphorus and nitrogen from the soil by burning and cultivating, opening the soil to the sun's direct rays, destroying the vegetation, and in sum causing soil breakdown and replacement of the climax vegetation by other types which are usually of less luxuriance and variety.

The humid tropics

Much of the Amazon Basin has selvas vegetation, a superb forest of very tall, large trees over 40 m high, mostly evergreen hardwoods, often supported by giant buttress roots, and substrata and lower levels of giant palms and bam-

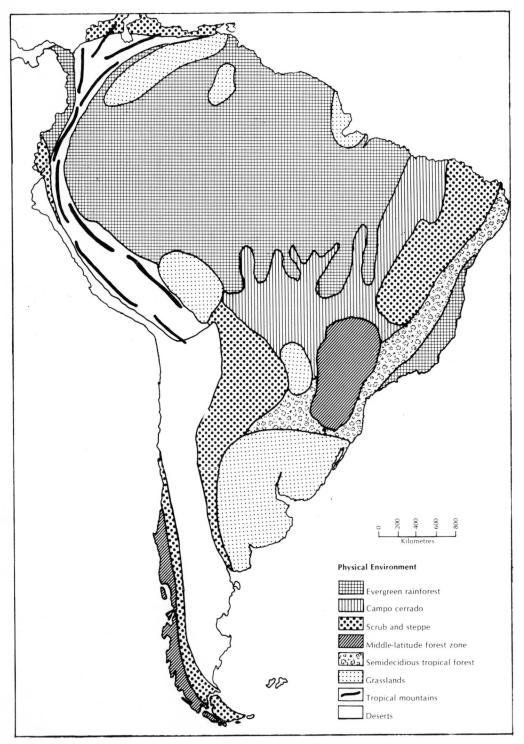

Fig. 1 Physical environment

boos, shade-tolerant hardwoods, and very little surface cover because of the dense shade conditions, so that the surface is quite open, giving a cathedral-like, vaulted aspect. Lianas and epiphytes of many kinds are common, a function of the need for light which drives plants up in search of the sun. Enormous variety of plant life is found, including at least 2500 species in the Amazon basin. Locally one giant tree type is fairly common, as in the Mora or Greenheart forests of Guyana, but more typical is a very wide species mix.

The soils underlying this exuberant vegetative cover are variable in fertility. On the alluvial flats they are good, rich soils, and permit the selvas to achieve full development. On upland areas, or even on high terraces above the rivers, forest cover is less abundant and soils are much poorer, tending towards lateritic types high in aluminium and iron sesquioxides and low in the soluble bases. They are covered with a thin humus layer which breaks down quickly from leaf fall under conditions of high heat and humidity and, when native forest is removed, there is rapid humus loss exposing the soil to the dangers of depletion and erosion.

Tropical woodlands and the campo cerrado
On the upland areas of the Brazilian Shield south of the selvas, there are climates similar to the equatorial but with a dry season, giving a unique vegetation cover intermediate between forest and savanna, with low gnarled trees and with substantial ground cover because the trees do not absorb all the incoming light as in a forest.

Something of a controversy exists over the origin and nature of this *campo cerrado* forest, which is an apparently drought-adapted vegetation in what is not a very dry climate, and alongside large stretches of forest which are intercalated with it. *Cerrado* was first studied scientifically in the late nineteenth century, and its xerophytic appearance attributed to seasonal drought and fires. This view was challenged in the 1940s when Brazilian scientists found that many *cerrado* plants do not wilt in the dry season and in fact transpire freely from their leaves because of their ability to tap water from the depth of two metres or more. Since then it has been shown that *cerrado* covers poorer soils and forest richer ones within the general *cerrado* area, and that this xeromorphic vegetation is

really an adaptation to lack of nutrients in an environment with abundant light and water. M.M. Cole in the 1960s showed a correspondence between geomorphology and vegetation since flat plateaux often had poorer soils and *cerrado,* while forest occurred on dissected slopes where nutrients were exposed. But the correlation is only moderate and it is perhaps better to show soil fertility as the main determinant, though fire must also enter into the equation especially at the edges where *cerrado* is maintained by man.*

South of the *cerrado* and along the river valleys tributary to the Amazon from the south, as well as along the southeast coast and in the Bahia mountains, there is a richer forest, intermediate between selvas and *cerrado.* It has many of the rainforest species, especially those of the understoreys, in more dwarf form. Forest height may reach thirty metres and the upper storey is of mainly deciduous trees, reflecting the annual drought. Below this, profiting from the more abundant light than in the selvas, are evergreen shrubs and low trees.

Dry lands
In the complete deserts of the Atacama and coastal Peru, there is virtually no vegetation at low levels except along watercourses and on the *lomas,* low hills which attract condensation water from the frequent sea fogs and allow ephemerals to flourish during the winter. At higher levels, the Pampa del Tamarugal of the interior Chilean desert is so named because of its former cover of *tamarugos,* xerophytes of the acacia family. Less arid deserts in Patagonia, western Argentina, the Chaco and northeast Brazil all have some vegetation cover.

In Patagonia it is typically bunch grass, though on gravelly soils this may be replaced by thorn scrub or bare surfaces. In western and northwestern Argentina thorn scrub is typical, waist high or lower in the driest regions, but reaching to a man's height where moisture is more abundant, though still useless except as firewood and feed for goats. A somewhat similar scrub is found on the red and ochre soils of

* The arguments are admirably summarized by Roberto Goodland, 'Ecological Studies of Cerrado Vegetation', pp. 40-53, in *The Savanna Controversy*, Savanna Research Series No. 15, Geography Department, McGill University, Montreal, 1970.

Brazil's Nordeste, where it is called *caatinga*, though with a tropical location there is a greater variety of species here including cacti, bromeliads and 'fat-bellied trees' which store moisture in their trunks. *Caatinga* presents a smiling aspect in the wet season, but during the drought as da Cunha describes it, gives an even more formidable impression of aridity than a bare sand desert.

> The searing drought settles on the backlands; the burning air is sterilized; the earth, cracked, grilled, turns to stone. The Northeaster roars in the desert; and like a lacerating haircloth, the *caatinga* extends over the earth in spiny branches . . . but with reduced metabolism, the plants, aestivating and holding life in store, feed on reserves made in the good season and live through the drought, ready to transform themselves in the sparkle of spring.
>
> *Euclides da Cunha,* Os Sertoes, *p. 120, in his* Obra Completa, *Vol. II (Jose Aguilar Editora, Rio de Janeiro, 1966)*

In the Chaco, on seasonally flooded land near the river there is a cover of savanna grasses, tall but not nutritious, and palms such as the caranday, but on drier lands the climax cover seems to be an open forest of quebracho, a slow-growing hardwood which is still being removed for timber and tannin extraction, and whose destruction must lead to irreversible deterioration of the already poor dry soils.

Tropical grasslands
Best known of South America's grasslands are perhaps the Llanos of Colombia and Venezuela, reaching through the Rio Branco country into the Rupununi savanna of Guyana. They are grass-covered without any tree cover over large stretches, because of a difficult combination of drainage and climatic conditions. Excesses of stagnant water during annual wet seasons kill the roots of trees, and in the dry season trees cannot easily survive without access to groundwater. Trees grow typically only as gallery forest, along the river banks, where drainage is better because of slight levees, and where the water supply is yet quite safe.

Similar tropical grasslands, all suffering from some seasonal flooding, are to be found in the Beni, in central eastern Bolivia, on the Brazilian Rio Negro north of the Amazon, and in the Pantanal zone of the upper Paraguay river in Paraguay and Brazil. Poor drainage is a common factor in their origin, with no doubt grazing, fires, and seasonal drought as accessory elements. Where savanna is maintained in well-drained regions, such as the Gran Pajonal of eastern Peru, fire and grazing must play a major role.

Pampas
The middle-latitude grasslands so typical of central North America, the midwestern prairies and the High Plains to the west, have their equivalent in the Argentine—Uruguayan Pampas. In the east the Pampas have neutral or slightly acid soils, deep, well supplied with nutrients and rich in humus. Their natural cover was a variety of tall grasses, somewhat coarser than the European ones which were introduced and now replace them. This replacement and improvement of pastures seem to have been in large measure due to the constant unselective grazing and fertilizing action of herds of cattle, though a certain density of cattle must have been necessary for this to happen since the wild cattle present since the 1500s had not managed to accomplish much. The process was still active when Darwin visited the Pampas, as he records:

> from a coarse herbage we passed on to a carpet of fine green verdure. I at first attributed this to some change in the nature of the soil, but the inhabitants assured me . . . the whole was to be attributed to the manuring and grazing of the cattle.
>
> *Charles Darwin,* Journal of Researches into the Natural History and Geology of the Countries visited during the voyage of H.M.S. Beagle *(Harper & Row, New York, 1846, p. 151)*

Further west there is a transition through a belt of low grasses and poorer, more alkaline soils, to the western thorn-scrub deserts.

Temperate forests
Very high rainfall and podzolic soils comparable to those of Western Europe permit a dense, fast-growing forest of conifers and deciduous trees in southern Chile south of about 38°S. The south Chilean forest is composed of species endemic to this area and unrelated, though visually quite similar, to their Northern Hemisphere equivalents. Several species of southern beech, *Nothofagus*, a deciduous broadleaf tree, are important, together with conifers such as

Podocarpus (*manio* and *llenge*), and the monkey puzzle tree, *Araucaria araucana,* on high mountain slopes. The so-called larch, *Fitzroya cupressoides,* is an excellent building timber of the region and reaches sixty metres in height.

Another forest resembling the Chilean in having important stands of timber-producing species, is the Paraná Plateau, where the widespread large member is the Paraná pine, growing to thirty metres or more, with understoreys of laurels and below them in valley sites the *yerba mate* tree, *Ilex paraguariensis,* whose native habitat extends west into Paraguay and more tropical climes.

ECOLOGY AND CONSERVATION

In both rural and urban areas of South America there is a need for more attention to the way in which man affects native flora and fauna, soils and water courses, and the reciprocal effects of nature on man's activities. Ecology is the study of relationships between different elements of the biosphere, tending to concentrate on the point of view of man and his specific relationship with the environment. Conservation signifies the rational use by man of the environmental resources, native and non-native, so as not to destroy them while using them. We may discuss separately for convenience, rural and urban aspects of the problem, though there are of course major overlaps between them.

Rural areas
Human use of the land of South America has extended over perhaps 50 000 years, and has therefore produced major changes in the natural environment of the most intensely occupied areas. In the present century however, the pace of exploitation and change has accelerated drastically and the effects are more fundamental.

One area of intense human use is in the Andean uplands. Here tillage and cattle farming on steep slopes with dry soils, often sandy or of loose volcanic ash, tree-felling for construction, fuel or land clearance, have resulted in a tree-less windblown landscape and parched, eroded soils. We have no information on the former extent of forest, but the ease with which blue gum (Eucalyptus globulus) and Monterrey pine can now be grown at heights of up to 4000 m suggest

that the valleys between the mountains, from Chile to Colombia, and even the lower *páramos*, were once tree-covered.

Today tree-cover is being maintained or increased in these areas, mostly with the species cited, but this leaves large areas unprotected from further degradation, especially where there are intensively worked farms. Fields are ploughed parallel to the slopes instead of across them, few animals are kept and there is little manure especially on the marginal fields, which can only be cultivated once every few years. In wetter areas this cultivation is preceded by burning off brush and coarse grasses, which causes a long-term loss of nitrogen from the soil. Correction of this situation requires farmer education, afforestation, and withdrawing of the worst areas from farming altogether, but most of all agrarian reform to give farmers an incentive for change.

A completely different environment is that of the Amazon selva, an area of 4.5 million sq km. It has been only lightly exploited before this century, and then only on the richer *varzea* soils. In this forest, the natural balance achieved is one now recognized as fragile, in which any major changes are likely to be non-reversible. Although the soils are inherently infertile on the *terra firme*, and carry little nutrients, the forest has various adaptive mechanisms. It has a storied canopy which reduces raindrop impact on soil and keeps out the direct sun's rays which would burn up humus. Epiphytes and forest trees can extract nutrients from the rainfall directly, thus relying less on the soil storage mechanism. Fungi in the soil feed on dead vegetation and the tree feeds on them, cutting out much of the need for nutrient solutions in the soil.

However, once the forest is removed these mechanisms are destroyed and the yield of any crops planted diminishes rapidly. Areas such as Bragantina in North East Brazil (see Chapter 14), where clearance took place a hundred years ago along the railway, have long become lands of shifting cultivation in secondary forest. Outside the immediate area there are broader implications of selva clearance. At the regional level flooding is more acute when forest is cleared to give rapid runoff. At a world level, there are unknown changes possible from major forest clearance, including global cooling and the reduction of carbon dioxide, oxygen and atmospheric moisture. Amazon rainforest exploitation is of course not as advanced as in the Andes — most of the Amazon remains as forest today despite rapid advances in colonization along new roads. The action appropriate here is thus more truly conservation, whereas in the Andes it is re-habilitation. But how far can the forest environment be conserved? Scientists suggest that *silviculture*, whereby the forest is not entirely cut over, but cut selectively so as to encourage the more useful species, is one answer. Another is *agri-silviculture*, forest clearance followed by annual crops, then shrubs like coffee or cocoa, then slower-growing useful trees, in a sequence which gradually restores a modified forest. A variation of this is to rotate crops, ranching, and forest, in one area, over a period of up to fifty years. Different policies stressing conservation above economic use are the creation of forest parks, forest reserves, and Indian reserves.

Some countries, such as Ecuador and Brazil, require a percentage of forest left in new extensions of farmland, but this is difficult to super-vise and does not ensure of itself that only the most appropriate soils, those of rich alluvium, are used for agriculture. Obviously careful soil and vegetation surveys are needed prior to settle-ment in order accurately to designate land uses of newly colonized areas.

The Orinoco Llanos

In the Amazon a fairly capital-intensive pro-gramme may be able to exploit and still conserve the environment. In many areas the best strategy for land management may be one of low capital investment and minimal interference even where abundant money resources are available. Such are the cases where there occur major natural catastrophes such as landslides, volcanic erup-tion, or flooding.

One example of the latter is the Venezuelan Llanos where the main hazard is floods. The Lower Orinoco runs through the Colombian and Venezuelan Llanos and is partially dammed in by the salient of the Guyana massif north of Cabruta. This plus the slight gradient from San Fernando (45 m to the sea at 1000 km distance, means flood liability all along the river but especially in the lower Apure. Floods covering thousands of square kilometres occur at intervals of about 10 years here in an area of savanna grasslands.

In 1976 this area was extensively flooded (Fig. 55) over July–August, to a total area of 65 000 sq km according to estimates from aerial photographs. Losses of life were minimal but roads and cattle and the small crop area were badly affected.

Apart from the basic drainage problem, new factors were noted as inducing exceptional floods. Forest destruction on the slopes around the basin helped, though most of the floodwater was pluvial, not fluvial, in other words the result of heavy rainfall on the plain itself and not brought down from the upper river. Engineering works also increased run-off and flood liability, since roads had been built across the Llanos on high embankments to keep them well above the floods; these embankments acted as effective dams for the floodwater, as on the road from San Fernando west to Mantecal, or that from San Fernando north to Calabozo, and increased the flooding behind them. Some ranches also ag-gravate flooding because they have perimeter banks built to keep out floodwater, which puts a greater flood load onto neighbouring property. Agricultural colonization schemes such as the Guanare–Masparro north-west of San Fernando, have also increased flooding though clearing vegetation and improving drainage.

Because of these negative effects of human intervention a policy of adaptation rather than control is now being advocated. Dams on the river are specifically rejected as a solution. It has already been noted that most flooding in 1976 was from rainfall in the plains area, uncontrol-lable by river dams. Dams and massive levées tend to hold back this kind of 'pluvial flood' and prevent it from draining into the rivers. In any case the large dams built at El Guri, Camatagua, Guárico and elsewhere control only 5% of the Orinoco's flow and protect 5% of its basin in Venezuela. Over 30% of the basin is outside all control, in Colombia.

Instead, the recommended strategy includes use of a warning system to protect urban popula-tions at floodtime and allow planned evacuation; elimination of all obstructions to flow on the floodplain near the river, such as buildings, bridges, and roads, which might hold back natural drainage; use of the traditional custom of transhumance of cattle from low meadows to higher terraces, and temporary cultivation for crops of *vegas*, fertile lowlands which are then abandoned in the wet season; general adoption of non-intensive land uses on the floodplain; and preservation of forest where possible. Such strategies might well be adopted elsewhere with variations to suit the case. A comparable flood area is in central Buenos Aires province, where massive floods of the Salado trough occurred last in 1979 and 1980. These floods were aggravated by the north–south alignment of the main road and rail lines between Buenos Aires, Mar del Plata, and Bahía Blanca, blocking natural drainage.

Parks and reservations

One important aim of conservation is to preserve intact the native flora and fauna in their natural surrounding, especially in areas of scenic value, historical or archaeological interest. National Parks had their origin in 1872 in the US Yellowstone Park. In South America, despite the presence of a tropical rainforest with a larger number of animal and vegetable species than all corresponding areas of the Old World, and a rapid rate of destruction of that forest, despite the existence of places such as the Galapagos Islands with their unique fauna, little was done before the 1940s, and even now the effort is uneven. Argentina has eight national parks occupying 2.3 million hectares, but largely restricted to the Patagonian Andes. These parks are protected from exploitation except for tourist use. Chile created national parks from 1931 and they occupy nearly a million hectares again largely in the southern Andes. In this country however, farmers have been allowed to come in and settle on good lands in the parks. This is a problem which must also be faced by colonizing countries such as Brazil: the need to compromise between park creation and colonists' needs for land on a farm frontier — such conflicts are not found in old-settled lands such as western Europe.

Bolivia lacks national parks but Peru has created several small ones to conserve archaeological and faunal curiosities, plus a larger one in the Cordillera Blanca. Ecuador has the Galapagos Islands effectively protected as a park since 1964, and has designated smaller areas in the Sierra near Quito. Venezuela has a number of large parks covering in all 500 000 ha, begun in 1937 with the Pittier park in the mountains north of Maracay. The Mérida mountains have another, and one lies between Caracas and the Caribbean, its most important function being possibly the restriction of urban growth onto the steep slopes of Mount Avila adjacent to the city.

Brazil's first National Park dates from 1937, and the large Iguassu Falls park from 1944, but most are much later, the biggest being at Bananal Island on the middle Araguaia river, with 460 000 ha and dating to 1973, and Amazonia, created at the same time in 1 million hectares of western Para state. It is noteworthy that Brazil's national parks are very largely in the southeast where there is more demand for recreation and more conservation awareness. The poor northeast, despite its population, is not provided. There are over 2 million hectares of National Parks in Brazil, plus over 1 million hectares of State Parks. A fundamental problem, here as elsewhere, is control over land use in parks occupying sparsely-populated and little-known regions.

Other parks are created with special functions. In 1966 Peru, followed by Bolivia, Argentina and Chile, created parks to protect the *vicuña* which had been almost exterminated through hunting for its fur-like wool. This action, helped by bans on export of *vicuña* wool from these countries and import bans in former markets, has been successful in saving this species.

Urban areas

In previous centuries the amount of land used by cities, their population size, and their capacity for pollution, were all much lower. In the last twenty years, South America has had not only many cities, but several of megalopolis size, creating demands on services such as water and sewage disposal which are not just larger but demand radically new technology.

In the big cities man has replaced large areas of vegetation with concrete and tarmac, and tunneled through the subsoil to a depth of 50 metres in places. Consequences are more rapid run-off to river, a special urban micro-climate, and a lowered water table. Cities also create noise, air, visual and water pollution to the point where they constitute major health hazards. Water pollution may be crucial where big cities are on small rivers. Caracas, with 3 million inhabitants, is on the little Guaire, which is consequently heavily loaded with silt from steep unprotected slopes round the city, and heavily contaminated as well, especially during the dry season. Other ultra-polluted waterways are the Riachuelo of Buenos Aires, the Machángara in Quito and the Rimac at Lima in Peru.

Atmospheric pollution is particularly important at the west-coast cities which, like Los Angeles in California, enjoy stable subtropical high pressure weather most of the year and occupy basin sites. Santiago in Chile, Lima in Peru, enter this category. Basin sites such as that of Caracas are less problematical because of a constant wind, here the Easterly trades. Buenos Aires and São Paulo, the largest cities, usually have some wind but when it fails suffer greatly from air pollution, much of it from the street traffic rather than industrial sources. Along with air pollution, noise pollution from the same traffic is of a higher intensity than in Europe. This problem affects small cities as well as large, as does the visual pollution produced by countless billboards and hoardings, telephone, power

and other cables, and architectural horrors.

There are solutions to these problems, some involving great cost and imported technology (underground railways for example), others the simple remedy of tree-planting wherever possible to moderate city climate and pollution. Urban planning can do much but has not traditionally been strong in these countries. One notable attempt has been the creation, in Buenos Aires, of an Ecological Belt of 74 000 acres over a 150 km strip connecting three existing green areas, from the Paraná Delta on the north side to Pereyra–Iraola on the south. In this belt city refuse will be used to fill in swamplands and create parkland.

In this way three purposes are served, the reclamation of swampland, creation of badly-needed recreation areas, and disposal of refuse, a problem, since rubbish burning has been prohibited since 1969.

2. Historical Aspects

BEFORE THE CONQUEST

Nineteenth-century archaeologists originally maintained that the Americas have been inhabited by man for a long time. On finding that early dates could not be proved, the opposite point of view, that settlement was very recent, became fashionable. Nowadays there is a trend to acceptance of a substantial antiquity for New World man, who is thought to have entered during a low sealevel period of the Pleistocene, perhaps as a hunter of mammoth and other big game, coming across a landbridge in the Bering Straits regions which may have connected Siberia and Alaska. The date of entry is still uncertain, but lies more than 20 000 years ago, for evidence of human occupation dating from that time has been found in caves near Ayacucho in upland Peru. The oldest finds, here and elsewhere in the continent, are of flint and obsidian choppers and scrapers used by hunters of extinct animals, mammoth, wild horses, animals related to the modern llama, and a giant sloth. Later hunters used more finely executed spearheads and blades. Their principal hunting grounds appear to have been cold grasslands, near the altitudinal limits for vegetation.

Changes away from this kind of life were only gradually achieved, with the introduction of gathered, then of cultivated plants into the diet. From 3600 BC onwards settled forms of life are known from the Peruvian southern and central coasts, based on both crops and shellfish. How and where agriculture began in the Americas is still in dispute, but its earliest locations were probably not on the coast, where most early remains are known because of the excellent conditions for preservation, but in other areas; one such is the Peruvian Sierra, another is southern Mexico, another on the southern shores of the Caribbean. In each of these regions a variety of environments, according to Carl Sauer, would have allowed the domestication of many species of plant, especially those which can be cultivated using vegetative reproduction (plant division as opposed to seeds), such as the potato and yam, requiring only a minimal level of technical expertise. However domestication came about, the effects were the same in all parts, the advent of settled village life, allowing much more of the paraphernalia of tools and equipment of modern man than ever could be used by nomadic man. Crafts such as cotton cloth making, which have been identified from the deserts of north Peru as over 5000 years old, and the making of pottery, were now possible. It has been suggested, largely from Mexican evidence (McNeish, *vide* Bibliography), that there was a Neolithic Evolution rather than a Revolution, and this may also be true of South America. Plant domestication in Mexico dates back to 5000 BC, but villages did not follow until 3000 BC and pottery only in 2300 BC. For some unknown reasons the pace of innovation seems to be slower than in the Old World.

Stages of social evolution

In the Old World, prehistoric stages of man's development are based mostly on technology,

Fig. 2 Culture types in South America about AD 1500

from the Stone Ages through the Chalcolithic to the Bronze and Iron Ages. This sequence does not easily fit the American experience, for the key materials are not the same — no iron was used, for example — and civilizations had different relations between social advance and technical advance. Instead, it is more meaningful, following Sanders and Marino (fig. 2) to order society into bands, tribes, chiefdoms and ancient states. Of these, *bands* were always the most widespread, as kinlinked groups of under 100 persons with relatively slight organization. Above them, *tribes* might have several thousands, and permanent settlements based on farming rather than the bands' hunting and collecting; they also had some social division into classes. Above these again in social complexity, the *chiefdoms* with 5000-20000 persons, had hereditary chiefs, a definite power hierarchy and considerable division of labour, often also ceremonial centres and palaces. *Ancient states* saw the final displacement of kinship links by organized control of territory as the social bond, and the rudiments of a commercial marketing system.

Tribes and a sedentary village life lasted without alteration until at least 2000 BC. From then, chiefdoms with their specialized urban centres of craft, administration and religion began to appear, earlier in the Peruvian culture hearth than anywhere else in America. The most colourful and splendid of the chiefdoms came later with the Chavín culture of 1200-750 BC, chronologically and socially the equal of the Olmec culture in southern Mexico, the other cradle of American civilization. Chavín is in the Northern Highlands of Peru, and has a stone-built temple and palace complex, together with a large residential sector adjacent to it, implying not just a ceremonial centre here but also organized agriculture producing regular surpluses for the urban population.

Ancient states
Chiefdoms are followed in time by the first ancient states, such as the Mochica state of AD 1-800, with its elaborate irrigation-based agriculture and fine development of arts and technology, exemplified in metal working using a variety of techniques, in gold, silver and copper; these people were followed by the Huari—Tiahuanaco culture in the culture-hearth area, and then by the Incas. The Tiahuanaco culture has recently been proved to have substantial depth at its name-site on the Bolivian altiplano above La Paz. Here the buildings show an evolution spread over a period from 1200 BC to AD 1000. Pyramids and temples dating from shortly after Christ are built with a high level of engineering competence, for, despite its burial in wet alluvial mud for many centuries, the architecture has not suffered much deterioration, having an excellent drainage system to keep the whole dry.

After AD 1200 the Inca empire grew up, first occupying a small area near Cuzco, then in the last century before the Conquest, spreading over an area which extended over 3000 km from north to south (fig. 3). More than a million people owed allegiance to the Inca, as visible ruler and deity. The Incas achieved remarkable attainments in stone architecture, using few mechanical aids — the wheel for example was not apparently known, though used in miniature

form for toys — and uncemented, and a variety of engineering works such as castles, irrigation canals and terraces are ascribed to them, though much must have been copied, extended, or merely taken over from earlier civilizations. The Incas' relation to their predecessors was probably like that of the Romans to the Greeks, that of a practical, militaristic, hierarchically more organized people, who invented little but used the astounding discoveries of their forebears to good purpose.

As a military empire their geographical limits were fairly well defined; they could occupy only the open grass-covered uplands, with some minor exceptions, and to east, north and south were delayed and halted by swamps and forests, where guerrilla warfare could indefinitely hold back an organized army. To the south they thus came no further than central Chile, and to the north to central Ecuador, while in the east their limits were those of the eastern cordilleras. In the southeast, they did not have a forest front, but a plains one, and seem to have shunned the Argentine Chaco simply because it was unattractive to them and held no resources.

Outside the Inca empire, large regions were occupied by chiefdoms, societies of a smaller total size and with less complex organization, in particular without the class structure that characterized the Incas. Figure 2 shows that one of these regions, occupied by many chiefdoms, was that of Ecuador—Colombia, on the north front of the Incas and no doubt influenced by the older upland civilizations. The Chibcha were perhaps the best organized of these chiefdoms, a group lying on the upland savannas of the Colombian Cordillera Oriental, with organized trade in textiles, salt and farm products. At a probably lower economic but similar social level, there were the people of the San Agustin culture of southern Colombia, responsible for elaborate ceremonial architecture in stone known from over thirty major sites, with features reminiscent of the Chavín culture formerly dominant in the south. The Beni region of northeast Bolivia also had chiefdoms with organized power of a military nature, and built causeways and canals across the seasonally flooded savanna.

Beyond empires and chiefdoms, Indian tribes practising slash and burn agriculture, which had gradually replaced an older gathering and hunting economy, occupied the tropical forest low-

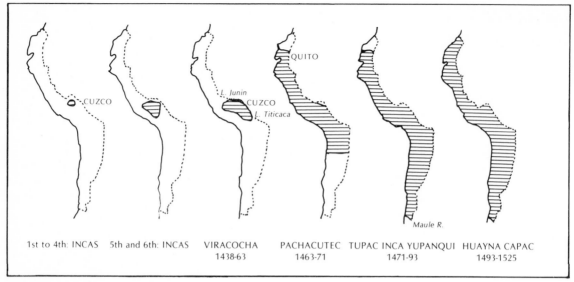

Fig. 3 The expansion of the Inca Empire

lands, while the Pampas were still the domain of wandering hunters, and hunters and gatherers lived in the Chaco, as they have done until the very recent past.

THE IBERIAN ORIGINS OF THE CONQUEST

Inevitably, the history of the Iberian peoples has had much influence on the course of American history. In particular, the secular battle against the Moors, over the harsh environment of the Meseta, quite different from anything else in Europe, could not but mould American events. Isolation of the peninsula made Iberia socially more traditional than most of Europe, so that while the Conquest of the New World belongs to Renaissance time, Iberian, and particularly Spanish, attitudes to life and the afterlife were medieval rather than Renaissance; faith in God rather than belief in human potential for achievement was the motif of the early years of the Conquest. The overseas empires grew up with many features of feudal, Church-dominated medieval Europe, despite the new environment of the New World, which could have permitted innovations and change.

Spanish — Portuguese differences
Although both Spain and Portugal grew out of

the Reconquista, the advance against the Moors, they evolved in different ways, which were reflected in differences in their New World possessions. First, the Portuguese were much earlier in forming a stable independent state, finally expelling the Moors from their south in 1249, whereas Spain did not oust the Moors from Granada until 1492, the year in which Columbus discovered America, so that for Spaniards, the fight for America was to some extent a continuation of the fight for Spain itself.

By 1500, the Portuguese were comparatively experienced in colonial rule, from their explorations and acquisitions in Africa; Spain had also expanded to Africa, but was less committed or interested in foreign parts in the fifteenth century while she still had enemies on home territory. Portugal had also become a cosmopolitan society, with many Negroes and Moslems incorporated and accepted in the country, contrasting with Spain's intolerance, later to express itself forcibly both at home and abroad.

In America then, the Spanish came with little experience of governing, and with a mixture of motivations among the young conquistadors that is quite surprising to modern minds. They had something still of the medieval Christianizing fervour and search for honour inherited from their battles in Spain, mixed with a greed for personal gain that was more consistent with the rest of Renaissance Europe. Portuguese colonists, though there were a few idealists among them, came with more strictly materialistic ideas of the possibilities of the New World.

The medieval endowment: feudalism and fantasy

In the late stages of the Spanish advance across the Castilian Meseta, especially in the thirteenth-century push south from the Tagus, the Spanish king adopted the policy of granting titles of nobility and land to the soldiers and religious—military orders who led the attack. Land and people were placed under the feudal protection of the new lords. This policy was effectively continued into the New World, with donations of great land areas and their dependent population to the leaders. Such a practice was not followed in Brazil, nor could it be with the lack of Indians and cultivated land worth giving to soldiers; but a similar land policy, following that used in Madeira and Africa, was adopted: this was the granting of great tracts of land with seignorial rights of taxation and land for the nobles who took control of it under the crown.

Another strain of medieval influence was that of fantasy: legends of unknown lands or cities and fabulous beings, most of them originating in European writings with no empirical foundation, pursued the Spaniards into the New World. They included those of the Amazons, tribes of warlike women, thought to have been seen in California as well as on the river Amazon; the legend of El Dorado, the gilded king, whose subjects regularly adorned him in gold paint, a legend which motivated exploration over the whole northern half of the continent; and the mysterious seven cities of Cíbola, placed anywhere from the Mississippi valley to Argentina.

The Conquest

The Spanish gained the upper hand in America, over all other potential colonizers. They were given rights to land west of 100 leagues from Cape Verde in a Papal Bull of 1493, amended to 370 leagues west in the Treaty of Tordesillas in 1494. After a relatively slow start in the West Indies, they expanded rapidly onto the continent from 1519, with Cortés' exploration into and conquest of the Mexican empire, followed by Pizarro's adventure into Peru, begun in 1530,

which obtained at one dramatic stroke the accumulated wealth of centuries of civilization, including gold, fertile land, and dense settlements of peaceful Indians. The Portuguese had no similar fortune to await them in their legally allotted section of the continent. In Brazil there were no densely settled Indian populations, nor mineral riches, as far as could be ascertained, and precious little fertile land in cultivation or awaiting the plough.

The geography of conquest was simple in outline. Closest to South America of the Spanish bases in the Indies was Panama. From here, Pascal de Andagoya sailed 320 km down the Colombian Pacific coast and explored the Rio San Juan in 1522. In 1524, Francisco Pizarro led a first trip with 80 men and four horses, and in 1526, a second one with 160 men, disastrous in its losses of men and goods, but serving to show for the first time the wealth of a civilized people living to the south, from the evidence of pottery, metal-working, clothing and domesticated animals.

In 1530, Pizarro launched a third expedition, with finance and men he brought from Spain. Moving slowly south from a landing in Ecuador he at last struck inland in 1532 with 170 men. His timing was lucky for the Inca* Atahualpa and a large army of perhaps 80 000 men were nearby at Cajamarca. To this town he went, occupied the square which is still modern Cajamarca's central plaza, and invited the Inca to a parley. Atahualpa accepted the invitation and entered the town with as many men as could squeeze into the square. He was surprised not to see any Spaniards, but these were in fact lying in wait in the houses around the square with their horses and cannon. First Pizarro's priest approached to read the Requirement, an impractical Spanish document intended to be read to natives and asking them to accept Christian faith and Spanish sovereignty or be massacred. On finding little reaction to this, a Christian breviary was shown to the Inca who at first could not even open it, let alone understand it, and threw it down. This was the signal for attack. The Indians, massed into the square, panicked at the sound of cannon and the sight of horses, and vast numbers of them were slaughtered

---

* The name Inca was strictly that of the king or one of his family, but was applied later to the whole civilization.

immediately. The Inca was captured, and the breakdown of the Empire, following a pattern established by Cortés in Mexico, had begun.

Everywhere Spanish arms held the advantage of horse against foot soldiers, armour against the cotton quilting used by the Indians, and firearms against wooden clubs, or bows and arrows. Following the conquest of Cuzco and most of Peru, lieutenants of Pizarro were sent out to finish the task of subjection. Jimenez de Quesada entered the Magdalena valley from the Caribbean and arrived at the Chibcha centre of Bogotá before Sebastian de Belalcazar from Quito and the German Federmann from Venezuela. Chile was conquered directly by Diego de Almagro from Peru.

Thus the Andean lands were brought into subjugation. In the river Plate the impetus for settlement came initially in the search for a western passage to the Spice Islands, a search continued long after it was discovered that America did not reach to Asia or adjoin it. Juan de Solis made a first landfall in the Plate estuary in 1513, though from contemporary maps it seems he was anticipated by undocumented Portuguese voyagers. On a second trip in 1515, Solis was killed on the Uruguayan shore by hostile Indians. He was followed by Magellan, though no settlement was made then, for the search for western sea routes was still uppermost in Spanish minds.

Settlement on the Plate only came with the large group brought by Don Pedro de Mendoza, which ended in near disaster because of famine and Indian attacks. It was learnt early that settlement was only possible where settled Indians could be made to work for their parasitic conquerors. Where, as in the Plate, they could not, the conquerors had to move on, in this case to the upper river, at Asunción, among the Guaraní farmer Indians.

In Portuguese America the tale of conquest was perhaps less dramatic but it was equally brutal and the results, for the native peoples, equally disastrous, resulting again in the total breakdown of native cultures. For the first 30 years the Portuguese engaged only in trade, like the French on the same coast. But thereafter, and for the remainder of the sixteenth century, they were engaged in a colonization policy which established permanent settlements only after all-out wars against the Indians. These wars usually ended in the almost complete elimination of the Indians, through the immediate war losses and burning of their villages, their flight out of the coast lands into the interior forest for protection, and through European diseases, which decimated them, smallpox and dysentry being important early killers. The Portuguese found it only easy to settle among and conquer the Tupi tribes of the coast between Bahia and Pernambuco. Further north they were hard pressed by the French and by a well-organised Tupi group of tribes; further south they faced non-Tupi tribes, at a more primitive level, without large villages or permanent residences of any kind, who fought a guerilla war against them, making colonization almost impossible. The Portuguese settlers and government were substantially aided by the Jesuit missionaries who in creating villages and in teaching the Indians also made them more controllable and totally dependent. Concentration in villages also probably helped spread European diseases more quickly.

Neither Spanish nor Portuguese advanced into the interior in the way that North American settlers were later to do. The Spanish especially were not farmer—settlers looking for land but knights on horseback, founding cities and claiming land without actually occupying it themselves. Only in the southern grasslands of the Pampas was there a frontier. Here wild raiding Indians were a reality, pressing on the frontier of military forts and tightening it, and making an impression on Spanish settlers, who were forced to occupy the land themselves for want of Indian farmers to do so for them. There was however none of the frontier experience of the North Americans, for the Pampas frontier was thinly peopled and static until the latter part of the nineteenth century. Latin Americans never experienced the socially democratizing influence of a small-farmer frontier.

COLONIAL ECONOMY AND SOCIETY

Land tenure

Arrangements for Spanish—Indian relations in America were complicated by the fact that the sovereigns who published laws of a humane nature governing the 'Indies', as they continued to be called, did not see them put into practice.

Thus, while Spanish monarchs genuinely desired the wellbeing of their new American subjects, and would never permit their enslavement, in practice the Spanish overlordship was often terribly harsh. One institution set up was the *encomienda*, for the protection and conversion of Indian peoples put under an *encomendero*; the term implies the commending of Indian souls to the teaching of their Spanish master, but more than this was involved — a regal ordinance of 1573 describes one facet that could lead immediately to exploitation of Indians:

> The Indians who offer us obedience and are distributed among Spaniards are to be persuaded to acknowledge our sovereignty over the Indies. They are to give us tributes of local produce in moderate amounts, which are to be turned over to their Spanish *encomenderos* so that the latter may fulfill their obligations [to the Crown], reserving to us the tributes of the principal villages and the seaports, as well as an amount adequate to pay the salaries of our officials.
>
> *cited in Lewis Hanke (ed.),* History of Latin American Civilization *(Methuen, 1969), p. 152.*

In fact many *encomiendas* were treated as land grants together with a serf Indian population to be used for labour. A highly stratified social relationship developed in the Inca territories, with Indians, imported slaves and *mestizos*, all set below the Europeans and *criollos*, Europeans born in America. True land grants, *donaciones* and *mercedes,* were also made, of so great a size that often the local Indians had to become serfs on them, for want of other land to work in the vicinity. Alternatively, they might move to new lands, but over the colonial period these were increasingly the marginal lands, away from valley floors and alluvial soils which were occupied by the estates. The *mercedes* were supposed to be for one generation only, but in fact tended to remain within the family granted them rather than reverting to the Crown.

The *encomienda* system broke down at different rates in different areas, in its transformation into the *haciendas*. These latter were large estates privately owned by Spaniards using Indian labour. They were introduced rapidly in such areas as the Peruvian coast where Indian population declined rapidly in the sixteenth century, less rapidly in the Sierra because a large Indian population could still be exploited under the old system. *Encomiendas* also declined because they were insufficient in number to support the demands of an increasing number of Spanish immigrants and their sons. *Haciendas* grew as the European system of private holdings replaced the communal ownership of most land in the old civilisations of Latin America. As communal holding was not recognized by Spanish law, communal lands could be taken readily in legal actions against it when there was no ready defender.

New crops and animals

The structure of farming was changed away from subsistence or semi-subsistence farming towards commercial farming. Important in these changes were the animals and crops introduced from Europe. The New World was not rich in domesticated animals, for, apart from the dog, it had only poultry, guinea pigs, llamas and alpacas as important domesticates. The introduction of sheep, cattle, pigs and goats to the region put a new value on unused pasture lands. The horse, mule and donkey brought a virtual transport revolution to the land. Llamas had been used for carrying burdens but they were weak compared with donkeys, and there was nothing to match the horse, as carrier of man or puller of the plough, which was here, as in the Old World, a symbol of its owner's prestige and power.

For crops, the Americas were richer and could even provide Europe with new commodities, such as tomatoes, maize and potatoes; but the middle-latitude grains — wheat, barley and oats — were an important innovation, replacing and supplementing the old crops of quinoa on the cold uplands and temperate south. Vines and olives were also important in these temperate lands. Sugar was easily transplanted and became an early export crop, associated with particular forms of society and farm organization, as is shown in later chapters. Citrus fruits also came to the tropics and subtropics at an early date, and spread so rapidly that it has been asserted until the present that there must have been a native, wild variety of orange.

Brazil

The Portuguese, after an initial period of interest only in trade with the coastal natives in manufactured trinkets which were exchanged for great logs of brazilwood, established their own landholding system, a little different from the Spanish, in fact comparable in form to the colony system used for the first North American colonies. Grants, *donatárias,* were made by the crown to nobles or rich men to exploit, in return for a tenth of harvests or a fifth of metals extracted. The lands granted were placed under the *donatário* for the purpose of internal taxation and lawmaking, and he received in addition half the income from brazilwood and a fifth of the land in his domain.

This system was intended to promote colonization; it had already done so in Madeira, the Azores and the Cape Verde islands. Here in Brazil it was more difficult to advance; Duarte Coelho, *donatário,* says in a letter to the king: 'We are obliged to conquer by inches, the land that your Majesty has granted us by leagues' (cited in Roberto Simonsen, *História Económica do Brasil* (São Paulo, 1957), p. 85).

A tropical climate, the hostility and the very lack of Indians, competition from French and Dutch to which the Spaniards were not exposed, all slowed down the process of expansion. For lack of a labour force, the Portuguese were forced to bring in slaves from their West African possessions, establishing the plantation system that lasted until the nineteenth century. The Dutch did similarly in their own sugar plantations in Guiana, finding few Indians willing to work for them on the coast.

The Church

Distinctive forms of tenure and production were occasionally established by the Catholic Church in America. Large land holdings all over the continent were owned by the Church, many of them bequests by repentant landlords on their deathbed. Some of the largest *latifundia* in the continent came into being in this way, to be expropriated finally by the state in nineteenth-century independence reforms.

While most church holdings were operated as ordinary cattle *haciendas* or crop farms, with the clergy exerting no influence on the form of economy, the Jesuits set up what amounted to complete economic and social enclaves in South America, in the Amazon valley, in eastern Bolivia and in eastern Paraguay and adjacent parts of Brazil (fig. 4). Their method was to build *aldeias* or *reducciones,* villages occupied only by the Indians with a Jesuit director, to produce goods for sustenance and sale, at the same time converting the Indians and controlling their whole way of life.

In the Amazon, the economic base was spices and cocoa, gathered or cultivated by the Indians and exported to Europe without paying tax. In Bolivia, cotton and craft products were sent to the altiplano from the *aldeias* while the Paraguayan *reducciones* produced yerba mate, tobacco, sugar and cotton for export. The Jesuits must be seen as a major force in colonial South America, organizing the Indians into villages, protecting them from slave attack or at least from the shocks of adaptation to lay European culture. They also served a strategic purpose, providing a buffer state or no-man's-land between Portuguese and Spanish territories, and even provided a good economic example to the rest of society. Jesuit rule has been criticized as domineering and autocratic; but this was also its strength, and what allowed it to become economically successful. It must also be remembered that Indians willingly entered the *reducciones* and welcomed their protection from the slave-catchers.

TRADE

Both Spanish and Portuguese economic policies were what may be called mercantilist, whereby the colonies were forced to trade with the mother country alone, to produce only raw materials and items of immediate consumption, and were not allowed to engage in manufacturing to compete with the mother country. In addition, most South American trade was channelled through the ports of Lima and Cartagena, if destined for Spain's colonies in the subcontinent. A convoy system was set up, ships travelling under naval escort across the Atlantic to the Outer Antilles, where the fleet split up into two, the northern part going to Veracruz in Mexico, the southern to Venezuela, Colombia and Panama, where it met a similar fleet from Peru travelling up the Pacific coast.

Further restrictions were the crown monopolies, in Spanish territory of tobacco and alcohol, in Brazil of brazilwood and salt; besides these there were many different taxes on trade transactions, which helped to raise, for example, the price of imported Spanish cloth from fivefold to eightfold between Lima and Buenos Aires. Such monstrous impositions encouraged corruption and contraband trade on a large scale.

The map (fig. 4) shows the major trade items and directions of movement in the early eighteenth century. Lima was the obvious focus of the Spanish South American economy, receiving goods via the Panama isthmus in the annual fleets which brought textiles, metal goods and luxury items such as fine furniture, and sending back gold, silver, and such durable products as hides and tallow. Lima received her stock of these goods from an enormous hinterland, within which only a few producing areas contributed the greater part.

MANUFACTURING AND DEPENDENCE

Before the eighteenth century, some of the tributary areas had produced much more by way of manufactures themselves; textiles in Chile and New Granada's Quito district, the upland region of present Ecuador; leatherwork, such as saddles and harnesses, carpentry, carts and carriages, in northwestern Argentina and eastern Bolivia; iron and other metal goods for farmers in many isolated regions.

After 1750 the Industrial Revolution and European manufacturing began to strangle this craft industry and reduced the peripheral areas to the status of raw material producers. A curious process of relative underdeveloping, holding back development while other areas went ahead, was put into operation. The Jesuit-controlled areas fared better, for their independence in economic matters meant that their surpluses could be chosen, and they were never hampered by trade restrictions. The Caribbean and river Plate also did better in trade than their remote positions would suggest, for contraband trade kept them busy with British and French buccaneers.

Brazil had similar mercantilist restrictions imposed by Portugal but it did not have the high-value trade items which permitted trade concentration at one great market as in Spanish America. Trade was rather of more bulky products, which necessarily moved out to Europe from the nearest port, and so went from a whole range of locations along the coast, not one great port. Sugar, brazilwood and even cotton required ready access to sea routes. Probably the most significant imports to Brazil, in terms of value, were the West African slaves. To the north of Brazil, another trading region was that of the Guianas, especially the coastal fringe of present-day Surinam and Guyana, which were under Dutch control and sent sugar out to Europe from slave plantations. The Guianan economic geography was similar to that of Brazil, with emphasis on the coast and relations to Europe.

POLITICAL ORGANIZATION

The administrative machinery of the Spanish American Empire was strongly hierarchical, and very important in most aspects of life, with independent structures for towns, large regions and for legal matters. The basic division was into several viceroyalties, of which the most important in South America was that of Peru. Lima held great power as centre to South America, exercising some authority over most of the inhabited land of the continent. Within its viceroyalty, several units preserved some separate administrative identity. The Captaincy-General of Chile, the presidencies of Charcas, Cuzco, Quito and Caracas, were all early units which had separate legal definition in the Audiencias of their district.

In the eighteenth century, Bourbon Spain attempted reforms in its Empire, and split off the northern and southern wings of the Peruvian Viceroyalty, as the new Viceroyalties of New Granada, first established in 1717, and of La Plata, 1776 (fig. 5), recognizing the real differences in interest and structure of economy between these lands.

Between these colonies and the Viceroyalty of Brazil, there was a *cordon sanitaire* of remote Indian settlements, under Jesuit domination until the expulsion of this order in 1767-8. Brazilian colonies were captaincies, under the nominal leadership of Bahia (Salvador), but, in correspondence with the economic facts of life, having no high degree of centralized power as in Spanish America. The northern region of Maranhão was for some time in danger of splitting off as a separate colony.

CULTURE AND SOCIETY

Given the feudal structure of the latifundia and the still more rigid division of labour on the plantation, social divisions were necessarily strong

Fig. 4 Colonial economy in 1700

between different classes of society in Spanish America. To some extent, division was along racial lines: the slaves were Negroes, the Indians were a servile population, the Spaniards and *criollos* formed an urban elite. Mestization permitted some breaching of the division, though mestizos tended to form yet another group, intermediate between whites and Indians.

Regional differences in culture were apparent across the continent, as was natural given the isolation of one centre from another, separated by hundreds of kilometres of near deserted territory. An index is language; Spanish as spoken by high-class Colombians was regarded as among the best Spanish spoken in the world, and was quite different from that of Argentina. In the altiplano of Peru, most Indians were maintained outside the Spanish-speaking community and spoke their native languages. In other countries where mestizos were more important, Spanish was spoken by nearly all the population. Only in one country, Paraguay, did an Indian language take over as the leading one. Guaraní language is still spoken today by all Paraguayans, and its prevalence indicates the deep penetration of Indian culture in this region.

South America is more notable now for cultural homogeneity than distinctiveness of regions; one colonial factor in this state of affairs was the refusal to allow other than Spanish and Portuguese immigrants into the area. Only in the Guianas, under North European rule, did different policies prevail. Another factor for unity was the Church, far more powerful than today, and influencing Indian as well as European. Old Indian religious beliefs and customs were adapted and moulded into Christian frames rather than completely suppressed; into the Baroque ecclesiastical architecture of Brazil and Peru, motifs such as snakes and monkeys, sacred to the Indians, were incorporated by clever Indian masons. Former holy days were given Christian saints' names, former holy places given legal existence as places holy to Our Lady or to a patron saint of the Christian calendar.

THE NINETEENTH CENTURY

It has often been asserted that the breakup of the Spanish Empire was due to internal decadence. Nowadays it is recognized that eighteenth-century Spain was not as much in decline as might be supposed; both economically and politically, Spain and her colonies made something of a recovery over the latter part of the century. Breakup was probably due more to external pressures, the rise of northern Europe and North America, than to internal problems. New ideas on politics, economy and society were beyond the control of Spain, and must eventually have wrought great changes even if Spain were to retain control. As it was, small groups of intellectuals, then the *criollos* of colonial cities, a disaffected group because they were kept out of high administrative office by Spanish rule, began to read the revolutionary writings of Rousseau, Locke and others, and foci of rebellion sprang

up in Buenos Aires, Caracas, Bogotá and Santiago. These provincial centres, after the wars of independence, became the capitals of new states, each with their own political leaders and administrative machines, developed in the late eighteenth century and revolutionary period.

Since the middle-class *criollos* were the mainstay of revolution, little was changed in the social order by Spain's overthrow, and the same social system as in colonial time, with some modifications, was carried over into Independence. Slavery was gradually abolished in the course of the century, though the released slaves were not always given an easier lot. Church holdings throughout Latin America were expropriated, but were taken over by *criollos* and other wealthy landowners, leading to no democratization of land holding. Prohibition on settlement by other than Spaniards or Portuguese was abolished, and this meant something of a change for the temperate countries, Argentina, Uruguay and Chile.

Independence and a new dependence

Freedom from Spain thus brought social change to only a few areas; economic change was similarly restricted, for the same kinds of exports and imports were maintained, ultimate control of trade merely moving from the Spanish metropolis to the English. This was a move which had begun in the previous century with the freeing of ports in the New World to more open trade. Now a strong English manufacturing sector was able to penetrate all parts of the continent, bringing cotton cloths from Manchester, knives and forks from Sheffield or Birmingham and furniture and other luxury items from northwestern Europe generally.

The entry of cheap manufactures finally doomed the old craft industries of areas such as Santander—Boyacá in Colombia, Mendoza and the northwest of Argentina, where cloths and metal and leather goods had continued to be made. Penetration of European goods was facilitated by gradual improvements in transport means; steamboats up the rivers helped, though there are few easily navigable waterways in the continent; more important were the railways, especially after 1880, and notably in Argentina, Peru and Colombia, lowering the real cost of transport four- or five-fold over mule packing, the previous norm in mountainous country.

Fig. 5 Administrative organisation of the Spanish American empire

Nineteenth-century Brazil

Brazilian transfer of power was peaceful, beginning with the removal of the whole Portuguese court and royalty to Brazil as a consequence of Napoleon's takeover in 1808. Effectively, Brazil could begin to turn her back on Portugal without losing her traditional respect for royal authority, in contrast to Spanish colonies where this duality of affections slowed down the Independence movements. From 1808 there were relaxations of colonial rule, with Brazil the centre of the empire. Manufacturing was now permitted,

trade completely freed, and a period of economic prosperity ushered in.

A question sometimes posed by historians on Brazilian evolution is how such a large country could hold together despite tendencies towards separation throughout colonial times and tenuous connections along the coast between the various rival centres. One reason for this keeping together into modern times may have been the presence of the king in the country, an important symbol of unity. Another reason was the very primitiveness of the country, with few centres of intellectual activity to compare with those in Buenos Aires, Bogotá and elsewhere in Spanish America. For revolution to occur, as has been observed in this century, a certain degree of economic and social development is necessary. Finally, we should note that the economy of Brazil over the colonial period focussed in one region at a time; first on the coast, then in the northeast, then in the southeast, so that economic unity and a single core was maintained.

Nineteenth-century Brazilian economic evolution proceeded much as in Spanish America, with dependence on Portugal transferred to Britain. In fact dependence had moved, in this case too, to England in the eighteenth century, when Portugal had become to some extent an economic colony of the northern state, exchanging military protection for unequal trade terms; under the Methuen Treaty of 1703, amplified by later measures, Portugal gave free entry to English textiles, and English manufactures or displaced Portuguese manufactures had to look for markets in Brazil and elsewhere. Direct entry of British goods became important in the nineteenth century.

Immigration of new European blood was slight until the late nineteenth century, coming first into Rio Grande do Sul and Santa Catarina, from 1840, then on a grander scale into Sao Paulo in the 1880s and 90s, with the rise of coffee. Slavery did not come to an end until the 1880s, forestalling labour problems for the sugar plantations and deterring what slight immigration might have occurred into the tropical regions. Formal declaration of a republic was also delayed until the 1880s, when the Emperor Don Pedro II was quietly replaced in a palace revolution of 1889, followed by the optimistic creation of a United States of Brazil, with a constitution based on that of the United States of America, giving strong rights to the state governments, though in fact centralized government was to be the norm.

TERRITORIAL ADJUSTMENTS

Colonial boundaries between the various colonial territories had not often been precisely defined, still less surveyed on the ground, so that there was room for considerable jostling between the newborn states, changing the political map during the nineteenth century. In the centre, Paraguay, controlled by a dictator with expansionist aims, made war on all its neighbours in the War of the Triple Alliance (1865-70). This war devastated the country, and caused it to lose land to Brazil and Argentina. The boundaries on the open plain of the Chaco, with few natural markers to use as limits, were still unsettled, and in the 1930s Paraguay again went to war, with disastrous results, in the War of the Chaco, fought partly for the economic interests in potential oil supplies.

Economic interests were also uppermost in the War of the Pacific from 1880 to 1884, interest focussing in this case on the nitrates of the Atacama, developed by Chilean entrepreneurs. In the war both Bolivia and Peru lost their claims to the nitrate lands. Other economic interests were present in the shifts of boundary pressed on Bolivia by Brazil during the century. The upper Amazon valley acquired a new value for its wild rubber trees, and Brazil found it easy to exert pressure on Bolivia for these lands, holding the transport key to trade, in the great river leading to the Atlantic and Europe. Brazil similarly expanded to take over Amazon territory in Colombia, Venezuela and Ecuador, in each case Brazilian occupation of the zone allowing a claim of de facto control. Brazilian *caboclos* moved in from the east, upriver, in a natural and unrecorded advance of the frontier, while the Andean states, with no tradition of lowland forest settlement and with no occupants for the frontier zones, found it difficult to enforce any claims to the Amazon lands. A common thread unites these territorial disputes or wars; while the excuse for battle was dispute over the true lines of demarcation between countries, the real interests were vital economic ones, pressed not by farmers on the frontier but by urban administrators and middle-class landowners or merchants who stood to gain most.

CONCLUSIONS

Two themes seem worth recalling in the history of the continent. One is the continuity of human patterns, another is its broad unity, increasing rather than diminishing over time. Continuity is apparent despite upsets and distortions produced by revolutions and wars. Part of this continuity is a reflection of environmental dictates, most notably the climatic and other effects of the mountain areas. These lands provided veritable islands of temperate climate in the tropics and open, relatively fertile land above the dense forests. Here the ancient civilizations developed to their highest levels, and here the Spanish found it easiest and most rewarding to impose their rule. To the present day the oecumene of the continent within the tropics is partially confined to the mountains, following old patterns, despite expansionary movements into the lowlands, which serve to occupy the mountain fringe, but not the main body of tropical lowland. Brazil provides the best exceptions to this rule, with a throbbing economic core in the Southeast, although this is only marginally tropical, in an area where no ancient civilization seems to have grown up. And the Brazilian Northeast has long had a dense lowland population and active economy, albeit based in good measure on African, not European, blood.

Economic and social patterns also have historical antecedents. Inca civilization involved strong class distinctions, which were taken up and utilized with racially determined groupings. On the economic front, continuity is found in the state of subordination to foreign powers, begun in the sixteenth century and remaining to the present despite political changes which have brought independence to nearly all parts of the continent.

Unity is as impressive as continuity in South America. Given control by the two Iberian nations alone over a period of more than three centuries, this is perhaps not surprising, but its special force must be ascribed to the power of the Church, in matters both spiritual and temporal, and to the strictness of Spanish and Portuguese colonial policy, allowing no other nation to influence their American wards, or to send settlers to the region with new ideas. Over a continent, similar language, culture and economy were imposed, similar relations to a mother country which insisted on uniform methods of government and administration throughout its domains.

3. Agriculture

South America is perhaps best known to Europeans through its agricultural products: bananas from Ecuador or Surinam, coffee from Brazil, wheat and beef from the river Plate and sugar from Guyana. These items are exported to the countries of the West, and represent important financial contributions to the economy of exporting countries, often comprising the leading exports of those countries.

Considering this reputation as a food producer, it is a little surprising to realize that less than 10 per cent of the continent is cultivated and, without substantial improvements, only 15 per cent of it is cultivable with present practices. The great volume of export products comes from a small part of what we see on the map, and many parts of the continent are not self-sufficient nowadays in agricultural production, or only just self-sufficient and with no useful surpluses.

Thus Brazil, with her enormous area, was until recently dependent on large imports of wheat and milk products. This might be taken as an index of tropicality, for middle-latitude farming has few convenient regions to take hold in Brazil. More glaring is the case of Chile, where imports of wheat, bananas, sugar, coffee, tea, oilseeds, cattle and milk products are all necessary. Here is a country dependent on the exterior for its food to a considerable degree, despite a large and active agricultural population.

The truth is of course that Chile's, and even Brazil's, agricultural area is quite limited, even with continuing efforts at forest clearing,

drainage and irrigation. The poverty of farmers allows them to use few machines, so that their ability to use more land is low; in addition, for the lands in production, there are institutional difficulties such as the ownership of land which currently hold back production levels below the attainable maxima.

FARMING CULTURES

There are three cultures in Latin America as far as agriculture is concerned: the Indian, the Iberian and the immigrant culture which dates only from the nineteenth century. Use of the word culture here implies that more than a distinctive set of crops or production systems is involved, that what we consider is a people's set of production priorities, their technology, and their perceptions of the world, as well as the social structure within which they work. The interrelationships of these cultures are complex; in some places they overlap one another, in others the Iberian or the immigrant culture has laid a new stratum, completely obliterating all foregoing types.

Indian farming, in the predominantly temperate areas of the Andean countries where it was sedentary agriculture, was of a very distinctive character. The small farm, *chacara* or *chacra*, possibly irrigated, but in any case intensively cultivated, produced a wide variety of crops mixed closely together in what a modern farmer would term disarray; in fact it was precisely organized and planned, with a careful rotation of crops and symbiosis which helped to maintain soil fertility and prevent disease. On the best land, in the warmer areas, maize might be planted with beans beside it that might use the maize stalk as a pole for climbing. Following maize, squash or manioc with their lower soil requirements might be used. Stratification of the crop in miniature reproduction of the natural forest environment, with an upper tree crop, grains or roots below, and vines climbing up the taller crops, was typical of these warm lands.

In the harsher parts of the *altiplano* in Bolivia—Peru, polyculture and interculture of different crops was perhaps less. A variety of crops unknown elsewhere was used here. It included many types of potato adapted to varying soils and climates. Other Andean tubers were the *añu*, *arracacha*, *oca* and *ulluco*. Cultivation was by means of the *chakitaclla*, a heavy wooden digging stick with a footrest; no animal power was used. Few grains were grown, the most common being *quinoa (Chenopodium quinoa)* and the related *cañihua*, plants more resistant to cold, hail and snow than European grains, and rich in protein, an important fact in view of the lack of meat-providing livestock. The llama was the most common beast, but could only carry a light load of 20 kilos for any distance; it was more prized for its excellent wool, as were the more unmanageable alpacas and the now nearly exterminated wild *vicuña*. Apart from these, the Indians had minor protein sources in hens, ducks and guinea pigs. Rather than in villages, the Indians lived in dispersed, often single, dwellings, among their fields, where human manure could be easiest applied to land and where their travelling time to their lands was minimized.

Outside the cooler highlands and generally beyond the influence of the Inca and pre-Inca higher civilizations, lowland cultures have had little hold in modern days, retreating before all other forms of agricultural enterprise, but they merit a word as their agricultural technology is being currently reappraised by anthropologists and others. Shifting cultivators were common in the northern Andes and on the lower Andean slopes further south in Peru—Bolivia. These men worked within the Indian tradition of a polyculture with many crops and few animals. But they had to key their enterprise to steep slopes and hot rainy climates which speeded soil deple-

tion and erosion, and their shifting plots, using a piece of forest for two or three years before allowing it to go to forest fallow for 20, 50 or even 100 years, maintained their tiny populations with no undue pressure on the natural environment. Slash-and-burn farming such as they used has been criticized as wasteful of land and forest, and has been overlooked as a technology for poor soils in the tropics, but it may have ecological lessons that have yet to be learned by modern farmers.

The Iberian culture thread

Spaniards and Portuguese brought new ideas to the continent, but more importantly they brought new crops and animals. Sheep, goats, pigs, horses and cattle were all new to the continent and all could be used, especially in the hitherto unoccupied grasslands of the Pampas, where they multiplied rapidly in the wild, and in other grasslands elsewhere. Using the new animals, ploughs could also be introduced and large areas worked under a new system of farming. Instead of small-scale intensive farming, massive ploughing and planting of single, monocultural crops was possible. A particular type of establishment grew up, the *hacienda* (or *fazenda* in Brazil) which combined the capitalist production of livestock or grains with a medieval social structure of a semi-servile labour force and all-powerful lords.

In the tropical lands where large-scale production was desired but few hands could be mustered from Indian sources, slavery was practised, and this became the standard system on the sugar plantations of Brazil, the Guianas, Colombia or Peru.

Nineteenth-century immigrants

A third culture thread is that of the migrant streams of the late nineteenth century, bringing in new blood, European peoples who, because of their very newness and because of the mixture of ideas which they could introduce to the country and to one another, gave new life to the agricultural regions where they settled. They brought in small owner-operator farming, a new system to Latin America, often producing the same goods as the great *haciendas,* but with a new intensity and with their own labour and that of their families, not with tenants.

It was these people too who were responsible

for the introduction of dairying on a commercial scale in Argentina and Chile, for French vines in Mendoza and for a variety of improved European stocks of known animals and crops. Under their aegis farmer cooperatives were set up in the same countries, allowing them to compete with the big farmers in economies of scale. By providing their labour, they also permitted the large-scale introduction of alfalfa in the Pampas, improvement of the livestock industries, and the extension of wheat growing throughout this region, both in Uruguay and Argentina. Often they could not become owner-operators, for difficult physical conditions, their own ignorance of local conditions, or financial difficulties in paying for their land could all delay or prevent successful settlement. In these cases, they were absorbed into a modified form of old systems, or left the land for the cities.

Communal tenure

One of the main ways in which the three cultures outlined above differ is in their attitude to land ownership. For the Indians, the system most commonly found in pre-Hispanic time was some kind of communal holding of land, wherein responsibility was shared and decisions as to land use were taken collectively as in the early medieval version of European agriculture. This system of landholding survives, in Chile, in Colombia and Ecuador, but especially in Bolivia and Peru, where indigenous communities have continued to hold onto their land, despite a long history of land takeovers on the part of Spanish landowners. Usually only part of the land is collectively owned today, often only pasture-land, and the communal system has long been eroded by and intermingled with the lati-fundio—minifundio system outlined below.

One reason for survival of the system is its communal sharing of responsibilities. Land cannot be sold in communities which are strictly managed, so that farmers cannot become landless through selling out; in cases of crop failure, the community maintains the farmer, perhaps very modestly, but it maintains him, until next year and a new crop. The system is not progressive, for it is ruled by village elders whose concern is largely welfare, not production, and who have to work within a tight framework of limited resources of land and other inputs. Innovations are in any case hard to achieve with the established system of collective decision-making. The system's great advantage is its social concern and ability to provide for each member, in hard years as well as good.

The Iberian heritage: latifundia

The essential features of the *latifundio* are a combination of great size and underutilization of the land resource. This combination was possible in most regions until the present because land was the cheapest resource, costing little or nothing to the individual, and because there was no effective competition from small farmers to limit it or force higher production levels. Attempts to give a comprehensive explanation of the origins of great landholdings have often been made for Latin America, but without entire success because of the extreme variety of sources. Some great holdings were in fact the remnants of original grants to the *conquistadores* from Spain, and *donatários* from Portugal. Others were lesser grants, *donaciones* by the leaders to soldiers in the ranks or to officers. Yet others were not intended by the Crown as grants at all, but permission to use royal lands (which were all those not held by some other body) for one or two generations; these were the *mercedes*. In fact, many of these were never returned to the Crown and continued as land holdings of private families on a permanent basis.

One property arrangement was peculiar to the New World. This was the *encomienda*, which placed Indians in the care of a lord. A controversy exists over the extent to which such entrustments of men became also grants of land, and for at least one region, Paraguay, race mixture and the division of *encomiendas* among various inheritors meant they were soon worth very little; but the possibility of converting an *encomienda* into territorial control was always there and must have been taken up on many occasions.

The Church too came into possession of great holdings throughout Latin America, and these tended to grow continuously because no land donated by men on their death bed to the Church was ever returned. Not all Church lands were unproductive *latifundia,* and the Jesuit holdings in Bolivia and Paraguay were intensive producers of such goods as cotton, yerba mate and tobacco, but other orders were less efficient and their lands were managed no better than those of lay owners.

Not all *latifundia* were colonial, and the nineteenth and even the twentieth century has seen further great domains arise, while old colonial estates have remained unbroken, merely transferred to mestizo or creole owners. In Argentina, the expansion of the frontier allowed expanses of fertile land, as well as Patagonian steppe, to be given away or sold at ridiculous prices, to army officers who had helped the campaigns against the Indians, or to capitalists who had financed it. Behind the frontier, other lands were given away to friends and supporters of the dictator Rosas, in the years before 1850. A public land policy like that of the United States, reserving lands for ordered settlement by small farmers after careful survey, was conspicuous by its absence. Even the ecclesiastical estates which were taken from the Church in the nineteenth century were not reserved for new family farmers but sold to existing landowners.

Minifundia: a dependent system
Great landholdings could not survive alone, without a work force, and this was brought except in thinly peopled lands from surrounding or included Indian settlements. Indians were forced to work on the great estates in the early days by a *corvée* or labour tax. Later this could be dropped as the Indian was forced into greater dependence on the *haciendas*. To earn enough to live, he was forced to work part-time on the *hacienda*. In the case of landless labourers, the *hacienda* could allot a piece of land, too tiny to provide a living, in usufruct to the Indian, in return for his work over part of the week, sometimes most of it, on the master's land. These tiny holdings became present-day *minifundia* in many parts of old upland America. Elsewhere, *minifundia* have emerged because of the simple rise in modern populations without traditional checks imposed by disease, war or climatic accidents. Modern medicine and disaster relief have the unfortunate effects of prolonging and extending the main problems while attending to the immediate and obvious ones.

Slavery and debt-serfdom
In areas where labour was difficult to attract because of slight population, two methods could be employed. In rubber, yerba mate, Peruvian sugar and some other zones, debt enserfment was practised. Unmarried youths in search of excitement and a new life were enticed away from home with promises and gifts of clothes, money and goods. They were then made to work in the forests or on the plantations, under the domination of gang-masters, and under the legalistic pretext of not having paid debts owed for the advance of goods, clothes or money. Since they were never paid enough to repay these debts, the system was self-preserving.

In the coastlands of Brazil, Pacific Colombia and the Guianas, where Indians could not be made to work continuously, slaves were brought in from West Africa. For Brazil, slaves were the most valuable item on the import list through much of the colonial period, and were traded for large amounts of money.

Immigrant tenure
Nineteenth-century introduction of Northern Europeans, from countries unused to oppressive forms of tenure, led to the rise of owner-operator small farms. This introduction could only take place, however, in the parts to which immigrants could be attracted, thus excluding nearly all of the tropics.

Migrants came especially to Argentina, south Brazil and south-central Chile. In these regions they were given, or had made available to them at advantageous terms, plots of land between 10 and 50 ha, on which they worked as families, initially without the help of tenants or labourers.

DISTRIBUTION OF LAND
The recent figures on land distribution among the continent's farms are the result of this history of different cultures and attitudes to land. It is apparent that concentration of land in very large holdings is a continuing problem, just as the crowding of peasant farmers on tiny holdings remains a drawback, for optimal production, of another kind.

Among the countries with the largest problem of this kind are those of the Andes, from Chile, through pre-revolutionary Bolivia (there is no post-revolution census) to Peru, Ecuador and Colombia. It should be emphasized that the existence of large and small farms, however extreme, is not a negative feature in itself; it may be useful and necessary to have large farms in dry pastoral zones, small ones in irrigated valleys. When these large and small farms occur together, however,

FARM HOLDINGS IN SOUTH AMERICA

Country	Smallest and largest size classes (ha)	Percentage of farms	Percentage of farmland
Argentina	0—5	15.2	0.1
	Over 1000	5.9	74.5
Bolivia	0—10	69.4	0.4
(1950)	Over 500	8.1	95.1
Brazil	0—10	44.8	2.4
	Over 1000	0.9	44.2
Colombia	0—5	62.5	4.5
	Over 500	0.6	40.5
Chile	0—5	48.8	0.7
(1965)	Over 1000	1.4	72.6
Ecuador	0—5	73.1	7.2
(1965)	Over 1000	2.0	27.1
Paraguay	0—5	46.4	n.a.
(1961)	Over 500	1.4	n.a.
Peru	0—5	83.4	5.8
	Over 500	0.4	75.1
Uruguay	0—10	29.6	0.7
	Over 1000	4.8	58.3
Venezuela	0—5	42.9	1.0
	Over 1000	1.7	67.0

Source: various. The data refer to 1960 unless otherwise given in the first column

on the same kinds of land, there is obviously something critically wrong in terms of the national economy's loss of potential production, and the inequity resulting to the small farmers themselves.

Loss to the national economy occurs because the large farms are almost invariably less productive than the small ones on a per ha basis, so that maximum production is not achieved. Large farms may provide a good profit to their owners, but they employ only a few people per unit area and do not produce enough. This is the situation implied by the term *latifundio,* a farm which is not only large but also underproducing.

LAND REFORM MOVEMENTS

To improve the agricultural situation has been a recurrent promise of governments in Latin America. Plans have included the establishment of modern forms of tenure, eliminating in particular the old forms where rent was paid by work, or by provision of goods or services, and re-

placing these with money rents.

Apart from tenure, unequal land holdings have been the object of reform, and this matter involves much more effort than tenancy reform, which may be based simply on legislation. Reallocation of land requires not only legislation, but expropriation of land, and allocation of this land among the landless and the *minifundistas*. It also requires granting of credits to new farmers, building of roads, farm houses, irrigation ditches and other associated works in order to settle new small farmers in zones where only cattle may have been before.

Chile

Reforms have been undertaken on the most extensive scale in Latin America in the countries of Chile, Cuba, Mexico and Bolivia. In Chile, the reform movement has been growing over a long period, starting with the opening of the Agricultural Colonization Bank in 1928 to help settle small farmers on unused land. Very little was done before the war, or until the money and administrative teeth were put into reform with the creation of CORA, a national reform agency taking over from the Bank in 1962. Even then progress was slow and settled only 4000 families a year between 1965 and 1970. Then Allende's left-wing government speeded the pace of reform and was aided or anticipated in its work by unorganized takeovers in the Frontera district, home of the still restless Araucanian Indians.

From its election in November 1970 to its deposing in September 1973 this government expropriated over 5 million ha, compared to 3½ million in the preceding six years, itself a large figure. Another way of describing the massive scope of land reform is to say that 64 per cent of the national farmland other than forest has been subjected to reform. There are of course deficiencies in the operation including the displacement of many experienced farm technicians and managers, some of the farm labour force, and a lack of infrastructural works such as roads and houses, but the reform remains basically intact under the new military regime, and production is expected to show improvement in the years ahead.

Bolivia

Here the premises, content and expectations of agrarian reform were different. Land was taken over wholesale, some of it before the enactment of an agrarian reform law in August 1953, a law which lagged over a year behind the takeover of power in 1952. During this year, Indians of the *altiplano,* organized into *sindicatos*, found themselves in sufficient control to be able to take over haciendas by force, and many killings took place. No compensation was paid for the takeovers despite provisions for compensation in state bonds under the reform law, and this disruptive change in control must have affected production. Certainly production levels seem to have fallen in the first post-reform years, though part of what happened was the retention for themselves, as home consumption, of a far greater portion of the harvests by the peasants. Quantities delivered to markets cannot reveal the total picture of change. In any case, as much of the organization of marketing farm products was in the hands of landlords, when these went a new system was bound to be slow in emerging. A study comparing the Peruvian and Bolivian sides of lake Titicaca in the late 1960s (Burke, 1970) found little or no increase in land or labour productivity due to reform in Bolivia, but that by cropping a greater part of the land the Bolivians had managed to put more peasants on the land; in terms of the national economy this may be a satisfactory trade-off against low farm productivity, in a country where urban industrial jobs are scarce.

In recent years Bolivian commodity production has been increasing, but the best improvements are in subtropical agriculture, coffee, citrus and other crops coming from the Oriente, from Santa Cruz, from the Yungas, from beyond the old agricultural heartland of the *altiplano*. Old forms of production, lack of machinery and tiny farms are all still in evidence, and in such a poor country must be slow in finding replacements.

Reform in other countries

Over the rest of the continent, the rate of reform has been much more leisurely, and has not solved the fundamental agricultural problems to date. In Venezuela, Colombia and Ecuador, land reform has taken at least in part the form of grants of title to land to already existing farmers. This is because many thousands of peasants in these countries had moved into subtropical or mountainous country where the owners have

little control over the land, or where ownership is by the state. Here, the role of reform agencies has been merely to legitimize existing farms by granting title. The squatter farmer is in this way given security of tenure, an important accomplishment but in no way constituting land reform in the sense of redistribution of land from large to small owners.

The pace of peaceful land reform by subdivision of large farms has been slow in these countries because of the agreed policy of recompensing landowners who suffer expropriation. No state has had sufficient funds to undertake the great burden of credit extension, farm building construction and road building, to name only major infrastructural needs, and at the same time pay *latifundistas* market values for their farms. Venezuela, with her oil revenues, has the most money for farmers, including budgeted funds for expropriation when mutual agreement on a takeover by the National Agrarian Institute cannot be achieved. The payments for expropriated farms vary and are larger for those farms which serve a social function, by feeding local populations or employing much local labour. The Institute has also taken a hand in various programmes designed to aid the productivity of small farmers, with extension services and small farmer credits and loans.

Perhaps the most forceful movement apart from Bolivia and Chile has been in Peru, where since 1969 expropriation of lands, both on the coast and in the Sierra, has been pushed through, to the surprise of the outside world, by a military government. On the coast the foreign companies which had dominated the sugar industry, and the foreign and domestic concerns owning cotton plantations, have been taken over by the state. This was a simple action, and far more complicated action has been necessary on the Sierra where Peruvians must take land from Peruvians, resulting in much bitterness and social disruption. Some form of cooperative venture is the norm in the Sierra, in an attempt to revive the old community spirit of the villages, but this very often still leaves underprivileged sectors of the community, those who could not be included in the cooperative, the landless, and those unable to work their land.

In some countries, the Guianas, Argentina, Uruguay and Paraguay, reform has not taken place at all, though reform laws have been enacted. In Argentina, an indirect line of attack is relied on, the taxation of land according to productive capacity rather than production levels, so that landowners who cannot improve their output are encouraged to sell. Fiscal measures must always be suspect in countries where tax evasion is as common as it is in Uruguay, where so little faith is put in the income tax that the state's revenue from it is no greater than that from the stamps which must be affixed to official documents.

COLONIZATION PROJECTS

Agrarian reform is the restructuring of farming on areas already occupied, with the aims of improving the lot of the rural poor and of increasing farm production. In the eyes of some governments both aims may be met by the alternative of colonizing new farm lands, so that it is necessary to ask here whether such an alternative can be viable.

Colonization has a long history in the post-independence period of Latin America. In Argentina, thousands of South European migrants were made into colonists on the edge of the Humid Pampas in Santa Fe between 1850 and 1900. In Brazil, many settlers came into the southernmost states in the late nineteenth century, 1.4 million of them between 1887 and 1898, and many became colonist farmers. But European settlers were not easily attracted to the low tropics and twentieth century colonists of the Amazon Basin have been citizens of the various countries concerned, except for special cases as with Japanese in Paraguay, Bolivia and Brazil.

Most colonization involves poor native farmers, moving out from densely settled areas into virgin or long fallow land, often into a region of different soils and climate from what they knew, either as spontaneous colonists, i.e. colonists who move of their own accord as individuals and families, or as sponsored or directed colonists under a government programme.

We may identify three broad kinds of problem in colonization projects: the natural environment, the human material, and the organizational and technical problems of colonies. Dealing with these in turn, the physical environment problems include the enervating physiological effects of hot humid climates, which may reduce

resistance to disease; the poor nutrient base of soils commented on in the first chapter; liability to flood and high water table in many regions; and tree weed invasion in natural forest lands. These physical problems are compounded by colonists' lack of experience. In the Colombian Putumayo, for example, colonists try to grow coffee though it is unsuited because of excessive moisture, lack of dry season, and poor soils; the farmers insist on it because it is a crop they are familiar with from the higher mountain slopes of their area of origin.

This leads us on to consider colonists character. Those best adapted are the spontaneous colonists, who migrate into the area because they know its potential, often have friends or relations in the area, and know about farming. These men stay longest in the frontier areas and are most successful as colonists. In contrast, former townsmen are not good colonists. In the Turen–Las Majaguas project in the Venezuelan Llanos 500 lots were set aside in the mid-1960s for slum dwellers from Caracas, as a gesture towards relief of their condition. By 1970 over 60% of these lots had been abandoned. Unrest and settler disputes have also been a problem in Las Majaguas, because the settlers were brought in from different areas with distinct cultural backgrounds, instead of making each group a homogeneous unit.*

Other disputes may occur, as for example in south-east Colombia, between spontaneous settlers who have entered the region without legal title to land, and colonists brought under government schemes. Another group conflict is between colonists and Indians, as has occured continuously in Brazil where ranchers have pushed tribal peoples off their traditional territories using the same tactics as the Wild West: threats followed by brute force.

Organizational problems are universal in settling new areas under government-directed schemes. Title to the land is not usually given at once, but made subject to conditions. In the Peruvian *montaña*, government surveyors have to survey the land before granting title, and survey costs may exceed the cost of the land. Size of holdings in planned colonies is often a difficulty. In Venezuela, a small colony at

*R.C. Eidt, 'Agrarian reform and the growth of new rural settlements in Venezuela', *Erdkunde*, **29**, (1975), pp.118–33

Barbacoas has been successful with only 5 ha holdings, because intensive vegetable and fruit crops could be grown and marketed in Barcelona. Further west in Barlovento, 5–10 ha holdings are formed on a shifting basis, using a hectare or two at a time, because of tradition and the type of crops grown. In contrast 5 ha lots were too small for rice and maize farmers in Turen-Las Majaguas in the poorer soils of the western Venezuelan Llanos. Obviously considerable flexibility is required in this matter as in others. Organizational failings go much farther than farm size and title; as with land reform, it is not enough to hand out land, and lack of credit, machinery, good road access, planned settlements with services, are constant complaints.

The broad question remains as to the overall desirability of colonization compared to agrarian reform. Colonizing new land may certainly increase farm production, may serve to reduce political and social unrest among small farmers on over-populated lands, and may have a strategic role in occupying land which lies too close to borders with aggressive neighbours for safety. It does not of itself however make any changes in land tenure or affect social relationships in the areas of colonist origin. Perhaps both agrarian reform and colonization are needed in any overall land policy.

The Green Revolution
Yet another alternative to agrarian reform may be thought to be the use of better technology. What has been termed the Green Revolution (not really a revolution in world terms but an application of advanced methods to poor countries) concentrates on plant breeding to provide high-yielding and resistant varieties of the main food plants.

This began in Mexico in 1943 under a programme financed by the Rockefeller Foundation of the USA. Later other countries were also helped to start similar programmes. Most attention was given to wheat and maize, and considerable success was had with new wheats, high-yielding, short stalked, disease resistant, and responsive to fertilizer. These wheats were adopted in South America in the 1950s and especially in the 1960s, but the Indian sub-continent and other areas have proved more receptive of them and in South America the new varieties are often grown only at and around agricultural experiment

stations. Maize has been gradually improved too, but not in the manner of wheat. The US hybrid corns are not desired by Latin American farmers because they provide no seed corn for sowing the next year. Rice has been more successful, a rice breeding programme begun in Colombia leading to total adoption of a new dwarf variety by 1974, and substantial adoption in Ecuador and Venezuela.

The difference in success between maize and rice illustrates the main problem in adoption and explains why the Green Revolution has passed by Latin America. Rice is a crop of commercial farms produced entirely for the market, and controlled by rice mills which may act as agents to introduce new varieties or indeed insist on their use. Maize is a subsistence crop of peasant farms, where the farmer may have little contact with the outside world, because he does not market the crop, or does so only locally in a village, not selling into a national network.

High-yielding crop varieties create their own problems for the small farmer. They require fertilizers to yield well, they may need irrigation, larger harvests may mean transport problems and storage building on farm. These things are well beyond the means of poor farmers and they often cannot obtain the credit which would be needed to start. Tenant farmers as many of them are, are unlikely to make investments in irrigation or drainage, in grain silos, or any other permanent improvements, because the owner may at any time dislace them and reap the benefits himself or charge higher rents. Green Revolution is thus only effective as a set of technical changes following agrarian reform.

PRODUCTION SYSTEMS

On the basis of the three cultural traditions outlined above, native, Iberian and immigrant, and a set of agricultural production possibilities, a regionalization of agricultural types is possible (fig. 6).

Upland traditional
This is the system of the Bolivian and Peruvian Andes, carried north also into Ecuador and Colombia. It is characterized by small farming among Indian and mestizo peoples, for subsistence crops of beans, maize, potatoes and other roots, and it involves few animals. Interspersed

among the *minifundia* are great haciendas, usually devoted primarily to cattle and sheep production. The type extends with little variation into northwest Argentina and into Chile where till the very recent past similar forms of production were found.

Tropical lowland

Outside the highlands this is the nearest approximation to the traditional system. It occupies parts of all the tropical countries. Because it occupies lowlands and thus areas outside the traditional settled lands, it differs from the highland traditional type, not only in crop type but in organization, tenure and commercial orientation. Farms are more likely to be owner-operator in type, more likely to market a good part of their production, their farmers enterprising and aggressive rather than cooperative. Indian *comunidades* are absent from these areas of no high Indian cultural tradition. The products of this farming are bananas, citrus and other fruits, vegetables in zones near to markets, and as subsistence crops cassava, beans, maize and rice on wet lands. The great pastoral industries, mostly for beef production, are considered separately.

Plantations

The degree of organization required in sugar production is sufficient to call into being a special type of production system, the plantation, and this is found widely but most importantly in northeast Brazil, in the Peruvian coastlands, and the Guianas, especially the republic of Guyana, former British Guiana. Sugar production in Tucumán, Argentina, is similarly organized: the central features are the dominance of the large farm, often owned by the sugar mill which thus controls farm prices on the small farms that also grow cane; the reliance on a large, poverty-stricken labour force which suffers because sugar field work is only seasonal; and the dependence on irrigation systems which often come under control of the large landowners.

Plantation systems may also be observed in the production of cocoa on the Venezuelan coast, in the former U.S.-owned banana plantations near Santa Marta, Colombia, and in coffee production in Brazil. In every case the advantage of the plantation is its ability to invest heavily and then wait several years for the harvesting of the first crops. Plantations have also replaced collection from natural forests in the cases of rubber in the

4 A vineyard in Mendoza Province, Argentina. Irrigation culture is vital to the economy of many Latin American countries

Fig. 6 An agricultural typology

The following labels appear on the map:

ANTIOQUIA

GUIANA

NORTH PERU COAST

NORTHEAST

TUCUMÁN

SANTA CATARINA
RIO GRANDE

Farm Production Systems

Immigrant small	
Traditional/Immigrant	
Upland traditional	
Commercial Pampas	
Tropical lowland	
Plantation	

0 250 500 750

Kilometres

Amazon basin, and yerba mate in the middle Parana country.

Immigrant small farm

Occupying areas on the edge of the Pampas and in Paraguay, south-central Chile and Colombia, is a farming type which might be described as 'immigrant small farming'. It was introduced to Santa Fé province in Argentina and to the Puerto Montt region in Chile by nineteenth-century migrants, and to Paraguay and northeast Argentina by twentieth-century incomers. Production includes milk and dairy products, meat and grains, from truly mixed farms as well as grain and cattle farms worked intensively. In the Paraguay—northeast Argentina case, production is of subtropical crops such as citrus and tea. The Antioquia area of Colombia is distinct, for here immigrants were very few, and small farming is more a product of the specific form of spontaneous colonization into the middle Cauca and Magdalena valleys for coffee production.

Commercial midlatitude

The natural grasslands of the Humid Pampas in Argentina, Uruguay and southern Brazil have been used for a combination of cattle and grain farming. This is not mixed farming in the western sense of integration, however, for cattle are not used to fertilize the lands or eat stubble remains, nor are they fed grain as a common practice. Instead it is a dual system with grain sold as such, and cattle grazed on grass in long leys, or alfalfa, quite separate from grain production.

This duality is quite logical, for the farmer may turn from crops to animals according to the markets, and has the financial resources to do so. Though the system is run by a largely immigrant population of the nineteenth century and is found in middle latitudes, it differs from the immigrant small farm type, being composed of large and often mechanized farms, especially the grain farms where tractors and combine harvesters are common sights.

Traditional—immigrant transition

Some areas which have received large numbers of migrants have not undergone a complete change of farm organization but merely adjusted to the immigrant. For example, the Bolivian Oriente has had many Bolivian peasant migrants from the altiplano and immigrants proper from East Asia. These have sometimes been taken into existing farms where they are tenants, elsewhere receiving their own land and becoming owner-operators, though in a somewhat traditional environment and using traditional channels for marketing and credit, only locally forming a genuine independent colonization movement.

Similarly in Brazil, the opening up of coffee lands has been by a combination of immigrants from Europe and Asia, absorbed in part into a *latifundio* system, in part and for a time seeking out their own land on the agricultural frontier. Other areas where comparable evolution has taken place are south-central Chile, the Argentine Chaco cotton lands, Mendoza—San Juan in western Argentina, and the Atlantic coastlands of Colombia. In these areas commercial agriculture on small farms is usual, but traditional control by large landowners places some doubt over the success of the projects as intensive farming on a permanent basis.

PASTORAL LANDS

Livestock production in South America is generally quite separate from crop farming. It is also very much more extensive in type, as opposed to the intensive cattle farming on small farms in Western Europe.

Perhaps the most productive area is that of the Pampas, already mentioned as a crop—livestock producer. Allied to this region and managed by a related immigrant group is Patagonia, where large *estancias*, owned by absentee landlords in many cases, produce sheep for wool and a little meat.

Outside these middle-latitude areas, grazing land is almost entirely natural pasture, and therefore generally very poor in quality, sufficient for raising steers over a period which may be as long as five or six years. This is the condition in the Llanos of Venezuela, in the Gran Chaco, in the *sertão* of Brazil, and on the *tierra fría* and *páramos* of the Andean altiplano. In general, livestock production may be seen as a residual landuse, occupying only those lands unsuited to crops and not really competing with them except in the artificial conditions of *latifundia* which own good land which they do not care to cultivate.

4. Industrial Infrastructure and Manufacturing

Latin America is not generally thought of as a major manufacturing region, but as provider of minerals and other raw materials, as well as farm products, to the world. Two world wars, however, and the trade restrictions and tariff barriers they engendered in order to protect home industries, have made for the emergence of new industrial centres of some importance, on a domestic and even a world scale. In the present chapter a review is made of these industries and of the transport, mineral and power infrastructure which they require. Agricultural resources which are used in industry are discussed separately in the chapter on agriculture.

MINERAL INDUSTRIES

Manufacturing industries rely on a variety of raw materials, fuel and power resources, for the most part highly localized and costly to make available at the sites of consumption. In South America, many minerals are mined primarily for export markets, so that locations for mining near the coast have been at a premium, and the interior regions are still little developed. Thus, of the two major regions with metalliferous ores — the Andes and the Brazilian Shield mass — the second has been tapped only to a slight extent, for it occupies a largely interior position. The intervening plains of sedimentation have no major metal ore deposits to speak of, so that

Argentina, Paraguay and Uruguay, dominantly plains countries, have unimportant metal mining industries compared to the wealth of Peru, Chile or Brazil.

The manner of mineral extraction varies greatly in the continent, even within one country, for the great modern mining companies have not displaced traditional small-scale producers. Often giant mines owned by foreign capital and producing efficiently can be seen alongside one-man enterprises using pick and shovel to scratch a meagre existence from the subsoil. The great companies have their own concentration plants for processing ore, their own transport arrangements for exporting it, their own power, water and fuel supplies, sometimes their own housing for employees. Thus the company forms an enclave of the world economy within a peasant landscape, a state within a state in extreme examples, where education, wages, health and welfare are attended to at a different level from the rest of the country, and it is natural that such a situation should arouse the antipathy of governments and people, forming an easy target for nationalistic outbursts and calls for expropriation.

In effect there arises a dual economy, in minerals as in agriculture, one sector well supplied with capital and modern, the other, composed of the poor single miners, completely without capital and relying on the only factor available, personal labour. Poor miners are the products of the local economy, where a whole set of different costs for factors is to be found, and where the cost of labour and capital must be compared, not with costs in other producing countries as in the case of the large mining company, but with labour and capital costs in agriculture and industry within the country.

An example: Chilean copper

The Chilean copper industry before the expropriations of 1972 is illustrative of the situation. Here, at the large mines owned by North American interests, was produced 90 per cent of all Chilean copper, yielding substantial excise tax income to the state and employing 15 000 workers. In addition, there were 400 medium-size companies with modern capital structure and thousands of one-man or very small operations. Medium and small mining employed about 40 000 persons, but produced only 10 per cent of the copper. The dilemma faced by Chile, and in different form by all countries in Latin America, was whether to allow foreign companies to continue and maximize short-term revenues, or to nationalize and have full control of the mines.

The aims of expropriation would be to help employment by using more local manpower, to help training of local engineers and administrators (the upper professional element in the big companies was normally foreign), and to direct all the profits into the national economy instead of having them siphoned off to the foreign headquarters of the company. It was also thought in the Chilean case that the level of production could be controlled, to meet national economic needs rather than the ups and downs of the international markets.

Net results of expropriation, which Chile undertook against the companies' will, have been negative in the short term, with disruption of production through the loss of technicians and non-availability of materials which were formerly imported. Long-term effects have yet to make themselves felt, and could be much more favourable if the copper profits are really devoted to national aims, though production and consumption of a commodity such as copper, capable of being stockpiled on a massive scale by market countries, cannot be controlled, nor its prices much influenced, by a single producer country.

Some major ores
COPPER

Copper is the most important of the region's metal ores, produced very largely to feed international markets. Chile, for example, exports all but 3 per cent of her copper to other countries. Concentrations of copper associated with great magmas are to be found throughout the Southern and Central Andes, and now Chile is being challenged in copper production by Peru, which in 1955 had only 1 per cent of world production, but in 1974 nearly 3 per cent, a result of foreign investment on a massive scale, opening up three major mines in the south of the country with reasonable access to the coast.

Massive investment is in fact the key to copper developments, because copper occurs largely as a 1 per cent or even smaller element mixed into a ground mass from which it can only be separated using modern large-scale methods. The mining of large volumes of ore also requires heavy investment in machinery. Thus copper mining has not yet come to Argentina and Bolivia, on a large scale, for want of permits to the international companies, or because of political uncertainties in the country which deter investors. Both these countries have known reserves of disseminated copper capable of supporting a major industry, and in the case of Argentina there are plans for a long-term development of the resource by the raising of internal capital.

TIN

Bolivia is the only large tin producer in the continent, and tin still dominates the Bolivian economy, providing the greatest single contribution towards the country's foreign exchange. Like Chile or Venezuela, Bolivia has had a one-product economy with the resultant crises and booms that this engenders. In the late nineteenth century the industry was developed here when there were no other world producers, and the difficulties of transport to the exterior were overcome, with rail lines to the Pacific to take out this vital ore. Tin came at a useful moment in time, when the decline of silver mining, because of a gradual disappearance of bimetallism and acceptance of the gold standard, was causing gloom and crisis in the local mining industry — an earlier example of the effects of a one-product economy.

Large investments soon became necessary in

Bolivia because of the depth of deposits and low grade of ores, so that three large companies, dominated by three leaders, Patiño, Hochschild and Aramayo, made the tin-mining oligopoly, and comparison with other countries became more direct over the years as these three companies came under foreign ownership. Small miners were never excluded, but their production was small and their control of the industry nil.

In recent decades the inefficiencies of the enormous industry compared with its world competitor, Malaya, which works accessible alluvial ores, have made for a modern situation of economic crisis. The industry, representing U.S., Chilean, British and Swiss interests, was taken over in 1952 after the revolution, but the basic physical problem of high extraction costs from deep mines and poor ores could not be by-passed or overcome.

In recent years a major effort at diversification and emphasis on the ores which are associated with tin — notably wolfram, bismuth, lead, zinc and silver — has had some effect in solving this problem. The share of tin in exports has decreased from 70 per cent in 1963-5 to 50 per cent in 1971 and 48 per cent in 1972. Petroleum and natural gas are helping this movement, and cotton from the agricultural sector.

IRON

Both production and markets in the case of iron are somewhat different from tin or copper: there are many producing countries all round the world; the mineral is not stockpiled in the same way as tin or copper; and there are substantial markets growing up in Latin America itself. All these are conditions leading to somewhat more secure and steady mining, though exports to industrial countries still account for a large share of production. As late as 1970, Chile, Brazil, Peru and Venezuela were all exporting 90 per cent of their ore despite large domestic industries. Thus coastal sites and the involvement of international companies have been normal.

Another factor influencing iron ore development has been that of national security. In Argentina, for example, low-grade ore from Sierra Grande (fig. 27) in Patagonia is used to supply the national steel industry though total delivered costs can never match those of Brazilian ores. For the most part, South American ores are of high grade, reaching over

65 per cent iron content in the major Brazilian, Chilean and Peruvian deposits, which fits them well for the international markets. The Brazilian deposits benefit from the fact that they are associated with manganese, the most important of the ferro-alloys.

Only one major iron ore deposit of the interior is likely to be developed in the near future, the Mutún deposit of southeast Bolivia. This remote ore has no markets in Bolivia or nearby Brazil which has more than adequate domestic supplies, but it is close to the river Paraguay, and experimental shipments by barge down to the San Nicolás steel mills of Argentina are being made. For most other interior iron ores which may be discovered, the transport costs are likely to prevent development.

Where other conditions are favourable, the use of an iron ore below 50 per cent iron may be warranted; the Colombian industry provides us with an example in the works at Paz del Río, built up at a site with ready access to coking coal, limestone and water all within the Chicamocha valley, and with fair access to the principal market of the country, Bogotá, for the steel produced.

BAUXITE

Until recent years the market for aluminium, and thus for bauxite, has been extremely thin, and concentrated in a few industrialized countries. Now markets are growing in many countries with transportation industries, and aluminium use is spreading out to other items, so that the location of mills in South America must be expected soon, producing for local markets.

To date production has been controlled by North American and Dutch interests, operating in Surinam and Guyana, the only large producers on the continent. These countries suffer from overdependence on a single product, and this is scarcely alleviated, in the case of Surinam, by the development of mills using hydroelectric power to produce alumina and aluminium.

In the long term the location of this industry, and of bauxite extraction, is likely to be controlled by power availability, because of the heavy demands for power in converting the ore to metal. Bauxite itself is widely distributed over the Shield areas as a product of long weathering in tropical conditions, and most bauxites must remain unused. Extractors are likely to seek loca-

PRODUCTION OF SOME LEADING MINERALS, 1977

| Country | METALS | | | FUELS | | |
	Iron ore*	Copper ore*	Bauxite	Coal	Crude oil	Natural gas†
Argentina	321	0.1		533	22,167	64,629
Bolivia		3.7			1,612	14,800
Brazil	56,600		1,000	3,859	7,810	9,720
Chile	4,879	1,053.7		1,228	928	13,560
Colombia	460			3,800	7,106	20,411
Ecuador		0.3			9,280	387
Guyana			3,223			
Paraguay						
Peru	4,021	343.6			4,496	4,590
Surinam			4,856			
Uruguay						
Venezuela	8,490			121	117,007	122,000

*Metal content of ore
†Natural gas figures exclude gas flared and vented at well head, and gas reinjected to maintain oil pressure. These categories account for much Venezuelan gas

All figures are in thousand metric tons, except for natural gas which is in teracalories (calories x 10^{12})
Source: United Nations Statistical Yearbook 1978.

tions near the large hydroelectric plant available in the lower Sao Francisco valley (Paulo Afonso Falls) and on the middle Paraná river, from Posadas—Encarnación up to Jupiá—Ilha Solteira, a line of power potential shared between Paraguay, Argentina and Brazil.

OTHER METALS
Associated with the major ores in the ore mix, or associated regionally because of the type of geological structures obtaining, are a variety of minor ores. The bismuth, wolfram, antimony and lead of Bolivia have been noted. In the case of Chilean copper, as in North American copper, there is an important associated production of molybdenum, and Chile, with 9840 metric tons out of the world's total of 88490 tons molybdenum content in 1974, is second only to the United States in the free world. Brazil holds a similarly important position with respect to manganese, in 1973 producing 1.14 million tons manganese content out of a world total of 9.15 million tons. Finally, Peru is still a world leader in silver production, with 1275 metric tons out of a world total of 9230 tons in 1974. It should be noted that none of these minor ores weighs heavily in the overall national production

structure. Peru, for example, only earns about seven per cent of GNP from mining, and this is spread over a number of minerals, from important and large mines of iron through copper, lead and zinc to silver and many minor products. Minerals, for nearly all countries of the region, are important because of the export trade and foreign currency earnings they provide.

FUEL AND POWER RESOURCES

Among fuel sources, as the above table demonstrates, petroleum has an overwhelming dominance in South America. Coals are produced by Brazil, Chile and Colombia on a moderate scale, but even in these countries the role of coal as a fuel is very much subordinate to that of oil and gas. In most cases the coals are relatively low-grade sub-bituminous types and not suited to the production of metallurgical coke, so that there has been little spur to their exploitation. Many small Tertiary basins with low-grade coal in the Andean countries lie unused for want of effective demand.

It is fortunate considering this reliance on petroleum that supplies are reasonably abundant. Until recent years production was heavily concentrated in the hands of Venezuela, and this country still has the lion's share of reserves and production. Some countries, like Paraguay, the Guianas and Uruguay, which have not yet found oil, and Ecuador, which only found significant quantities recently in dramatic discoveries in the Oriente following decades of drilling dry holes, have seen their twentieth-century economies suffer for want of ready fuel and power in comparison with the oil producers. In the long term, countries such as Argentina and Bolivia, owning large sections of sedimentary geological basins between the Andes and the Shield where oil is likely, may produce considerable amounts and be able to become major exporters. Brazil has high hopes too, based on recent offshore finds reported in the northeast and near Rio, but Petrobras, the state oil firm, only produces a quarter of national requirements at present.

Oil and Venezuela

This country is the closest approach to a Middle Eastern 'oilarchy', with one product providing 90 per cent of exports, though even in this extreme situation the mining sector of the country only contributes in direct form about 8 per cent of GNP (1979). Overdependence on a single product has become a matter for concern as the oil wells produce increasingly heavy oil, as international firms have been excluded from production, and as the search for an alternative to oil for governmental revenue continues to bring up no real answers. Over time, too, Venezuela's economic strength relative to its neighbours is being eroded because of the stagnation in production since 1960. Whereas in 1960 Venezuela contributed 32.7 per cent of all LAFTA exports, in 1969 it was 22.6 per cent, symptomatic of a general economic decline prior to the rapid increase in oil prices of 1974. Venezuela is now only gradually shifting her economy away from oil because of the OPEC price rises; diversification of exports has been a minor feature and industrialization has been advanced by using oil in petrochemical industries, on lake Maracaibo and the Caribbean coast.

In Peru, expropriation of oil firms held back the development of rich country in the Oriente for a while, though the selvas is now being developed and foreign firms are working under contract to Petroperu, the state oil firm, an Argentine firm for example helping to build an oil pipeline from the selvas out to the Pacific at Bayovar. In Bolivia, expropriation came after a period of oil development, and recuperation of production under national control has been possible. For Argentina, there has been an alternation of permissive attitudes towards foreign participation and harsh controls or expulsion. This has done nothing to encourage new foreign investment though it has made the state company YPF an experienced oil producer and marketer.

In Ecuador, political thinking at present is towards increasing national control of an industry which has recently become prominent, and Venezuela has taken complete control of her production, refining and petrochemicals industries. Harsher attitudes towards foreign investment are of course part of a world pattern emanating from the Middle East, which Latin America is able to follow with difficulty because her industries are younger and less experienced. Only Venezuela and Argentina with strong and mature national oil companies, can afford to exclude foreign finance and technology from the industry.

Total energy production

The table shows the dominance of oil in the overall energy picture, as well as the enormous contrast in levels of production between countries like Venezuela and Paraguay or the Guianas, which latter are not represented in the table for want of data, but have only a tiny output. In one or two countries, notably Brazil, there is more reliance on hydro power, reflecting both the lack of alternative power sources in the country, and

TOTAL ENERGY PRODUCTION
(Million metric tons coal equivalent)

Country	1955	1963	1971	1976
Argentina	7.00	22.92	37.63	41.82
Bolivia	0.49	0.59	2.46	5.04
Brazil	4.04	11.55	20.39	26.47
Chile	2.99	6.15	9.08	15.73
Colombia	9.36	15.37	21.63	18.73
Ecuador	0.64	0.47	0.31	14.10
Paraguay	—	—	0.02	0.08
Peru	3.44	5.53	5.27	7.06
Uruguay	0.08	0.11	0.18	0.15
Venezuela	153.92	228.72	155.11	199.00

Source: U.N. Statistical Yearbook, *1978*

the excellent sites for power production from the rivers, notably the middle Paraná and the lower Sao Francisco, at the Paulo Afonso falls. The five-fold increase in energy production in Brazil shown over the period 1955-71 in the table is the most remarkable feature of it, and has been achieved with very little recourse to oil or coal production. The equally impressive potential for hydroelectric power in the other countries, especially in the Cental Andes, has been more difficult to utilize, and without considerable aid from international agencies still less would have been achieved.

Means of increasing energy production
South America has large untapped fossil fuel reserves. Among those currently being used, natural gas is wasted in colourful extravagance by being flared at well head in most wells that are not near a large market. Venezuela is currently making efforts to use some of her Lake Maracaibo gas, and Chile is planning to make liquefied gas from her Magellan Straits deposits.

Another major petroleum resource for the future is in heavy petroleum and oil shales. South Venezuela has a strip of country just north of the Orinoco with perhaps 2800 billion barrels of which 10–30% is recoverable by new techniques which involve steam injection into the beds at regular drill points, a method already tested in secondary recovery of oil from the Maracaibo region. Brazil has large oil shale deposits in its far south, Río Grande, which it is trying to find ways of exploiting.

It is also likely* that conventional oil supplies have themselves been underrated in Latin America for a number of reasons, primarily because international companies have not been made welcome in the area, and have always worked under the shadow of possible expropriation and interference from local governments. National agencies, when they have taken over from the internationals, have been constantly restricted by shortage of capital and lack of technical expertise. Large potential oil-bearing areas have still not been surveyed, and within existing areas there are many recent finds extending the life of old fields.

Non-petroleum energy resources are still mostly untapped. The hydroelectric resource is only used to the extent of about 5% of total potential. Even if we exclude a half of the remainder because it is undesirable to use it for one reason or another, this leaves large resources. Nuclear power is only beginning to be developed, with a functioning centre in Argentina and two more under construction there. Technological and capital requirements for this industry are the main drawbacks.

Non-conventional energy resources, using low technology, are obviously of interest to poor countries in South America, with its relative lack of capital and manufacturing skills. Brazil, with much land and little oil, has been prominent in vegetable alcohol production, from wood and recently from cassava. São Paulo state has a 10% alcohol component in fuel sold at petrol pumps, and it is rising in other states. Experimental biogas producers from vegetable waste are in use in the tropical lowlands in various regions, and lack now only an efficient marketing system to become an important rural agency source.

Some countries such as Brazil and the Guianas, have large wood-waste resources that go unused. From 1981, wood-waste from large mills near Georgetown, Guayana, is to be used in a 5000 kw power generator, disposing of the problem of where to put the waste, replacing expensive oil imports, and producing fertilizer in the form of wood ash.

Wind and solar power, like biogas and vegetable alcohol, are potentially important but distributed over a very wide geographical area. The principal market of such power sources is thus the widely distributed rural population rather than towns. Unfortunately the rural target areas are often at such a primitive level of development, lacking all infrastructure (e.g. electric power installations and roads) that even this intermediate technology is difficult to apply. Solar, wind and biomass energy should obviously be part of integrated rural development schemes.

Electric power
Provision of electric power is an important element of the manufacturing infrastructure, and the existence of a power grid is especially useful for small manufacturers who may use it as an external economy. This factor is often overlooked by observers familiar with the industrialized countries, where a grid is universally available,

---

*Peter R. Odell, 'Energy Prospects in Latin America', *Bolsa Review* **14**/II (1980), pp. 98–112.

ELECTRIC ENERGY PRODUCTION

Country	1965 Total	HEP	1974 Total	HEP	1977 Total	HEP
Argentina	15 383	1 225	27 990	4 820	32 477	5 771
Bolivia	566	433	967	747	1 150	890
Brazil	30 128	25 515	70 480	66 960	99 869	92 943
Chile	6 131	3 954	9 297	6 049	9 776	6 502
Colombia	5 824	3 900	11 950	8 200	15 223	10 350
Ecuador	572	249	1 270	440	2 145	630
French Guiana	11	(thermal)	55	—	75	—
Guyana	220	—	387	—	416	—
Paraguay	135	—	504	—	626	595*
Peru	3 839	2 625	7 530	5 582	8 557	6 098
Surinam	244	85	1 588	1 006	1 421	1 215
Uruguay	1 744	—	2 458	—	3 040	1 567*
Venezuela	8 197	1 369	18 396	7 299	23 051	11 934

Source: U.N. Statistical Yearbook, *1975, 1978*   *Public plant only*   *— unknown*

but the alternative, private small generating sets, often very inefficient, has to be accepted in many parts of Latin America. Reliable systems are by no means universal, and irregular supply or blackouts are frequent occurrences in all countries of the South American continent. In addition, most countries do not operate their electric power systems under a single controlling body, but have a motley combination of federal, provincial, municipal and private concerns generating and transmitting electricity to the public.

THE EMERGENCE OF NATIONAL GRIDS
No really national networks of power lines are yet in existence, but there are several countries with grids on a macro-regional scale. In Argentina, high-voltage lines connect the Pampas cities, Buenos Aires, Cordoba, Rosario and Santa Fé, to one another and to power sources on the Rio Negro and in Mendoza.

In Brazil, a network has also emerged in the industrial core, the Belo Horizonte—Rio—Sao Paulo triangle, fed by thermal and hydro plants in the core and also by the Ilha Solteira—Jupiá plants on the Paraná. Some planning has been done to integrate the network, a particularly desirable process in south east Brazil where many companies operate. In Minas Gerais, for example, 359 companies were in operation in 1950, most of which have now disappeared or

amalgamated. The vast power of the north-eastern Sao Francisco river has yet to be brought to the centre, and perhaps it will be best for regional development that this power be made available first to industries in Recife or Bahia.

Colombia provides another example of regional integration, in the industrial triangle of Cali—Medellín—Bogotá, also linked to Barrancabermeja on the Magdalena, but with no links to the northern thermal-based electricity of the Caribbean cities. Integration of a national scale here and elsewhere is necessary to balance and share loads so that one region can make up deficiencies elsewhere, or take up slack in demand.

A considerable amount of the electrical energy (as opposed to total energy) comes from HEP installations, much more than is common in the major industrial countries of the Northern Hemisphere. The table shows the dominance of hydroelectricity in the Brazilian, Chilean, Colombian, Peruvian and Bolivian economies. It also shows the spectacular growth of Brazil, again outperforming all other countries in percentage growth, except for the minor cases of the Guianas, growing from a near-zero base in the 1960s. Venezuela also stands out in the way in which it has increased the participation of HEP in its electricity production despite huge petroleum reserves, with the harnessing of the Caroní river.

5 At the Paulo Afonso Falls the river Sao Francisco leaves the Brazilian plateau, producing a highly concentrated hydro-electric potential which has been gradually harnessed since the 1950s

In the long term, the concentration of power from rivers is likely to be in two major regions, the middle Paraná valley, where the gorge section of the river produces excellent heads of water and basin shapes for retaining water, and where there is ample flow; and on the Sao Francisco river, notably at the Paulo Afonso Falls, where similar conditions obtain. In addition there are thousands of individual sites in the Andes south of 35°S and north of 10°S, between which parallels the mountains are too dry for very large rivers. Sites on the middle Paraná, which are shared by Paraguay with her two large neighbours, Brazil and Argentina, are likely to convert this country into a major exporter of power within a few years.

FOREST RESOURCES

On world vegetation maps South America is usually depicted as mainly forested, which is accurate enough in botanic terms, but must not be taken to imply a wealth of timber or other products merely awaiting the logger and sawmill.

Over many parts collection of wild forest products is still the only way of utilizing the forest. In Brazil, *yerba mate*, from a member of the holly family which inhabits the Paraná Plateau region, carnauba wax from a palm growing in the northeast, Brazil nuts from the Amazon valley, are all still collected from wild trees. Not long ago, wild rubber from the Amazon was responsible for a brief but spectacular boom in the northern interior of Brazil, halted only by competition from plantations in the Old World.

Much forest has poor timber value as it is today, being composed of secondary growth following slash-and-burn farming for a few years by migratory subsistence farmers. Where cutting has taken place, it has been destructive, with no replacement, and no concern for conservation. Farmers and ranchers seeking new pastures have set great fires on the forest frontiers of the continent, eliminating major tracts of virgin forest. Some attempts at conservation are being made now — in Argentina, with poor resources of timber, planted eucalyptus, willow and pine are replacing natural forests in the delta of the Paraná and in Misiones province in the northeast. In Chile, on the southern fringe of the central Mediterranean belt, there are increasing plantations of Monterrey pine (*Pinus radiata*) to serve the needs of pulp and paper mills. In Colombia, substantial plans exist to convert the central Magdalena valley into a great timber producer for sawmills and paper mills in Barrancabermeja. In this country, as in others, tree planting could well be incorporated into general plans for river basin management, to conserve soils and help control flooding and silting of the rivers, but organizational problems have prevented the emergence of this type of thinking in the continent.

A problem in forest use held in common with other tropical regions is that of species mix; much forest is selvas with enormous abundance of species, so that the exploitation of any one is quite difficult. This is part of the reason for concentration of forest utilization on two regions, southern Chile and the Paraná Plateau of southern Brazil. In the former, pine-laurel forests, with good stands of single species, are available, and make Chile an exporter of timber to other countries. In the latter, *Araucaria* forests produce wood suitable for either paper or construction; in foreign markets the wood is known as Paraná pine. Even in these major forest industries, there are problems of management. In southern Chile, for example, the industry of sawmilling is in the hands of small forest owners who are often also farmers, and do not devote their full attention to the business. They lack capital for large installations and for transport to take out their product.

TRANSPORTATION

The peripheral pattern

Although the continent is apparently entered quite easily along the major rivers, to judge superficially from the map, trade and population have always kept close to the coast so that most long-distance movement has been by sea. Important physical reasons exist for the coastal orientation of transport — the rivers are in fact not readily navigable by large vessels, in the case of the Amazon because of many rapids both on the

main stream in its upper course and on all the principal tributaries. On the Paraná-Paraguay system, it is the silt load that deters river traffic, and makes the river fit only for shallow draft steamers and barges or rafts of timber. The line of the Andes has also helped to orient countries outwards, to either the Pacific or the Atlantic ocean, and links across the mountains have always been difficult.

The other factors in peripherality of transport are economic ones; trade orientation has always been with overseas countries, predominantly those of North America or Europe, and transport has been improved mainly to serve this trade. The Spanish policy of divide and conquer meant in effect very little trade between her subject colonies, each of which required roads only to the ports leading to Iberia.

Railways

In colonial time, oxcarts and mule trains — or in difficult country human carriers—sufficed for transport. During the nineteenth century, the

6 Peasants in a landscape — a scene on the middle São Francisco river. This river is still the principal means of transportation in the region, as well as a food and water resource to the local populace

steamer, operating on the rivers, made some impact in changing and improving movement, but it was the railways, superseding river travel and taking new overland routes, that really changed the pattern. Rail development was made, however, during the period of maximum dependence on the transport of goods to and from South America, rather than among the member countries of the continent. Rails served more often as dividers of regions than connectors, for, while agricultural interiors might be linked to port cities, the ports remained separate and isolated from one another, as did the interior regions.

Railway expansion went through the stages of main line construction to ports, followed by feeder extensions to either side, but failed to complete a final stage of filling out a complete net with multiple-direction main through lines. Under nineteenth-century conditions there was no need for such filling out, given the export orientation of transport. In any case, construction was never unified under a national plan, but entrusted by provinces or governments to private, foreign firms whose responsibility was only for individual lines.

After the private construction stage, governments attempted to fill in the gaps by building 'developmental lines', but these were doomed to unprofitability as they were built quite generally with more political and strategic motivation than economic. Such developmental lines were built in the Argentine Chaco and the northwest, and in Patagonia to the south. Strategic interest accounts in part for the construction of the north Chilean line, which helped to link the nitrates region won in the War of the Pacific to the centre at Santiago. Similar interests were uppermost in the building of a railway through Brazil's far south in Rio Grande do Sul.

The end of the railway era

Figure 7 shows the cycle of railway development, starting in 1850, rising to a peak around 1930, and declining thereafter. In most countries it was almost inevitable that railways should lose importance, for they were composed, for example in Venezuela, of single-purpose lines linking mines with ports and dependent on a single type of trade. Construction was usually lightweight, often of a type which would not permit the later

adoption of heavy diesel locomotives or of high running speeds. Rail gauges were varied, and some of them were even abandoned in the countries of manufacture so that new rolling stock could never be acquired easily, and transfers from one gauge to another were another obstacle to development of a network.

After the Second World War, most railways were expropriated by local governments, which meant a further run-down of the equipment: worn-out track, ancient locomotives (steam is still common even in advanced Argentina) and rolling stock, inefficient and excessive manning of the railways. All these mean that the rail systems are great loss makers for their countries and have been losing traffic to roads. But is the railway age over?

In some cases, apparently not. In Brazil, where at present only the iron ore line down the Rio Doce valley is profitable, a 970 kilometre line is to lead from the Serra dos Carajas iron ore body, discovered in 1967, near the Transamazon Highway, out to Itaqui near Sao Luís in the northeast, and the government has a five-year plan involving 3800 kilometres of new line, gauge widening of 3200 km, and electrification of 1439 km. Further north, Venezuela has finally settled its plans for a railway system, and is to build over 3000 km of track, eventually linking San Cristóbal in the west to Ciudad Guayana in the east, and connecting with the short line linking Barquisimeto to the coast at Puerto Cabello. Bolivia too is expanding her rail lines into the flat Oriente, linking to Argentine and to Brazilian lines, and so forming a transcontinental line across the wide tropical section of the continent, as well as giving Bolivia an outlet to both oceans.

Roads

In the countries whose standard of living does not demand a massive road-building programme, and where national planning can direct infrastructure and manufacturing, the railways may yet present a viable, perhaps even optimal, solution to the transport problem. But roads and lorry traffic have seen the greater development over the last thirty years, and for the extension of farming areas into the interior as well as for the development of intra-continental trade, roads would seem to have an advantage. Brazilian road-building has been the most rapid

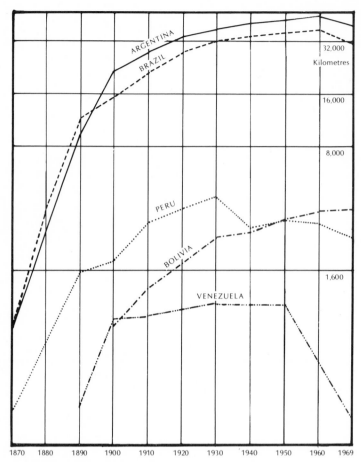

Fig. 7 Trends in railway development in South America

and far-reaching in the continent, and has had the advantage of no competition from rail or water since neither achieved a real penetration of the deep interior.

Roads and economic development

An important question is whether there can be a genuine fostering of development by road construction alone, or more generally by improvement of the economic infrastructure in any way. There are two quite different types of situation which may be considered: first, that of the farming frontier, where new lands, usually tropical lowlands, are being opened up by small farmers; secondly, there is the case of an already densely peopled region making investments in roads or transport of some form.

In the first of these cases, provision of a road has value as giving an outlet for lowland produce. Plenty of examples, such as the road to the Bolivian Yungas from the capital La Paz, may be cited, showing the direct benefits of the road, without which the citrus fruits, bananas or coffee could not be marketed. Here the road has an absolute value, and in its absence a semi-subsistence economy would prevail. On the other hand, success of the peasants in this frontier situation is not assured merely by having good transport. Marketing problems and the action of middlemen in marketing, insecure land tenure and the breakup of farms into *minifundios* may all constitute barriers to economic progress.

In the second case, that of densely peopled areas such as the Nordeste of Brazil, roads inten-

7 The Santos-São Paulo motorway. Only locally, as here and in the case of the Caracas Motorway in Venezuela, were such roads possible before 1970. But a network is now beginning to emerge

ded to help the movement of farm products and industrialization have led instead to a migration out of the region to Rio and Sao Paulo. Improvement in transport and communications has led to rising expectations and information about better-off regions, in advance of local improvements in employment or social services. There is perhaps a case here for the bettering of social services and the building of farm-to-market roads before the construction of giant inter-regional highways, so that local levels of living can be raised before the raising of information levels concerning opportunities in other regions and increased ease of travel to them.

Stated aims of the Brazilian government have been to bring settlement to new zones via the Transamazon and Belém—Brasília roads and their like, and also the reduction of inter-regional differences in standards of living. The priority

given to motorway construction and to roads in isolated peripheries with tiny populations may however remind us more of the *autobahn* plans of prewar Germany with their strategic implications, than of any plan for economic and social development.

The Carretera Marginal de las Selvas
This is one example of the dramatic roadbuilding projects in the western selvas (fig. 8). Under the inspiration of Peru's President Belaunde, Peru, Bolivia, Ecuador and Colombia agreed to make the Selvas Flanking Highway, a road providing international links north—south and connecting to the highlands and west coast. This road was expected to lead to the opening up of much new farmland and to add, according to estimates, 5-12 per cent to national totals of cultivated land, as well as allowing nearly a million farmers into

Fig. 8 The Carretera Marginal de las Selvas

the region. In fact only a fifth of the 5500 km road has been built, mostly in Bolivia, and it is pertinent to ask why enthusiasm waned. According to one enthusiastic proponent of the scheme:

> The role of the Carretera Marginal de las Selvas is both permissive, in that it makes possible the elimination of regional differentials, and compulsive, in that it forces a realignment of the use of resources.
>
> *C.J. Stokes,* Transportation and Economic Development in Latin America *(Praeger, 1968), p. 127*

The road would in fact only permit elimination of differentials if other improvements were made, in the fields of education, social services, the creation of town centres and perhaps the introduction of industries. These phenomena cannot be expected to accrue naturally to a new road in the wilderness. There are technical and broad economic difficulties in achieving the results hoped for from the road; the physical potential of much of the land is suspect, or even known to be low, with highly infertile soils in some regions. The road runs in a north—south direction which does not meet the needs of the majority of farmers, who would wish for links to the highlands, rather than links to their neighbour tropical zones, with which there can never be much agricultural trade.

MANUFACTURING

Factors in the localization of manufacturing

Nearly all manufacturing in the subcontinent is concentrated in the great metropolitan centres. Exceptions are to be found, as in Colombia, where population and industry are more dispersed, and manufacturing is shared between Bogotá, Cali, Medellín, Barranquilla and others, and there are several examples of twin centres, capital and port, such as Quito—Guayaquil, Santiago—Valparaiso, Lima—Callao, but these scarcely alter the validity of the statement.

There are many reasons for concentration, some of which may be enumerated:

1 The nature of manufacturing in the continent encourages metropolitan location: much of it is light manufacturing, such as textiles, food and drink manufacture, consumer goods for which the dominant location factor is usually markets and labour. Capital goods manufacturing, steel, chemicals and the like, though often decentralized, is little represented in most countries and scarcely affects the pattern.

2 Foreign control of some industries, and the dependence of manufacturing on distant decision makers, probably constitutes a strong centralizing force. These decision makers have few prejudices, family ties or affections regarding regional preference, and will always tend to place their investments according to economic as opposed to social optima. The international car firms, with their assembly plants near the great cities of Brazil, Argentina or Venezuela, exemplify this feature. It is difficult to attract such firms to remote rural or urban locations, though government action has occasionally brought them to smaller cities such as Arica in Chile or Trujillo, through generous credits and tax remissions. The case of Arica is apposite in this discussion. Tax exemptions and effective prohibition of car plants being established elsewhere from 1958 to 1967 meant a great concentration at Arica. But when Santiago was allowed plants in 1967 much of the industry migrated there, to take advantage of vicinity to

markets and suppliers. Evidently government action has to be longterm to be effective.

3 A third factor has been the historical process of centripetal industrialization, from colonial times onwards. Under Spanish and Portuguese rule, industry was either banned or allowed in remote parts where supplies could not be brought in, but gradually concentration of colonial industry came about in the few ports of note. In the post-colonial period, concentration at these ports or nearby cities has continued under European influence.

STAGES OF INDUSTRIAL GROWTH

Though the development of industry in the continent has little immediately apparent pattern, there are certain time—space regularities which must be pointed out, and which may be defined in terms of stages of growth. The scheme outlined below is only indicative and approximate, but it charts a real process.

Colonial history

Mercantilism of the Iberian variety tended to reduce industry to a minimum in the colonies, making them raw material providers and importers of manufactures from Europe. There was a definite pattern of colonial industry, however, with certain regions specializing in products for regional populations. In the Northern Andes, artisan industries were well known in Quito and nearby towns of the highlands; there were also important craft industries in Santander—Norte de Santander in present Colombia. In both regions, textiles were dominant, especially woollens, with Panama hats and basketry other typical products. Further south, the Bolivian Oriente had organized industry in the Jesuit mission villages: these supplied textiles, metal work, leather work, and milled sugar, all for the altiplano markets. Related to the same industrial core of mining in Bolivia, northwestern Argentina had its craft industries, transport-oriented (saddles, harnesses, carts) for the trade to the altiplano, in towns such as Tucumán, Salta and Jujuy. Further south still, isolated Mendoza and San Juan had a number of craft industries, as befits a region where communications to both east and west were quite difficult. Iron working, leather industries, wine and barrel making were among the crafts practised here and to some extent also in Cordoba. In Portuguese America this pattern of craft industry was less advanced, a reflection of the coastal concentration of all population and lack of any economic advance in the interior.

Nineteenth century

The first stage described above lasted until Independence, with a gradual decline of the craft industries through European competition. Following independence, and with the emergence of free trade, the new republics were unable to develop manufactures and old handicraft industries were all virtually eliminated by Manchester and Birmingham. The revolutions had been led by the *criollos,* whose wealth was in land, not in manufacturing, and they had little interest in new industrial processes; indeed, the whole social climate was against the entry of upper-class men into industry, and gave prestige only to administration and the military services.

Modern industry thus came late in the century and from the exterior. Early industries were the processing plants for goods moving out to Europe, flour mills, sugar mills, meat packing and meat extract factories, all of them near or on the coast. This second stage might be termed that of Port Processing. It lasted till about 1930, and brought a considerable concentration of industry to the main ports, to Valparaiso, El Callao, Guayaquil, Rio, Santos, Montevideo and Buenos Aires.

Import substitution

The effect of the 1930s' depression was to reduce trade substantially, so that port industries were also reduced in importance. Tariff raising at this time, carried out in all parts of the world, served here to help the growth of a number of industrial types, by protecting newborn domestic industries from foreign competitors. Industries now established were those requiring little capital or technology to start up, textiles, toys, kitchenware, furniture, printing and publishing. Again, geographical concentration as in the previous stage was an important feature. This stage of import substitution is still being traversed by some of the countries and the very high tariffs originally established in this stage make current trade unification among the countries very difficult.

General industrialization

In recent years the largest countries, Argentina and Brazil, have been able to move on to a fourth stage of general industrialization, producing capital goods and consumer durables, notably the motor car. These countries have substantial iron and steel industries, oil refining, petrochemicals, heavy engineering. These resource-oriented industries tend to lead to a deconcentration of industry, to sites close to deep-water transport or to bulky and heavy raw materials. With the advent of this stage, a complete range of manufacturing is found and Argentina and Brazil may already be ranked as important industrial nations.

One important shadow hangs over this swift advance in manufacturing: many of the industries are not strictly speaking homegrown. The firms are often subsidiaries of foreign companies who set up within South America to avoid tariffs imposed against foreigners and use some cheap factors in manufacture. Since finance, engineering and enterprise remain outside the country, such industries are not the boon that a truly domestic industry would be. Brazil's recent 'Economic Miracle', with very rapid advances in GNP and exports, is particularly affected by this problem, which makes the economic sparkle superficial and somewhat fragile.

The four stages mentioned have not of course replaced one another entirely, but coexist in a country. Interesting patterns of old craft industry, such as the old leatherworks of San Luís or Catamarca, may survive despite manufacture of the same articles by mass methods in the capital of Argentina. In the Nordeste and the Peruvian Oriente, ancient ox-mills produce coarse brown sugar while on the coast modern mills make sugar for international and urban markets of a quite different quality.

A KEY INDUSTRY: STEEL (fig. 9)

For steel the twin factors of national security and prestige have been important. A steel industry has been regarded as a badge of the developed country and has been developed in part because of this, and also because of a desire by governments to establish independence of other countries in steel manufacture, a strategic industry. This helps explain the steel industries of Argentina, Venezuela, Colombia, Chile and

Fig. 9 Integrated steel mills, coal fields and iron ore deposits

Peru, which have state backing despite many negative economic features such as high material costs and small markets.

The Chilean and Venezuelan cases have curious similarities; in Chile there are good ores in the north, coal and limestone in the far south. Despite great distances, sea transport makes total assembly cost reasonably low, and the tiny market which in 1945 could not absorb a large mill's output, has grown to economic size since then. In Venezuela, ore and HEP were found together on the Caroní river, together with coal from the coast; transport by sea for coal and finished steel was possible and a market restric-ted largely to pipelines for oil has broadened to take all kinds of steel products. The venture has also allowed some regional development of the Guyana region in the southeast.

The market factor

Two countries with substantial and broad markets capable of taking all products of a modern integrated mill are Argentina and Brazil. In Argentina, the high cost of raw materials has been a drawback, but the chief mill, at San Nicolás above Buenos Aires, has a market location and open water to bring in ores. Brazil has both markets and materials at low cost, with iron ore, limestone, manganese and wood charcoal in Minas Gerais. Some movement away from these resources has however taken place, and the integrated plants, apart from Ipatinga on the Doce, are near or on the coast — Volta Redonda, Santos and Porto Alegre — where they have immediate access to large industrial markets. Brazil intends to increase steel production to supply export markets, and this intention also brings coastal sites, in this case at the mouth of the river Doce, into prominence.

At the other end of the market scale, small countries such as Bolivia, Paraguay, Guyana or Uruguay cannot contemplate steel industries, unless export demand supplements that of the home market, which does not approach the output of a modern mill.

Colombia, with its excellent combination of resources for steel in the Chicamocha valley, has not been able to expand its industry, despite the continent's lowest assembly costs, for want of markets. Peru's small industry is similarly confined.

Obviously future steel developments will depend on international rather than internal markets, and it is likely that only a few steel centres will emerge, the question being whether these will all be market centres, or sites where material assembly costs are low, such as Colombia or Venezuela. Market sites are now in the ascendant, and must maintain an advantage as long as free movement of goods is promoted.

INDUSTRIAL REGIONS

Steel industries with their associate engineering and other user industries tend to form industrial complexes which occupy much of a region's population and make it an industrial region. While industrial regions of the Northern Hemisphere type are not to be found, two zones, the Plate from La Plata to Rosario, and the industrial triangle Sao Paulo—Rio—Belo Horizonte, might be defined as emerging industrial regions. They are examined in detail in the regional chapters. Outside these two, there are only large single centres or conurbations, such as Lima—Callao, Santiago—Valparaiso, Caracas

or the big cities of Colombia, and these tend to have a less broad spread of industry than the two first mentioned.

OVERALL VIEW AND OUTLOOK

Manufacturing has come to the region only recently, but its impact is already considerable, providing as much as 35 per cent of GNP in Argentina, and 13 per cent even in Bolivia. This impact is not apparent to the outside world, for most industries cater solely to domestic markets, but it is nevertheless real.

One observable feature has been the geographical concentration of industry, which is explicable in historical and economic terms. What is now needed, for the benefit of the countries concerned, is perhaps a more vigorous policy of regional deconcentration — moving industries out to growth poles outside the metropolitan cities. Given that industry must be the major future revenue earner for the region, it is important that its inevitable growth and dynamism be guided to the best effect, both in terms of industrial type or sector, and in terms of location.

Another feature which has earned comment is foreign ownership and influence. Simple expropriation is not an answer to this problem, especially in a world where trade between countries is continually increasing and international connections are made ever closer at the commercial level. In any case, administrators and entrepreneurs will not grow up overnight to replace those expelled in revolutionary movements. What seems to be needed is an arrangement between foreign investor and home government, whereby nationals of the country are brought into high executive position or trained as technologists, as well as profit-sharing policies which earn the home government some revenue from the industry. Instead of such an arrangement, the usual and depressing story is of little profit or skill sharing, until a moment of revolutionary takeover, and subsequent decline of the industry in question. Such problems must slow down and undermine the stability of Latin American manufacturing industry.

5. Population Patterns

Population in Latin America is mostly distributed in the vicinity of the coasts, and the far interior of the continent still has very few inhabitants. Reasons for this concentration are not far to seek. Physically, the interior presents difficulties for agriculturalists, especially in the Amazon selvas and, to the south, drought in the Chaco and poor soils are long-term problems. Historically, the status of economic and political dependence on Europe has enforced concentration of all activity at or near the coast, accessible to Spain and Portugal. Aboriginal settlement too, at least at the time of the Conquest, did not penetrate much into the interior, though evidence of Indian fields from the pre-Hispanic era in the Oriente of Bolivia and Llanos of Venezuela—Colombia suggests that savanna lands with reasonable fertility may have had permanent occupation by organized groups.

The potential of these interior lands assumes a growing importance for modern nations, since today the most obvious thing about Latin American population is its rate of increase, though even within South America there are contrasts in demographic trends, so that some countries are presented with immediate food supply problems, while others stand in need of more people to occupy their peripheral regions.

RACIAL AND ETHNIC PATTERNS

Before the Conquest, the racial makeup of the Americas was simple, for the continent was populated in archaeologically recent times, and by only one major group, the 'Indians', who migrated out of East Asia and occupied the whole continent. This human group has been substantially modified by European contact and miscegenation. Only in one area, the highlands of Bolivia—Peru—Ecuador, has there remained a dense population of reasonably pure Indian blood. In Bolivia it is estimated that 50 per cent of the population is pure Indian, against 40 per cent in Ecuador and 45 per cent in Peru; these figures must always be estimates in view of the impossibility of checking everybody's pedigree, but they give an idea of the mix. Apart from this highland group, there are tribal Indians living in the Amazon basin, often without any permanent contacts with civilization, but these only number a few thousand and their domain is rapidly diminishing in the face of modern ranchers and farmers, who have been responsible for real atrocities in removing Indians from their lands — in some documented Brazilian cases hunting and shooting them like wild animals.

Spaniards and Portuguese came as minorities into the New World, nowhere forming a dense rural mass as in North America. They and their descendants, however, formed a sizeable part of the urban populations. In contrast, the Negroes brought in from West Africa were, and remained, largely rural, forming the bulk of the population in two areas, the Nordeste of Brazil, where they were the work force for the sugar plantations, and the Pacific coastal regions of Colombia, where they formed the mine labour force.

European settlement restrictions
Iberian policy did not permit foreigners to settle in their possessions, so that Europeans in South America are mostly Spanish or Portuguese in origin. Only in the temperate countries, Argentina, Chile, Uruguay and southern Brazil, and only after 1800, has there been any settlement by north Europeans, and even here this group is outweighed by south Europeans, Italians and Iberians, who formed a very distinctive group as they came into the Pampas and Southern Chile, into regions from which the Indian had been totally eradicated, so that racial mixture could not take place.

Race and class
Elsewhere, Spanish and Portuguese have mixed with the Indians to a considerable degree, the result being a blurred colour distinction and the claim by Latin Americans that colour bars are not to be found. This is true in a formal sense, but because of historical distinctions between white masters and black or coloured serfs and slaves, there remain very decided differences between the prospects for coloured and white persons. In the colonial period, only first-generation Spaniards were allowed to hold major offices, a source of resentment which was one cause of the independence moves of the nineteenth century led by the *criollos*, American-born people of pure Spanish blood.

At the other end of the social scale, the Negroes were almost entirely used as slaves until the mid-nineteenth century, and, only slightly higher up the ladder, the altiplano Indians were held as serfs, working for the Spanish at least as hard as for the Incas in olden times. In the twentieth century the results of these old limitations are to be seen in the fact that Negroes, mulattos, Indians, mestizos and other mixed groups occupy socio-economic niches much lower than those of Europeans, in part because of the poor regions where they live, in part because of continuing discrimination against them.

The Guianas
In the northeast of South America there is a slightly different story to tell. Here, as there was no fixed Indian population near the coast, African slaves were brought in as in Brazil, to work the plantations for sugar and cotton. Another group however came in and partially re-placed these during the nineteenth century, people from what is now Pakistan and India, from China and from Indonesia, as servants on several-year contracts after which they were free men. This group has given greater racial diversity to Surinam and Guyana.

In the Guianas too, British and Dutch policy did not restrict immigration by other nationalities, and the result is that the little towns of the region have a diverse, cosmopolitan population of many nationalities, a factor that has no doubt helped to alleviate inter-racial tensions, while the varied skills derived from the different cultures contribute towards overall economic and social development.

DEMOGRAPHIC CHARACTERISTICS

The most significant Latin American population statistic is the growth rate, which for the LAFTA countries generally is 2.9 per cent per annum, a figure higher than that of any other continental size unit, and one which calls forth numerous demands for regional and national population control policies. The Catholic Church's opposition to most forms of birth control is often adduced as the reason for such high figures. On inspection, however, the relationship of high birth rates to Catholicism seems slight. Uruguay and Argentina are, like all Latin countries, nominally Catholic, yet their birth rates, currently about 2.1 per cent per annum, stand well below the average and a long way behind Brazil, with 4 per cent, Venezuela with 3.6 per cent, or Bolivia with 4.4 per cent. A host of factors is related to the level of births and deaths, including the provision of health services, social attitudes towards family size, and the degree of emphasis put on material wealth as opposed to production of the next generation and enjoyment of a family. Evidently, population changes occur as a part of the general process of modernization and socio-economic change towards western standards. In any case, the influence of the Church is difficult to gauge because most people are only Catholic by baptism. There is little Church influence among either the anticlerical Italian nineteenth-century migrants to Argentina, or the peasants of the Andes where Christianity was never much more than a veneer over older faiths.

BIRTH AND DEATH RATES PER THOUSAND, 1960-5 & 1970-5

Country	Crude Birth Rate		Crude Death Rate		Infant Mortality	
	(60-65)	(70-75)	(60-65)	(70-75)	(60-65)	(70-75)
Argentina	22.5	22.9*	8.5	9.4	59.1	59.0
Bolivia	44.0	44.0	21	19.1	73.3	77.3
Brazil	42.0	37.1	11	8.8	n.a.	n.a.
Chile	35.3	26.0*	11.5	8.7	91.6	77.8
Colombia	42.5	40.6	13	8.8	89.6	62.8
Ecuador	48.5	41.8	14	9.5	48.5	70.2
Guyana	39.7	33.4*	9.5	7.2	48.1	42.3
Paraguay	43.5	39.8	13	8.9	44.3	38.6
Peru	44.5	41.0	13	11.9	93.2	65.1
Uruguay	24.5	20.9*	9	9.6	41.6	45.4
Venezuela	47.0	36.1	9.5	7.0	52.9	46.0
Mexico	44.5	42.0	10.5	8.6	60.7	52.0
United Kingdom	18.3	13.3	11.5	11.9	19.6	16.3

*One year only

Source: United Nations Demographic Yearbook, *various years*

Death rates are seen to be at or even below European levels, at first glance a surprise but in fact to be expected, for the large proportion of young people in a growing population means an artificial lowering of the death rate until these people age. In Colombia, Chile and Brazil, over 40 per cent of the population is under 15 years old, because of continuing high birth rates, which are showing slight tendencies to decline; from what is known of the 'demographic transition' (the change from high birth and death rates to low rates as socio-economic development takes place), birth rates will take another twenty years to fall to stable levels, accelerating in urban areas where new ideals about family life and economic opportunity are accepted, slow in conservative rural areas.

COLONIZATION

Most modern migrations are citywards, and rural colonization faces great problems of isolation and limited opportunities. Despite official support for colonization programmes in the eastern lowlands of Bolivia, Peru, Ecuador and Colombia, achievement has been slight and limited to the Andean fringe. Brazil has had perhaps the most successful colonization programme, supported by active roadbuilding, and regional figures indicate in part the process, though they are also an index of high rural fertility rates. Only the industrial and urban Sudeste has suffered rural decline in the face of massive migration to towns.

Little research has been done on the nature of the migrants to new farm lands, as compared to that done on migrants to the urban frontier. It seems from casual observation by the author and from other sources* that the rural-to-rural migrants differ substantially from rural—urban migrants. They seem to be older, often with families, less well educated than those who migrate to towns, theoretically less mobile, in fact little different from those who are left behind. One implication of this is that agricultural extension services, the provision of technical and general education to the settlers, is essential to maintain their impetus in colonization, if in fact colonization is a desired feature.

* D.A. Eastwood, 'Observations on the nature of intra-rural migration in Mérida State, Venezuela', paper read at Conference of Society for Latin American Studies, Southampton, 1974.

URBAN MIGRATION AND METROPOLITAN GROWTH

Large-scale migration from rural to urban areas is causing major changes in the overall distribution of population, so that dense settlement is accumulating in a few relatively small zones, such as the Plate estuary, the Sao Paulo— Rio—Belo Horizonte triangle, and the Lima—Callao conurbation. Until this century, most people could be classified as rural in the strict sense of living in small settlements or isolated houses and working the land. Now large cities are growing up rapidly because of migration, leaving a stagnant ageing population in the rural areas. In Brazil, as late as 1940 the population was 70 per cent rural, but by 1975 it was only 38.6 per cent. In Colombia, the rural population percentage declined from 71 per cent to 36 per cent in the period 1938-74. Yet the natural rates of increase are universally lower in cities, so that migration on a massive scale is taking place.

In the countryside, many regions maintain rural growth, as the table shows for Brazil, but in the south-east region outmigration to towns means an absolute decline in rural numbers.

BRAZIL: RURAL POPULATION 1940–1980

Region	1940	1970	1980 (estimate)
Norte	1 057	1 977	2 466
Nordeste	11 053	16 359	19 054
Sudeste	11 114	10 889	8 346
Sul	4 145	9 193	11 464
Centro--Oeste	988	2 636	3 548

Source: Anuario Estatístico do Brasil, *various issues.*

Rates of growth: the hierarchy balance

Urban geographers have long established a hierarchical structure of cities, following such descriptive models as the rank—size rule, or Christaller's more analytic approach through hinterland demarcation. The findings of such models, based on the interweaving of a large number of economic and social factors, are that

8 *A shanty home on the outskirts of Popayán. Rural-urban migration affects even the sleepy colonial towns of the Andes and, in the absence of either sufficient income or public housing, leads to shanty construction*

a pyramid grouping of cities occurs, with one or two very large cities at the top, followed by a larger number in the next lower size group, and a regular progression of larger numbers of towns in each lower size class.

In Latin America, some commentators have remarked on the unbalanced, top-heavy nature of this pyramid, with one 'primate city', followed at a great distance by the smaller settlements. An index of this primacy, the degree to which one city dominates, may readily be constructed from the ratio of the largest city's population to those following: the table shows some results for South America using as the index the 1970 population of the largest city divided by the next three cities' population.

Index of Primacy

Country	Index	Date	Country	Index	Date
Argentina	4.503	1975	Peru	4.927	1972
Brazil	0.939	1975	Venezuela	1.551	1976
Chile	2.095	1978	Bolivia	1.179	1976
Colombia	1.005	1973			

Source: United Nations *Demographic Yearbook 1978*, Table 8, pp.214–217.
Note: Valparaiso is included with Viña del Mar as the second city in Chile, and Concepción with Talcahuano as the third. Lima is counted with El Callao as the largest city of Peru. In every case where they are given figures for the whole urbanized area, rather than the political city, are used for the city size.

An example of the uneven structure is the comparison in the table, of the sizes of cities in Ecuador estimated for 1980, and the sizes that would obtain if they followed the rank-size rule, the nth town having a population of A/n where A is the population of the largest city, Guayaquil. Quito, the capital, is evidently a second metropolis, but the others are far smaller than this model predicts.

There are many reasons for this structure. In part it is a historical legacy from the colonial past when a few towns were made centres of political power and trade, and other neglected. But to ascribe metropolitan dominance to history is insufficient. Current growth is based on political centralization, but also on economic power, and the main cities are the foci of industrial growth, which itself is highly centralized because it is mostly market-oriented, and the market is in the urban centre. In part the locational decision

CITIES IN ECUADOR

Rank number	City	Population 1980	Rank/size population
1	Guayaquil	1 116 280	1 116 280
2	Quito	807 665	558 140
3	Cuenca	139 209	371 093
4	Ambato	100 046	279 070
5	Manta	89 468	223 256
6	Esmeraldas	87 464	186 046
7	Portoviejo	84 574	159 468
8	Riobamba	71 104	139 535
9	Loja	61 610	124 031
10	Ibarra	54 116	111 628
11	Sto. Domingo	51 377	101 480

makers may be blamed — professionals such as doctors, and industrialists, will not seek locations where infrastructure and social provision are poor. In poor regions even the larger towns that exist have a limited function and that function shows imbalance between them and their region. Portoviejo in the Ecuadorean list, for example, has many doctors, dentists, and markets, bazaars and shops providing essentials such as sugar and rice, all for the surrounding region, because these commodities and services are not available at all in smaller towns. Country folk here will make a weekly or monthly trip to town to find all their needs.

In this way the vicious circles of international imbalance are repeated at various scales, national and regional. Mobile (i.e. urban) functions are concentrated at central points and help bolster their wealth, peripheral areas are poorly provided, and because of the initial advantage of the centre there is no tendency to even out disparities.

SOCIO-DEMOGRAPHIC CHARACTERISTICS

Economic differences between urban and rural areas are apparent over the whole continent, for higher standards of living are generally observable in towns, though urban poverty makes the cities areas both of great wealth and great poverty, often in close proximity. The expression of poverty is varied, and a fascinating set of symptoms is that of various diseases. The map (fig. 10) shows as an example some aspects of

Fig. 10 Causes of death and infant mortality, Brazil

Brazilian medical geography. Two kinds of region emerge, central and peripheral. Circulatory diseases, including strokes, heart and circulation system diseases, are the leading cause of death in the centre, appropriately enough for a region of relatively good diet, resistance to infection, and sanitation, but high living stress and a larger percentage of old people. In the peripheral regions, gastro-enteritis, dysentery, tuberculosis, and other infectious diseases are dominant as killers. Another index of regional difference which is shown is the infant mortality rate, again high in the periphery, all regions, that is, outside the south and southeast.

Apart from disease, the urban areas are characterized by the relative youth of their populace, higher levels of education, and often by social instability, shown in crime, delinquency, prostitution and other social deviations. All these features distinguish them from the countryside. To understand these characteristics, it is necessary to revert to the migration process.

Migration attracts younger people, because of better job opportunities, better use of qualifications, and fewer ties to family, house and other commitments. This leaves the countryside with an older group, a stable society where little is changed by migrants coming in with new ideas, while towns open up new horizons and at the same time make social abnormalities much more likely, for the checks of the rural hierarchy are gone, unreplaced or poorly replaced by public authorities in the city.

SETTLEMENTS

Population patterns over the countryside are a reflection of economic structure and social groupings, physical environment and sometimes administrative fiat. In South America rural settlements include a good number of pre-Columbian towns, especially in the civilized parts of the Inca empire, but for the continent as a whole, settlements mostly date from the colonial period. A limited number of settlements postdate the Independence movements of the nineteenth century.

Old Indian settlements have been most frequently maintained in use in the dry Andes, where water is at a premium and most settlements must seek riversides. Here the Spanish took over the old towns, partly because this allowed them to control the surrounding rural population and make the hinterland produce for its new masters. Thus the Inca settlements, Cuzco and Quito, were made Spanish centres, as were Bogotá and Tunja in the Chibcha area of Colombia, although little is usually to be found

9 Peasants transporting canes for thatching and craftwork at Capachica, on the shores of lake Titicaca. Concentration of settlement into villages was brought about largely by Spanish administrators

of the Indian settlement form.

Apart from taking over intensive Indian agricultural areas, the Iberian newcomers brought in new domestic animals, sheep and cattle, which required a new settlement form, the *hacienda* (Portuguese *fazenda*), an isolated and specialized form of settlement, with ranch and outhouses for peons; the horse was another animal which allowed such dispersed settlement to come in despite the great distances which had to be covered. In some areas, notably in Peru, royal and viceregal ordinances caused concentration of settlement, bringing Indians together in new villages for better control (plate 9); the Jesuits and other fathers practised a similar concen-

tration in their *reducciones*, villages where they taught the Indians and protected them from slavers.

Most of the colonization and settlement described above was into land occupied to some extent by Indians. In the nineteenth century a new move began, into land devoid of settlement or nearly so. This was the movement into the Pampas grasslands, involving a usually dispersed settlement pattern but occasionally European-style villages (fig. 11). From the late nineteenth century a further plunge has taken place, into the selvas, starting from the Brazilian side and now vigorously pressed on all fronts, usually following linear forms along the roads of pene-

Fig. 11 Rural settlement in a part of Entre Rios, Argentina. The Aldea Protestante is exceptional, a village built for a community of German settlers who wished to maintain traditional forms. More common is the surrounding country with dispersed farms and a road system like that of North America. The area to the right is one of older settlement before careful surveys on grid pattern has been established.

tration into the forest.

It is hard to reconcile this linear pattern of settlement with the standard geographers' model for settlement, that of 'central place theory', in which complete areas are occupied with no gaps, by a regular lattice of hexagonal hinterlands or trade areas. In colonization areas the settlements are farms necessarily strung out along or near the roads which lead to the small towns providing services and essential goods, and the merchants who buy and sell farm products. It is perhaps desirable to refer to another kind of settlement model in which the role of the merchants and of the long-distance trade that they dominate is made explicit, allowing that large areas are not incorporated into the market network at all during the colonization phase.*

URBAN SETTLEMENT

For the industrial city of the West, one development model is that under which extension spreads outwards from the centre in a concentric pattern; the centre becomes a business and retail zone, surrounded by successive rings of lower quality housing, manufacturing, inner and outer suburbs of better housing. Another model is based on radial, spoke-like expansion in long fingers of growth along transport arteries. On some spokes, residential development is prominent, on others industry or commerce.

In the non-western or pre-industrial city these rules do not hold, or they are modified by other features. For smaller colonial cities of South America, the residential pattern is of decreasing quality outwards, with the upper classes central and the poor peripheral, rather than the reverse. The centre has fine mansions, or nowadays luxury flats, while further out land is occupied by middle- and then lower-class dwellings. On the outskirts are shanty towns, the *villas miseria* of Buenos Aires, *barriadas* of Lima, *tugurios* of Bogotá and Medellín (plate 10). The variety of names expresses the recency of the phenomenon, a fact of significance to its study. The *favelas* of Rio and the shanty developments at Asunción are not physically at the periphery, it is true, but they occupy similarly marginal sites. They are

*Walter Christaller, *Central Places in Southern Germany* (1966), transl. C.W. Baskin, Prentice-Hall, first presented the central place model. James Vance, in *The Merchant's World* (1970), Prentice-Hall, has outlined the alternative linear model referred to here.

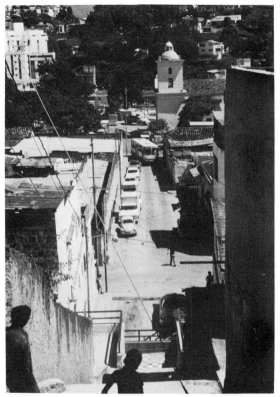

10 This barrio, *a shanty town in Baruta, Caracas, is located adjacent to an old village centre. It is accessible only by steps or narrow lanes, and shoppers or vendors must go on foot*

found in the case of Rio on little hills which were nearly empty before the *favelas,* and on the Paraguay river floodplain in Asunción, another site shunned by ordinary residents.

Apart from high-quality residences, the centre tends to dominate commercial structure, and in small and medium-size towns there is very little spread of lesser shopping centres such as occurs in the West. Public buildings are also central so that the core area has a good mix of functions apart from manufacturing, and even this is sometimes to be found, for land-use zoning has had little impact even where, as in Buenos Aires, it has been in force.

URBAN GROWTH AND LAND USE

For North America several descriptive models have been used to represent urban growth over space and time. One is the *concentric ring model*, whereby the city grows through the accretion of onion-skin rings around its original core. Each ring takes on a different land-use character, the centre becoming the area of shops and offices, the intermediate zone one of industries and poor residences, the outer one high class residence. Another is the *sector model*, the city divided like slices of a cake and each slice having its own character especially in terms of residential growth. Yet another is growth through coalescence of *multiple nuclei* into single urban mass, with a lack of any unified pattern of land use.

The concentric ring model has little applicability in Latin America because of topography

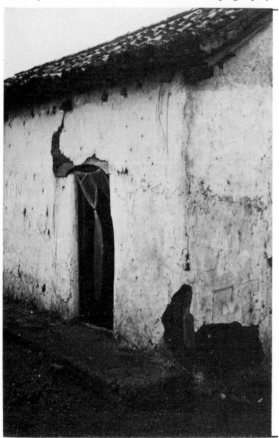

11 Rural housing at El Quibor, a small town in Venezuela. This typical building in bahareque, *sun-dried daub and wattle, with no improvements, is unhealthy for many reasons. One is that it allows carrier insects of a form of sleeping sickness,* mal de chagas, *to live in the cracks in the mud walls.*

and other physical factors that distort city shape, because of an unbalanced socio-economic structure, and perhaps also because what rings do exist are of different character. This last point is not so crucial, because a simple redefinition of the zones would leave the model viable. For example, in traditional towns of South America, central areas were high-class residential and public buildings, peripheral areas were low class, i.e. the reverse of what North American rings produced, so that these rings would simply be renamed for our region. Coalescence of multiple nuclei is also dubious as a growth process, for it really only applies to developed countries where there may be several large cities, for example a group of textile and chemical manufacturing towns sited together on a coalfield, in close proximity to one another. In Latin America big cities are surrounded commonly by open land and only small towns.

Sectoral growth does approximate the kind of pattern seen in many South American cities. This is because residential land use is by far the dominant agent — industrial functions are more limited and as light, market-orient industries are the most frequent, can be set up in most parts without the need for location on power sites, near other linked industries, on water courses or by railway lines. The sectoral growth model for our region is however a special one, being controlled largely by the decisions on where to live made by the upper class which has the resources to buy and develop outer suburban areas. In this sectoral expansion, the role of transportation is not fundamental as has been assumed in the original model. Since it is an *élite* class choosing its residence, transport costs are not too important.

In Caracas (Fig. 57) the dominantly eastward, then south-eastwards expansion, has been led by the growth of *urbanizaciones*, planned suburbs of villas with gardens, through the flat Caracas valley and neighbouring hills. For Quito, the growth has been mostly onto the shelf of flat land north of the old centre. Buenos Aires has grown north in elite suburbs along the river Plate shore towards Tigre at the Parana mouth, though here other sectoral fingers have grown out along the rail lines, south and west. The most important factor is the concentration of wealth in the hands of this relatively small class that can afford suburban housing on a large scale, a much

Fig. 12 Mendoza, Argentina: a transitional pattern of urban land use

more extreme concentration than is to be found in industrialized countries. A secondary factor is the physical restraints which have strongly conditioned urban growth. Topography has controlled urban expansion in towns such as La Paz, Caracas, Quito and Lima, with spectacular mountain walls, while the sea forms a barrier at

Buenos Aires, Lima and Rio, the river at Guayaquil or Asunción.

Shanty towns

At the other end of the scale, a phenomenon characteristic of all poor countries today is the shanty town, called by various names — *villa miseria* in Buenos Aires, *barriada* in Lima, *tugurio* in Bogotá, *barrio* in Ecuador or Venezuela, *callampa* in Santiago. These have been described as 'peripheral' in location; a better term is marginal, for many are not on any geographic periphery. In Asunción, these settlements are close to the city centre on the annually flooded river plain. In Rio, they are on steep slopes of the *morros* or by railway tracks. In Quito, some are within half a kilometre of the centre on the slopes of Mount Pichincha. All these sites are marginal in the sense of unsuitability for housing, but not peripheral. Central characteristics of the shanty towns are usually their illegal origins, through invasions of public or private land which is currently unused (this may be anywhere in the city) and their lack of any standard urban infrastructure. They are thus unimportant to an understanding of overall urban growth because they tend to fill in sites rather than to open new urban ground. They are also densely crowded and occupy little space.

Migration and urban areas

The model above is thus one of sectoral growth led by high-class residential suburbs. The poor of the shanties have a much more limited role. We may ask now how the land use zones relate to migration as this frequently distinguishes zones in cities, and especially as a large proportion (more than half in some recent estimates) of big-city growth is through in-migration. The best approximation to a model here is that of rural migrants, moving either directly or through a series of moves to larger towns, arrive at the central city where they replace the old upper classes that have moved out, occupying tenements which may be formed from the original old mansions of the rich. They become a poor tenant population, but after some time the more enterprising move out to the shanties to build their own homes, often with their own labour.

The role of the shanties is thus not as once thought, that of a parasitic, unemployed, unadapted group with high rates of disease and criminality. *Barrio* dwellers are commonly stable citizens, moving upwards in socio-economic status, and most have acquired urban jobs and experience prior to arrival in the shanty. Nor may it be claimed that the shanties are a burden on municipal services. As they are 'home-made', often to the extent of providing their own water

supplies and laying out their own streets, the cost to urban government in providing infrastructure is lower than for other kinds of suburb. Over a period of time most shanties have their houses improved e.g. by replacing oildrums, plywood and tin roofs by permanent brick and concrete, and the city normally capitulates by agreeing to supply all infrastructure, so that they turn into standard workingclass suburbs. It may of course be argued that shanty building is an inefficient way of using the labour force, using amateur in place of professional builders and still leaving permanent housing to be done later as a second stage, producing poorly planned suburbs that must later be corrected, and sometimes providing poor shelter and sanitation to the inhabitants. But there are often no alternatives given the lack of municipal funds, and in any case these comments do not deny the overall view of shanties as a dynamic movement with sound moral and economic motivation.

Mendoza: An example of transitional landuse patterns

This is a medium-sized city (fig. 12) in Argentina, the total urbanized area population reaching about 470000 in 1970. It is a transitional city in various senses, with a long colonial history but a considerable modern industrial complex, with old traditions but also the new elements given it by immigrants over the last hundred years, and by new resources. In land-use terms, one can see from the map something of the traditional decline of residential values away from the central high-class dwellings, and low-class housing is mostly peripheral, in all directions except west. Squatters form compact groups here and there outside the city, concentrated by the need to be near water sources.

There is some tendency to a modern sector pattern too, high-class housing extending out to the west, towards higher slopes and the city park, an identifiably aristocratic situation, where vegetation is made to flourish in the desert; poor housing tends to run fingerlike along the rail lines, north and south. Pressure on central space has also forced public buildings away from the centre into non-traditional sites; the Universidad de Cuyo is now mostly on a large new site west of the city, on former squatter territory.

THE POPULATION AHEAD

Within Latin America itself, population problems are not generally seen to have the same urgency that is claimed by the outside world. It is felt by many of the nations concerned that they have no problem of feeding their populations because vast reserves of unused land are available. Birth control programmes initiated from abroad are looked at somewhat askance, for they are often seen as instruments of the major powers, who would seek to maintain their numerical superiority and thus their power. By some, birth control is seen as an agent leading to immorality and breaking up the family bonds which centre on the children.

Looking at the purely demographic facts, and at some of the sociological phenomena behind them, there is no cause for optimism in the continent. For the remainder of this century, it is likely that the present areas of high mortality, especially infant mortality, that is, most of the rural tropical areas where poverty, disease and lack of public services are most apparent, will see a decline in these death rates, through improving medical services, so that population increase will continue as at present, through the imbalance of births and deaths, doubling the population every 25 years, the highest rate for any area of this size in the world.

A very large questionmark must be placed over birth rates. Most of the continent is nominally Catholic and, despite a deep-rooted anti-clericalism, is likely to be slow to adopt birth control unless a change in the Church's attitude is also made. Real moves towards birth control are limited to some urban areas, where high rates of illegal abortion are found (estimated in Chile at 40 per thousand), because of the lack of alternative controls and the inconvenience of large families to these city people. Public programmes for birth control, apart from clinics to avoid the unhealthy practices of illegal abortion, are absent from the continent except in Colombia, and of little effect so far in that country.

The present coastal pattern of population may be expected to remain. Pressure by farmer colonists on the Amazon Basin may provide that land with a moderate scatter of settlements, but the superior physical infrastructure of transport, irrigation works, power and better soils must always remain an attraction near the coast. Soil erosion and soil depletion limit the viability of settling the Amazon, compared with the use of more productive lands outside it.

> The problem, how to obtain a labouring class for a new and tropical country, without slavery, has to be solved before this glorious region can become what its delightful climate and exuberant fertility fit it for — the abode of a numerous civilized and happy people.
>
> *Henry Walter Bates,* The Naturalist on the River Amazon *(London, 1863), p. 178*

This quotation from the nineteenth-century English naturalist shows the old optimism of early visitors to the deserted heart of the continent, an optimism unjustified by physical potential. The encouragement of immigration to the region is indeed difficult, but for good reasons.

Development of industrial zones and urbanization in general also favour the continuation of a coastal concentration of population, for nearly all metropolitan growth is near the coast, focussing on ports and administrative—industrial centres. Despite energetic programmes to populate the interior, such as the foundation of Brasília as an interior capital (similar proposals have been made for the capitals of Argentina and Venezuela), and the extension of roads and railways into the wilderness, economic and social forces pull out to the coast. Trade linkages to Spain and Portugal have been replaced, but by other links to the exterior, not links between the countries of the continent. The difficulty seen in building up intra-continental trade within LAFTA and similar economic groupings of countries reflects the long-established orientation of each country to the exterior, not to its neighbour.

THE HIGHLAND CORE

6. Peru — The Heartland

Peru with Bolivia, or Alto Peru as the latter was known, was the cultural and economic heartland of South America from pre-Conquest times till the nineteenth century, centre of an empire and home to the highest civilization on the continent. There is no longer any economic or political centrality to the country, but it is still a heartland in another sense, in displaying all that is most typical, most quintessentially the continent's problems in internal relations, between Indian, mestizo and white man, and in external relations, between foreign companies and states seeking its riches, and the home needs of a poor nation. In the forms and purposes of exploitation of man by man, region by region, country by country, it is typically Latin American, and seems destined to remain so despite drastic measures towards nationalization in recent years.

ECONOMIC AND SOCIAL HISTORY

The early civilizations have been mentioned already, but here their forms of social and economic conduct may be outlined. The pre-Inca highland economy, to judge by its remains among the Aymará, the dominant Indian cultural group apart from the Quechua-speaking Incas, was communal; the term *ayllu*, still in current use, signifies a community with close social ties, where land was held in usufruct by the village members, ownership being held by the whole community. The land area of the *ayllu* was the *marca*, a word which still occurs in the place

names such as Cajamarca. Cooperation in village life was typical and some forms of it, especially in crop harvesting or road and bridge building and maintenance, have survived to the present, despite later governments' insistence on private property as the only legal possibility. This communalism was scarcely communism as modern writers have sometimes insisted, but a forced cooperation for survival, to farm a difficult land. Later, under the Incas and perhaps for some centuries earlier, it was organized still further but not in communal form, rather in a despotic way in order to build the great palaces and temples of kings, to construct irrigation systems and level terraces. It may have been, as Karl Wittfogel suggested, that there is a strong causal relationship between the rise of civilizations needing massive hydraulic engineering feats, and despotic, intensely hierarchical political systems, where the king or leader is elevated to the position of a god.

The Incas

Chief of the pre-Columbian Peruvian state was a god-king, the Inca, surrounded by a large court, military leaders and a bureaucracy of priests. This strongly structured administrative order probably kept most of society in great poverty, because all cultivated village land was divided into three parts, one designated as lands of the Inca, and used for his purposes, another as lands of the Sun, feeding the priesthood, and the third for the *ayllu*. This third part was adjusted so as to suffice for the *ayllu* population, but poverty was the norm for all but the upper classes, a poverty derived in part from the unbalanced and limited diet. Protein foods from animals were generally scarce, and there were few wild animals to make up for the lack of domesticates. Potatoes and maize seem to have been twin staffs of life, and a variety of plants unknown outside the altiplano were also minor food sources: quinua, a useful grain because of its high protein content, oca, olluco, añu (tuberose plants), mashua, lupins and canihua, all of which could be grown on the difficult lands at over 4000 m altitude.

Inca engineering feats are well known, especially their ability at drystone wall construction using great irregular-faced rocks. In Cuzco and elsewhere these have proved earthquake- and decay-proof over the centuries, more so than Spanish buildings built above them. They were skilled in irrigation works, terraces, drainage and irrigation canals passing long distances across irregular ground. Inca knowledge must have been largely an inheritance, for the builders of Tiahuanaco and other military—ceremonial cities before the Incas had used similar techniques and massive labour organization to build their monuments. The ultimate origins of altiplano civilization are uncertain; old civilizations are found on the coast but this is partly due to better preservation than on the uplands. The oldest Tiahuanaco architecture has stone designs based on timber design principles. Timber was in short supply both on the deserts of the coast and in the sierras, which leaves the Amazon region, rich in timber, a mysterious possible source for later high cultures. More immediately the heritage is from the Moche—Chimu state of the northern coastlands in the Moche valley, a hierarchically organized state with its centre at Chan-Chan near modern Trujillo, where 23 sq km are covered in adobe remains. Chimu culture was dependent on elaborate irrigation techniques and flourished from the thirteenth to the fifteenth centuries.

Conquest and resistance

Spanish conquest was rapid and crushing, but not entirely complete despite a great superiority in arms. From Pizarro's 1533 entry into Cuzco up to 1572, there was continuous resistance by the last of the Incas and their followers. This rearguard action concentrated in the Incas' Anti-Suyo (the name which gave the Spaniards their Andes) or Eastern Empire, located in the moun-

12 *Machu Picchu and llamas. This isolated mountain-edge site was probably only an occasional royal residence, at the subtropical margin of the empire*

tains north of Cuzco which border the montaña, and in the montaña itself. Here a guerrilla war was possible because of the impossibility of access on horseback to parts of the rugged region, so that a few thousand Indians could hide from Spanish arms and make occasional sorties. A remnant state of Vilcabamba was beginning to emerge, and might with more diplomacy have remained as a native state, but it was destroyed in 1572 by a Spanish war party. The subsequent search for a mysterious lost city of Vilcabamba, home of the last Incas, led to explorations from the mid-nineteenth century on, and to the discovery of the famous and spectacular ruins of Machu Picchu (plate 12) above the Rio Urubamba northwest of Cuzco. Hiram Bingham, who found Machu Picchu, thought it must be Vilcabamba, but it now appears likely that it was a royal Inca residence, on the edge of the subtropical montaña and perhaps producing coca, a royal monopoly, from surrounding plantations. The true lost city was further to the northwest, lying at 1100 m altitude right out of the upland core, at a place called Espiritu Pampa, the Plain of the Spirits, an appropriate name for the resting place of a civilization.

Colonial economy and society

Inca hierarchy was rapidly replaced by Spanish hierarchies; the Lands of the Inca were given out to the conquistadores in distributions (repartimientos), while encomiendas, entrustments of native people, became effective land grants despite royal edicts from Spanish monarchs and the efforts of Viceroy Toledo in the sixteenth century. Peasants were collected into hundreds of new villages (reducciones) to make them more accessible for control and tax payments than in their former hamlets and farms. Such shifts in settlement caused further loss of land, ayllu land which slipped into Spanish hands. In any case control over land was difficult for Indians whose population was almost literally decimated, the decline in numbers being very severe on the coast where old irrigation canals fell into disrepair and the economy consequently collapsed. The Inca system of forced labour, the mita, and European diseases such as scarlet fever and smallpox helped in the decline of population from 20 million to 8 million in 1548. Although Lima gained in importance continuously as capital of the Viceroyalty and the trade centre, the rest of the land suffered.

Huancavelica

Mining was another drain on rural resources, especially of men. At Huancavelica between Lima and Cuzco a mercury deposit was found in 1563 which, following the 1570 introduction of the amalgamation process for silver refining into Peru from Mexico, led to what Viceroy Toledo, its introducer, called 'the most important marriage in the world, that between Potosí and Huancavelica'. Huancavelica's importance was as the only source of mercury in America, and thus a controlling factor over silver production. Other mercury mines were closed and Huancavelica made a royal monopoly, so that it could be carefully controlled. Taxes were raised on production by concessionaires, royal profits were made on sales of mercury from the mines to the silver refiners at Potosí, and taxes on silver could be checked against the amount of mercury used rather than on silver mined so as to prevent any cheating on claimed production. A mita was established to work the mine and was fed by Indians from nearby provinces. Abuse of this labour, mercury poisoning, tuberculosis and other pulmonary diseases from the exposure of miners to cold altiplano air after hours in an overheated mine, and deaths from poison gases in the mine, all accounted for many thousands of labourers. The provinces around the mine were depopulated by natives fleeing the dreaded mita, and it was only possible to maintain it under technically crude conditions because of its monopoly position in the continent, and the vital financial role it had.

Post-colonial history

After Independence in 1825, a population of 1.3 million had little importance in the new continent. Land redistribution was planned but never enacted, the growth of latifundia continuing into the present century. No immigrants came to alter what was still a strongly Indian country, and only on the coast were there changes in outlook. Short booms from guano exports and from mineral nitrates caused momentary prosperity and financed railway construction in Peru, but the slump following Peru's loss of her nitrates in the War of the Pacific brought back national poverty.

PHYSICAL REGIONS

Peruvian geography is one of great regional contrasts, between Costa, Sierra and Selvas, and even within these divisions; the division is not precise nor always the determinant for other geographical facts but it is a real and convenient division (fig. 13).

The costa
This is a narrow belt of desert some 45 km wide, opening out to 160 km in the north, reduced to a few kilometres where the Andes approach the coast. It is in no sense to be thought of as a coastal plain, but as a series of terraces in an enormous staircase up to the steep wall of the mountains, at 2000 m. Through the terraces forty rivers have cut their way, in deep alluvial-floored valleys; between the valleys the Costa has a completely desert aspect, though, despite low rainfall and a tropical location, temperatures are kept low through the year by the cold water of the Humboldt current, often producing seafogs which drift in and keep out the sun for days at a time. These fogs, known as *garua*, are common in winter and may, like their equivalents in Southern California, cause smog conditions in enclosed basins along the coast.

The sierra
This lies largely at inhabitable levels between 2000 and 4000 m. At 3600–5000 m the vegetation is mostly an open grass-shrub combination. From 5000 m to 5250 m there is a frost desert, between the vegetation limit and the snowline, and above about 5250 m permanent snow. Sierran topography is comprised of two elements, a gigantic dissected tableland, and irregular volcanic or fold mountain systems rising above it to peaks at 6000 m on both flanks.

The sierran landscape is mild and relatively inviting in the north, where altitudes are lower, where heavier rains allow a cover of trees and good grassland, and a more rolling topography is common. Further south a more hostile environment emerges, higher, colder and drier, with only *ichu* bunch grass and low *tola* bushes on the interfluves (plate 13). Nearly all drainage is eastwards into the Amazon system, the upper rivers cutting canyons into the sierra; such is the upper Apurimac, flowing in a gorge which formed a major military barrier when its rope bridges, made by the Indians out of local materials, were cut or burnt. The Titicaca Basin of the far south is a land of internal drainage, where in consequence there is no rapid down-cutting of river gorges into the plateau, and it presents an un-

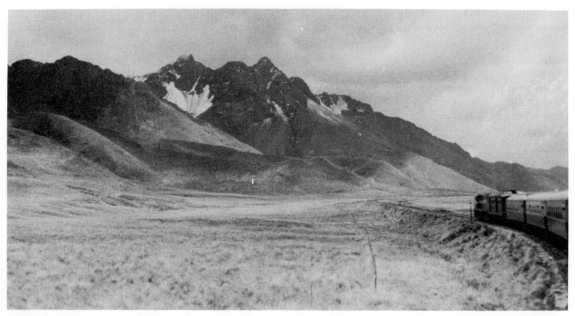

13 The cold dry southern altiplano area at 3500 m, north of lake Titicaca, with ichu vegetation, near the port of Puno

broken windswept surface. Lake Titicaca, a lake of tectonic origin, with a constant surface temperature of 10–12°C, acts as climatic moderator and thus helps the farmer. It is fed by rivers and remains fresh, draining out to salt lakes in Bolivia through the river Desaguadero.

The Andes, in geological terms, are recent mountains in their present form, having been uplifted in epeirogenesis to raise coastal sections rapidly up to 2000 m and more, as shown in well-formed pebble beaches and terraces at that height. Pleistocene glaciation reaches down to 3500 m in the north and 3000 m in the south; on the slopes at 2500-3200 m there are thick masses of loose periglacial material which are subject to continuous danger of mudflows, as well as landslides and avalanches. These mass movements are most dangerous and frequent on the steep slopes of the western cordilleras, as in Ancash in the Callejón de Huaylas between the Cordillera Negra and Cordillera Blanca, because of over-steepening through river downcutting and heavy precipitation on these western mountains. The 1970 mudflow into the Callejón, due to an earthquake activating the material, which caused several thousand deaths, was a recent example of the type of devastation possible.

Montaña and selvas

East of the Sierra lies a zone of intense river dissection and spectacular scenery, which the Spanish called the *montaña*. The name signified both the wooded character and broken topography of the mountains, in contrast to the bare sierra. Along the *montaña* front, with high continuous rainfall over 1000 mm except in intermontane situations, and moderate temperatures, there are luxuriant rainforests. In the intermontane cases the natural cover is dry, thin tropical forest. As the *montaña* is an altitude level rather than an area, it is found in long fingers of country along the main rivers between ribs of the Sierra. Along the valleys there are narrow, fertile floodplains, above them several erosional terraces. Far out to the east narrow outliers of the Andes form a limit to the *montaña* beyond which is the true rainforest or *selvas*. Where the rivers cross the outliers rapids develop, forming the heads of steamer navigation. One famous rapids section is the 12-kilometre canyon of the Pongo de Manseriche, on the river Marañón, just navigable to powerful

and light craft with favourable conditions on the river.

The *selvas* (sometimes the term is applied to the whole of *montaña* and *selva*), lying below 200 m altitude, comprises a huge stretch of country — half of Peru — mostly in the northeast. The *selva alta*, upper selva, is distinguished by better drainage and more slope land, while the *selva baja*, low selva, is mostly floodplain, poorly drained and all flooded except for some low terraces which form the only inhabitable land. Iquitos, centre of the Peruvian *selva baja*, lies on such a terrace formed out of old lake deposits standing 15 m above high water on the Amazon. Not all of the *selvas* is forested: on the upper Ucayali on the left bank above Pucallpa, is a region of savanna, the Gran Pajonal, occupying the ridgetops of hills which are forested below. This land is occupied by the Campa Indians, a primitive tribe with a mixed economy that places its settlements on the grassy ridges and keeps back the forest by fires.*

MODERN ECONOMY

To the physical contrast we may add contrasts in social and economic terms. The Costa is a relatively rich region (fig. 13), it is the home of most industrial—urban agglomerations in Peru, it has modern commercial farming and an important fishing industry. The Sierra, even with recent agrarian reforms, is still economically and socially a land of minifundios, of Indian peasant farmers, while to the east, the lowlands are little developed and have few inhabitants. Symptomatic of the national imbalance is the hypertrophy of Lima—Callao, with 3.6 million out of a total population of 14.1 million in 1972. Migration to Lima is disruptive both to the recipient and donor regions.

PRIMARY PRODUCTION

The Costa

Costa agriculture is of a dual nature, commercial cash-crop production on one side and small-farmer diversified farming on the other. This is

---

* This large savanna on well-drained slopes is unusual in the tropics. Human factors in its development are stressed by W. Denevan and S. Chrostowski, *The Biogeography of a Savanna Landscape: the Gran Pajonal of Eastern Peru,* Savanna Research Series No. 16, McGill University, Montreal, 1970.

Fig. 13 Peru: income per capita and major regions

the only region where farm production is oriented to international markets and where subsistence farming is subsidiary.

SUGAR

This crop is highly concentrated, notably in the Chicama river valley north of Trujillo, with 45 per cent of national production, and most of the rest in neighbouring valleys. Prior to the 1969 agrarian reforms there were great foreign-owned estates here in Chicama, four of them holding almost 90 per cent of the sugar land in the valley. Plantation-type production with the usual economies of scale in production and processing,

and even in this case a specialized port, Puerto Chicama, helped a profitable operation. The largest estate owned, in addition to sugar land, 420000 ha of land in the Sierra of Cajamarca, thereby controlling its own supply of labour from the overpopulated hinterland. Men were brought in for the harvest by the *enganche*, an advance of money or goods made to entice penniless Indians to the coast where they worked to pay off debts and, if they cleared them, returned penniless home. Growth of large holdings on the Costa was aided by the traditional water law which gave pre-emptive rights to upstream farmers, and allowed water rights to be

Fig. 14 The principal agricultural regions of Peru

Legend:
- Cotton
- Sugar
- Rice
- Cattle
- Sheep
- Railways

held separately from land, so that downstream farmers, or farmers without water rights, could be subjected to pressure and eventually taken over by their upstream neighbours. Since 1969 the sugar lands have been expropriated and formed into production cooperatives, while a second-level cooperative, a cooperative of co-operatives, has been formed to market the products and supply inputs such as machines and fertilizer.

COTTON

This crop is admirably suited to the desert climate and to irrigation, producing fine long-staple cotton of high quality; its cultivation goes back to prehistoric times, as is demonstrated from archaeological finds in the desert. Production is wider spread than in the case of sugar, over the northern and central Costa, and the crop expanded greatly during 1900-50, thereafter falling somewhat and occupying 147 000 ha (average 1973-5) compared to 54 000 ha of sugar cane in the same period. Like sugar it tends to become a monoculture with the attendant evils of soil destruction and susceptibility to market irregularities. There are many small farmers producing cotton, but there were also some large pre-reform estates with hired labour. As in the case of sugar, the government has set up and supported the growth of cooperatives to manage post-reform estates, and for both crops it will be interesting to see whether diversification is possible under the new structure of ownership, and whether the producing area will expand to include other small farmers who may benefit from cooperative membership. Most of the cotton crop is exported, providing an important contribution to foreign exchange earnings.

RICE

A third commercial crop is also grown as a monoculture on estates but also locally as a peasant subsistence crop. Rice is produced mostly on the north coast from Piura to Pacasmayo (fig. 14) and it is sent largely to nearby cities, for rice and fish are basic elements of the costeño diet. Rice cultivation follows standard forms, using large amounts of irrigation water, despite a desert climate, and in view of its water requirements it may have to give way in future years to other less thirsty crops which can make better use of limited water sources. Rapid expansion of the rice area from 51.5 thousand ha in 1951 to 72.8 in 1963, and to 122 thousand ha in 1979, has made this crop the major competitor with cotton for land, and as long as near-subsistence farming is practised the area is unlikely to drop, especially when population is rapidly increasing.

PEASANT FARMING

The second sector of Costa agriculture is that of the small farmer, dominant in the south and near cities, often using irregular or poor water supplies, producing mixed crops of beans, vegetables, maize, potatoes, and fruits. Most production is for home or very local consumption, but those farmers with more land and luck can send food to the urban markets. Many of these small diversified farms are in the suburban areas and can be classified as market gardens, though they lack the technology and capital that term implies in the West.

Throughout the twentieth century, laws have been necessary to protect this small-farmer sector from the encroachments of cotton and sugar estates, but they now stand on firmer ground with the protection of agrarian reform laws. One noted area for small-farmer production was always the lower Rimac valley and nearby valleys, but because of urban expansion this area has been shifted out of farm production in large measure, and now supplies to Lima must come from areas many kilometres away, brought by truck along the coast road.

WATER SUPPLIES

All Costa crops depend on the river floods from January to April, when the snowmelt occurs in the mountains. In 1978, 1.18 million ha were irrigated, making Peru third after Argentina and Chile in irrigated area, within South America. Improvement of the irregular supplies is however difficult, because each river is short and independent of the next, so that many small schemes rather than a few giant ones must be the format for development. The need for improvement is clear, for many irrigation systems are old and achieve only flood-farming, using rough structures to divert water without any attempt at storage. There is evidence which suggests that much more could be watered, in the old pre-Columbian systems which are now lying derelict, such as those near the city of Trujillo.* The northern plain has most of the land suited to expansion of irrigation, and in the rest of the Costa, alluvial flats are too narrow, while larger flat surfaces, the high terraces, are above the reach of river water. Underground water could be supplied but its costs are still high compared to river water.

Several major projects are in hand, one on the Majes valley in the south, another in Lambayeque in the north, begun as long ago as 1926 with a dam on the Chancay river, and now being extended by diverting the unused eastward-flowing Chotano into the Lambayeque plain north of Chiclayo, a land of slight slopes ideal for canal construction. This scheme, known as the Olmos project (see also below, p.83), is to provide water for 110000 ha more irrigated land in the area. Additional work is in hand to build a reservoir at Tinajones to control water flow and irrigate another 60000 ha of land. Lambayeque lies on the south edge of the Sechura desert. On the north side the Chira has been dammed and partially diverted since 1975 into the Piura, increasing supplies to 60 000 ha in that valley, and 40 000 ha of new irrigation land in the Chira valley.

The sea's resources

GUANO BOOM

An important adjunct of costeño agriculture has long been guano, which is still brought in from a

* Gonzalo de Reparaz, in an article entitled 'La Zone Aride du Pérou', describes and maps these systems at Trujillo; *Geografiska Annaler* (1958), pp. 1-61.

number of islets lying within a few kilometres of the shore and used by cormorant-like birds for nesting while they prey on the enormous fish resource of the sea. Guano was important to the pre-Inca Moche—Chimu state, for many objects belonging to that culture have been found in the deposits, up to 47 m thick, which covered the islands before the nineteenth century. Guano was also used in farming by the Incas, who had punishments, including even the death sentence, for anyone found guilty of killing seabirds going out to nest on the island! The Spanish abandoned guano exploitation and it was only 'rediscovered' in the early nineteenth century, when the markets became largely European, especially Britain. In the third quarter of the century there was a guano boom in Peru, a boom which served to bring temporary wealth to the state and to bring American railroad constructors to lay Peru's first railways, through the difficult Andean passes into the Sierra. Like all classical booms it turned to bust as suddenly as it had grown, through the rise of a competitor, mineral nitrates from the Antofagasta and Tarapacá deserts. The Peruvian nitrate boom was also of short duration, for it ended with the War of the Pacific in 1883, when Chile took control of the main producing areas.

THE FISHMEAL BOOM

Guano is an inefficient way of using a vital protein source, and more direct ways were practised by the Incas, though they were not great fishermen. Besides eating the fish themselves, they planted a fish head or two beside each grain of maize in the fields. In the 1950s, agriculturalists and others, pushed by rising world prices for fertilizers, finally took effective notice of the fact that less than a tenth of the fertilizer value of fish is available through guano; to meet growing world demand for fertilizers, a thriving fishing industry grew up, based mostly on the little anchoveta, an oilrich fish which was made into fishmeal in small factories along the coast. In the 1960s, this industry experienced another boom like that of the guano industry before it. The fish catch expanded from a negligible figure in 1950 to a record 12.3 million tons in 1970, under the impulse of investment by small fishermen, foreign firms which soon came into the business, and the state which gave credits to stimulate fishing.

Technically the industry was backward, with small boats and factories and an unwieldy marketing structure, but rapid building of large boats of over 50 tonnes allowed longer trips and tapping of the whole Humboldt current reserve out to 80 km or more. Employment expanded to around 30 000 and beginnings were made in fish-oil production, replacing expensive imports of vegetable oils, and canning and freezing. The most important port for landings was Chimbote in the north. In 1970 the government took over the fishmeal industry and began construction of large fish terminals and factories at Paita, El Callao and Pisco, with room to accommodate wholesalers who traded directly with the fishermen instead of through middlemen as before. In 1973, the fishing fleet was also taken over by the state.

Boom led rapidly to bust. In 1973 the government was forced to ban fishing except in March and April because of poor stocks, and only 1.7 million tonnes were caught, in 1974 five months fishing produced 3.6 million tonnes, and in 1979

14 A general store in Abancay, in the Peruvian Sierra. Western commercial marketing in the Sierra is little advanced and most peasant goods are sold in shops such as these or in the open markets.

3.6 million tonnes. In this year the fishing fleet was returned to private ownership, and many anchoveta boats have been converted under a government-sponsored programme to trawl for food fishes such as hake, tunny and *corvina*, in an attempt to diversify the industry and reduce a food shortage in Peru.

Physical reasons for the decline, apart from overfishing, were the southern penetration of the current which opposes the Humboldt, the Niño or Child, so called because most often seen at Christmas time, time of the Christ Child. This current is low in oxygen and nutrients, and is lethal to the ocean fish life, and restriction is evidently still necessary, for yields have not recovered to their peaks and the sustained yield level now seems to be well below the 10 million tonne mark. Southern ports, such as Ilo, have in fact been able to maintain more of the traditional anchoveta industry, simply because they are further south and thus less subject to the Niño.

Sierra agriculture

AGRICULTURAL SOCIETY

Visually the Sierra is an attractive land, a landscape of villages and small towns of adobe houses, with Spanish tiles or reed thatch in more rural areas, the fields carefully enclosed by stone walls, by hedges of broom, or by terrace walls where the earth is held in by deep-rooted aloes. Most towns have a standard Spanish chessboard layout, with everywhere eucalyptus trees for shade in the plazas. Outdoor markets, either daily or periodic, provide scenes of colour and bustle, selling goods for the peasant population, food, farm goods, sometimes secondhand, clothing from factories or from craft industries.

The pace of life is not fast, but life has not been easy either. A report from distant colonial time, on Jauja, in the productive Mantaro valley east of Lima, stated that:

In the valley there are no pastures: it is of a dry disposition, but suffers of rheumatism; that in

15 *Making adobe bricks in the Peruvian Sierra*

many years the frost takes the food and the sown land before the winter comes.

> *Justicia Mayor de Jauja, cited in A.M. Quesada, Costa, Sierra y Montaña (Lima, 1969), p. 162*

Poverty remains a problem, to the point of engendering serious malnutrition diseases, partly from lack of food, partly because the food base includes very little animal or vegetable protein.

In the Sierra there was the classic rural polarization, between great *haciendas* on the one hand, and traditional Indian communities of small farmers on the other, a *latifundio-minifundio* division exacerbated by the *haciendas'* control of most good land, leaving steep slopes and isolated areas to the communities. With this structure it is no wonder that the Sierra produces only 25% of Peru's food, and 10% of its farm exports. Indian communities have preserved some collective ownership, usually of pasture lands, and some work-sharing in the *minga*, for example in harvesting and housebuilding. These groups must supplement their income from tiny farms with work on the *hacienda*, which also employs permanent labourers and sharecroppers.

AGRARIAN REFORM

The military regime ruling from 1968–79 introduced a comprehensive agrarian reform in 1969, first in the Costa, where the plantations saw a relatively rapid and complete transfer of power from capitalist firms to large cooperatives with indirect State control, leaving however many landless workers and small private farms without any benefits. In the Sierra, the expropriation of *haciendas*, their combination into larger units, and reallocation to cooperatives formed mostly of the permanent workers on the estate, was

16 *Pitumarca, near Cuzco. Some common elements of the rural Peruvian landscape are present: the ox with primitive scratch plough, walls of stone and adobe, roofed in tile or straw thatch. Behind the settlement are eucalyptus trees, and in the middle distance terraced hillsides*

more difficult because of legal complexities, such as the existence of several different claimants to a piece of land, or the lack of any proper survey of the *hacienda*. The *hacendados* were also often well connected in local society and able to influence adjudications.

By 1976, only 23% of some 960 000 Sierran farm families had received land in the 7 million ha transfer, and the remainder, mostly labourers and communities, were unaffected. An extension of reform from 1973 introduced Integrated Rural Settlements (*PIAR*) on the Costa, covering several thousand hectares of irrigated land each, and including both cooperative members and landless labourers and communities. On the Sierra, Social Agricultural Societies (*SAIS*) were set up with indirect State control and finance, to bring in the groups who had not received benefits. In both areas, these huge new land units and organizations, covering several thousand farmers and areas up to half a million hectares, have proved unwieldy so that integration has been slow.

SIERRA CROPS
A wide variety of domesticated plants are known and were perhaps first domesticated here: potatoes, beans, quinua and maize are important, among native crops, and wheat and barley have made some impact as introductions. Many different varieties of potatoes are known, some of them extremely hardy and capable of surviving on the highest levels of cultivation above 4200 m, where the poor soils will support only one crop in five or ten years. Potatoes are particularly important in the cool moist area around lake Titicaca, but are a major element of diet throughout the Sierra, a standby in time of need, as *chuño*, dried and frozen potato. *Quinoa* and *cañihua* are grain grown in the same regions as the potato. Maize is more common in the hotter and more fertile lands of the montaña edge, and cannot tolerate the altiplano climate.

Sierran farmers, unlike *costeños*, have animals as well as crops. Sheep are the best suited of the European livestock to the dry cold climates and poor pastures, and are concentrated in the high lands of the south. Some cattle are raised too, to be fattened on the irrigated valleys near the western city markets. The whole livestock industry remains poor and backward, because most stock are in the hands of peasant farmers,

with no access to good pastures, and making no use of breed improvement techniques. Animal dung is not used on the fields nor are the cattle fed with grain, so that there is little of the Western mixed cattle—arable farming with its mutually advantageous results. Cattle dung is in fact still collected on the dry treeless highlands for fuel to feed house fires.

Three species of auquenid animals are found, llamas, alpacas and vicuñas. Of these the llama is the most domesticated and is primarily a beast of burden for the peasant. The alpaca provides a superb wool; it is somewhat wilder than the llama and is reared by shepherds rather than peasant farmers, for its pasture zone is in the high slopes above 4000 m where no other animals can prosper. The vicuña lives in the same Alpine zone near the snowlimit, but it is wild and has a coat intermediate between fur and wool which is highly prized. It survives continual hunting less by the laws enacted to forbid hunting than by a rabbit-like fertility and the natural defence of its mountain habitat.

Montaña and selvas
In the upper *montaña*, in parts most accessible by unmetalled roads out of the Sierra, subtropical crops are grown both by small farmers, many of them colonists on the farming frontier, and on large *haciendas*. Coffee, maize, sugar, rice, bananas and plantains, yucca, mangoes and citrus fruits are common. The crops of tobacco and coca, the latter sold to foreign drug companies, are perhaps the best-kept of the selection. Because of their isolation, farmer families live on their own crops of plantains and rice, with no more protein foods than those on the Sierra, for livestock have not been generally established despite a considerable potential.

As colonists move in, seeking land and cash income, there is an increase in commercial crops such as tea, oil palms and coffee, in the lands between 800 and 1800 m. While tea is a minor crop, coffee covers some 150000 ha, reaching into zones where there are no roads and the coffee must be brought to roadheads on the backs of farmers. Some colonization has been under government supervision, but most is from individual initiative.

Lower *montaña* farmers also produce sugar in a few localities, not generally in competition with the Costa but for alcohol and traditionally for *chancaca,* the coarse sugar-cake formerly used as food in rural areas. There remains an atmosphere of the frontier about sugar production here, because of the tax on alcohol and attempts to evade it by hidden stills and plantations far into the *selvas.*

The *selvas* still have a sizeable population (100 000 in 1961 according to the census) of pure Indian stock living in primitive tribal conditions, little modified by contact with white man. Most live in fairly settled conditions, building wooden huts with hardwood frames and palm leaf covers, and have a mixed economy based on tiny cultivated plots, hunting with bow and lance and fish trapping. They live near water, dependent on fish for protein food and the rivers for canoe movement. The mestizo and white population also lives near rivers, either in tiny self-sufficient hamlets growing rice, plantains and sugar, or around the few steamer ports, of which Iquitos is the most important (plate 17). The continuing isolation of the whole region is indicated in such items as a 1974 newspaper report that natives of the southern selvas were found being exploited in conditions of virtual slavery for the panning of gold along a remote river.

MINERAL INDUSTRIES (fig. 15)

In Peru, as in other Andean countries, the mineral industries have long been a world apart, controlled by foreign capital and enterprise, and respondent not to local needs but to those of world markets. There is a curious continuity in the mining industry, controlled first from Spain, then from Europe and the United States, now also from Japan, but always a key to the economic health of the nation and always under foreign control until 1974 when the Cerro de Pasco Corporation, a wholly-owned subsidiary of the Cerro Corporation of the U.S.A., was expropriated with payment of some compensation money. This is a giant firm with six mines and smelters and refinery in the central Sierra, and it commits the Peruvian state to a definite involvement in mining. Before this, foreign interests were dominant in silver and mercury mines, important in guano and nitrates, then in copper.

Because of the isolated and remote location of much mining, foreign companies could dominate the economy and society of their region, forming local enclaves. This was the case with the colonial *mita* and still more in the present cen-

17 *Pucallpa, river port of the southern Peruvian selvas. Shanty construction here uses the abundant timber and cane supply*

Fig. 15 Urban locations, mines, railways and river transport lines

tury with copper and iron mining. Copper first became important in the central Sierra with many mines in the late nineteenth century around Cerro de Pasco, which came under North American control about 1906, and led to copper concentrating and smelting at Cerro de Pasco and La Oroya. One key to this growth had been the Central Railway, built on guano and nitrate revenues in the 1870s and connecting the Sierra to Lima.

The central Sierra has been overtaken by the South since 1950, with the development on a massive scale, calling for heavy international investment, of disseminated copper deposits. Toquepala is one of these, connected by rail to the port of Ilo where there is a smelter and refinery in operation since 1975, using hydro-electricity. This mine and another at Cuajone, recently opened, are owned by the Southern Peruvian Copper Corporation (SPCC), United States owned. Cerro Verde and Santa Rosa are other giant deposits in this area, controlled by Mineroperu, the state mining corporation. Copper is usually found in association with lead, zinc and silver which are subsidiary resources.

Iron-ore production is substantial, mostly going to export markets, though increasing amounts are absorbed by domestic steel plants at Chimbote. The ore comes from Marcona in the south, and production is also under Mineroperu following a state takeover of the North American Marcona Company's operation in 1975. Peru does not have large coal supplies and coal production has been declining, in 1972-4 averaging only 85 000 tons. One field, that of the Alto Chicama valley in the north, is to be developed for thermal electric power.

Apart from coal there are significant petroleum and hydro power supplies in the country. Electric energy is increasingly from hydro sources (in 1963 63 per cent, in 1974 74 per cent), largely because of efforts by the state. Before 1960, most electricity was produced, not by public services but by mining and other private firms producing for their own needs. This inefficient stage is being passed with the use of large sources in the Andes, the focus of new work swinging dramatically from the smaller Pacific-slope rivers to the great Amazon tributaries, where Russian technology is being employed. A new line distributing power is being laid between Lima and Chimbote. Reversal of flow from Atlantic to Pacific is being employed at some plants like the Huinco station above Lima, which also helps irrigate the Rimac valley. The Mantaro valley supplies are being harnessed by diverting water to cut off a great bend in the river and run it through a 15 km tunnel. Substantial development of the Santa river above Chimbote is used to power its steel mills and other related engineering industries. The Olmos project on the north coast is another large scheme with both irrigation (100 000 ha) and power (520 MW) uses from a diversion of the Chotano and Huancabamba rivers, a scheme which is using Russian assistance and finance.

Petroleum

Oil resources are still incompletely known, but are large enough to make Peru an oil exporting country with exports of about 6 000 barrels a day. South America's first oil was extracted in the north Peruvian coastal oilfields of Talara, after the War of the Pacific. Talara has continued up to 1974 as the main producing area, and old wells there have even been reopened following the 1973 increase of oil prices, while new ones have been drilled to expand output. But a redirection of effort to oil-bearing regions on the Ucayali, Marañon and Aguaytía tributaries of the Amazon, deep in the Peruvian selvas, has been taking place, under the control of Petroperu, the state agency which has taken over the concessions formerly held by international firms. There are small refineries in the east at Pucallpa and Iquitos which are now being expanded, but most oil will be taken out via the Nor-Peruano pipeline opened in 1976 from the lower Marañon region, 855 km across the Andes to Bayovar where an oil terminal for large tankers allows ready export of oil (Fig. 15).

Bayovar

It is perhaps appropriate that Peru, supplier to the world of fertilizers from guano, nitrates and fishmeal, should have a massive phosphates resource. In the northern desert of Sechura there are an estimated 10 000 million tons of phosphates, one of the world's largest deposits. A planned development of these deposits as fertilizers has begun at Bayovar. As the Nor-Peruano pipeline also ends at Bayovar, a massive energy-based industrial development is possible too, and a new port, oil refinery, metals refinery and petrochemicals complex is coming into being. These, with the phosphates industry, must attract a rapid urban development, and the whole has been placed under a regional development agency for Bayovar.

TOWNS AND INDUSTRIES

The Costa

Peru's urban population is scattered through a multitude of small towns, a few cities of medium size, and the metropolitan area of Lima—Callao. Urbanization, and indeed population growth generally, is most rapid on the Costa, with its varied processing industries and ports. Without attempting complete coverage, some of the more important towns may be discussed further.

Chimbote

This is Peru's steel town, with a state-owned mill since 1957, the only one in Peru, though another is planned at San Juan on the southern coast near the iron-ore mines of Marcona and Acari. Chimbote uses local hydroelectric power from the Cañon del Pato dam on the Santa river, where the potential is being increased from 100 mW to 150 mW. Its coal and iron ore must be brought by sea, and its products also sent out in the same fashion. Chimbote produces high-cost steel because of these transport costs, but also because of the small size of the national market for steel; yet with recent expansions it can produce wire, tinplate, steel stampings and structural steel. Heavy engineering is also appearing at the city, to produce pipeline for the booming oil industry. Chimbote is also the country's leading fishing port, followed by El Callao and Supe. The 1970 earthquake hit the city tragically, but it has been partially rebuilt some 20 km to the south, and has gained some light industries because of its designation as a growth pole by the government.

Trujillo

This town has had changing fortunes. As a

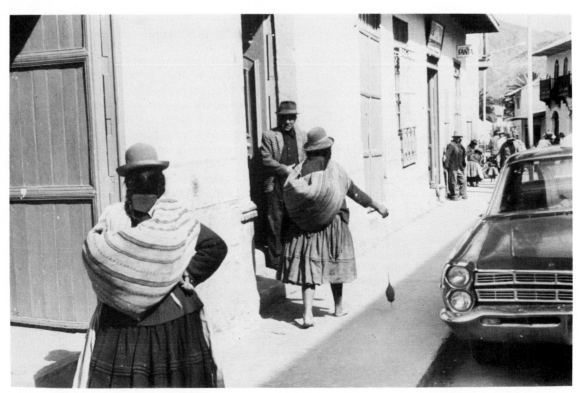

18 The old and the new, Sicuani, Peru. Modern vehicles and the age-old peasant system of a shawl for carrying goods

former sugar-milling town it lost its importance when sugar milling became part of a vertically integrated industry and was done on the estates rather than in town. Trujillo however attracted paper factories and a newsprint factory, using in part the cane bagasse of the estates. Planners now seek to make the city another growth centre, along with Chiclayo where there is a pulp factory, and Chimbote. Although the paper industry is not a fast-growing one and domestic demand is small, other industries have been attracted, including machine tools, milk processing, motor cycle and diesel engine manufacture, mostly foreign investments.

Lima

Cuzco soon ceded to Lima after the Conquest, a more central and strategic site between the northern cities at Piura and Cajamarca and southern foci around Cuzco. This new site was also symbolic of the change in orientation away from the interior, towards the sea and Europe. Institutional bases were strong, including the archbishopric from 1545, university of Saint Mark from 1551, administrative centre of the viceroyalty of Peru, and jurisdictional centre with its Audiencia from 1543. These established and maintained Lima's primacy as collecting centre monopolizing trade with Spain from the Viceroyalty. The South Seas Armada took all official trade from El Callao to Panama, where it met the Spanish (Atlantic) Armada for trade. By 1600, the town had nearly 60000 inhabitants, half of them negro slaves for wealthy citizens. Manufactures, spices, fabrics and jewels were brought from Europe and exchanged for native silver.

The old city, along with the port El Callao, was virtually destroyed in 1746 by a violent earthquake, and present architecture entirely postdates this time. Lima is now a dusty, relatively lowbuilt city, with flat roofs and uninspired architecture, though many fine churches retain colonial gold and treasures. Most of the colonial façades of three-storey noblemen's and merchants' houses are also gone, because they had wooden balconies which allowed fire to spread along a whole street. New balconies were forbidden in the early nineteenth century and only now is there an attempt to restore the remaining ones. Perhaps the finest visual aspect is the great Plaza de Armas (plate 19), central

square flanked by cathedral and government offices. After booms and depression in the last century modern growth (figs. 16 and 17) has been dramatic, using up nearly all the flat land of the Rimac delta, linking Lima to El Callao (plate 20), and spreading up adjacent hillsides, a growth stemming both from rural poverty and from industrial growth in the city; 90 per cent of the national textile industry is located here, and in Lima—Callao is half the fishmeal industry. The port is by far the most important in Peru, with three-quarters of its imports, and one third of its exports. Allied to the fishing interests and the port are shipbuilding industries and ship-repairing. Lima has a major industry in car assembly works, and has attracted most of the light industrial investment from overseas. The commercial role of the city as main port and

19 *Wooden balconies of the Archbishop's Palace in the central Plaza de Armas, Lima. Most wooden balconies like this have now disappeared, and the one shown is a replacement*

administrative centre is also dominant, and its links to the Sierra are the best in the country, making Cerro de Pasco and the mineral industries part of its industrial hinterland, though rail and road links do not connect it or any other coastal city to the whole of the highlands.

Cuzco

This was the Inca capital, lying on a small river, the Huatanay, which the Incas had tamed, running its clear water in stone culverts through the paved streets of the city. It was built in traditional Inca megalithic form, with the solid appearance that results from lack of knowledge of the arch, instead of which massive lintels were employed in gateways and doors. Inca buildings were mostly low, roofed in thatch, the largest being the palaces around the central square.

The essential lines have been preserved in the Spanish colonial town, because Inca stonemasonry proved too difficult to change to the orderly geometric lines of the Spanish planned towns. Streets remain narrow despite the Spanish love of open, wide avenues. The central square, Aucaypata, surfaced by the Incas in fine gravel, remains, but the palaces have gone, to be replaced by churches and public buildings. The old central walls of diorite and andesite still stand as well as the fortress of Sacsahuaman outside the town. Within the city the Temple of the Sun, Coricancha, once clad in gold which was stripped for the ransom of Atahualpa, is marked by remaining walls of interlocking masonry, although overlying Spanish work has crumbled from earthquake damage.

POLITICS AND ECONOMICS: THE CONTROL OF INDUSTRY

A new political scene was set in October 1968 when a military regime took over power. This regime was anxious to show its pro-Peruvian intentions by expropriating or controlling the international firms which have traditionally owned large sectors of the economy. Investment was traditionally in agriculture where, for example, the Grace Line of the United States owned plantations, paper and chemical plants on the north coast, and other firms were engaged in sugar, cotton and rice production in the region. These great estates were taken over by the agrarian reform of 1969, which concentrated its effort on the Costa before moving to home-owned latifundia on the Sierra.

20 *A street in El Callao, port of Lima. Wooden façades were common in colonial Lima*

Fig. 16 Lima and surroundings in 1928

Fig. 17 Lima in 1950

Minerals constituted the second area of foreign ownership; the Cerro de Pasco Corporation was principal owner till 1960, based on the copper of the central Sierra. In the early 1950s, Toquepala began production under the SPCC, also North American, and Marcona iron ore was exploited by another North American firm. Cuajone, Cerro Verde, Quellaveco and Michiquillay also came under North American control without any mining being attempted. An enclave situation grew up in which the company could prevent, for example, unionization of labour.

The present government's actions here have been to allow continued foreign exploitation (Cuajone is now being developed by the SPCC), but to assert state control over processing and marketing, through a state agency, Mineroperu. The Cerro de Pasco smelting and refining operations therefore came into government hands, though the southern mines did not, apart from the Santa Rosa deposit.

In petroleum there was a dramatic move to expropriate one North American company, IPC, operating in the Talara area, and this action served to alienate U.S. opinion and governmental aid for some years. The company was turned over to Petroperu, a state agency which with its other deposits now became main Peruvian producer of oil, though many foreign firms remain; contracts to extract oil are being tightened to give Petroperu a 60/40 share in the enterprises.

Policies and mechanisms
Peru seems to be seeking, not a total nationalization but state control of the basic industries, and a guiding hand on the rest. Among the basic industries are steel, refining, smelting of metals and cement production. Most manufacturing is left in private hands. Expropriations are made, but with payment in full, in the cases where the firm suffering loss will invest in industry within Peru.

The effect of this kind of pressure is to move foreign investment from agriculture and mining into a new sector, manufacturing, which had not previously been its forte. This is a bold attempt to cut a difficult new path, encouraging foreign investment but only under controls that will inevitably limit its attractiveness. In fact, rather than a path it might be called a tightrope, between total nationalization and loss of all foreign investment, on the one hand, and free entry for international firms, bringing plenty of money in but no control for Peruvians, on the other.

In some areas there has been a decline in state intervention. The fishing industry has been returned to private hands and the agrarian reform has effectively come to a halt. With a civilian government after 12 years of military rule, further denationalization of major industries is possible, though such changes are unlikely to affect the basic incongruity of a country whose relations with the outside world are based on capital-intensive raw material production, and which yet has a large mass of humanity living in dire shortage of food, land, and other resources.

7. Bolivia

Bolivia's landscape is to many the most striking in the continent. In the southern altiplano, there are desert regions resembling the surface of the moon more than any terrestrial landscape, dry white salt flats reflecting harsh sunlight in the rarefied atmosphere, and contrasting with the naked black rocks of island mountains sticking up through the lake-flat surface. Further north, and nearer to lake Titicaca, the landscape is less bleak but still barren-looking. Long low adobe huts covered in thatch are the northern farm houses, with an occasional new corrugated iron roof indicating new influences from abroad. Around the southern desert there are only igloo-like round huts bearing silent testimony to a natural poverty. Despite its bleakness, the altiplano has attracted most Bolivian population since before the Conquest. Within the plateau, though admittedly sheltering within a deep ravine on its edge, is La Paz, the capital, a solitary indicator of prosperity and active development, excentric to the country but not to its economically and culturally determined core area, crowding its constricted valley and climbing up its sheer surrounds in a shanty town sprawl.

On the edges of the altiplano are sharp contrasts; a few kilometres from La Paz's cold, luminous landscape is a zone of subtropical rainforest, the Yungas, a wild medley of palms and hardwoods interspersed with little farm clearings, and constantly bathed in warm air and Amazon rains. Further east, there are luxuriant forests in the Upper Amazon tributaries, park-land savanna in the central plains and semi-desert in the Chaco to the south.

PHYSICAL FEATURES (fig. 18)

In the central Andes, a western range, the Cordillera Occidental, and an eastern Cordillera Real enclose the altiplano. The Cordillera Real is Palaeozoic in age, much eroded so as to expose the granites which form its core, as well as the important minerals of magmatic separation, tin, bismuth, silver, lead and zinc. The Cordillera Occidental is of Tertiary age, and has had less of its cover rocks stripped off, so that minerals are less important, except for some copper. Volcanic peaks form the greatest heights, at 6000 m rising well above the altiplano's 4000 m. Peaks over 5000 m are generally above the snow line, though snow is often absent because of low precipitation and direct evaporation under strong dry winds. Pleistocene glaciation has left its marks down to 4000 m, as near Potosí and around Chorolque, with glacial lakes, moraines, rock striations and other marks. There is also evidence for a great interior lake, lake Ballivián, an expanded lake Titicaca, from the Ice Age's periods of greater precipitation and less evaporation. Today, lake Titicaca is fed only by small streams and drains out through the Desaguadero into a salt lake, lake Poopó. Salt flats further south are occasionally filled by exceptional rains.

The altiplano has a vigorous climate for man, with slight seasonal changes but strong diurnal change, and cold winter nights. The writer

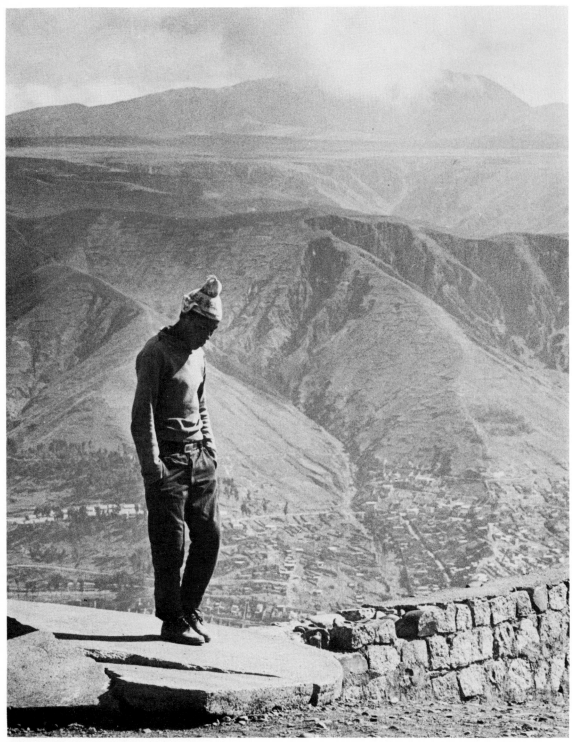

21 La Paz city from the edge of the altiplano

22 *Llamas and alpacas grazing on the* ichu *bunch grass above the limits of cultivation on the Bolivian altiplano*

remembers a night in an unheated train crossing the altiplano, during which the local peasants' habit of taking a blanket on all travels was made completely intelligible! Minor hazards are the very strong sunlight, deceptive in the cool air, and *soroche*, the altitudinal effect which attacks those who arrive suddenly from low altitudes but which wears off after a week of acclimatization. For agriculture the climate is more difficult; in the south, a large region has 50 mm or less precipitation, and rainfall is only sufficient around lake Titicaca for cultivation without irrigation water.

Oriente
Below 1000 m, the land slopes away to the Amazon and Paraguay, though the water divide between the two is imperceptible and the whole plain is flat with few interruptions. Summer rain brings huge floods from midsummer to late autumn, floods which are particularly noticeable in the Beni section of the north where the rivers are held up by the rock outcrops around the outlet of the Beni to the Madeira; these outcrops are responsible for the rapids or *cachuelas* of this section. Above the rock barrier the water and silt is impounded on a completely flat plain between

Beni and Guaporé, where water surfaces are more common than land during the flood season. In some parts of the flat lands, poor drainage and seasonal flooding induce a savanna vegetation except for isolated gallery forest on river levees and terraces. To the south, the shield rocks come to the surface and form the rolling Chiquitos uplands with a dry woodland cover. Further south still, the Chaco Boreal has a desert climate and no permanent streams though there are many wide dry river beds used by seasonal floods. Along them grows a thin gallery forest of palms such as Caranday, *Copernicia cerifera*, carobs, quebrachos and other xerophytes.

Valles and Yungas
Between lowlands and altiplano, intermediate altitudes belong to the Yungas in the north, to the Valles in the south. Annual rainfall on the Yungas is over 3500 mm, and their steep slopes have near-selvas vegetation. Further south are the Valles which are drier with a long dry season. Because of this, and also because of gentler slopes and the clearing which has been done for cultivation, they present a much more open aspect.

Fig. 18 Physical regions of Bolivia

- **Selva**
- **Yungas**
- **Gran chaco**
- **Llanos**
- **Altiplano**
- **Valles**

HISTORY OF SETTLEMENT

Bolivia's pre-Conquest history is closely tied to that of Peru, outlined in the last chapter. In fact, the political boundary between the two countries runs through the very heart of the old culture region, for lake Titicaca, which it bisects, was the Incas' holy lake; north of Copacabana lie the famous islands of the Sun and the Moon, sacred to the Indians.

There was a dense population on the northern altiplano, based on settled and organized agriculture and using only the *chakitaclla* (digging stick) as a tool. The older civilizations left little more

than their presumed language, Aymará, and even this was partially replaced by Quechua, the speech of the Incas who spread their influence rapidly over the region during the two centuries before the Conquest. Inca policy was to move loyal soldiers and farmers out from the centre to areas of dissidence or disaffection, and thus Quechua became dominant in the Valles and Yungas and in the south, while Aymará remained uppermost in the central lands around lake Titicaca.

In the Oriente, there were peoples living at an intermediate level of civilization, in the chiefdoms. These were the Arawak chiefdoms and other groupings of the Beni. They built no great architectonic monuments of stone to match Cuzco or Tiahuanaco, but used very considerable civil engineering skills and organized labour to overcome flood problems by placing fields and villages on artificial mounds, laying causeways and canals across the plain, and ridging fields to plant on the ridge tops, over thousands of hectares. This mysterious civilization offers an exceptional example of the possibilities of farming the tropical savannas without the aid of the plough, and it may have supported half a million people before the Spaniards; its affinities to the altiplano cultures are still uncertain.

The Spanish

A large Spanish contingent in Alto Peru, as the land became known, was never necessary or possible. Here Spaniards came only as landowners, merchants or miners, and the dense Indian population suffered only moderate miscegenation, so that about half the present population is classified as pure Indian, another 35 per cent as mestizo. Since no European immigrants were ever brought in, pure Spanish blood is the only other important component of race.

Changes wrought under the colonial system were gradual, and only occasionally radical. Some new towns were created: La Paz, the capital, was founded on the all-important road from Potosí to Lima in 1584. Its name, meaning 'peace', signified the celebration of total conquest of Inca territory in Peru, a premature celebration in point of fact, for resistance movements were to continue for a long time. To the south, Chuquisaca, Cochabamba and Tarija were all founded in the sixteenth century, and prospered in the reflected light of Potosí, supplying it with food, manufactures and services. Chuquisaca also achieved a certain prominence as juridical centre, with its Audiencia or High Court from 1559, a powerful authority because it was remote from Lima, centre of the viceroyalty. Potosí itself grew up from the silver find in 1545 as a true boom town, with world-wide fame for the wealth and extravagance of its inhabitants, endowed like any Wild West town with its whore houses and gambling dens, populated by hard-drinking, financially reckless and quarrelsome miners. Fortunes were made and lost in a day by these men,

though the silver boom continued for over a century, serving thus to fill the Spanish royal coffers through the tax of a fifth, more than any miner's individual pocket.

In the Oriente, Santa Cruz was first founded in the far southeast on the Chaco edge, then progressively moved 320 km west to the present position, to form an agricultural centre and trading post for the region. To the north, only missionaries attempted colonization. Jesuit control from 1668 to 1768 in the province of Mojos allowed some development of an exchange economy, centred on mission villages, and producing surpluses of cotton, rice, sugar and cacao for upland miners. In the longer term the Oriente's economy was to see a decline, in the face of a continual increase in the focus on the Pacific coast, making this region increasingly isolated. After the departure of the Jesuits much of the region became ranching country with a tiny population.

PROBLEMS OF POLITICAL GEOGRAPHY

National identity

Political geographers have long recognized the need, to ensure the survival of any state, of some cohesive force such as a well-defined territory or a state idea such as religion or language, to bind together the nation. Bolivia came into existence in 1825 with little in the way of unifying principles. She was certainly well isolated from centres in Lima or Buenos Aires, and there was a separate Audiencia. But this was not a unit which normally formed an independent state in the nineteenth-century divisions of the continent under independent rule. The name Bolivia is itself somewhat ironic, for Bolivar, Liberator of northern South America from Spanish rule, himself firmly opposed the idea of a state created out of Alto Peru on such flimsy historical bases, and indeed looked to the day of a multinational federation of states in South America. Only the outspoken attitude of the *criollos,* the American-born Europeans of La Paz and Chuquisaca, and support from General Sucre, who defeated the last Royalist armies in the area, established Bolivia as a separate state.

Such inauspicious beginnings were matched by difficulties in holding together the state newly created. It was large, at 2.2 million sq km twice the present size, and its four provinces, La Paz, Chuquisaca, Cochabamba and Potosí, showed persistently individualist tendencies. In particular, there was a rivalry which lasted the whole century between Sucre (Chuquisaca) and La Paz city, for leadership. Sucre had been the old administrative and ecclesiastical centre, but La Paz at independence was already the economic key and had best access to the important Pacific coast, so that it was finally to be confirmed as capital in 1898. The problem of size was to be partially solved in a drastic manner, through the nibbling away of peripheral territories by Bolivia's neighbours on all fronts.

Exit to the sea

Under the nineteenth-century economic system, it was important for countries to have access to the ocean, sole means of long-distance transport. Bolivia could only claim a narrow appendage out to the southwest (fig. 19) from the Loa to the Salado at about 26°S. This fact had mattered little in colonial time because other ports catered to Alto Peru, and Arica especially was the port to Potosí, linked to it by mule trails.

During Bolivia's century and a half of existence, a series of excisions of Bolivian territory have been made by neighbours attracted to minerals or other riches, provoking a revanchist attitude in Bolivian politics, under the name of claims for a *salida al mar* or exit to the sea. On the west, Bolivia tried to build up a port at Cobija, but it was too far from La Paz and unprovided with fresh water. Arica, the main port, maintained its dominance until the construction of the Antofagasta and Bolivia Railway in the 1880s, following the nitrate boom in the desert. Nitrates cost Bolivia all her coastal strip, but paradoxically at last gave her access to the sea in the southwest, by the Antofagasta railway, which was long but with easy grades. In addition, as compensation for loss, Chile financed the Arica—La Paz railway, unfortunately not of great value because it had excessive gradients which enforced the use of rack and pinion track. Further north, yet another railway, the Mollendo—Puno line built by Henry Meiggs for Peru gave yet another outlet to Bolivia, though again its value was diminished by the need to cross lake Titicaca by boat and transfer goods from rail to boat and back again.

To the east, Bolivia never had any access to the great rivers, but this did not prevent her raising claims. On the Paraguay, Portuguese missionaries and merchants trickled in long before Bolivian attempts at settlement, and in any case Brazil, Argentina and Paraguay were hostile to Bolivian use of the river and effectively controlled it. From eighteenth-century claims to a Spanish front along the whole upper river, Bolivia was reduced to a tiny window onto the river above Bahía Negra, 50 km long.

In the northeast, the rapids on the Madeira isolated the Beni river from the Amazon which was opened to trade by Brazil and, when value was finally attached to the region with the rubber boom of the 1890s, and settlements came to the Madeira, the Beni, Madre de Dios, Orton and Acre rivers, Brazilian dominance in numbers of settlers soon meant a Brazilian takeover in what was known as the Acre territory. Again, repeating the Chilean events of the War of the Pacific, a rail access to the Amazon was promised by Brazil in part-compensation for the loss of the Acre in 1903, and indeed was built by 1913; again, as in the case of the Arica—La Paz railway, it proved to be of little use, in this case because by the time it was finished the rubber boom was already collapsing with the competition from other regions.

In all, the present-day Bolivian quest for a *salida al mar* may be viewed as something different from a simple recovery of the lost lands. It has been, rather, a political slogan to unite a country with little natural coherence. It has also been a way of putting pressure on neighbour states for good ocean access through free ports, but without any real attempt to recover land. Bolivia has good access to the Pacific, considering her difficult topography, provided by her western neighbours at modern ports. She is also promised access to the Atlantic and Plate, something she has never enjoyed.

We may legitimately ask whether Bolivia is really disadvantaged by lack of a coast. She certainly has not had the benefit of guano, nitrates or copper, nor of irrigated subtropical oasis agriculture along a coastline. But these are gifts of the lowlands behind the coast, and not the same thing, arguably, as access to the sea. Bolivian prominence in the use of these resources might have been greater in any case, had she ever shown any ability to initiate exploitation, but this

Fig. 19 Maximum claims and present Bolivian boundaries

was always left to other nations. Bolivia's *mediterraniedad*, her interior location, has been claimed as a reason for lack of immigration and colonization. This is scarcely fair comment either, for Paraguay, equally lacking a coast, has attracted many colonists, and Bolivia herself has some new colonists in the southern Oriente around Santa Cruz. Rather it is the dense pre-existing Indian population that has deterred possible immigrants, along with the poverty of the Altiplano and the isolation of the Oriente.

THE ECONOMY

It is usual in economic discussions to classify a national economy into primary, secondary and tertiary sectors. This division in Bolivia is less meaningful than the division into a traditional, semi-subsistence sector, and the modernized sector of the economy which has a market economy. These sectors and the unutilized areas of the country have been sketched in on the accompanying map (fig. 20), from which it is evident that large parts of the country are either void of any important economic activity or are used at only a semi-subsistence level, as negative or at best economically neutral areas. They are areas certainly for future use when resources have been identified, but at present they may only be presented as indices of the difficulties of modernization in a country where islands of development are separated from one another by hundreds of kilometres, often without road or rail connection.

AGRICULTURE

The altiplano
In the northern altiplano rainfall could suffice for Northern Hemisphere commercial farming of grains like barley, wheat and oats, and these are in fact grown using dry-farming techniques, in particular barley, which is used for malting and beer making in La Paz. Small farmers however are more concerned with the traditional subsistence crops of potatoes and quinoa, the latter growing under similar conditions to barley and replacing it where subsistence is more important than commercial sale. Its richness in protein helps eke out the miserable animal protein supply from a few scraggy chickens or the rare sheep or llama. Quinoa grain is made into biscuits, porridge, soups and steamed puddings, and the leaf is also eaten as a vegetable by country folk. *Canagua* (in Peru *cañihua*) is a related grain of the chenopod family. Both *quinoa* and *canagua* are grown on plots following potatoes, which latter may be fertilized. Near the margins of cultivation at 4200 to 4400 m, the land is rested after the *quinoa* crop from 10–20 years.

Altiplano peasants live in conditions which are still very primitive, despite some improvements since the 1952 revolution which overthrew landlords' power. Adobe huts and a few hectares of land are still their main possessions, though more western clothes, radios and bicycles are appearing everywhere. Goods are still carried to market, without any animal or machine aid, in many places. Most peasant families have three or four llamas and perhaps some alpacas for their wool and meat; the llamas can carry light loads. On high slopes above the limit of cultivation, herds of llamas and alpacas may be seen, minded by full-time shepherds with fifty or more animals. Towards the south sheep are most important, their degree of dominance being indexed by the gradual decline of mutton in price

along the Antofagasta railway. Their coarse wool is important for the making of carpets, rugs and ponchos to sell in La Paz. A good deal of the trade in llama and alpaca wool, skins and garments goes as contraband over the high lonely passes to Peru, Chile and Argentina, unrecorded by national customs posts.

This is probably even more common in the case of the vicuña and guanaco skins, which are obtained by hunting in the high *puna* grasslands of *ichu* bunchgrass, near the snowline. Vicuñas, once protected by Inca laws which only allowed royalty to wear their ultrafine wool, twice as fine as the wool of merino sheep, have been subjected to increasingly intensive hunting to the point where in 1969 it was estimated that only about 10000 survived, mostly in Peru but with some in Bolivia, Argentina and Chile. Now it is hoped that the vicuña will be saved, for national parks have been created in all of these countries with special concern for their preservation, and all hunting and trading in vicuña has been forbidden for a recuperative period of ten years from 1969. Illegal hunting still goes on, but guards in the mountains are at least ensuring a steady increase in the vicuña population at the present and it is hoped that after the ten-year interval controlled hunting and trading will again be possible.

Valles and Yungas
In the Cochabamba and Tarija valleys, intermediate levels of 2000 to 3000 m with strongly seasonal rainfall of 400-600 mm produce wheat and maize, potatoes, oats and alfalfa, in part under irrigation using small private irrigation schemes. Farming here is more prosperous than on the altiplano, but there remains the problem of the subdivision of farms to minifundio size, and most farms are under 10 ha. Commercial crops are important and cotton, flax for seed, and market garden products are sent by road to Potosí, Oruro and La Paz. Cochabamba has a relatively advanced dairy cattle industry, importing Argentine Holsteins to improve its stock, and has a growing cattle-feeding function. Oxen replace the altiplano llamas as beasts of burden in the region.

The Yungas, with good access to La Paz for those parts near the roads, has developed a strong commercial agriculture, based on coffee and coca. Coffee is a new crop and covers some 7000 ha in the region. It meets local demands and

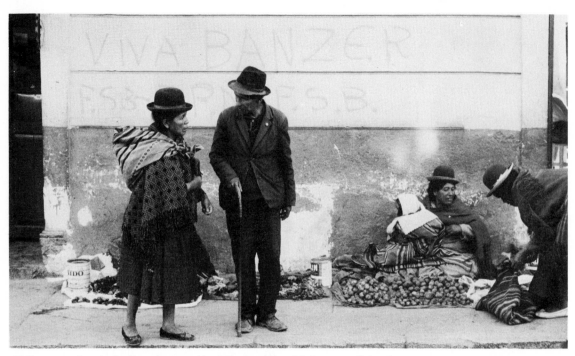

23 Street vendors in La Paz who travel in daily from the altiplano to sell food

could be extended for export, but the marketing is not well organized and profits go to middlemen rather than to producers or transporters. Citrus fruit, bananas and vegetables are also brought up to La Paz to be sold on the streets or in the central market by the peasants who bring their loads and often their families on lorries from the production areas. Coca, from the leaves of which the drug cocaine is extracted, is the most carefully tended crop of the Yungas, produced on tiny plots of less than quarter of a hectare, cleared of all weeds and precisely terraced on the steep slopes. Its high value—weight ratio, and steady markets — it is still chewed by the Indians as a stimulant, pain-killer and reliever of hunger, as well as being bought by foreign pharmaceutical firms — make it an ideal crop for the Yungas farmer. It is unofficially reported that cocaine illegally exported, some through Colombia to the USA, is Bolivia's largest export in value, exceeding tin.

Oriente

Extensive ranching is dominant here except for islands of intensive crop cultivation. Cattle ranching is especially important on the Llanos de Mojos, which sends its cattle upriver to the city markets; the cattle are a mixture of tough Spanish longhorns with zebu stock for extra insect and heat resistance. Many cattle are lost in the annual floods, though their numbers are unrecorded on the great unfenced latifundia, the *fincas*. On such ranches there are no capital installations apart from the ranch house itself, and the cattle receive little attention. All this of course stands in contrast to an apparently thriving agricultural economy here before the Conquest, which survived somewhat under Jesuit rule. Nineteenth-century historians used to speak of the 'civilizing rails'. For the Oriente, the railways were a means of reducing the region to a barbaric backwater state, unrelieved until the last two decades.

Santa Cruz growth pole

One of the changes introduced recently has been the upgrading of cattle and of ranches, and attempts at flying out beef by air. But the most important changes have not been on the *fincas* at all, but among the modern colonies in the Santa Cruz de la Sierra region. Here too the colonial economic scene had been more prosperous than in the nineteenth century, with commercial production of sugar and rice, but transport means declined in relative terms with the arrival of the western railways onto the altiplano. In 1954 the big change came to this sleepy backwater with a road to Cochabamba built with U.S. financial aid, allowing lorries to ship goods in a day to La Paz and Cochabamba, instead of the week or more formerly necessary. Settlement has been by a mixture of altiplano Indians, Okinawans and Japanese, and Mennonites; these people receive plots of land of 10-50 ha, and grow rice, mostly without irrigation, on seasonally flooded land; rice occupied 60000 ha in 1972.* Sugar cane is also important with 42000 ha, compared to a few thousand in the 1950s, and yields of 40-50 tons per ha are competitive with Argentine sugar to the south. Cotton is a third commercial crop, and maize is also grown where conditions are suitable. The whole region benefits from substantial credits and assistance from the U.S. governmental Point Four programme, including the establishment of experimental stations, to aid farmers unfamiliar with the region.

The district has effectively become the Oriente's regional growth pole, with not only the road to La Paz, but rail links to Argentina, at Yacuiba, Corumbá on the Brazilian frontier, and the soon-to-be-realized rail link to the altiplano. Agriculture feeds industry, with rice mills, sugar mills and farm machinery at the city of Santa Cruz, which had a population of 42700 in 1950 and 108700 in 1969, a growth rate faster than that of any other Bolivian city. The oil industry is another local booster to the economy. It should be remembered however that this is not the only area of opportunity in the east. The Upper Beni has also been colonized, with roads leading out from La Paz and, although there have been many setbacks in the programme of colonization, its closeness to La Paz may prove a deciding advantage over Santa Cruz. On the flat plains further out, mechanical means for drainage might well make available a new major agricultural resource.

* Data for 1972-3 are from estimates given by Ingeniero Villegas of the Agricultural Experiment Station at Saavedra, Santa Cruz.

THE MINERAL ECONOMY

Bolivian dependence on ore extraction for export is of long standing. In Potosí, a literal mountain of silver ore, the Cerro Rico de Potosí, attracted immediate attention from the Spaniards who brought Indian miners, first as paid volunteers, then as forced labour, to work under frightful conditions in the mines, already in 1600 reaching a depth of 200 m, bringing out ore painfully on ladders made of hides, after shifts at work lasting several days (including breaks for rest and meals). The death rate was phenomenally high, including losses from exhaustion, accidents on the ladders or in the mine, and lung diseases like pneumoconiosis. Ore smelting was initially carried out by means of tiny furnaces using wind funnels, a slow and irregular process. The discovery and use of mercury from Huancavelica allowed a speedier and more effective smelting process.

Potosí and some smaller mines acted as a powerful vortex of economic activity, employing thousands of Indians, in the transport of silver out to the ports, and in bringing mercury, food, fuel and mules from a distant hinterland. The whole area of Alto Peru, including the Oriente, and places such as Arica and northwest Argentina, were all part of this hinterland. The city itself grew to have a population of 120000 by 1600, the largest city of the Western Hemisphere. From 1572, the demands for power to grind the ores led to the construction of an elaborate reservoir and aqueduct system to bring water to Potosí, based on the cirque and other glacial lakes of mountains east of the town. Some of these lakes are still used by the city today, for the dry climate, with 600 mm annual rainfall which is concentrated in the summer, means long periods of drought and potential shortages.

Silver mining flourished until the late eighteenth century, to be followed after a gap of poverty by tin, suddenly in demand for new industries in the late nineteenth century. Simon Patiño was the central figure in this industry, gaining possession of the great Catavi deposit which long yielded over 50 per cent of Bolivian tin. The tin belt (fig. 21), following lines of silver mineralization north—south through the Cordillera Real, was developed at many points in small and large workings. At Potosí, tin ores

Fig. 21 Mineral production locations and potential oil-bearing regions

were found below the silver levels and still provide employment to its miners. Today, the industrial structure is one of very large firms, reflecting the heavy capital costs and economies of scale in the industry. Mines in the mountains far from civilization have caused whole mining towns to be created, which by their isolation and distinctive management were real enclaves of

foreign powers. Three firms only, Patiño, Hochschild and Aramayo, owned most of Bolivian tin resources before 1952.

The requirements of organization for tin mining, large firms and large operating units, led both to the rise of the great capitalists and to the overthrow of their power for, despite rigid company controls in mining towns, miners' unions led the movement of 1952. The Movimiento Nacionalista Revolucionario (MNR), initiated in 1939, based its policies for change on the support of organized labour, which in 1952 armed itself, defeated regular army forces, and instituted something quite different from the palace revolutions that have been the hallmark of South American politics since independence. Mine nationalization and agrarian reform were both undertaken by this government.

Comibol, the national mining agency, holds all the big mines and over half the total production, from the main mines at Llallagua (Catavi), Colquiri and Huanuni, in the zone east of Oruro (fig. 21). Hundreds of smaller enterprises are still privately owned, including primitive peasant —miner workings of short adits and alluvial gravels. The central importance of the industry, as a primary employer and as an earner of foreign exchange, continues to colour any discussion of national development, and much anxiety must derive from the industry's position of high-cost production, compared to Malaya with easily worked gravels as her main source of production.

Taking the minerals industry as a whole, i.e. including byproduct or even main product workings of silver, copper and zinc, a slight tendency for diminishing reliance on the sector is evident from the table, though this is of little comfort to Bolivia for such trends are to be expected in the absence of major wars and the stockpiling they engender. Diversification is the watchword of the day, more and more urgently as mining spreads from the deep mines to old tailings which are reworked as ore at under 1 per cent tin content, and as old machines are allowed to fall into disrepair without any replacement. One form of diversification is the growth of processing. Concentration plants for ore have been built at Porosí and Oruro, and tin and antimony smelters operate at Vinto near Oruro. Bismuth is to be smelted and there are plans for lead, silver and zinc processing. Comibol is also interested in diversification into other minerals, especially wolfram, copper and lead, and in moves away from the altiplano to use the alluvial ores of the Oriente. Copper development, if it could be induced, would cause a genuine geographical dispersion of mining, for the ores are low-grade disseminated coppers all along the Cordillera Occidental. The only major mine

today is Corocoro, for competition from foreign producers and lack of local capital has hindered expansion.

MINERAL EXPORTS EXCLUDING PETROLEUM

Year	Mineral value in millions of US dollars	Minerals as per cent of total exports
1952	138	97.5
1960	60	88.4
1964	108	94.8
1968	139	79.1
1972	194	80.8
1978	488	76.3

Minerals in the east

Petroleum is the counterbalance to the depressing story of Bolivian metals. A major petroleum zone (fig. 21) runs at the foot of the Andes, and within it a number of producing fields have been developed around Santa Cruz and to the south, starting from the U.S. investments of the 1920s at Camiri, taken over by the state in 1937, as an embittered and impoverished Bolivia sought funds to recuperate from the Chaco War of 1932-5, fought with these same oil deposits in mind. The industry was small in scale until 1952, when the revolutionary government rapidly expanded Camiri, followed by Caranda and Madrejones. In 1970, a second expropriation of US interests led to temporary decline in the industry, but this has been followed by expansion and continued discoveries. Associated refineries at Camiri, Santa Cruz and Cochabamba handle oil for domestic consumption, while exports of oil go by pipeline to Yacuiba and Argentina. Gas is also piped out to Argentina, moving from the gasfields near Santa Cruz through a processing plant at Colpa and then to Yacuiba. The oil pipeline to the Pacific at Arica is less important and has remained idle for much of the time recently.

In the far southeast, a recent interest has also developed in iron ore. The deposits of Mutún and Urucum, which are huge masses of haematite and manganese ores spreading over both Bolivian and Brazilian sides of the international boundary, may be mined opencast, and their only major disadvantage is transportation cost. Bolivia hopes to send the ore downstream to Argentina through Puerto Busch, though the existing port at Corumbá on the Brazilian side would be more logical and already has rail connections. It must of course be admitted that neither oil nor iron ore of themselves can provide a secure base for massive settlement in the east, for they will never employ large numbers. Farming is likely to employ more, and it too can scarcely become a vital sector in the isolation of the far southeast, outside the foothills.

TRANSPORT NETWORKS

The lack of a good rail and road network is both a symptom and a cause of underdevelopment. In Bolivia's case it is perhaps more the latter in the wide plains of the Oriente, and more the former on the altiplano where there are social and historical roots to poverty.

Railways

The rail network (fig. 20) is thin, and covers only 3542 km. Perhaps the most peculiar feature is that the western sector on the altiplano is quite separate from that in the Oriente, so that regional isolation has been compounded. A link between the two is of some interest, for it would also be a transcontinental link, a long-dreamed-of project in Bolivia and, when completed, a link between Arica and other Pacific ports, and Santos on the Atlantic, a line of 3952 km. To the north of these lines, there is no rail network. The only line is the notorious Madeira—Mamoré railway, from Pôrto Velho to Guajará Mirim, first attempted and abandoned as a project in 1878-9, and finally built only in 1909-12, by an American firm contracted by the Brazilian government. The history of the line's building shows some of the reasons for the lack of other rail extensions in the area. Many died from malaria, from beri beri disease caused by poor diet, dysentery carried in the rivers and even from Indian attacks. By the time of its completion, the fine grade of rubber from the Bolivian trees had become less desirable a commodity since lower grades could be used, and plantations in the Far East were already providing competition. Thus the railway, abandoned for some years and now run at a loss by Brazil, has little function, for it does not connect to any important centre in Bolivia, only to river navigation on the Ichilo and Beni, a steady trade worked by small steamers, but unconnected to the altiplano.

The older links to the exterior, mentioned in the section above on Political Geography, can only handle a very limited traffic. To the north-west, the Mollendo—Matarani outlet is not viable unless good rail or road links round lake Titicaca are found. To the west, the Arica railway is very difficult. Southwest, the Antofagasta line carries most Bolivian trade, and a spur joins the Argentine system at La Quiaca—Villazón, but the distances are very great. In no case are the lines adequate, with narrow gauge and single track, and using outdated rolling stock, though they are being replaced by modern Japanese and German equipment. The writer has seen carriages built at Gloucester in 1910 alongside Japanese stock of 1968 and later.

Roads are notoriously bad, but are in heavy and constant use by open lorries carrying goods and passengers, often together, over long distances at relatively low cost. Roads in fact carried 55 per cent of ton-km freight traffic and 78 per cent of passenger-km in Bolivia during 1965-9. Of most striking importance has been the Santa Cruz—Cochabamba paved road, initiated in 1954 and completed in 1963, a link between the eastern and western transportation systems capable of handling heavy traffic and providing a key to agricultural development at Santa Cruz.

BOLIVIAN OUTLOOK

Reviewing Bolivia's inauspicious first century and a half of separate existence, one might be tempted to conclude that the questions of sea access and lost territory would be most in need of solution. But these have been shown to be somewhat unreal problems, for Bolivian sea access is better than it has ever been, perhaps as good as it could have been had Bolivia in fact retained a coast. As to territorial parings, these may be claimed to make Bolivia today a more coherent and united country and to give her greater credibility as a political unit; no more than a shadowy control was ever exercised over the peripheries.

There are of course problems, but they are of another order: one serious question concerns the *campesinos*, as the altiplano peasants are officially termed, their lack of education, their lack of integration in ideals and way of thought into the national life, their separation, marked by language and culture, their extreme poverty. Related to this matter is that of a failing mineral source of wealth in tin mining and related activity, in the absence of massive international investments; agricultural resources which are totally inadequate to feed the population, requiring periodic injections of North American wheat and other foods; and the lack of any sound manufacturing development. Alto Peru, once the colonial jewel in the Spanish king's crown, has become, finally, the Sick Man of South America. This country's hopes must be pinned on new assignations within the Andean Pact, which promise it the regional monopoly of a small but growing number of industries on which there have been Group agreements.

THE MIDDLE LATITUDES

8. The Pampas Countries: Argentina and the Pampas Core Region

INTRODUCTION

Over the middle-latitude grasslands of both Northern and Southern Hemispheres, during the course of the last century, there occurred sweeping changes in landscape, reflecting other changes in economy and society, changes linked to the rise of early industrial nations and to the new technologies these countries introduced. What had been the untamed Prairies and Great Plains of the United States and Canada, the almost unsettled Ukrainian steppes, and the little known grasslands of the South African Veldt, of eastern Australia or New Zealand, rapidly became settled, prosperous farming regions tied in to a world economy. In South America, the same phenomenon occurred in the Pampas region in Argentina and Uruguay, possessing like the other regions a plains topography ideal for mechanized agriculture, or for transport by railways, fine deep black or near-black soils, and a climate eminently suited to the production of wheat or other grains as well as for grass.

For this South American zone, the settlement and economic rise of the Pampas meant a substantial reorientation of the space-economy of young nations. The economic concentration on the Peruvian altiplano and Lima throughout colonial time, emphasizing the role of northern and western provinces as providers of raw materials to the centre, now changed to a new focus on the river Plate, with direct access to a new Europe. The political creation of Uruguay, an economic nonentity, to serve as buffer between Argentina and Brazil, was now seen to have economic significance as the little country became part of the growth region in the Humid Pampas. Over the last hundred years, the dominance of Pampas society and economy in the life of Argentina and Uruguay has stamped a special imprint on these countries, distinct from any other Latin American group. They have shed some of their colonial structures of society and economy, and in the central area of the Pampas a totally new socio-economic being has emerged, neither European nor *criollo*, though in terms of physical race almost entirely European since the Plains Indians, as in America, had to be eliminated rather than incorporated into a new life which they totally rejected. The immigrants from Europe of the nineteenth century did not entirely displace traditional socio-economic structures, as will be seen, but they modified them in various ways, helping the advance of education, of democratic government, of intensive agriculture on owner-operator farms, of small industries and urban life in general.

The Indian word *pampa* refers to any kind of a plains surface, and in reality it is more appropriate to speak of the Humid Pampas in respect of the area undergoing the transformations just mentioned. These Humid Pampas, in central-eastern Argentina and Southern Uruguay, are the core area of the river Plate basin today, concentrating most farm and manufacturing production for the region. Round the core are grouped a set of drier, poorer lands, each individually linked in more or less well to the core but with few direct connections between them. These are the regions of Patagonia in the far south, Cuyo in the west, the northwestern provinces in Argentina, the Chaco in both Argentina and Paraguay, eastern Paraguay, northeastern Argentina and northern Uruguay.

The country is large by any standards, covering 2.8 million sq km or, if its claims to a slice of the Antarctic between 25° and 74° west are recognized, 4 million sq km. Within these bounds, there are all kinds of physical environments, from subtropical to arctic, and it might be expected that some pronounced regional divisions would occur. The most important is that between the Pampas, including Buenos Aires, and the Interior, which is covered in the next chapter. Another important division might be made between Buenos Aires city and the rest of the country, for in population, economy and culture the capital is of comparable importance to all other regions combined, and is certainly distinctive, if only occupying a tiny fragment of the area of a great country.

The Pampas—Interior division has its roots in physical differences, emphasized by the colonial policy of concentration on Peru and Lima, which brought only the northwest into prominence. The division continued into Independence times despite a complete changeover of relative importance with the development of the Pampas region for agriculture. Integration of the two macro-regions is still in progress, after a stormy period in the nineteenth century when even political unity of the Argentine provinces was threatened. Integration has been in terms of links to the single city of Buenos Aires, and this in itself has been a weakness for the national unity of Argentina, and has converted Paraguay into an entirely dependent state which must reach the outside world through a foreign capital acting as its outport. Neither economic nor cultural integration has been entirely possible, for there are deep gaps in level of education, of income, and employment prospects, between the poor lands of the Interior and the wealthy littoral provinces.

THE LAND

The Pampas landscape is a comparatively new one, with little of the overlay of history, old cathedrals, churches, university buildings and *cabildos*, nor the brown mestizo skins and bright garments of the people of the northwest. It is a landscape of flat fields, straight fences and roads, mechanized farms and small uninteresting towns, more reminiscent of the North American Midwest than of South America. Even the city of Buenos Aires, spreading over an enormous area with its low flat dwellings, great open expanses and straight streets, is an expression of the abundance of flat land and of its recent ordered occupation by man.

The Humid Pampas is a low plain, interrupted by hills in the sierras of Tandil, Ventana and Córdoba. It has been formed as an enormous surface of deposition, crossed by broad modern alluvial floodplains, occupied by sluggish streams and frequent shallow reedy lakes, the home of marsh birds and frogs, and described vividly by many a nineteenth-century writer in the period before it had been tamed and cultivated:

> Around Huincul, the country spread untilled and undivided, with its traditional air of pastoral *latifundio*, with no other visible sign of human appropriation than some flock of sheep, or the cattle scattered around a rustic hut. It was the almost untouched prairie of the recent conquest, not long ago the Indian frontier, where now any tiled ranch might occupy an Indian campsite . . . the monotonous landscape offered its few accidents in the form of nominal streams, endowed with an ephemeral existence by yesterday's rain, destined to die tomorrow, leaving only the bed in which they ran. More permanent, the lagoons filled by the flood, displayed their liquid mirror, occupied by widgeons and shrieking *teruteros*, dusty *chajas* and rose-coloured flamingos, and all framed deeply by the jonquils and reedmace on their banks.

> *Paul Groussac,* Relatos Argentinos *(Victoriano Suarez, Madrid, 1922), p. 131*

A higher portion of the plain is that in Entre Rios, with a rolling landscape and generally better drainage, while the other extreme, a dead flat and permanently ill-drained plain, is that of the Salado river in central Buenos Aires province.

Climatically the region is comparable with the southeastern United States, hot and humid in summer, temperate and wet in winter, with little frost but a constant succession of frontal storms from depressions moving north up the east coast, giving frequent changes in wind direction, humidity and cloud cover such as are common within the world's west-coast middle latitudes. Climate sets the limits of the Humid Pampas near the 500 mm annual isohyet, an approximate limit to continuous grass cover and to cultivation on the west, while in the north the winter (July) isotherm of 15°C is a limit for tropical forms of vegetation and land use, between Pampas and Chaco.

The natural vegetation of the Pampas is a thick grass sward, perhaps not a true climax vegetation but the result of frequent fires during dry periods. Now this grass cover has gone from most areas, either to cultivation or more frequently simply improved by grazing of cattle and the introduction of European grasses and especially clover. The maintenance of a good grass cover has meant less erosion problem on the dry margins than in the North American equivalent on the Great Plains margin of cultivation.

SETTLEMENT AND COLONIAL ECONOMY

A South American frontier

Figure 22 shows the progress of settlement through time, from a linear and river-tied occupation in early times, through the occupation of Entre Rios and southwest Uruguay, to a final swift march across the remainder during the nineteenth century. This settlement and its expansion is of interest as presenting the only large-scale case of a true frontier in South America. In other regions the Spaniards normally occupied pre-existing towns and thus extended their control over the surrounding territory without actually having to occupy it in person; they merely replaced the upper echelons of administration and set the Indians or mestizos to work for them.

In the Pampas there was a frontier, because no settled Indians were to be found over whom control might have been extended, and because the Pampas Indians were actively hostile, requiring

stockaded buildings for the *estancias* surrounded by deep ditches to hinder Indian attack on horseback. In this region a direct confrontation was made, over three hundred years, between untamed Indians and Spanish settlers. This confrontation, and the final expansion of the frontier, did not however lead to a new democratic society forged by frontier life, as was claimed by Frederick Jackson Turner for North America. Here in the south, great landowners held the land privately before the wave of settlers arrived, there was little public land, and in any case they came too late to experience much frontier life. Instead, Argentina's 'Wild West' was experienced by only a scanty old-established Spanish population, soldiers defending little forts against Indian attack on the frontier, coaches and coachmen carrying mails or carters with high-wheeled slow oxcarts taking wine or textiles across the plains, ranchers with their primitive *estancias*, any and each of these groups liable to sudden, unannounced attack by marauding Indian horsemen from the *desierto*, the untamed interior. Settlement was thus based on an insecure tenure of the land.

Trade in mules, hides and leather to Peru, and contraband trade out through Buenos Aires were both important, and required only the maintenance of the overland routes to the north of the main Indian concentrations in the Pampas. The land base was the unfenced and unoccupied plain, where cattle and horses, introduced by the Spaniards, multiplied rapidly, leading to a peculiar industry, that of cattle-hunting. This had begun with the *cimarrones*, but it expanded to include any wandering cattle in the interior, for cattle were not always marked and in any case they were not to be brought back, merely slaughtered in the field.

The system adopted was for a number of horsemen to hunt down a herd of cattle, incapacitate them while still at the gallop by cutting their tendons with long knives on poles, until a sufficient number had been brought down, after which they would return to kill off and strip the hides from their victims, leaving the carcass as a useless byproduct of the operation except for some delicacy they might eat themselves, lightly cooked and eaten alone, apart from a little *yerba mate*, which they considered the only necessary accompaniment of their meal.

Fig. 22 The spread of settlement on the Pampas

ESTANCIAS AND SALADEROS

Limits on this primitive form of economy were set by the cattle, which eventually became scarce and moved out of the hunting range and into Indian country. This forced some care in cattle husbandry and more *estancias* were set up, temporary gathering places for the animals often conveniently placed in a curl of a river or some other site which confined the herd. From these semi-permanent sites, both hides and tallow could be obtained, and in the eighteenth century meat too became important. It was sun-dried, forming *charqui*, and often in addition salted at the *saladeros*, which brought salt from Patagonia or from the interior for the industry, exporting the product to the slave colonies of Cuba and Brazil. The frontier was extended gradually from the Paraná—Plate line, occupying Entre Rios from an early date and then reaching out to the Salado, a defensive frontier against the aggressive Pampas Indians from about 1770 to 1820.

Trade

While the cattle kingdom expanded and became more sophisticated in techniques and products, towns grew little. Spanish hegemony in foreign trade meant that all colonial exports and imports went through Lima. This trade monopoly was a serious drawback for Buenos Aires, three or more months' journey overland from Peru. Naturally, a large contraband trade grew up on the Plate, utilizing the city's natural accessibility to Europe compared to Lima. British, Dutch and French vessels were involved in the trade in gold and silver, hides and tallow, all commanding good prices in Europe.

NINETEENTH CENTURY: THE TRANSFORMATION OF THE PAMPAS

The drive to settle the southern Pampas after Independence came initially from military leaders, but was taken up and given a true frontier atmosphere with the mass arrival of European immigrants after 1850, coming not as *estancieros* but as small farmers to cultivate the virgin soil of the Pampas. The colour and romance of the frontier and its savagery were fleeting moments captured by only a few writers who knew and could describe the primitive grasslands. Here is a description of an Indian raid:

> Soon afterwards Indians and cattle galloped over the line of frontier forts, through the virgin pampa equidistant from Trenque Lauquen and Guaminí, an area covered in *puna* grass and thickets of low brushwood. At the noise of this avalanche, the ostriches and deer fled in close-packed groups as did the wild cats which lived among the tall grasses . . . . It was like an undulating river of backs and rumps, an immense mass, sombre against the sun, illuminated here and there by the manes of the white, bay or roan horses.

> *E. Acevedo Diaz,* Cancha Larga *(Editorial Sopena, Buenos Aires, 1939), p. 201*

Successful settlement by the small farmer began in central Santa Fé and Entre Rios, then quickly extended to all the Humid Pampas. Tenure systems varied; in a minority of cases, notably in Santa Fé, ownership of the land was conferred on the small farmer, because the provincial government aided settlement and overlooked early debts of the settlers, and because of basically favourable physical conditions. Elsewhere, similar colonies failed, sometimes for want of effort on the part of farmer, owner or colonizing agent, sometimes through total ignorance of the problems of the region, such as locust attack spreading out of the northern deserts, droughts and floods, lack of roads or transport. Many colonists were not farmers at all but recruited in towns and ignorant of any kind of farming. In many places migrants were brought in merely as tenants, cultivating the land for four years and then handing it back with planted alfalfa to the owner, who thus had land rents plus a ready-made pasture of improved grass for his cattle at the end of the contract period. Under such conditions, expansion of the frontier and introduction of small farmers had no democratizing influence on society, as had been hypothesized for North America. *Estancias* continued to grow into the present century, and to control a subordinate labour force of considerable size.

Tenants had a special role in improving pastures. They were part of a technological revolution, which began in the 1830s with Merino and then improved British breeds of sheep, followed by British breeds of cattle, imported to replace the Spanish longhorns and provide good quality meat for European markets. They required good pastures to fatten well, and the tenants would plant alfalfa for the purpose at no cost to the owner of land. To avoid mixing their pedigree cattle with others, and to control pasture use, fencing was needed and this was introduced during the 1870s in massive imports of wire. Railways were extended across the plains to bring the animals to market, and ships using steampower to take them to Europe. For a while there was an active trade in live cattle, but it was superseded in the 1890s by the frozen meat ship, the result of yet another technological development, the use of refrigeration.

Railways also helped the cultivation of crops, and were essential to ship out the wheat surpluses from the 1880s onwards. Rosario was the first port with good rail access to its hinterland, but it

Fig. 23 Railway map of Argentina

was soon overshadowed by Buenos Aires, which gained the termini of most rail lines through commercial advantages and influence with the British constructors of railways. Figure 23 shows that the centrality of Buenos Aires is not as great as might be supposed. There are five different gauges of railway and most interior provinces are on metre-gauge lines, unconnected to the capital.

PRESENT-DAY POPULATION

Argentina is today a largely urban country. Buenos Aires alone had 9.7 million in 1978 (2.98 in the city proper), or a third of the total national population. This urban concentration is remarkable in a large country where many other major urban regional centres have long been powerful, and is to some extent an expression of the country's ties to foreign markets, and of the fact that national administration is based in the same place as the national port and manufacturing centre. The Argentines have contemplated the removal of their capital to an interior site for some time, in the interests of spreading development and asserting interest in the provinces, but until now the pull of the coast has proved too great.

Perhaps concentration in the major urban location is comprehensible if we examine closer the national employment structure.

EMPLOYMENT BY SECTOR IN PERCENTAGES

	1970	1975 (estimated)
Primary	20.5	18.2
Manufacturing	18.9	19.5
Construction	7.6	8.5
Transport	6.5	7.7
Public services	0.8	0.8
Government	11.3	10.4
Retail, Services	34.4	34.9
Total	100.0	100.0

Source: Plan Nacional de Desarrollo y Seguridad, 1971-5, *Consejo Nacional de Desarrollo, Buenos Aires, 1971, p. 36.*

Even in the rural areas there is little truly dispersed population. The relative dispersal of the nineteenth century has been generally replaced by concentration of farmers in the small towns, from which they travel by car to their work. Most families have either a pickup or a car, an index of an agricultural system standing above the normal Latin American level.

Racial makeup in the Pampas is also distinctive, with no Indian or Negro component. Indians were eliminated in fighting, while the few negroes imported in colonial time were mostly domestics who never mixed with the rest of the populace. Spanish and Italian immigrants of the nineteenth and early twentieth centuries are the largest contingents, Italians having provided some 55 per cent of the 3.4 million immigrants during 1860-1910, a total reduced to a still impressive 2.5 million if those who returned, the *golondrinas* or swallows as they were called from their seasonal habits, are subtracted. Small minorities of many European nations, English, Scots, Irish, French and German, are also found in both town and country, having come in to take up cheap land offered by railway companies, or with commercial enterprises from Europe. Today immigration from Europe has ceased, but for the capital at least has been replaced by a large flow from the interior of Argentina and from the poor neighbouring countries, Bolivia, Chile and Paraguay.

Modern migration from the interior to Buenos Aires is usually done by stages. Rural people move to small towns in their region, then to large cities and so to the capital, where they form an active, energetic group, poorly educated but not without skills, so that unemployment is not a primary problem. As a rich city, Buenos Aires has also been able to tackle vigorously the housing problem of the immigrants, upgrading and replacing shanty towns, the *villas miseria*, with solid economical housing.

AGRICULTURE

The governmental body in Buenos Aires which deals with farm matters is called the Ministry of Agriculture and Livestock, firmly separating the two. This Spanish language distinction is an index of the continuing differences between cattlemen and cultivators; there is little mixed farming for a region where it might well be expected, and those who belong to the *estanciero* class regard themselves as a separate class whose dignity might be lowered by bringing arable cultivation into their ranches. This distinction

N

Smallholdings   Urban area

Alberdi

Vedia

L.N. Alem

0 1 2 3 4 5
Kilometres

Fig. 24 Agricultural colonies and estancias in Leandro Alem partido

however is between individual farmers and farm types, and not between land-use regions and, as fig. 24 shows, a mixture of farms may be found in many parts, of great *estancias* with small farms producing grain, vegetables or milk.

There are certain areas of specialization within the agricultural system predominant on the Pampas. Up to the 1930s, a division could simply be made between zones of beef cattle breeding or fattening, and zones of grain production. These are still on the map (fig. 25) as the northern maize belt and southern wheat belt, though changed in form and reduced from their maximum extent. There are however large areas under new products, symbols of a new transformation of the Pampas. Dairy regions have sprung up in several places, while potatoes, fruit and vegetables have all made incursions onto Pampas land; such changes are partly in response to growing urban markets, partly a result of the difficult world markets for traditional wheat and beef. The grain and beef producing zones continue to hold most of the area, fluctuating with world markets, but they give way to the new crops wherever small farms are available, where there is a good transport network and dense rural labour force, and where organization of farmers in cooperatives has been successful.

On the traditional *estancias*, and on many medium-sized farms, grain-farming tends to expand with good prices and a stable political situation. During more difficult times, such as that of the Perón government of 1945-55, cultivation is replaced by ranching and tenant farmers by cattle, the land being turned over to a small labour force of *gauchos*, or cowboys. At all times farming is extensive with minimal inputs, a system that shows land to be the cheap input and the one that can still be squandered. Low inputs of capital in buildings or machinery are of course useful to the Pampas farmer in giving him flexibility; he may change easily from one form of farming to another, having invested little in specialized equipment. The system's disadvantage is that production is low and tends to rise only slowly over pre-Second-World War levels. Wheat provides an example of this feature.

WHEAT AREA, PRODUCTION AND YIELD

Year	000 ha Area	000 metric tons Production	Metric tons per ha Yield
1934-8	6783	6634	9.8
1948-52	4487	5175	11.5
1955	4062	5250	12.9
1960	3599	3960	11.0
1965	4601	6079	13.2
1970	3332	4250	12.8
1975	5339	8560	16.0

Source: FAO Production Yearbook, *various editions, United Nations, Rome*

Fig. 25 Areas with over 20 per cent of farmland in wheat and maize, 1937 and 1960

INDUSTRY AND CITY DEVELOPMENT

In the twentieth century Argentina has become an industrial power, most of her industry collected in Buenos Aires and other Pampas cities. Industry began with the processing of farm products for export, specifically the freezing and chilling of beef in the great foreign-owned *frigoríficos,* slaughterhouses and meat-packing factories. This first stage of foreign-led industry was added to through the 1920s and 1930s by all kinds of consumer goods industries in the drive for import substitution by domestic production. Nowadays industry has a well-rounded aspect, with not only these consumer industries but those of a third stage of industrialization, including steel, chemicals, heavy engineering and other capital-goods manufacturing.

The geography of industry is simple. Three-quarters of it is concentrated in and around Buenos Aires city. Within the city there are several industrial districts, but the major one is from south of the modern port area to a big zone on the south side of the Riachuelo, in the industrial suburb of Avellaneda. Light industries have come into some old residential sites in the older parts of the city, while large modern industries like car assembly have taken up open-field sites around the peripheries of the capital.

Southeast of the city, there is another industrial concentration at Ensenada, a port originally developed for La Plata, but now with large petrochemical works and an oil refinery. On the northwest side, industry continues upstream with Rosario (810 840), second city of Argentina and a major industrial centre. It is still the port outlet for part of the northern Pampas, milling and shipping much grain, and processing gas and oil

24 The cathedral at Tucuman. This city is not only an industrial centre but a cultural one of long standing

from northern Argentina and Bolivia (fig. 27). Further upriver there are other industrial districts, most notably at Santa Fé (244 580) and Paraná, now closely linked by a new tunnel under the river Paraná. Santa Fé is another port with terminus facilities for grain, but Paraná has only a minor port. Below Rosario, San Nicolás is Argentina's steel city, lying within easy reach of Buenos Aires markets and accessible too, to ocean steamers bringing raw materials.

Far to the south, Bahía Blanca has port functions and provides the main outlet for the southern grain belt; its port has bulk-handling facilities and new grain terminals, and suffers less from silting than the muddy Plate estuary. Bahía Blanca also benefits now from the oil industry, lying at the confluence of lines from Neuquén and Patagonia, and it is building up new petrochemical and derivative industries.

The only major Pampas city not on the coast or with ready access to it is Córdoba (798 660). In fact, Córdoba is not strictly in the Humid Pampas region if we judge solely by the 500 mm rainfall line. Historically it has had an intermediate, transitional situation, as the great interior routeway focus and point of contact between the Northwest and the Pampas. Appropriately enough with this situation, it has large transport-machinery factories, making cars, buses, railway rolling-stock and locomotives.

OTHER URBAN FUNCTIONS

Apart from manufacturing, the administrative function is important in the provincial capitals, especially in La Plata (506 300), capital of Buenos Aires province, richest of the Pampas provinces. This city came into being by governmental fiat in the 1880s, as a replacement for Buenos Aires city which had become a federal district and could not at the same time govern a province. La Plata is thus a planned, open, clean city, with no industry and with its university, of high reputation, the only competitor to government. Provincial government in the other cities, Santa Fé, Paraná, Córdoba and Santa Rosa (La Pampa), is a less important but not negligible industry, linked in to a regional service and marketing-centre function.

Another distinctive town function is tourism, again evidence of Argentina's sizeable middle class, for the tourist resorts, apart from the capital, are fed by domestic holiday makers rather than foreigners. Mar del Plata (299 700) is the largest tourist centre, with good road and rail links to Buenos Aires. It houses an increasing number of permanent dwellers, mostly retired persons, who are changing its character from a purely summer resort to an all-year centre and a large city. Other smaller resorts crowd the coastline to the south from Mar del Plata, on uncrowded beaches of fine sand.

Tourists can also go to Córdoba for open air, as the city stands under the Sierra de Córdoba, a hill range with open country, forests and some old colonial settlements. The city itself provides much of interest to the traveller for, as the colonial centre of trade and administration, it has many old buildings, including a baroque cathedral, and many monasteries. It boasts the country's oldest university, though it was scarcely more than a school, under Jesuit supervision, until the nineteenth century. Santa Fé has similar colonial origins and some old architecture, but its subtropical heat and the marshlands near the Paraná do not attract many tourists.

BUENOS AIRES

This city cannot be classified as industrial, administrative or commercial, for it has all these functions. It grew up, however, as a commercial rather than a manufacturing centre, and its manufacturing function is still limited in scope, if not in absolute size. There are no steel mills or other heavy industries in the city, a reflection of national shortcomings in this direction. Administration is important in the life and landscape of the city; the Congress building and the Casa Rosada, the rose-coloured presidential palace on the Plaza de Mayo, are twin symbols of administrative power and, on the same plaza, the old colonial *cabildo* or town hall remains as a reminder of the fact that this was one of the first foci of colonial revolt against Napoleonic Spain. Governmental power is strongly held in Buenos Aires, although the country is constitutionally a federation of provinces.

Governmental control is matched by the private industries, which all have their main offices at Buenos Aires, even those with little association with the capital. In addition, there are the financial and management companies, and those of transport and communications networks, most with offices near the Plaza de Mayo in the centre of the city.

Culturally, Buenos Aires has always been a world apart from the interior. In the nineteenth century, the city and its province were only precariously linked to the rest of the country. The city was the home for all those with any kind of literary or intellectual aspirations or pretensions, because of its associations with Europe, as culture followed trade. Today the city still houses most of the theatre, opera and artistic life of the nation. To its residents, the distant interior is still an uncivilized region, the land of barbarity that people of vision such as Domingo F. Sarmiento, educationalist and nineteenth-century president of the country, sought to change through the civilizing influences of the city, and by replacing local feudalism with a nationally effective government. The viewpoint of city dwellers is no doubt extreme; but it remains, and still has some basis in reality.

9. Argentina: The Interior

A second Argentina lies beyond the city of Buenos Aires and its Humid Pampas hinterland. This is an open, empty land, much of it desert or semi-desert, where man has never had a firm hold. Its landscapes, however, are not monotonous for, apart from the Dry Pampas, the western extension of the Humid Pampas plains, there are many mountain ranges standing up from alluvial piedmont fans at their foot, like cliffed islands in a grey—brown sea, displaying rock formations in sharp contrast of colour and form to the dun of the plains. The cities, whose intense activity stands in contrast to the thinly-peopled countryside, differ from those of the Pampas and from each other. In the northwest and west, they have darker-skinned people, some remnants of old traditions in custom and dress, and are architecturally distinct. Their social milieu is not quite in tune with the twentieth century.

An Argentine joke is that 'God is in all places, but his office is at Buenos Aires', and this expresses something of the relative poverty and resentment of the inhabitants of the Interior towards the richer littoral and especially Buenos Aires. Figure 26 shows the differences in wealth of the Interior, except for Patagonia, where the wealth is held by a few *estancieros* and industrialists, who in any case take much of their earnings out to Buenos Aires, leaving the region as poor as its neighbours.

PATAGONIA

The land south of the Rio Colorado is a high plateau region, standing generally over 300 m above the Atlantic, to which it slopes gradually down, a harsh windswept environment with scanty vegetation, the desert increasing in strength rather than diminishing towards the coast. Here and there tabletop mountains or volcanic cones break the monotony of the pebble-strewn flat surface, and the through-flowing rivers, the Chubut, Colorado and Negro, have deep, almost canyon-like valleys. The Andean fringe of the region is a lower and less impressive range than further north, but has spectacular scenery in the region of Bariloche, an Argentine Lake District with similar origin to the English Lake District in scouring by Pleistocene glaciers.

Historical factors

This region was claimed by Chile in colonial times, but no control was ever exerted, and no exploration made apart from the visits of a few missionary priests. It held neither settled Indians nor, despite many rumours, any gold or silver that might have attracted settlers. The few inhabitants were warlike Indians who lived on hunting guanaco (a wild relative of the llama), and the little American deer, mostly in the vicinity of the Andes where there is most moisture and vegetation. In the far south, some of the world's most primitive economies were to be found, among them the shellfish collectors of the Magellan Straits.

After Independence, the question of ownership became urgent, but Patagonian Indians could not be dominated until the 1880s, when

Fig. 26 Per capita Gross Domestic Product of Argentine provinces

Argentine troops conducted the 'Conquest of the Desert' campaign, which effectively secured them the right to all land east of the Andes, and virtually eliminated the Indian population of the region. Colonization of the distant shores of Patagonia by Europeans was not attempted, except for a Welsh group which was enticed by poorly informed leaders to the lower Chubut, where it nearly came to total grief because of misconceptions about the environment and

25 The Iguassú Falls, formed where a Paraña tributary leaves the basalt plateau. At present they are a growing tourist attraction on both Argentine and Brazilian sides of the frontier

possible farming methods. Meanwhile, most of Patagonia was given away in great grants to landowners who had bought bonds, to be redeemed in land, for the financing of the desert campaign, or given in smaller blocks to soldiers of this campaign. Such grants merely extended the traditional estancia system into a new area.

Modern economy

Mineral resources are important to modern Patagonia, with oil, gas and coal as fuels, and iron ore in the north. The coal of Rio Turbio (fig. 27) is of low grade, unsuitable for steel-making except for a small percentage mixture in the coking ovens, but useful for heating purposes, and its production is expanding under government plans, from under one million tons in recent years to over four million; the coal is shipped out by a narrow-gauge railway to Rio Gallegos, a little port from which freighters take it to the river Plate.

More important than coal are the oil and gas of Comodoro Rivadavia, an area developed since 1913, the oil again moving north by coastal tankers, the gas by pipeline to Buenos Aires. Large gas fields have also been discovered in Neuquén and Tierra del Fuego. The iron ore of Sierra Grande is a lowgrade (under 50% iron) deposit, but in ore-deficient Argentina is of great interest and is now being developed with foreign aid at a highly mechanized extraction and concentration plant.

Water resources have considerable importance for the region for power and irrigation, though the potential is still little used. The largest water project is that on the Negro, or rather on its tributaries, the Limay and Neuquén. This is the giant El Chocón—Cerros Colorados scheme, using dams on the two rivers to produce power which is presently taken out via a high-tension line to Buenos Aires, the only consuming market for it at the moment. It is significant that

AGUA BLANCA
ZAPLA
Antofagasta
Salta
Metán
Asunción
San Juan
Córdoba
Santa Fé
Mendoza
San Lorenzo
San Luís
Campana
LUJÁN
Montevideo
Buenos Aires
La Plata
Mar del Plata
Punta Alta
PLAZA HUINCUL
Bahía Blanca
SIERRA GRANDE
Comodoro Rivadavia
RÍO TURBIO
S. Sebastián
R. Grande

■ Iron deposits

◆ Coal field

— Oil pipelines

— Gas pipelines

-•- Product pipelines

Oil and gas fields

REFINERIES
Capacity in barrels per day

▲ Less than 10 000

▲ 10 000 to 100 000

▲ more than 100 000

△ under construction

0   200   400

Fig. 27 Argentine mineral resources and the oil industry

regional development is not yet affected by the dam, despite this being a stated aim of the government-supported agency set up to manage the project. Power is taken out to the capital, and water sufficient to irrigate a million hectares is unused for want of demand by the small farmer community.

The other important Patagonian river is the Colorado. In this case interprovincial dispute between the riverine provinces has held up utilization for decades, the principal contestants being Mendoza, which would divert water for use in its own irrigation system, and Buenos Aires, which already uses a substantial flow for supplementary irrigation in the lower valley. No large dams or hydroelectric projects have been attempted because of the disputes between upstream and downstream users, finally solved by a compromise agreement in 1976.

Another river development of importance is that of Futaleufú, on the upper tributaries of the Yelcho, a river running out to the Pacific. Power from a new scheme here is to be sent via 330 kV lines to Puerto Madryn on the Atlantic, and used there for manufacturing aluminium.

Agriculture
In the dry Interior, agriculture tends to polarize into two extremes, intensive cultivation on irrigated land and extensive pastoral land use on dry land. In Patagonia, the irrigated lands are mostly those of the upper Negro valley, where some colonization by small farmers has taken place in this century and marketing of the product in Buenos Aires is possible, using trucks on a modern asphalt road all the way to the capital, or the General Roca railway which runs up the valley to the regional centres, Neuquén, Plaza Huincul and Zapala. Apples, cherries, pears and even grapes may be produced in the warm summers of the protected valley, and cooperative organization aids an efficient marketing of the product.

Outside the irrigated valleys, only sheep farming is practicable and even this is excluded from the true deserts of the northeastern half of the territory. Grass cover is best in Tierra del Fuego and near the Andes, and in both areas there are great *estancias* with hundreds of thousands of head of sheep, some of them Merino and Merino cross-breds.

Industries
There has been little basis for urban growth in Patagonia, and the little towns of the region are either ports, like Puerto Madryn and Rio Gallegos, handling export of wool and some frozen mutton, coal or oil; agricultural or oil centres in the upper Rio Negro valley, Neuquén, Zapala and Plaza Huincul, Neuquén province's oil centre; or the tourist centres of the Argentine Lake District, especially Bariloche itself, which

has attracted some permanent retirees as well as the summer visitors for camping, fishing and hiking in the mountains.

THE CUYO REGION
North of the Rio Colorado, the plateau aspect of the landscape gradually disappears and the bunch grasses of Patagonia are replaced by thornscrub, a still more difficult environment for farmers than the arid grasslands to the south. The region of Cuyo comprises the three provinces of Mendoza, San Juan and San Luís; its historical basis is a province of this name, held by Chile until 1776, when it finally became part of the river Plate viceroyalty. Before the Spaniards came, this land had had a certain unity under the Huarpe Indians, settled agriculturalists on the fringe of the Inca empire and with a modest irrigation system, which attracted the sixteenth-century Spaniards exploring from Santiago in the 1560s.

Under the colonial regime, Cuyo developed a prospering vineyard economy and also fattened cattle for driving over the pass of Uspallata to Chile, but the region was economically independent to a considerable degree, as it had to be with the high passes blocked by snow for at least six months of the year. Leather and ironworking, textiles, pottery and woodworking were all practised here because of the impossibility of relying on outside supplies.

This economy declined with the nineteenth-century attachment to Buenos Aires, for the port became the centre, Cuyo part of a remote periphery, and transport over the plains by lumbering oxcart was almost as painful as crossing the Andes to Chile. The rescue came in 1884 with the rail line from Buenos Aires to Mendoza, which allowed vineyards and olive cultivation, as well as alfalfa production, to expand rapidly in Mendoza, sweet grapes for drying into raisins in San Juan along with olive groves, though this province was always a little more isolated and less well provided with irrigation water.

The other mainstay of Cuyo's development, besides the rail, was the building of new concrete dams, and general upgrading of the whole irrigation system from a primitive colonial state, in which a multiplicity of water owners had their own derivatory canals taking a little water from

26 Careful cultivation is apparent in the vineyards of Mendoza, which now provide a surplus of wine for export from Argentina. Lines of poplars provide both a windbreak and a useful source of wood for fruit packing cases

rough partial dams of loose stones. Irrigation was organized centrally under a provincial authority which ensured rapid development and reasonably equitable provision of water to farms. No colonists were to be attracted to frontier lands, but there were new settlers, mostly northern Italians who came in during 1880-1900.

Loss of autarchy
The development of vineyards, olive orchards and alfalfa fields was a help to Cuyo but placed her in a subordinate position relative to the new centre and market at Buenos Aires, which acted as importer of goods from Europe, entirely displacing the old craft wares of the Interior. Mendoza, San Juan and San Luís became the home of wine and olive merchants, traders and shopkeepers, not of the host of small manufacturers who had formerly been so important.

Modern economy
Cuyo retains this agricultural orientation to the present, with a still expanding area under vines and alfalfa as well as new intensively irrigated areas with vegetables and fruits. Added to farming is a variety of light manufacture in Mendoza which give the city a fairly rounded economic structure.

Water and agriculture
Water is all-important, for rainfall in most of the region is under 300 mm annually, insufficient for any unirrigated crop. The rivers, San Juan, Mendoza, Tunuyán, Atuel and Diamante, provide five-sixths of the farm water, pumped ground water the rest. The river water reaches maximum flow in late summer, as it derives from snowmelt in the high Andes, and this is useful for agriculture, though water control leaves much to be desired as sudden floods and long droughts can still cause havoc.

The Rio Atuel has high dams already controlling its flow and helping electricity production in a province which has important power-based industries. Now high dams are being constructed on the Diamante and in the south of the province, and will soon be built also on the other rivers.

Using the river water and increasing amounts from wells, Mendoza continues to concentrate on her vines, used for wine production which serves all national markets and a growing export trade (plate 26). There is a dynamic vegetable production sector too, for sale as quickfrozen, canned or dried food. Most of the farms are small, under 5 ha, but there are also large estates of over 2000 ha, implying enormous wealth when it is remembered that this area is all under irrigation. San Juan is more conservative, and has progressed little towards crop diversification away from the traditional vines and olives. Western San Luís has a more primitive economy, some of its isolated oases producing at a semi-subsistence level. Outside the irrigated lands, throughout Cuyo, there is at most only pasture for goats, whose meat is sold in local markets.

Towns and industries

Mendoza is largest of the Interior's towns, with a population of 470 900 in the urbanized area, extending far beyond the administrative limits of the city. It functions as major regional centre to Cuyo, for retailing, administration and government, with a large state university, and for manufacturing. The *bodegas* producing 80 per cent of Argentine wine are in or around the city, largest among them a government-owned one which acts as price guarantor to the small vineyard owners.

The city also has power-based industries, electrochemicals and explosives manufacture, using local hydroelectric power and also that from a big new oilfired plant, fed by oil from Mendoza's own oilfields; these fields are of growing importance to the nation, and the province has become the largest producer in the country in recent years. A large oil refinery is located at Luján, to the south of the city.

San Juan (224 000), the other large town of Cuyo, is economically less important, and more dependent on farm-based industries, as are San Luís and San Rafael, in southern Mendoza province. These cities are not major tourist resorts; Mendoza attracts some travellers, lying as it does on rail and air lines between Buenos Aires and Santiago, and this city has considerable attraction in its well-kept streets, tree-lined for shade and with ornamental parks and squares, all kept verdant with constant irrigation. San Rafael and San Juan are not so accessible, nor have they so much to offer.

Both San Juan and Mendoza are old colonial cities, but nothing remains of this period except ruins, because of disastrous earthquakes, Mendoza's in the 1860s, San Juan's as recently as the 1940s. In consequence they are modern cities in appearance, most modern construction being in reinforced concrete capable of withstanding some earthquake activity.

THE NORTHWEST

This is a landscape of alternating hills and enclosed basin flats, of dry forests and grasslands, and of old cities with a largely mestizo population, the centre of fertile irrigated lands. The Indians of the region were the most advanced of those in Argentine territory, settled farmers growing maize, beans and squash, and rendering tribute to the Incas of the altiplano.

Colonial links

The region became tributary to Lima in political terms, and in economic terms too, for it was a supplier of materials to the mining industry of Alto Peru, sending up mules and cattle, horses, carts and leather, much coming from Córdoba or even the Pampas and passing through the northwest in an enormous trek to the plateaus of the north. Principal centres to emerge included Salta, where great fairs were held each year for the sale of mules and saddlery to Peru. Salta was also centre to a rich agricultural region with many settled Indians. Jujuy was another centre, a transhipment station on the route to Peru, where oxcarts and carriages had to be exchanged for pack mules and horses, as above the town there is the long climb from the plains to the altiplano, through the dramatic canyon of the Quebrada de Humahuaca, the narrow valley of the Rio Grande. Jujuy at the foot of the valley was also a military site of some importance, guarding the approaches to the altiplano. Santiago del Estero and Tucumán were other important colonial centres, and there were many smaller towns with Spanish settlers, located wherever Indians formed dense rural populations capable of supporting overlords. Some of them had important craft industries as in Cuyo, such as leather and textiles, which declined in the nineteenth century.

Reorientation to Buenos Aires

Changes in this scheme of things came with the rise of Buenos Aires and the decline of mining in Alto Peru in the late eighteenth century. The region was no longer an essential contributor to the altiplano, and was separated from it by a political boundary.

Instead, it became a remote area in a new state based on Buenos Aires and geared to new markets in Europe. Industry and commerce declined until, as in Cuyo, the railways arrived in the 1880s, allowing a new commerce. Tucumán's sugar, important under the Jesuits in colonial time, was revived in this period and exported to Buenos Aires from big new plantations and mills, while crops of tobacco and cotton were possible in the fertile valleys. Few settlers came in, and the population thus retained its mestizo flavour and to some extent its poverty, for the amount of irrigated land did not expand much and few new ideas to change the economy or society arrived from abroad.

MODERN ECONOMY

Infrastructure

The northwestern oil is located in the Chaco plains of Salta, near the Bolivian frontier, with considerable amounts of natural gas, which is sent by pipeline down to the Paraná river at San Lorenzo near Rosario, where there is a large petrochemical industry. There are old silver, lead, copper and other mines in the sierras, but little of commercial interest.

Water resources are relatively poor, for even the highest parts of the Andes in the subtropical latitude are arid, and there is no snowmelt water as a result. Major dam-construction projects may improve the situation, and one big plan is that for the Bermejo, but for the most part there will never be enough river water to supply new irrigated lands and, though subterranean sources may help, their contribution is not likely to be permanent in such an arid environment.

Agriculture

Sugar is the key to Tucumán's economy, and is also the most important crop in the northwest. It is grown on large factory-owned estates, and the concentration of production in a few hands is a long-established feature of the economy, with

severe social effects. Small farms are to be found, but they are necessarily dependent on the mill owners. An economic problem for sugar producers is the degree of monoculture, which has led in crisis years such as those of the late 1960s to large-scale searches for new alternatives. Sorghum for cattle feed has had some success in recent years. In the smaller irrigated oases, there are more varied crops: in La Rioja vineyards are prominent, in Salta maize and vegetables, in Jujuy tobacco, and there is much semi-subsistence farming in the *minifundio* farms, which can barely support their owners.

Urban centres

Tucumán (365 800) is the main centre of the northwest, and has a considerable colonial past, with an old cathedral and other religious monuments, though most of the city is of recent construction. Part of the tourist current to the northwest enters the city and the hills behind it. It is financial and commercial centre to the sugar trade, and even in the heart of the city one may see an occasional tractor followed by a line of six or more rubber-tyred carts of sugar cane, rumbling through to the mills during the cutting season. Derivative industries have also been located around the city producing alcohol and sweets, and newsprint from bagasse. A few other industries, such as domestic electrical goods, shoes and clothing, have been attracted to the city on account of special tax credits given to encourage new industry, and the availability of a large labour force; Tucumán retains the unenviable position of having the highest level of unemployment — over 10 per cent on average — for any large Argentine city, a feature that is related to the cyclical nature of employment in the sugar mills which work for only half the year.

Salta, Jujuy, Catamarca and smaller centres in the northwest share in the tourist trade with Tucumán, but they have no industrial vitality. Jujuy in particular depends on its tourist trade and a relatively slight retail and service function to its province.

THE CHACO AND NORTHEAST

Crossing the desert of the southern Chaco, vegetation becomes thicker and greener again towards the Paraná river. Quebracho and other hardwoods form an open forest on high land,

and swamp savanna of palms occupies the flood-plains. Further east there are plains too through the province of Corrientes, with swamp forest and grasslands where forests were easily cleared from the sandy soils. The swamps have made this some of the most isolated country in South America, and seasonal flooding makes any kind of habitation around the swamps difficult. Further eastwards, Misiones is a province of rough hill lands and a tropical hardwood forest vegetation.

These northern lands were little occupied till the nineteenth century. The Chaco Indians were always hostile and deterred any settlement in what was in any case a physically difficult region, with no resources for agriculture. In Misiones, settlement came earlier, for Jesuit missions, pushed out of the Paraná plateau region of Brazil by the marauding *bandeirantes* from São Paulo, crossed over into the region during the seventeenth century. After a period of pros-perity, the mission villages declined and their churches became ruins in the forest, when the Jesuits were ejected from South America by the civil authorities in the eighteenth century.

Most of Misiones and Corrientes came under large landowners who either had no use for their lands or maintained herds of lean cattle on the grasslands. Another stage of occupation came to Misiones with the nineteenth-century expansion of the *yerba mate* industry, based on wild plants, trees related to our holly to be found as an element in the understorey of luxuriant *selvas* vegetation in narrow, protected valleys of the region. Because of the isolation of the area, poor labourers could be enticed into the industry, then held there under fierce overseers with the pretext that they could not leave till their debts to the company for clothes, food or drink were repaid. This exploitation of manpower only ended with the better transportation means available in this century.

Modern economy
The northeast is not in general a water-deficit region, and Misiones receives throughout more than 2000 mm of rainfall annually. Temporary droughts may affect production but are not severe enough to warrant irrigation schemes. Water for power is present as an enormous resource on the middle Paraná; the gorge section of the river ends just above Posadas, and here, at

Yaciretá—Apipé, is planned a large hydro-electric plant to be built in conjunction with the Paraguayan government.

Fossil fuels are not known in the northeast, but there is a very considerable timber resource in the forests of Misiones, useful to Argentina as a country poor in forests. The natural mixed tropical hardwood forest is being replaced by eucalyptus and pine plantations, which grow exceptionally quickly in the region and reach cutting size for use in paper mills within fifteen or even twelve years. Quebracho trees in the Chaco provide another natural resource, but they are in effect irreplaceable, for the tree requires over a hundred years to reach commercial size, so that no planting programme is contemplated by quebracho extractors.

Agriculture
During the 1920s cotton production in the eastern Chaco began a rapid expansion, under a government-sponsored colonization scheme which attracted some immigrants, but also many migrants from other parts of the country. Cotton farming on the small farms set up then is still flourishing and the area under cotton has under-gone considerable expansion, with associated industries such as cotton-ginning and cotton-seed pressing. There are long-term problems in its production, including salinity of the water and soil resulting from poor drainage and the high evaporation rates of this hot region.

Subtropical agriculture in Misiones has a special place in Argentine markets. The province reaches into subtropical latitudes where crops such as tea can be grown. Tea is a comparatively new crop for the country, and is carefully culti-vated on small estates and farms, among others which produce citrus, tung nuts or *yerba mate*. Tung, tea and *yerba* all require some processing before transportation to markets, and thus there are a variety of small industries in the region.

Settlement and towns
While the remaining *estancia* country retains a traditional flavour, with no new blood or impor-tant changes in the economy, colonization has had some impact through Corrientes and Misiones. In the latter province, many colonists are immigrants, having come to the country during 1900-20, and many are from eastern

Europe, Poland, the Baltic countries, European Russia and eastern Germany. The colonists came to small farms on colonies set up with national encouragement on land which in some cases was available simply because of mistakes in surveying the old latifundia which allowed open ground between them! In Corrientes colonies were planned all along the rivers Uruguay and Paraná, but few came into real existence; these have been colonized in recent times by a mixed small-farmer population, including Japanese, who are usually the most hardworking and successful of the farmers, producing citrus crops and vegetables.

There are no large cities in the northeast, though two agglomerations are being brought into being by new bridges at Resistencia and Corrientes, on either side of the Paraná, and at Posadas—Encarnación, where the twinned towns are forming an international conurbation. In both these twin cities, the industries currently serve only an immediate hinterland, and there are no larger industrial complexes, but the new links and industrial promotion efforts may be able to change this.

PLANNING AND THE REGIONS

Argentine central government has made only tentative steps towards encouragement of regional development, with simple financial incentives to move out of Buenos Aires before the Second World War, followed by more complex credit schemes and industrial estates at Córdoba and Rosario in the 1950s, and in the 1960s the creation of some growth poles for focussing the development process. In the north, there were to be three growth poles, at Resistencia—Corrientes, Posadas—Encarnación, and Salta—Guemes, with special treatment for the problem city of Tucumán, with its pool of unskilled labour. In none of these centres was there much attraction for industrialists, who found social and psychological drawbacks to a location so far from Buenos Aires, quite apart from the material economic disadvantages such as transport costs.

Three further centres were designated in the south, another peripheral area but with a quite different order of problems from that in the north. Here Puerto Madryn—Sierra Grande is seen as one focal area, with aluminium refining and ore extraction. Another is the upper Rio Negro centre at Neuquén—Zapala, and in the far south there is Rio Turbio with its coalfield. These centres must be judged as having contributed only in a very limited way to regional development. Their key industries being in the area of mineral extraction and power production, gives them few local links to other industries, and favours the movement of their commodities to Buenos Aires instead. In addition, the designation of three centres in the distant south, virtually unpopulated, suggests a strategic function was seen by the military government of the time, rather than social or economic improvements. New centres in peripheral zones could help consolidate Argentina's claim on lands she conquered only a hundred years ago.

Under the second government of Juan Peron/Isabel Peron, 1973-6, there was a concentration on industrial and energy sectoral planning, effectively abandoning the regional planning and allowing concentration in the centre again. Huge growth plans for the steel mills at San Nicolás are typical of this last phase. It must be admitted that regional deconcentration from Buenos Aires has to some small extent occurred; but it has very largely been to the other cities of the Pampas, and not to the distant interior, helping places such as Bahía Blanca, Córdoba and Rosario. The old problem of strains and divergence of interest between littoral and interior continues to plague the modern nation.

PROSPECTS FOR ARGENTINA

A considerable wealth of resources and a favourable population—resource balance make Argentina the wealthiest country in the subcontinent, on most reckonings. As old ties to European markets are thrown off, and the national economy achieves a certain maturity, one is tempted to expect a smoothing out of the old regional imbalances between Interior and Pampas, or even between Buenos Aires and the rest of the country. That the imbalance has not been corrected, despite the measures that have been taken, shows that deep-rooted processes causing polarization on the capital and vicinity are continuing to operate.

Apart from the internal processes of migration to the capital in search of work opportunities and advance, and the concentration at the city of all important industries, there are external reasons for the Pampas and Buenos Aires to maintain their leadership now and in the near future. In LAFTA, the favoured products of Argentina will be those of the Pampas, middle-latitude farm products and manufactures. The subtropical food products of the north will have to compete with cheaper production from more truly tropical regions, in Paraguay, Bolivia and Brazil.

Superficially, it might seem that there was scope for a flourishing exchange between Interior and Pampas — the latter's manufactures and farm products could be exchanged for the power and minerals of the Interior. This is in fact being done, but the point to be noted is that mineral and power exploitation do not have any regional multiplier effect, that the products are too easily exportable, and that the ultimate gainer from the process remains the central city.

10. Uruguay — The Small State

Uruguay has suffered for many years from its smallness, sitting as it does between two large neighbours and coming into being as a political body to form a buffer between them rather than because of any solid cultural or economic identity. Smallness, and the lack of any strong historical tradition, are in fact sometimes given as excuses by Uruguayans for their failings as a nation, and in particular for the lack of progress in recent years.

National area is in fact quite large by European standards (186 900 sq km), but very small compared with Argentina or Brazil, with 2.8 million and 8.5 million sq km respectively. Uruguay suffers however more from the smallness of its population of three million, and the smallness of its development in resources or population skills, than from any lack of land, which by most standards is in abundant supply. Small population and small purchasing power mean a small market, which might not matter had Uruguay been able to trade with other South American countries, and export manufactures to them, but, under the prevailing conditions of trade only with Europe, has hampered development of anything but a traditional agricultural economic structure, set up under British influence in the last century.

The theme of smallness is echoed in the resource base. Uruguay totally lacks coal, petroleum and gas, and has only limited hydroelectric power potential, because of its gentle topography. Among useful minerals, only building materials have been produced on any scale; commercial timber is scarce and metal ores virtually unknown. This still leaves a vast agricultural resource in the soil of the Pampas, but this wealth has yet to be properly tapped and its development will require a new attitude to the land on the part of both farmers and townsmen.

PHYSICAL FEATURES

The geological base of Uruguay is unremarkable, for the most part consisting of a southern extension of the Brazilian Shield, covered thickly in the north by sediments and the Paraná Plateau basalts which reach a thickness of 540 m in the northwest corner. Sedimentary cover to the shield increases to the river Uruguay, covering also the basalt which dips west under the river, except for local exposures such as at Salto Grande above Salto city, where rapids formed by the resistant basalt provide the physical basis for new hydroelectric development.

In the south, rocks of the shield complex are at the surface, except for a loessic cover which has been reworked by streams and deposited thickly in the valleys of the rolling countryside. Because of the crystalline rock influence, southern Uruguay has a slightly hilly topography, with ridges and swells, not the monotonous flatness of the central Argentine Humid Pampas. Along the Atlantic and Plate fronts of the country, recent marine deposition gives rise to flatter land and a fertile base for arable farming. For great distances along the Atlantic coast, there are lagoons, most notably lake Mirim, retained on the seaward side by sand dunes of great size. The landscape is thus one of table lands in the north-west, formed by the sandstones or basalts, and including most notably the Cuchilla de Haedo (fig. 28), and rolling country in the southeast, where the principal ridge is the Cuchilla Grande.

In terms of climate, the country is halfway bet-ween the midlatitude climates which may be experienced in eastern Argentina, with their definite winter, and the subtropical conditions of southern coastal Brazil. There is a cool season, but it is insufficient to allow a real rest period for

vegetative growth, and does not eliminate many insect forms of life, so that for example tropical ticks are a constant trouble to European breeds of cattle. Rainfall is around 1000 mm over the whole country, with a fairly even distribution through the year. This means that droughts are an irregular but recurring problem, for summer temperatures are high and any shortfall in preci-pitation is soon felt in water supplies to plants. Few farms have proper water-storage tanks and they suffer severely when real droughts come, so that cattle may have to be slaughtered *en masse*

Fig. 28 Agricultural economic regions of Uruguay

or left to die by their owners. Temperature and rainfall are adequate for tree growth, but much of the country has been grass-covered since Europeans arrived, while other areas have been cleared for charcoal making or for construction, leaving an almost entirely herbaceous cover today.

SETTLEMENT AND ECONOMIC GROWTH

Uruguay's aboriginal population consisted solely of a number of nomadic tribes, of which the best known were the fearless Charruas, hunting Indians like their neighbours on the Argentine side. These fierce men forbade early settlement in what was the Banda Oriental, or eastern side (of the river Plate), until the founding of Jesuit missions at Soriano in the southwest around 1625, in a region isolated from the main mission country lying on the Paraná Plateau within Brazil, but probably quite accessible to sources of cattle and cattle hands from the Entre Rios area of Argentina.

In the seventeenth century, Portuguese expansion out of São Paulo led to an early settlement in Uruguay, at Colônia do Sacramento in the 1680s, set up as an advance post against Spanish power in Buenos Aires and staking the Portuguese claim to cattle lands in the rich Pampas. This settlement finally goaded the Spaniards into action in the founding of a rival settlement, Montevideo, in 1726, though Colônia remained a thorn in the Spanish side and indeed changed hands frequently between Portuguese and Spanish in the course of the eighteenth century. Meanwhile, the economy of most of the interior was restricted to cattle hunting for the *cimarrones* and direct robbing of owned cattle from the unfenced *estancias* in the settled southwest of the country.

The wildness of the country districts was notorious, occupied as they were for the most part by *gauchos*, a group which was romanticized and to some extent legitimized in the next century but which had its beginnings in vagabonds and escapees from prison or military service, who lived here by robbing either Spanish or Portuguese of cattle to sell to the opposite side. Most of the contraband trade in cattle went to Brazil, finally reaching the great fairs of Sorocaba near São Paulo, and through them the

gold-mining settlements of Minas Gerais, a food-deficit region where the gold boom brought in thousands of Negro slaves under their masters to work the mines, without any corresponding development of farming. The *gauchos* were paid in money, in clothes or in alcohol, but obviously such a trade had to be irregular as a source of income and at other times the *gauchos* attacked *estancias* or settlements. Vigorous measures had to be taken against them, such as that recorded at the little village of Las Víboras, in 1801, where attacks of *gauchos* on the village were followed by their capture, beheading and the setting up of their bleached skulls at the village entrances as an awesome warning to their like.

The opening up of the interior during the late eighteenth century led to the founding of most of the inland towns (fig. 22). In general, this was an expansion northeast from bases along the Uruguay and Plate rivers. At the end of the century, the Banda Oriental came under Buenos Aires and it was in part the pressure of Argentine estancieros which led to the inland expansion. However, in the wars for independence from Spain, the Uruguayans led a separate campaign for independence under their own national hero, Artigas, who maintained a slender Uruguayan independence from all parties, and claimed the support of Argentine provinces west of the river Uruguay. With the fall of Artigas, Brazil and Argentina warred over Uruguay until a settlement was reached in 1828, leaving a tiny new republic with 70 000 inhabitants, with only an externally determined raison d'être and quite poor prospects for future development or even independence.

RECENT DEVELOPMENT

Montevideo grew immediately after Independence, attracting French and Italian immigrants who formed a merchant class and stimulated the town's commercial functions and administrative centrality. The interior was still quite untamed, because of isolation and the primitive cattle economy, and because of political instability. Civil wars between the two political parties, Colorados and Blancos, only ended in the 1900s and, as campaigns were conducted in the rural areas, were a considerable deterrent to economic advance. The economic base was still cattle, either hides or *charqui*, until a transformation began in the 1860s with the first meat-extract plant of the Liebig company at Fray Bentos. This kind of processing was particularly well suited to the primitive transport conditions of the time. Its raw material was the lean longhorn cattle, which could deliver themselves to the factory without road or rail, and its product was a liquid or solid extract relatively unaffected by storage and with a high value—weight ratio well able to stand the cost of movement to Europe. As an industry it was largely replaced in the 1890s by the *frigorífico,* relying on good-quality steers for freezing and thus on a whole new technology which could fatten such animals and bring them easily to the processing plant. Introduction of new breeds, conversion of estancias into surveyed and fenced ranches, the improvement of pastures, were all applied as in Argentina, though only a limited labour force was brought in and in fact labour needs in the country declined in many regions relative to the previous system.

Even taking into account the size of the country, Uruguay seems to have had a much smaller influx of migrants than Argentina, to judge by population growth from immigration. It is not immediately apparent why this should have been so, but one factor is likely to have been official and private attitudes towards migrants. In Argentina, the establishment of independent farmer colonies was found to be almost impossible without considerable financial and organizational aid, and various disappointing experiments in Uruguay which failed for want of such aid may have deterred further attempts. Tenant farmers could be brought in for wheat farming as in Argentina, on four-year contracts, but even these migrants were less important than in Buenos Aires, where wheat speculation went hand-in-hand with railway development.

A somewhat different pattern was established in the hinterland of Montevideo. Near the city are most of the small independent farmers and many tenant arable farmers, a great number immigrants of the 1900-30 period, when most of Uruguay's immigrants arrived. Some of these farms are quite prosperous, especially in dairying and vineyards, though near the city the *minifundio* has arisen and the dispersed rural population suffers from underemployment most of the year.

The most notable demographic phenomenon is of course the growth of Montevideo itself, which has become centre of all economic activity. Its population of 1.5 million out of a national total of 3.1 million is exceptional even within the Latin American context. It is not approached by any other town, for the next centres in order of size are Salto and Paysandú, each with about 60000 inhabitants.

THE ECONOMY

Metropolitan dominance
There are many reasons which might be advanced for Montevideo's dominance, among them the necessary concentration of settlement on the coast because of links to foreign markets and suppliers, which makes the major port city also the metropolis. In this light Montevideo is just an intensification of the general trend of all Uruguayan population to locate itself near either the Plate or the Uruguay river shipping axis. Another factor is the smallness of the country; given a wholly rural economy and the relatively small distances from any part of the country to any other, only one centre might be expected to emerge for trade and administration of the country's interests.

Contrast between city and *campo* (country) has long been a focus of interest for Uruguayans themselves. Martinez Lamas, an Uruguayan economist, likened the relationship between the two to a suction pump, operated by the city in order to draw off the lifeblood of the *campo* for its own parasitic growth. He claimed that traditional arguments about the poverty of the *campo* as being related to poverty of resources, lack of transport, *latifundio* dominance or the like were unfounded, and that all these could change given the appropriate encouragement from the government.

In fact the government, for most of this century, has indeed discouraged farm production, by export taxes which hit Uruguay's traditional exports of wool and meat, while manufactures have gained from a policy of tariff walls to protect them as young industries against foreign competition. This tax structure has no doubt been responsible for some of the metropolitan dominance, as it has for the general malaise which has increasingly affected the Uruguayan economy.

This divergence in regional fortunes between city and *campo* may seem odd in a country with a reputation of democratic government better than that of any other Latin American country, dating back to the beginning of this century, when Jose Batlle y Ordoñez, leader of a government independent of both urban and rural pressure groups, introduced a variety of welfare measures with a very modern flavour, such as pensions, farmer credits, unemployment pay and an eight-hour working day. The truth is that this welfare state never penetrated very deeply into the social structure of the country, because of the absence of central government funds, in a state where from 1905 to 1961 there was no real income tax and where the stamp tax on official papers still yields more than income tax. Under these conditions, it is impossible to reduce the gap between rich and poor to any significant extent.

AGRICULTURE AND INDUSTRIES OF THE CAMPO

Agriculture in Uruguay is largely devoted to livestock production rather than crops. Crop production is increasing, as the table shows, due to governmental encouragement and internal demand, but it is still small and little integrated with livestock. Argentina, it has been noted, has a Ministry of Agriculture and Livestock (Chapter 8, p.100) but Uruguay has a Ministry of Livestock and Agriculture! The dominance of the *estancieros* is expressed in the title. A regional division of farming may be made between the southwest, including Montevideo and surrounds, with 85 per cent of annual cropland, and the remainder of the country.

VALUE OF FARM PRODUCTION
(percentages of the total)

Years	Crops	Livestock	Total
1935-40	25.0	75.0	100.0
1950-2	28.6	71.4	100.0
1962-4	27.3	72.7	100.0
1973	40.6	59.4	100.0

Source: Banco Central del Uruguay, Cuentas Nacionales, *various years*

The southwest

This region (fig. 28) is one both of grain farming and cattle fattening. The *estancias* in the *departamentos* of Soriano, Colônia and San José in the southwest have a third of national rotation-grass area, used for fattening local calves and steers brought in from the northeast, driven along cattle tracks or by rail. Fattening is largely on alfalfa, rye grass and hybrid sorghums, giving a slow maturing animal which is sold at four to six years of age. Dairying is also practised in this zone.

Cash grain farming is for wheat, mostly grown by medium-scale farmers with 50-100 ha. Wheat came into prominence after 1945, with the ploughing up of open plateau lands along the middle Uruguay in the Paysandú and Rio Negro *departamentos* (fig. 29). Mechanized farming and the use of dry-farming techniques in places to conserve soil moisture and fertility are typical. Oats is an important secondary crop on the plateau, though not grown in rotation but used on poorer land as a dual-purpose crop, for grazing in early months, then harvesting if and when other feed becomes available to the cattle. Oilseeds, especially sunflower and flax, are important and were also originally expanded to relieve post-Second-World War shortages of vegetable oils.

The metropolitan hinterland

The region around Montevideo differs from the rest of the country in the intensity of farming and in a focussing of all production on city markets. In San José and Canelones *departamentos* there are many minifundios producing vegetables, maize, fruits, milk and potatoes, without the aid of machinery. Most farms are operated by their owners, many are less than five ha in size, and they suffer from soil erosion due to overworking and a lack of fertilizers to maintain soil structure. Some have already been abandoned through soil destruction. On larger farms, sugar-beet and dairying, which are both linked to industrial processing, are more common.

Towns

There are no large towns in the *campo*. The urban network is denser in the southwest than elsewhere because this region is densely populated and has some commercial products. Mercedes, San José and Fray Bentos are small

Fig. 29 Administrative divisions of Uruguay

centres with services to their hinterlands and rural industries such as flour milling, sugar milling and oil extraction from seeds. Fray Bentos has in addition meat packing and grain terminals.

Some towns are becoming tourist centres, a little surprisingly for a country with little tradition in this direction. Uruguay now earns over 10 per cent of her foreign exchange from tourists, a figure as high as anywhere in South America. Montevideo itself is the major attraction, but Punta del Este, at the limits of the Plate's brackish waters, is fast growing up as a resort town. La Paloma, Atlantida and Piriapolis are other resorts growing up along this coast. The most important tourist current is from Argentina, now coming by ferry to Colônia, and the bridge to be built over the Uruguay at Fray

Bentos and coastal road improvements should enhance the attractions of the country. There are distinct possibilities along the coast north towards the Brazilian frontier, to be realized with new road improvements linking into the rapidly expanding Brazilian road network.

Well up the Uruguay river lie Salto and Paysandú. Salto is a city of small houses trimmed in local marble, one of the important industries of the town. Apart from this it has the usual complement of mills for processing agricultural goods. Paysandú has a more industrial aspect with its breweries, cotton milling, leather working, cement factory and distilleries, and has a small but active port.

Salto's name comes from nearby falls on the river Uruguay, which have now disappeared under a huge lake behind a dam built in a joint

Argentine–Uruguayan project, named Salto Grande, over the period 1974–81, and having an eventual power output of 1.8 million kW. This dam also provides for industry and domestic supplies, irrigation for 130 000 ha of land, navigation through lateral locks for vessels up to 2.5 m draught as far as the Brazilian border. With this installation the Argentine and Uruguayan electrical distribution systems are effectively integrated, with high tension lines to Santa Fe and Buenos Aires in Argentina as well as to Montevideo. It is also a means of transport integration because the crown of the dam is used for new rail and road links between the two countries.

The northeast
Three-quarters of Uruguay is still open Pampas, a landscape little altered by man. In the far northeast there are good cattle lands and the region has become important for beef production (fig. 30). Over the remainder sheep are more important, monopolizing in particular the heights of the basalt and sandstone escarpments in the northwest, and *cuchillas*, low ridges, in the crystalline rocks of the east, where lack of surface water makes beef production difficult. Sheep are produced primarily for wool, so that rustic types with good drought resistance can be bred on poor pastures. Often sheep are grazed on the same land as cattle so that proper management of pastures and herds is impossible.

Cattle raising is also extensive in style, with little care for improvements or advanced forms of technology. Agricultural planning by the government now includes finance for improve-

Fig. 30 The relative importance of sheep and cattle in Uruguay

ment of breeding, pasture and fertilizer use, but land productivity remains low and many diseases are endemic, including foot and mouth and many parasitic diseases.

Islands of more intensive agriculture are appearing, notably rice growing in the ill-drained saline lands around lake Mirim. Sections of the flat plain have been drained for rice production in the last decades, and areas under rice grew from 17 800 ha in 1961 to 226 000 ha in 1978. Like sugar, which has been introduced on a big scale in the northwestern *departmentos* on cane lands owned by large landowners, rice has come in with capitalistic forms of exploitation using machinery rather than labour whereever possible. Another move in the same direction has been with citrus crops, though these can also be grown on small farms with little capital. Over all these subtropical crop developments, a big question mark must be placed, as LAFTA tariff reductions and the improvements in transportation means now coming into being may make Brazilian production more competitive and even eliminate the local crop which is in a physically marginal position on the edge of the tropics.

MONTEVIDEO

Montevideo is a city of parks and squares, an open city of relatively low buildings, a result of its relative youth and of its planned expansion with liberal allowances of space, only possible in a situation where new urban land has encroached only on open pastures and on flat land with no particular building problems. The aspect of openness and space is enhanced by the expanses of sandy beach to the south, a major summer attraction for tourists and local workers, and a special advantage over the muddy estuarine condition of Buenos Aires's front.

This is of course the economic hub of the country, housing within its *departamento* limits three-quarters of all manufacturing in the country. Its port is a vortex of transport routes, for the old city grew out of port trade and manufacturing has always had close connections to this trade, using the transhipment point between interior and foreign ports. Traditional industries are thus tanneries, flour mills and *frigorificos*. To these have been added under tariff protection a variety of other manufactures for final consumption markets. Textiles have come in

through such protection, as have a number of light engineering industries producing for example electrical domestic appliances.

Montevideo maintains its industrial dominance party through a superior infrastructure: its railway network, built from the 1860s by British companies which started work from Montevideo outwards, and its road network which was built (rather unimaginatively) to the same pattern, the roads often running right by the railway for many kilometres. This road network was built up after the First World War with the idea of providing competition to the railways; while not really doing this for a long time, it did help to consolidate the centrality of Montevideo. Now there is the further centrality provided by air services. Electricity supply is assured to Montevideo from the large hydroelectric plants on the Rio Negro at Rincón del Bonete and Baygorria, brought to the city by a 150 kW line. Since 1981 a large increase in power output has come from Uruguay's share of the Salto Grande scheme.

Apart from industrial strength, Montevideo is administrative and cultural centre to the country, monopolizing university education, national government, hospitals, libraries, museums and theatres. Socially, this is a complex city, its largely European population an amalgam of upper-crust merchant and *estanciero* families, a large lower middle class of office workers, some factory workers, and a last group of *marginados,* migrants from the country occupying peripheral areas of the city or old central residential sectors where they live in *conventillos,* rambling old houses converted into slum quarters. Immigrants to the city serve to complicate the geography of poverty for in earlier decades poor people did not typify the city. Now the *campo* has come to the city to remind urban government of a social responsibility yet to be wholly accepted.

CONCLUSIONS

Uruguay is still a country of opportunity. Despite resource limitations it still has enormous possibilities for intensification of agriculture where the basic resource is under used to date, though proper use will only come with a thorough going reform of agriculture. Specifically, the Uruguayan pampas can produce much more grain and other arable crops, and this they should be made to do whether or not industrial development is fostered. Concerning the latter, there is a total lack of decentralized industry, or any growth points outside Montevideo, though again government action could bring change.

Wedged between Brazil and Argentina, with favourable treatment from L A FTA it should have a key position on the axis from the river Plate to industrial São Paulo, and already the beginnings of transport improvements to aid connections between the two giants are helping Uruguay's own economic development. With this geographical situation and a relatively well-educated workforce, Uruguay's future as an industrial corridor country is not assured but becomes a definite possibility.

11. Paraguay

Paraguay holds a position much like that of Interior Argentina with respect to the city of Buenos Aires and the Pampas. It is poor, short of water over the greater part of its national territory, and dependent on the regional metropolis, Buenos Aires, for manufactures which it exchanges for its own raw-material exports. Paraguay, however, merits separate discussion on the basis of its independent status, as well as on the grounds of its distinct cultural and historical identity, stemming from such factors as the exceptionally complete mixing of Indian and white blood here, the special position on the Paraná—Paraguay river system, and the bitter history of national mismanagement since 1811, the year of its declaration of Independence.

PHYSICAL GEOGRAPHY

Geologically, as in many other respects, Paraguay is composed of two sections. The eastern two-fifths of the country is a rolling, grassland and forest region, formed basically of Brazilian Shield rocks, though these are covered by thick sandstones and basalts of the Paraná Plateau series. The western limit of these rocks and the hilly topography they produce is roughly at the Paraguay river.

Beyond the river, and immediately visible from the heights of Asunción, the Paraguayan capital which is built on outliers of the eastern hills, there is the vast, unending plain of the Chaco, spotted with palm trees or quebracho near the Paraguay, but open and uninterrupted

desert scrub further west, with no permanent water courses.

The climate is difficult for middle-latitude man. Given the subtropical latitude and location in the interior of a continent, and altitudes under 600 m, very high summer temperatures are to be expected, and annual maxima well over 36° C are experienced throughout the Chaco. In the east, temperatures are a little lower, but equally uncomfortable because of the higher humidity.

These conditions are alleviated in spring and autumn by the occasional cold fronts which sweep in from the south as the continuation northwards of the Argentine *pamperos*, associated with cyclonic depressions deriving their energy from the Atlantic seaboard and passing along the coast into Brazil. *Pamperos* cause temperatures to fall 10-20° C within a few hours. In winter, temperatures are very comfortable, between 15° C and 25° C, attracting tourists in increasing numbers from Argentina, especially Buenos Aires.

Rainfall is fairly evenly spread over the year, decreasing a little in the cool season; the annual total declines from highs over 2000 mm on the Brazilian frontier, through moderate levels around 1500 mm in the longitude of Asunción, down to levels which are quite insufficient for agriculture, (between 1000 mm and 500 mm), in the Chaco.

HISTORY

Asunción was an old core of Spanish settlement

in the continent. It had one important advantage which attracted settlement, its peaceful and dense agricultural population, capable of supporting Spanish overlords and producing a further surplus for sale. The first settlers on the lower Paraná in Argentina organized excursions upriver in search of riches during the 1530s, and Asunción was founded as a result in 1537, its importance soon confirmed when the lower river settlements had to be abandoned in the face of Indian hostility.

Despite several expeditions made from this base, no finds of gold or silver were made, and the Spaniards merely discovered that there were great deserts between them and the fabulous land of Peru, deserts capable of killing through the simple effects of heat and thirst, or through the actions of their hostile and treacherous Indian population. Asunción became an early backwater with the rise of Peru, its Spanish lords becoming impoverished and marrying or mixing with Indian girls, to form a unique *mestizo* race, in which the landlords, just as much as the poorest peasants, belonged to one new amalgamated stock, so that racially based class differences are less important in modern Paraguay than in other countries of the continent. An index of the historico-cultural importance of the Guaraní Indians is the strength of Guaraní as a language, still spoken by 95 per cent of Paraguayans, though Spanish is increasingly the language of private and official business, and is the language now taught in schools.

The Jesuit impact on the country was also of substantial historical importance. In the eastern borderlands of Paraguay, Indians were gathered into mission villages, called *reducciones,* and fine stone churches and other buildings were built as centres for economic units which produced important surpluses of cotton, *yerba mate*, cloth, tobacco and hardwoods.

From the 1767 expulsion of the Jesuits, their centres were abandoned and their laboriously cleared farmland reverted to woodland, a disaster for the regional economy. Soon Buenos Aires, declared centre of a viceroyalty of the Plate region in 1776, imposed itself as commercial as well as administrative centre and Asunción, the inland river town, was made an insignificant gathering point for its own poor agricultural region.

In the nineteenth century, development was in a negative direction. The effects of Independence in opening up trade possibilities with Europe were brought to nothing by the works of several dictators, Dr Francia (1815-40) and the two López presidents, father and son — the latter brought Paraguay into the War of the Triple Alliance, 1865-70, versus three powerful allies, Argentina, Uruguay and Brazil. Paraguayan military prowess was of no avail against these three and war devastation reduced the national population from 525 000 to 219 000, in addition causing much damage to agriculture and town settlements. A large part of the country was given up to the victors, in the northwest Brazil taking a section between the Paraguay and the Paraná, and in the south Argentina retaining land south of the Pilcomayo.

This war aimed at finding an independent access to the sea for Paraguay, but this could never be tolerated by neighbours who owned the seaboard. Expansionist aims also came to the forefront in the 1930s, finally exploding in the Chaco War with Bolivia in 1936-9. This was fought for possession of the barren Chaco country, and won by Paraguay, though it was truly a hollow victory, for the territory won proved to have no current value, the only oilfields to be found to date lying on the Bolivian side of the modern frontier, though hopeful exploration is in progress on the Paraguayan side.

PRESENT SETTLEMENT PATTERNS AND POPULATION

Settlement in the Chaco was not undertaken before the present century and it remained *terra incognita*, even the intrepid Jesuits having been unable to tame its wild inhabitants, or often to return alive from their exploratory ventures into the desert. It was finally subdued by Protestant missionaries but this led to no massive settlement, only a Mennonite group, settling around Filadelfia, being able to tolerate the extreme conditions. Some small Indian groups continue to live in the traditional semi-nomadic manner, but most are absorbed into Western civilization to some extent.

In the east, in Paraguay proper as it has been called, lives the great majority of the population, concentrated very largely in the southwest corner of the country near Asunción. The character of

Fig. 31 Asunción city and surrounds

this population is homogeneous, 95 per cent of it being the old *mestizo* group, with a minority of Japanese in some rural areas. Typical of an underdeveloped country, it has a very broad population pyramid, 45 per cent of the total being under 15 years of age, so that the growth of population, 3.1 per cent per annum, is very high. Despite this youthfulness of the population, indicating improved medical conditions and protection of young children, there is a high level of infant mortality (84 per thousand); another index of backwardness is the low level of literacy, with 25 per cent unable to read, though this is changing rapidly with the advent of universal education and better school facilities.

Settlement concentrates especially around the city of Asunción, which has a population of over half a million in its urbanized area. Despite its size, it presents the aspect of an overgrown country town, with predominantly low buildings and a function which is more administrative than industrial (fig. 31). The old colonial type of chessboard street pattern still remains here superimposed on a fairly hilly topography which makes it less than ideal; the spread of settlement is confined to the hill site, for there is the river to north and west, and marsh land to the southwest. Urban migration is apparent in the shanty town developments which occupy large areas, especially in the localities marked as temporary

27 *Shanty town at Asunción, subject to flooding from the Paraguay river*

housing on the map, along the floodplain edge. As elsewhere in South America, shanty town development has not been by recent immigrants but by established city residents, often with good jobs in offices and industries. The miserable huts put up by these people represent a first attempt at independence and an improvement on rented accommodation in the old city.

THE ECONOMY (fig. 32)

Asunción today gives us a fair idea of national economic status. Rather than skyscrapers there are two- or three-storey buildings. In place of organized bus services there are minibuses, converted trucks and the like, overstaffed with conductor and driver though only carrying half a dozen passengers. Disguised unemployment is rife and many people hold two or more jobs, since a one-job salary does not suffice to support a family.

Underemployment and unemployment are themselves indices of rapid urbanization, equal to anything on the continent, and forming a fast-growing town population which stretches public services beyond breaking point. Urban growth is due, not to urban boom conditions — the only boom industry is the government — but to the lack of any rural opportunity, so that migrants are constantly moving into town in the hope, not the sure knowledge, of finding jobs.

Agriculture

No agricultural production of note comes from the Chaco, except some cotton and vegetables from Filadelfia, marketed out to Asunción along the rough road. Most of this land is unused, or only used on a very extensive basis for beef-cattle production, supplying canned beef factories which constitute one of Paraguay's more important export industries. Production techniques are geared to the ultraextensive use of land; few attempts are made at cattle selection, for fences to guard cattle are not in use, nor rich grasses to

Fig. 32 Paraguay: the land use, road and hydroelectric power sites

feed them. Serious diseases including foot and mouth are endemic to the country and can scarcely be controlled using present techniques.

In the east, agriculture is a mix of various food crops produced on small owner-operator farms (46 per cent of all holdings are under 5 ha) interspersed with a few large *estancias*, the remnants of old *latifundia*, where cattle are reared on a more intensive basis than in the Chaco. Maize, cassava, beans and other vegetables, as well as cash crops such as cotton, are grown on the small farms. Where there are alluvial soils, tobacco and cotton are remunerative, but for most of the

east, despite the usual guidebook references to fertile soils and great potential, soils are thin and, as is common in continental subtropics, yields decline rapidly with continued cultivation.

ECONOMIC INFRASTRUCTURE

There is no road or rail network in Paraguay. The only railway, apart from some private lines constructed on the quebracho properties, is a single-track, standard-gauge line from Asunción to Encarnación, so slow that lorry transport competes successfully with it even for heavy

28 *President Stroessner bridge across the Paraña, linking Brazil and Paraguay*

freight, and poorly supplied with antiquated rolling stock.

There are only two well-paved roads between Asunción and Encarnación, and from Asunción east to the international bridge over the Paraná and into Brazil (plate 28). The Encarnación road is to be continued by a bridge into Argentina, linking to Posadas, while the eastern road already leads through Brazil to Paranagua where Paraguay is given free port facilities.

The Chaco has no metalled roads, though money has been made available for a trunk route from the Bolivian frontier through Mariscal Estigarribia to Asunción, constituting Paraguay's part of the Pan-American Highway system. This road will be brought across the Paraguay river on another new bridge. River transport has historically been of overriding importance, and continues to be of much use for the settlements above Asunción on the Paraguay, not currently served by road. For long-distance movements, however, this river is not so useful, for it is a long haul of 1640 km from Asunción to Buenos Aires, and there are substantial disadvantages in its great variation of seasonal level and heavy silting. The Paraná is much less used,

and the height of new dams to be placed on it must diminish its future potential as a waterway.

Power and minerals
Within the country, the plant at Acaray is the largest HEP installation in operation, its 90 MW capacity being doubled in 1975 to 180 MW, and supplying electricity to both Brazil and Argentina. The Acaray river is a tributary of the Paraná, whose main stream has much greater potential. Yacireta–Apipé, with 3 300 MW, is one of the two major projects to be built jointly with Argentina. With Brazil, Paraguay is building Itaipú on the Paraná just above the Iguasú mouth, with a huge dam of 7 km length, a flooded area of 1400 sq km, comprising a reservoir which reaches back over the whole 200 km canyon section of the Paraná and drowns the famous Guayra Falls (Sete Quedas). Its power output is 12 600 MW.

The need for these great power projects is not self-evident. Paraguay has no coal and as yet no oil worth extraction, despite continuing exploration. But neither does she have any industrial development capable of absorbing huge increases of unstored power — even Acaray's moderate contribution must be exported at present. Power development along the river seems rather to respond to the aims of the two big neighbour countries, and to provide a field for active competition between them, in which Paraguay is likely to be a pawn, though now benefiting greatly. I return to this matter at the end of the chapter.

Most of the saw timber comes from eastern Paraguay. Beyond the Paraguay river there is a separate resource in the red quebracho tree, *Schinopsis Balansae,* a particularly tough hardwood with over 20 per cent tannin content. Tannin has been extracted on a large scale since the 1880s, by cooking chips of the heartwood in great boilers. Much of the industry belongs to an Argentine firm, Casado, which alone has 3 million ha of land in the Chaco. An enclave economy has been operated along the east edge of the Chaco north of Resistencia in Argentina, with company villages, private railways into the forest, and private provision of water and electricity.

In recent years, competition from some synthetic tannin sources makes this a declining industry. In any case, the trees themselves provide an irreplaceable reserve, for they grow extremely slowly and once gone are replaced only by low scrub of very little value. Conservationists see much advantage in leaving the remaining trees and concentrating on the alternative tannin sources.

Industries

Manufacturing industry and urban development are very slight in Paraguay. Timber provides some material-oriented industries such as sawmills on the Paraná and the quebracho extractors on the upper Paraguay, but the tannin industry is not healthy and saw-milling suffers from Argentine unwillingness to receive prepared timber rather than raw logs.

In Asunción itself (fig. 31) and on the road axis out towards Caacupé to the east, there are industries designed to make use of cheap labour. Apart from meat processors, the city has cotton mills, cigarette, glass, soap and various food and drink manufacturers, items typical of first-stage

29 Nanduti, a traditional Indian craft weaving industry, at a roadside site near Asunción

industrial development, and using little advanced technology (plate 29). As university town and administrative centre the city also has printing and publishing industries. There are no true industrial zones in the city, only a tendency to concentrate near river or railway, and in the suburbs.

Outside the capital, besides the timber-based industries, many small-farm product processors occupy the small towns, making tung oil along the Paraná at Encarnación, *petit grain* oil from the wild orange, and vegetable oils from cotton seed, coconuts and oil palms. Asunción dominates the urban structure, with no other towns having more than 30000 inhabitants, but current plans by the government are for several new regional development centres, at Concepción, Encarnación, Pedro Juan Caballero, Pilar and Villarrica. Government interest in spreading effective occupance away from the Asunción core has long been a Paraguayan characteristic, expressed at times in expansionist war, and in the last twenty years in drives to settle people along road axes out from the capital, and in recent attempts to create urban growth points outside Asunción.

THE PARANÁ: AN ECONOMIC AND POLITICAL FRONT

In at least one area, the eastern frontier, the drive to settle Paraguayans has assumed critical importance. It is along this front, long an economic and political vacuum after the demise of the Jesuit missions and their advanced economic and social organization, that Brazil has pressed forward her secular advance to the west and to the very margins of the river, in a move spearheaded in the southern sector by spontaneous small-farmer frontiersmen, with maize and pig farms, backed by São Paulo firms who have bought land here, and in the northern sector by the advancing line of coffee farmers.

With the establishment of Brazilian coffee and other plantations on the western, Paraguayan side of the river since about 1960, this whole region has been moving noticeably into the Brazilian sphere of influence before Paraguayan control could be asserted. The existence of a tarmac highway from the Paraguayan frontier at Foz do Iguaçu to Paranagua, built supposedly to help Paraguayan exports bypass the river Plate

outlet, has in fact reinforced the alignment of the whole region to the east. General Stroessner's government in Asunción has seen a threat in this development, and has encouraged the eastward thrust of colonization along the road from west of Asunción to Puerto Presidente Stroessner, from 1966, as well as on the road being built north from 1968. Lots of 20 ha have been given to settlers by the government, but no infrastructure such as roads or buildings is provided. Evidently the primary concern has not been agricultural production to feed the cities, but establishment of a firm claim to land in imitation of Brazilian strategy. Paraguay's occupation by isolated subsistence farmers on minifundios contrasts with the organized commercial enterprises on the Brazilian side of the border.

On the question of power production, Brazil and Argentine vie with one another to partner Paraguay in hydroelectric schemes for the middle Paraná. The principal quarrel between Brazil and Argentina has been over Itaipú, placed on the Paraguay—Brazil sector of the river but provocatively close to Argentina.

In April 1973, a treaty to build the Itaipú dam was signed between Brazil and Paraguay, following an earlier agreement in 1968, the Iguassú Act, in which these two countries made a bilateral arrangement for powersharing on their sector. This agreement and the later treaty have irritated Argentina, particularly the lack of consultation with her over an international river. Fears were voiced in Buenos Aires that this action represented a recrudescence of Brazilian imperialism, that the river would be polluted by factories using the power, or that the turbines at Itaipú could send through a volume of water in excess of that recorded in the worst floods experienced in Argentina's provinces of Corrientes and Entre Rios. On the other side, Brazil did not want a high dam which is planned for Corpus (Fig. 32), which would have an output of 4000 MW and whose reservoir would back up to Itaipú and reduce its output. Through the late 1970s verbal battles were waged over how many turbines Itaipú should be restricted to, and how high the Corpus dam should rise. In late 1979 an agreement of 18 turbines for Itaipú and 105 m for the dam height at Corpus, originally negotiated in 1975, was agreed to. Corpus, however, has yet to be started.

Paraguay seems at first sight to have done well

out of the Paraná, with her share of Itaipú's building financed by Brazil under the terms of the agreement, to be paid back after eight years and then only over a fifty-year period, while she shares equally in the power produced which is to be sold to Brazil or other customers. Further still, Brazil has given financial and technical aid to Paraguay, to build a road from Encarnación to Iguassú, and a future rail link from Asunción into the Brazilian rail net, as well as setting up a Paraguayan steel industry which she will co-own, and other industries. Argentina, for her joint scheme at Yaciretá—Apipé, has similarly had to offer 50 per cent shares in the proceeds, and inducements such as help in construction of the bridge from Encarnación to Posadas and in a cement works and aluminium plant.

Yet Paraguay's technique of playing one great neighbour against the other for internal advantages may be a dangerous one in the long run. When Itaipú is finished in 1983 it will produce 12 600 MW, and form the largest hydroelectric installation in the world, outstripping Krasnoyarsk (5000 MW) and Bratsk (4000 MW) in Siberia. This may create dificulties in disposal of the energy, for Brazil can command large supplies from her own section of the Paraná, from sites developed in the 1960s, at Jupiá (1250 MW), Ilha Solteira (3200 MW) and others, while Argentina has her share of Yaciretá—Apipé (3300 MW) to absorb. Paraguay must thus dispose of electricity, at least initially, to Buenos Aires and Sao Paulo, and compete against various other sources of energy, so that the price she can charge may prove too low to cover the costs of maintenance and amortization of her capital charge. If this should be so there may be a political price to pay in the yielding of influence over the country to either Argentina or to Brazil, pursuing a long-term geo-political offensive towards the interior neighbours, Paraguay and Bolivia, no longer through direct occupation of territory but through extension of their economic control.

OVERVIEW

Paraguay is still hindered by its interior position and great cost-distance from cheap ocean transport, as compared to all other South American countries apart from Bolivia. Because of this isolation, Paraguay has attracted little attention from foreign governments, institutions or private firms, until very recently. Change in this position, as suggested in the section above on the Paraná, will depend on developments within South America rather than pressures from Europe or North America. River Plate Basin country agreements, or those under LAFTA, could help if managed in favour of small countries, but experience such as Itaipú, kept out of the River Plate Basin international cooperation movement by the interested parties, suggests that the big countries that bound Paraguay on the south and east will control her destiny to a considerable extent.

Historically many factors weigh heavily against the country. An uninterrupted dictatorship has allowed a social and economic structure to remain in this country which shows little advance over that first set up by the Spanish, and the landowners and military who back the present regime can have little genuine interest in social progress for the mass of the population, even if pressed on them by the outside world.

12. Chile

One version of the origin of Chile is that at the Creation, after God had finished His Labours, as a final task, He asked the angels to sweep some leftover pieces behind a high wall in an out-of-the-way corner of the globe; the wall was the Andes, and the leftovers, a motley assortment, formed Chile. The story is doubtless apocryphal, but it does underline a real state of isolation, as well as the diversity of the Chilean landscapes. Inevitably, in a stretch of 4300 km from north to south, there is room for physical contrasts; but even across the country, in the narrow 150-300 km width of Chile, there are profound contrasts between Andes, Central Valley and Coastal Cordillera. Corresponding to the major physical divisions, there are significant cultural and economic differences between the old-settled Mediterranean core and more recently occupied peripheries.

THE LAND

Structure and landforms

Structural units in Chile run north—south, parallel to the shield edge of Brazil and Patagonia. The Andes, backbone of the whole country and maintaining an impressive height throughout, are deepseated igneous masses, with some volcanics, rather than fold mountains; recent faulting and uplift have given them their present height, leaving the great Longitudinal Valley to the west as a fault-lined trough or graben. This igneous origin is responsible for the abundant mineral deposits, originating at the edge of the magmas and consolidating in contact zones. Continuing fault-line movements make earthquakes a constant peril and there has been repeated destruction of major cities throughout the country.

First of the three longitudinal elements of physical geography are the Andes. Because of their great height it is sometimes forgotten that they are also a broad mass, generally over 80 km wide, and composed of several parallel ranges. In the north, they open out to enclose high desert basins like the Salar de Atacama, with salt flats the only outlet to small streams. The Southern Andes are lower than the north, ranging around 3000 to 3500 m, and, in contrast with the northern deserts, are well carpeted with forests. They are dissected by deep valleys, carved out by glacial action during the Pleistocene era. The mountain chain continues beyond the mainland into Tierra del Fuego, of which Chile owns a half.

West of the mountains, the Longitudinal Valley has varied form. In the north it is a high desert basin with drainage into the salt flats of the Pampa del Tamarugal north of the last permanent river, the Loa, and is marked by typical desert pediment slopes. From Copiapó it disappears, to re-emerge at Santiago and form the enclosed basins of the capital and, to the south, of Rancagua, then open into a low trough reaching south to Chiloé Island, covered increasingly to the south by glacial and proglacial deposits giving a hilly or rolling topography.

The third element is the Cordillera de la Costa, another hilly or rolling topography, lower than

Fig. 33 Chile: the regions

the Andes, and generally under 3000 m, but for all that a continuous barrier and negative factor for transportation. Marine terraces all along the coast of Chile, and cut into this Cordillera, are a reminder of the rapidity of geological events here.

Climate, soil and vegetation

The fame of the northern desert is as one of the world's driest places, if not the driest of all; on the coast there are long records, covering over twenty years with fair accuracy, which note no rainfall. There was once a vegetation cover inland, however, in the desert country of the Longitudinal Valley, probably fed mostly by ground water seeping through from small mountain streams. The woods were *tamarugos* for the most part, a kind of mimosa which gave the name Pampa del Tamarugal to the· northern desert.

The northern desert land is called the Norte Grande by Chilean geographers. To the south of 30° S, there is the Norte Chico, the Little North; this region is a patchwork of contrasting extremes, with long runs of open desert like the Norte Grande, alternating with deep transverse valleys, green and lush in comparison to the uplands. From an airliner, seen through the cloudless desert skies which are nearly always found in these latitudes, the Norte Chico shows such valleys as the Copiapó, Huasco and Elqui as clearly as if marked out by pencil on a map.

From the river Aconcagua south to the Bío Bío is Mediterranean Chile, a land similar to the Mediterranean in climate, soil and vegetation, though the natural dry forest has been eliminated gradually by urban and agricultural expansion. Rainfall increases continuously to the south in this zone but a winter concentration typical of Mediterranean climates is found to the south in Valdivia and beyond. South of the river Bío Bío in the Sur Chico, this high rainfall combined with seasonality gives a unique vegetation of mixed Mediterranean and temperate forms, a dense evergreen and deciduous mix.

South Chile is temperate forest with podsolized soils, and a vegetation which includes some useful species in the northern margins, notably the 'larch', *Fitzroya cupressoides*, and the 'oak', *Nothofagus obliqua*. The Chilean monkey-puzzle tree is a member of this southern mixed forest, but its quality as a good constructional timber and the old Indian practice of collecting its cones for nourishment have made it a rather scarce species in its country of origin. Further south, extreme wind velocities, and lack of sunshine and heat, mean an impoverished forest cover of scrubby nature. In its extreme representatives in the far southern islands and coasts, it is a mat of ground-hugging vegetation; there are interesting descriptions of how exploring parties have had to crawl over the woods rather than walk through them in this zone! In the lee of the mountains, there is a small section of Chile which belongs to Patagonia and thus has a completely different physical aspect, dry, open and treeless.

THE SEA

To Chile, the ocean, producing food, providing employment, acting as road and railway, tempering the climate, is as important as to any small island in the Pacific. Most notable among its features is the Humboldt current, actually composed of two elements, a coastal section of cold, green—brown water moving at only 1 kph, and an outer section beyond 50 km out of deep blue, warmer and faster water moving at 2-3 kph. The coolness of the coastal water is due to upwelling more than its southern origins, for the cold spots are those where upwelling is strong, and temperatures scarcely rise before it reaches Peru.

Historically, the current was an important separator of Chile and Peru; and Juan Fernandez Islands, still in Chilean hands, were named after their discoverer, a pilot on the Valparaiso—El Callao run seeking to avoid the current by going out to sea on his return voyage. Today, the current is most important for the quantity of nutrients brought by upwelling and mixing into the life zone near the water surface. Hake and sea bass are important in the south, *anchoveta* and sardines in the north, while shellfish are found throughout. Mussels were the staff of life for the primitive Indian populations living around the Magellan Straits until recently.

OCCUPATION OF LAND

Claims and realities (fig. 34)
The effective occupation of Chile was by Pedro de Valdivia, lieutenant of Francisco Pizarro,

Fig. 34 Chilean boundary changes and claims

conquistador of Peru; he was sent out in 1539 to found a colony, and soon made its base at Santiago, founded in 1541 in the centre of a prosperous agricultural region where there were many settled Indians and where gold could also be gained from placer workings on the rivers.

Valdivia's colony, later the Captaincy General of Chile, had pretentious claims to a hundred leagues of country from the Pacific inland, a claim which made it trans-Andean and extending well into present Argentine land. Northern and southern limits were set only in vague terms, for no solid occupation of the north and south could be considered.

In reality, occupation was only of a central *oecumene*, the core area of Mediterranean Chile, where settled Indians, good land and security were possible. Across the Andes, the province of Cuyo, with the cities of Mendoza, San Juan and San Luís, formed a linked section, but the high passes over the Andes meant that the links were tenuous and could not be held indefinitely.

Trans-Andean territories in fact were gradually given up, starting with the area of Tucumán, already lost to Argentine interests in the 1560s; passing to the loss of Cuyo, in 1776, when the Viceroyalty of the Plate was formed; and ending with the loss of Patagonia in the 1880s when Argentina finally subdued the southern Indians and incorporated this territory.

On the other hand, cis-Andean lands could readily be maintained against all comers, and expansion was possible; to the north, it was easy to extend Chilean hegemony over the northern deserts in the War of the Pacific, using the open road of the sea for access; to the south, there were no other claimants to the land besides the Indians, and once these were defeated the land was Chile's. Thus in all cases, territory and frontiers were defined by the natural wall of the Andes, to which decrees and claims had to defer; only in the southern extremities, where a substantial difference between mountain line and water divide existed, and where in addition the mountains were lower, did a serious transgression of the Andes occur and become a supported political frontier. In this case, Chileans had settled through the low glacial valley troughs into Patagonia in the nineteenth century and had anticipated Argentine settlement. On this substantial basis they were allowed to remain east of the mountain peaks, in a treaty celebrated in 1901 between the two countries.

Colonial economy

A typical Latin American colonial economy and society came quickly into existence in Chile. The land was divided into great *latifundia*, leaving only small areas for the Indian and mestizo villagers. From the *latifundia*, cattle produced tallow and hides, which were sent to Peru from the earliest days. While Peru was supplier to Spain, Chile, with its abundant farmland and temperate climates, could be supplier of middle-latitude products to Peru's urban populations. A chain of dependent relations existed from the *inquilino*, semi-serf on the great estates, through owners and merchants all the way to the Spanish metropolis.

Nineteenth-century economy

This hierarchical economy was not broken by the advent of independence for the country, but later, by the arrival of migrants from the overcrowded farmlands of Europe. Immigrants were attracted to the Sur Chico, between the river Maule and Chiloé Island (fig. 33) to make clearings in the dense woodland and cultivate small farms. Chile never received large numbers of migrants but those who came had considerable impact, coming as they did into new, unsettled lands, and able therefore to maintain their own institutions and technology.

The colonists started from bases around Valdivia and Puerto Montt, first Germans, who had a tradition of forest clearing in eastern Europe which suited them well for this task. It is of interest to ask precisely why the migrants were successful here, when they were so unsuccessful in other places. One factor must have been their title to land, given freely or for a small sum, so that there was no fear of permanent indebtedness for land, or clouded title which might come from previous purchasers in the area before it was surveyed. Another factor was the plot size, 75-100 ha, big enough to support any reasonable farming family in this area. Finally, one must give credit to the group spirit and cultural provenance of the people. Their traditions, and the way they were permitted to retain them in Chile, meant no creeping demoralization such as could occur to a lonely family in a strange country elsewhere in the continent.

In a sense, the Germans (there were also some French and other European groups later) were allowed to preserve their identity so well because of the Indians; to the north of them, between 38° and 40° S, the Araucanian Indians, the Mapuche, had led a guerrilla war against the Chileans to the north for a 150-year period, only ending in 1883. This area, the Frontera (fig. 34), formed a *cordon sanitaire* between traditional, colonial Chile, Spanish Chile, and a new small-farmer, immigrant and democratic society to the south. Historically and even today, there is something of a duality between Spanish Chile, the centre, and the northern and southern fringes whose culture is from other sources, Indian, European, even North American in the case of the mineral workings.

Modern economy
Colonial Chile sent farm goods to Lima; today, the man—land balance has changed and Chile is a food-deficit country; the new key element is mining. Extractive industry employs only some 3-4 per cent of the work force, but it brings in 90 per cent of national export earnings. Such lopsidedness in the national economy is matched by regional imbalances, for the variation in means of support of the population is extreme, between mining and smelting, logging, manufacturing and urban employment, and farming. Chilean economy cannot be discussed without reference to these regional contrasts.

NORTE GRANDE

Nitrates
In colonial times the Peruvians mined silver at Huantajaya (fig. 35) and a host of smaller mines in the coastal hills north of the Loa. To break up the ores, explosives were made from the *caliche*, hardpan on the edge of the *salares*, desert salt flats. This *caliche* was locally in high concentration and directly used by the Indians for fertilizer with good results. In the first decade of the last century, the royal powder mill at Lima was desperately short of saltpetre for gunpowder production, and while sodium nitrate, the product from *caliche*, was not immediately usable as a replacement for true saltpetre, potassium nitrate, a formula for converting it was obtained and the ore began to be extracted on a modest scale.

The first crisis in the nitrate industry came after the end of the Revolutionary Wars, when no further use could be found for the mineral, and the problem was enough to close down many of the small-scale operations; a longterm solution came when its properties as a fertilizer were recognized abroad. Peter Aikman was a Glasgow merchant with trade in little ships to South America from 1825. In 1829 a ship of his put in to Iquique for ballast, and was given nitrates which it brought to Liverpool. The port authorities were determined to throw it into the sea as a dangerous and explosive material, but Aikman became curious and took ten sacks of it away to give to farmers around Glasgow, thus beginning a new era for the Chilean nitrates.

Swiftly Chilean and British enterprise moved in to the Tarapacá deposits all along the salar edges (fig. 35), using first a primitive technology of melting down the caliche or desert hardpan in great copper pans, with the aid of *tamarugo* wood, both standing and as trunks found under the desert sand by 'wood diviners' amongst the Indians; this was the only fuel available. Soon technical advances in refining and the use of coal brought back from Europe in the nitrate vessels, allowed much more rapid production and use of thinner nitrate ores further south.

In the desert section claimed by Bolivia, between the river Loa and 24° S, and the Chilean section to the south of this, development was slower than in the north because there was little earlier mining industry, the nitrates sector poorer, and water was a constant problem. Thus the Bolivian sector only saw extraction from 1869, the Chilean from 1879.

The nitrate boom
The rise of the industry was particularly rapid after 1860, when nitrates began to take the place of guano. A growth centre began to emerge in the desert, with mines and ports both attracting men. Iquique, Antofagasta and Pisagua became important ports, populated by a largely Chilean miner and merchant group; in 1878, Antofagasta, in the Bolivian sector, had a population of 8500, of which 6500 were Chilean. Besides the influx of men, inflowing food and material came from many quarters. A large and constant movement of cattle, trekked over the mountains from Salta in Argentina, and originating from the Gran Chaco and Córdoba

Fig. 35 The nitrates regions of Northern Chile and neighbouring lands

as steers, came to the mining camps where no food was produced. Vegetables were grown also on local patches of irrigated land, flour and sugar brought on coasting steamers.

Politically, the industry was subject to international frictions: in 1875, Peru nationalized her nitrate industry to finance railway construction, a move she had previously made in like manner with the guano industry; soon after, the Bolivian sector of the desert fell under Peruvian control. Such events alarmed Chile, for the nitrates industry was in the hands of Chileans whose livelihood was now threatened. Chile also rightly suspected a secret alliance between Bolivia and Peru, which could turn against her. For Peru, the progress of Chilean enterprise was menacing, and for Bolivia, there was an additional irritation over the political boundary with Chile, set at 24° S but with a band from 23° to 25° S in which mineral rights were shared.

New focus: copper

The War of the Pacific settled the disputes conclusively, and allowed the industry to go to new heights. Control passed very generally out of Chilean hands, a pattern followed with the copper industry, and British firms made good profits till the rise of synthetic fertilizers in the 1920s. Now the nitrate workings are reduced to one *oficina* in Tarapacá, and two in the sector south of the Loa; ghost towns remain as reminders of former wealth. A new industry was soon found to replace nitrates, copper, from the giant open-cast mine of Chuquicamata, known and worked since before the War but never developed. This now became a growth industry, replacing nitrates, with associated smelting, refining, and power production industries. Chuquicamata itself grew to over 25 000, endowed with modern housing, electric lighting and modern plumbing. The mine, a huge hole 3 km long and 300 m deep, has reserves to maintain its present rate of extraction, 100 000 tons of ore daily, for a hundred years, so that it may be expected to dominate regional economy for some time.

Apart from copper, developed with private funds, various manufacturing industries, notably chemicals, electrical goods and car assembly plants, were fostered at Arica in the Norte by government action from 1953. At this time import duties were lifted in Tarapacá province

and in the southernmost Chilean provinces. This move, it was hoped, would promote economic expansion and help political support for the regime, as the peripheries were centres of anti-government voting.

Car assembly was particularly boosted from 1958 by the virtual prohibition on location at other places, so that by 1963 there were 20 different companies in operation at Arica, producing in no case more than 2000 vehicles per annum. Inefficiency in scale of operation was compounded by distance to Santiago, whence came an increasing percentage of components, poorly made by national firms but up to ten times the price of unavailable imports. As well as bringing up components from Santiago, trucks had to be used to take the finished cars back to Santiago, the main market. Finally, the ban on assembly in Santiago was lifted and much of the industry moved, quite rationally, to that city.

What next as the export base?

Douglass North* and others have contended that many pioneer regions did not develop gradually out of a subsistence economy into commercial production as did the European countries, but depended from the start on finding and utilizing viable export base industries, the mechanism being that these basic industries would bring in capital, labour and enterprise via local multiplier effects, and that these new factors of production could then promote further growth in a snowball effect. The local or regional multiplier effects were those indirect effects of an industry on the local economy, growth because of the need to establish accessory or supply industries, growth of local demand from the labour force and its own needs for service industries, construction, etc.

This theory of the export base has application to the Norte; here a capitalist, exploitative economy was set up from at least the eighteenth century with silver as the export base, followed by nitrates, then by copper, and finally, spasmodically, by manufacturing industries. The earlier bases had however only limited regional multiplier effects. Chuquicamata has had little impact for, though there are links to the high

*Douglass C. North, 'Location theory and regional economic growth', *Journal of Political Economy,* Vol. 63, 1955, pp. 243-58.

Andes via pipelines, electric power comes from Tocopilla, and copper moves out along the Antofagasta railway, the mine does little for the region; employment is small because of heavy mechanization, and supply or market industries are absent. The same applies to silver working, to guano or nitrate mining in previous booms.

The 1953-67 policy of tax incentives to industry might have provided a better export base because regional multipliers would have been bigger, from larger labour forces and supply industries, but the lack of permanent control over industrial location meant this could not be. As an alternative agriculture has been put forward as an export base, using water from elsewhere. Since 1950 there have been discussions with Peru and Bolivia over possible diversion of lake Titicaca waters west into the coastal desert; in 1971 a longterm plan to bring water from Chile's own South, paralleling plans on the Pacific coast of North America, was announced, though no source of funds has been apparent, and this plan can scarcely be made operative in the near future. Thus the search for a viable export base remains a problem for the Norte.

NORTE CHICO

Farms and mines
Economic activity in river oasis Chile, from Copiapó south to the river Aconcagua, is a mixture of farming and mining. Historically copper mining was concentrated in the Norte Chico's interior, especially in Coquimbo province, and mostly in small and medium-size mines, forming over a thousand separate enterprises. As these mines cannot afford their own smelters there are government smelters at Paipote, Copiapó and Ventana near Santiago, which purchase ores and process them in competition with the big smelters. Today, iron ore exceeds copper as an export mineral, an industry located in the Coastal Cordillera between Coquimbo and Chañaral, owned by both Chilean and foreign, including North American and Japanese, enterprises.

Most population and agriculture is concentrated in the valleys, owned in part by large farmers, who use the irrigated meadows for feeding cattle with alfalfa, to complement hill grazing above. Some areas also have small farms producing a wide variety of crops: maize and

vegetables on valley floors, vineyards and orchards on the dry slopes. Traditional Indian *comunidades*, communal agriculturalists, are a third element, working tiny plots which afford little surplus. Outside the valleys, dry scrub provides a little grazing for the *comunidades* and for big graziers, and grain is grown in places along the more humid coastal hills, the Coastal Cordillera.

MEDITERRANEAN CHILE: THE CORE AREA

Farming
Here all land may be put to some farm use, except on the steepest slopes, and a landscape of straight irrigation ditches and poplar avenues, dispersed houses of brick and tile or *ranchos* of mud and cane, framed by stark eroded hillsides, forms the scene. Until recently, a sharp contrast was to be seen between the large *fundos* and small farms, the minifundia growing subsistence crops. Prior to the agrarian reforms which limited farms in the irrigated belt to under 40 ha, the big farms often had more than 1000 ha of irrigated land, used in many cases for alfalfa, rather than for intensive crops of grain, fruit or vegetables. Darwin described this traditional economy when he saw it in the Quillota valley near Valparaiso in 1834, on the round-the-world voyage of the *Beagle*:

> Each landowner in the valley possesses a certain portion of hill country, where his half-wild cattle, in considerable numbers, manage to find sufficient pasture. Once every year there is a grand *rodeo*, when all the cattle are driven down, counted, and marked, and a certain number separated to be fattened in the irrigated fields.
>
> *Charles Darwin,* Journal of Researches in the Natural History and Geology of the Countries visited during the voyage of H.M.S. Beagle round the World *(New York, Harper, 1846), vol. 1, p. 329*

Such farms have been taken over by their workers, who operate them as cooperatives. The economic results are not yet clear, though production has fallen following reorganization as in Bolivia and Cuba. An index of total agricultural production shows a continuous decline from 118 (1960-5) in 1970, to 95 in 1973, thereafter recovering in 1974-5 to 1970 levels. Partly this fall resulted from strikes and bad weather, partly from farmer uncertainties and the interruption of production through the lagging of infrastructural works such as roads and houses behind the formation of new farms. In the post-Allende period of military government, about 20 per cent of the expropriated farms have been restored to their former owners, helping to restore confidence on the part of larger farmers.

On the Coastal Cordillera's dry lands, large farms are operated with machinery to grow wheat by dry-farming techniques, on the broad gentle slopes of marine terraces and piedmont slopes of the mountains. Amongst such farms, occupying steeper slopes and areas with access to stream irrigation, there are clumps of small farms producing sometimes at a semi-subsistence level. As they depend often on water from streams that have only a seasonal flow and cannot build dams to store water, their livelihood is always subject to risk and few such farms will indulge in the further risk of commercial production for marketing in the cities. This is a landscape where the dual economy is directly visible, commercial and subsistence sectors side by side.

Santiago de Chile

The site (fig. 36) of the capital is a gentle, westwards-sloping piedmont, within a small hill-ringed basin. The city is sprawling, low, composed mostly of single-storey buildings, and occupying as much land as Paris which has twice the population; earthquake hazards have caused a fear of high buildings. The city, growing out of the colonial chessboard on the south side of the river Mapocho, has spread mostly to the south, to the river Maipo. To the northeast, the Cerro San Cristóbal presents a barrier, though construction is encroaching on its lower slopes.

The city's economic structure is reflected in its buildings. Nothing remains of colonial architecture, for earthquakes have destroyed it. Nineteenth-century expansion was as a residential, commercial and administrative centre, with fine housing and offices near to the centre. Industrial growth came later, in the twentieth century for the most part, as a result of crises in the nitrate industry and in agriculture, which forced the setting up of manufacturing industry under tariff protection, to provide for home markets when no foreign exchange was available to pay for

30 *Wooden and corrugated iron housing of a* callampa *in Santiago. In the background is a new three-storey housing scheme, part of the government's plan for increasing urban residential densities, while improving housing conditions. Chile's record in dealing with rural-urban migrants is better than that of most Latin American countries*

Fig. 36 Santiago city and environs

imports. The industrial structure established in this way was largely of consumer goods, using few local resources apart from labour and some foods.

Economic growth continues apace in the city, for 800000 immigrants came during 1950-70 to be housed in the *callampas,* the 'mushroom towns', as Chileans call their shanty towns, as well as in government-built flats west of the city to balance middle-class extension up the piedmont to the east (plate 30).

The metropolitan region

Valparaiso, second city of Chile (620 000 in

urbanized area in 1978), developed as Santiago's port in colonial times, though it was small until the mid-nineteenth-century boom. It achieved 100 000 inhabitants in 1880, acting as trade centre for the entire Pacific coast in the period when many ships came round the Cape Horn route before the Panama canal was opened. It grew up on a narrow discontinuous coastal terrace between shore and fossil cliff, with the addition of a little land won from the sea for rail line and warehouses. Expansion however forced other lands to be taken in further north, and Viña del Mar (262 000 in 1978) was occupied in the 1850s, soon growing into a residential suburb of Valparaiso. Now it is geared directly into the capital's orbit, as commuting suburb and week-end centre, with many chalets, hotels and lodging houses. There are other substantial towns in the metropolitan complex, including some dormitory suburbs on the Santiago—Viña railway, and the port of San Antonio, south of Valparaiso, which provides an alternative outlet for the capital and exports the copper from the El Teniente mine.

Migration: push and pull*
In 1978 Gran Santiago, the capital's urbanized area, had 3.69 million, 30 per cent of the national 10.25 million people. If we include the other towns of the metropolitan complex, and thus the two provinces of Santiago and Valparaiso, there is a massive 42 per cent of national population occupying only 3 per cent of national territory. The city's population growth rate is also higher than that of any group of smaller towns, reaching over 1940-75 to 3.5 per cent annually, compared to a rate of 1.8 per cent for towns of 100 000-1 000 000.

What does this massive concentration mean? To some observers, making the analogy with other cities in Latin America, the 'push' factor in migration has helped swell city population and migration is seen as an escape from rural poverty. While some truth in this viewpoint must be accepted, most facts seem to favour another explanation, in terms of 'pull' factors: the migrant stream, first of all, is not from country to metropolis — it is rather a stage-by-stage progression, one generation of migrants moving

from country to small towns, the next generation going on to the metropolis. Thus arrivals at Santiago are mostly accustomed to city life, an important fact because it means they have skills which give them employment opportunities. They are attracted into the city, by a strong manufacturing sector — Santiago is pre-eminently an industrial town, more so than most provincial towns — and they create no unemployment problems because with the skills they have acquired in other cities they can be readily used; the migration is in any case selective, taking the younger, better educated and trained persons.

It seems safe to conclude that the 'pull' factor, the city's attraction, is most important in Chilean migration. If other indicators of the city's industrial health were required to support the thesis, they could be the facts that unemployment has not been higher in the capital than elsewhere, and that the tertiary sector of the economy has not grown excessively large, as it might in situations of disguised unemployment such as exist in other cities, where minor jobs are created with miserable pay in shops, construction, transportation and offices, to take up cheap labour.

SUR CHICO

The economic structure of the South is generally, like that of the north, dependent on minerals. In the case of the Sur Chico, coal mines and forests are the leading resources, though agriculture is also important and gives rise to a distinctive landscape, especially around Puerto Montt and Valdivia, in what Weischet called *Waldrodungs-Chile*,* 'Forest-clearing Chile', a near-European landscape of small hedged fields, stumps marking old clearances, a hilly land of glacial deposits and little lakes, spotted with the neat wooden houses of small-farmer settlers.

This is prosperous farm country, with 50-100 ha properties producing beef, wheat and barley, milk, cheese and butter, and middle-latitude fruits. To the north of it is a different land, in the old Frontera zone, where a major socio-economic problem has arisen in the reservations set up for the Mapuche and other Indians, because of their rapid population increase and lack of land, so that takeovers of

---

* This section draws heavily on B. Herrick, *Urban Migration and Economic Development in Chile* (MIT, 1965).

* W. Weischet, *Chile* (Darmstadt, 1970), p. 11.

nearby estates have been made, anticipating government action. The regional centres in the Sur Chico include some agricultural market towns, notably Osorno and Valdivia; Osorno is sometimes credited with a German atmosphere, but little apart from shop names and social clubs remains of this; Valdivia is more industrial and has many small wood-based and farm-processing industries as well as a university. The city was badly hit by an earthquake in 1960, its wooden buildings then being replaced by new wood or concrete ones to form a smart centre, but the loss of economic status that occurred through this disaster only helped on its longer term relative decline, as one of the provincial towns, compared to overweening Santiago.

Forests
The region's forest resource is large but still under used. Good stands of single species and rapid growth rates under high regular rainfall are physical advantages, but economic backwardness is holding back the industry. At present, tree exploitation is purely destructive in most parts with little concern for conservation measures. Afforestation has begun on the northern fringes near Concepción, where Monterrey pines have been introduced from North America and planted on eroded farmlands for soil conservation and as feed for the paper pulp mills in Concepción, Valdivia and on the river Bío Bío. Further south, as for example on Chiloé Island, there is primitive lumbering on a small scale and poorly organized, often on the basis of hired temporary workers during the summer months and using little machinery. Graziers, illegally setting light to trees to produce more feed for their nomadic herds, often destroy large blocks of forest before it can be cut. In the longer term this industry must change, and may thrive as a provider of timber, woodpulp and newsprint — new factories are being built for the last product — to other countries in the continent.

Steel
From 1840 a metallurgical tradition was built up around Concepción, smelting copper on the basis of local coal and, from having a coaling station for steam ships, to providing general ship repairs. The coalfields south of Concepción provide a low-grade coal of Tertiary origin, but one which is useful in a continent of tiny coal

supplies. Based on this coal and on sea-borne raw materials, a very substantial investment has been made at Huachipato on the Talcahuano peninsula (fig. 37) to bring into being a national steel industry, at first inefficient but now capable of supplying steel as cheaply as any other country of the region.

The industry demonstrates how Chile's apparently awkward geography is economically logical if we bear in mind the possibilities of sea transport. What appears to be the enormous distance of 800 km from the iron ore deposit mined for the industry, at El Romeral near Coquimbo, and 1500 km from the limestone source in the far south, an island in the Madre de Dios archipelago, makes sense because of cheap sea freight and good harbourage. The industry, controlled by a state agency — the CAP, Pacific Steel Company — has grown in capacity from 250000 tons in 1950 to a million tons in 1970, though production is far less.

More than the mineral-based industries of North Chile, steel provides plenty of jobs in subsidiary industries: steel alloys, heavy engineering, zinc and tin production, and agricultural fertilizers use the steel directly. The coal attracts other industries — pottery, glass, textiles and woollens — at Tomé on the north side of Concepción bay and at Concepción itself, while there are cottons at Chiguayante. Most Chilean china comes from Penco, most glass from Lirquén. Coal itself is the greatest problem, for the Lota—Schwager mines have thin seams, and lie up to $1\frac{1}{2}$ km deep under the sea; production has declined from a peak of 2 million tons to 1.25 million in 1976, and heavy use of oil is now made with a refinery located at San Vicente. There are however newly discovered coal reserves in the far South, in Magallanes province, estimated at 5000 million tons, and a change back to coal use is being fostered, of vital importance in an energy-deficient country.

SUR GRANDE

Beyond Chiloé, the island archipelagoes and the fjord country of the adjacent mainland, steep tree-covered slopes and deep water, form a region of scenic grandeur and extreme isolation. The railway line ends at Puerto Montt, and further south there are only short unmade roads, most links being made by sea. Settlement is

Fig. 37 The industrial region of Concepción. This city, with Talcahuano and Huachipato, forms a single urbanized area of over half a million inhabitants.

sparse and either scattered over fertile patches at low level, or clustered in the little ports. The only really useful farmlands are strips along the glacial valleys cutting through the Cordillera, linked thus to coast and interior but isolated from one another.

Wool
On the opposite side of the Andes an abrupt change of landscape occurs, to Patagonian steppe with prosperous sheep farming. Mineral exploitation has become the economic base here, both oil and gas being important on Tierra del Fuego and in Chilean Patagonia. In this dry land sheep thrive and produce wool, Merino and Romney breeds being common on the great ranches, an industry that first started in 1878 with immigrants from the Falklands. Most of the grazing is unimproved, carrying only one animal per ha, but improvement and higher stocking rates are in hand and are raising wool and mutton production.

The oil industry
Continuous expansion in oil production has been possible since the first strikes made in 1945 under

the impulse of wartime shortages in fuel. Most of the oil is taken out by pipe to ports and shipped to refineries at Concón, serving Santiago, and San Vicente, for Concepción, leaving only little refineries in the far south for local needs. The oil basin around the Magellan Straits where active exploration is still going on has been linked up by modern all-weather roads, and provided with various public services, but its influence on the regional economy is limited. Natural gas is to be liquefied here for export to the USA!

REGIONAL DEVELOPMENT PATTERNS

Economists and others formulate models of economic regions with, as their main components, the central, metropolitan regions, and the surrounding peripheries. In such models, the centre is relatively rich, attracts migrants, and controls the periphery, on whose resources it lives; the periphery is poor and overpopulated, and has few resources which are exploited in any way apart from extraction.

For Chile such models do not hold without substantial modifications. First, there is indeed a centre at Santiago, and around it a 'peripheral' development in the poor provinces of central Chile, which send in migrants from overpopulated rural areas to the towns. Further afield, however, in the Norte and the Sur Chico, are relatively prosperous regions of low population and good resource endowment. They do not send many migrants to the centre; they do not in some cases send much of their production to the centre at Santiago, for copper and iron ore, and before them nitrates, were export products passing directly to the exterior.

Perhaps the best that can be done in centre—periphery relations is to describe the north in general as peripheral to the industrial metropolis in the Northern Hemisphere, not to Santiago. The south, including the wood-based industries of the Sur Chico, its steel and related industries, and petroleum in the far south, may be described as the true Chilean periphery, though it is not the problem area that peripheries are in other countries.

The regional problem in Chile is not one of helping poor people in distant provinces, but in those near the centre. It is certainly true that one

way of solving the problem of *minifundia* in central Chile could be the transference of water into the northern deserts for more irrigation and the creation of new farms, as well as opening up the remaining forest land for farmers in the south. Such possibilities must be placed against the international background, and Chile's possible role as an industrial nation within the LAFTA group of countries must be weighed against agricultural expansion. Chile, with a fairly advanced manufacturing sector but small local market, should be able to produce many manufactured products for her neighbours. In 1976 she withdrew from the Andean Pact, leaving intact only a few of the Pact's agreements concerning transport, taxation, and multinational firms, and this might be expected to prejudice her industrial future. But the withdrawal reflects a long-growing dissatisfaction with industrial protectionist policies which are seen as having distorted manufacturing industrial structure, and allowed inefficient and monopolistic industries. A high Andean Pact common external tariff and direct restriction on foreign investment were two items expected to continue the protection of such industries, in exchange for the rather dubious and non-specific promise of an Andean market for a few industries where Chile would be given the regional monopoly. Now Chile hopes to follow Brazil in industrialization through foreign investment, and looks towards the River Plate Basin countries for markets and capital. She is expected to become a member of this group.

Industrialization would provide no diversification to the peripheral provinces for it would inevitably be centred in Santiago, regardless of regional planning. But in such cases the regional benefits must be weighed against national advantages with concentrated growth. It may be argued that the peripheral regions are best left as resource areas with low population, and industrialization concentrated at those places with greatest external economies in the shape of labour force, capital, markets, transportation, and greatest economies of scale. Instead of moving industries to the regions, a national willingness to migrate, evidenced in the existing patterns, may be capitalized on by a loose concentration of industries in the central core region of Chile.

BRAZIL AND THE GUIANAS

13. Introduction to Brazil

Brazil is a country of continental proportions, occupying 8.46 million sq km, over half of South America. In spite of her size, Brazil has a certain unity, and there are not, for example, the sudden contrasts to be seen while travelling through the Andean countries, between high plateaus, mountains and selvas, and lowland deserts. The entire Brazilian landscape displays the mark of its firm foundations, the crystalline shield mass which has changed little over recent geological times. This shield produces a landscape of flat horizons, with few imposing mountain peaks. Homogeneity extends into climate and vegetation, with only gradual change from forest to wooded savanna to open plain, and the whole area is under the constant influence of tropical atlantic air apart from the occasional cooler wave along the east coast.

Man's use of this giant territory has also exhibited a certain homogeneity; Portuguese occupation has been dominant and has imparted Portuguese language, religion and culture to the country. Far in the interior there are islands of pure Indian communities, scarcely affected by the European invasion, but they are dwindling and now only preserved by governmental decrees protecting tribal land from further incursions, decrees which can only delay, not prevent, the eventual incorporation of all the land into the national culture. Unity is emphasized by the political integration of Brazil with few active separatist interests. It is a feature commonly remarked on that the many races of Brazil have all been absorbed into the national entity, a

remarkable accomplishment considering the size of the country.

A second feature of Brazilian human geography is the fact of its rapid and recent settlement, for the population has grown ten-fold, from 9.9 million in 1872 to 113.2 million (estimate) in 1977. A growth rate of over two million inhabitants per annum has been matched by enormous strides in industrialization, the building of cities, roads and power schemes. Inevitably, large sections of the country have experienced lesser growth and remain backwaters of subsistence agriculture and poverty, for agriculture has not been able to modernize in the same way as industry.

THE LAND (fig. 38)

The two elements of physical unity, shield structure and tropical climate, deserve some further detailing. Shield rocks do not occupy all Brazil, for in the north there is the Amazon valley, a giant rift valley separating the Guiana and Brazilian shields, and part of the Guiana shield in Amapá and Roraima also belongs to Brazil. The Brazilian part of the Amazon valley is not all alluvial floodplain, or *varzea*, as might be imagined; *varzeas* only occupy 1-2 per cent of the Brazilian part of the Amazon plain, though this still makes them very large in absolute terms, perhaps 65 000 sq km.* Over large areas there is low rolling topography, as suggested by some old

* H. O'Reilly Sternberg, *The Amazon River of Brazil* (Wiesbaden, Steiner, 1975), p.17.

Fig. 38 Physical regions of Brazil

explorations. Road construction on the Transamazon highway from 1970 has been made difficult by the continuing alternation of hill and dale encountered.

Over the southeast half of the country the shield rocks, gneiss and schist, are near the surface, determining landforms. These forms are of broad plateau type, lightly dissected by the rivers which cross them. On the Paraná (fig. 38) and locally elsewhere, geological events of more recent time have produced the still more level plateaus of basalt and interbedded sandstones. Both sandstones and basalts are rimmed by imposing cliffy scarps, hindering road and rail construction, but presenting great hydro-electric power potential. In a line parallel to the coast from São Paulo northwards, the eastern edge of the shield loses its plateau character with ancient fold mountain systems now exposed through uplift and differential erosion; such are the Serra do Mar and Serra da Mantiqueira near Rio.

The low general level of the land allows deep penetration of humid Atlantic air, and gives a tropical or subtropical climate to broad expanses. Rainshadow effects are slight, except perhaps in the Nordeste, the northeastern bulge of Brazil, where mountain slopes are wetter or drier according to their orientation, and vegetation and agricultural potential follow the same pattern. Climatic homogeneity is most impressive over the great Amazon lowlands, where the thick mass of tropical air enters with no topographic hindrances. The products of tropical humid climates on the plateau surface in soil and vegetation are also found over wide areas. Weathering is rapid because of the acidity of the vegetation cover, and penetrates deeply, producing a clay regolith which accumulates because stream erosion is so much slower. Soil fertility is low because of rapid decomposition of humus and solution of mineral bases, except where erosion locally outpaces weathering or where alluvium is brought regularly to floodplains.

Figure 38 presents a physical regionalization of Brazil into zones of different potential for man. The open grasslands are: those of the *campanha*, in Rio Grande do Sul, an extension of the Uruguayan pampas; the Rio Branco country, which also has some wooded savanna; the Pantanal and Campos de Vacaria in Mato Grosso; and the savannas of Marajó island in the Amazon delta. These grasslands occupy flat plains and owe their grass cover to poor drainage and floods rather than lack of rainfall. The intermediate region between forests and grasslands is shown as *campos cerrados*, wooded savanna which covers huge areas of Central Brazil on the plateau surface with 1000-1500 mm rainfall and a short dry season. The *campo cerrado* becomes wetter and more forestlike to the west and north, but is increasing its extent with the progressive burning and depletion of soil fertility by colonists. There are two high-rainfall tropical regions, the Amazon selvas and the Eastern Mountains extending from São Paulo state through the rugged and forested coastal mountains of Espirito Santo to the Nordeste, with a narrow discontinuous coastal plain to the east. Within the selvas the lower basin has the more tolerable climate for man, with frequent dry spells and lower humidity, while the west is continuously humid and hot. The Caatinga region is one of low irregular rainfall and has thin scrub forest, covering the whole interior of the Nordeste. Finally, the only middle-latitude type of forest region is the Paraná Plateau, with its cover of Paraná pine and strong seasonality of climate.

Early settlements

The second element of Brazilian unity is its people and culture. Brazil was discovered by the Portuguese soon after the first Spanish arrivals on the South American mainland; in 1500 Pedro de Cabral voyaged down the east coast by error, after losing his course to the East Indies. Cabral's trip and the Treaty of Tordesillas, however, laid the basis for a Portuguese claim to a vast territory, over which little effective control could ever be maintained in the colonial years.

There were substantial differences between Spanish and Portuguese forms of occupation, relating to their different motivations. Spanish religious fervour was never matched in Brazil — the first bishopric was not established till 1546 —

and the Portuguese came with fewer illusions and a less emotional attitude to colonial enterprises, with the political maturity of over 200 years' independence and colonial experience in West Africa and Madeira. In Brazil, all had to adapt themselves to a region with little mineral wealth and few inhabitants, the main resource being the land, not an easy prospect in a tropical climate where no previous agricultural advances had been made. The hardheadedness of Portuguese settlers reflects itself in the very name of the land, Brazil, named after the wood which was the land's first export commodity, sent as a valuable dyestuff to Portugal and northern Europe. This name replaced the early names of Santa Cruz and Vera Cruz.

The focus of this merchant and agricultural settlement was at first very much on the narrow coastal plain. While the Spaniards had won half a continent to the west, and were free from major attack throughout the colonial period, Brazil was always subject to attack from envious European powers, because it was so much easier to reach. First France, joining in the brazil-wood trade, then Holland, setting up coastal factories or trading stations, threatened Portuguese hegemony and forced the settlers to guard this coast with walled towns and castles, which are not seen in Spanish South America except along the Caribbean coast where pirates always lurked. Thus until the eighteenth century, Bahia and Rio were both walled towns. This forced focus on the coast was a blessing in disguise, for it kept the people together in an identifiable culture group, in touch with one another and with Portugal, instead of dissipating national energy in occupying the interior.

The form of settlement was in great grants of land, *donatárias,* given to landowners from Portugal to work in exchange for one-tenth of the harvest and one-fifth of the metals but, although these stretched indefinitely inland, their effective occupation was confined to the 16-km band next to the coast.

The sugar cycle

Brazilian economic history consists of a long series of speculative and dynamic waves of expansion in agriculture, leading to subsequent depressions when markets or production fall. Lucio de Azevedo, a Brazilian historian, termed these 'cycles', and recognized the sugar cycle,

31 A colonial sugar engenho, *from an engraving by Rugendas*

followed by those of gold, cotton and coffee. Sugar growing proved the only long-term successful economic basis for settlement in the sixteenth century, for the brazil-wood supplies were soon exhausted. By 1560-70 there were at least 60 sugar mills or *engenhos* spread out over the long coast from Pernambuco to São Vicente, the island near São Paulo in the south, and sugar was earning twice the income of brazil-wood. The old *engenho*, powered by oxen or by water (plate 31) with three wooden rollers, was placed close to its supplies of cane, from a plantation which usually formed part of the enterprise. In the seventeenth century, the industry concentrated in Pernambuco and Bahia and, as it could never be carried out by the few Portuguese and settled Indians, thousands of Africans were brought into the Northeast, forming to this day a large element in the racial makeup of the Nordeste. The industry was associated with a particularly strong plantation type of society, highly stratified, and dominated by the owner, who with European or mixed-blood foremen dealt in a patriarchal manner with the slave labour force. To some extent, this society has survived to the twentieth century in the Northeast.

While sugar was the Nordeste's driving force in the seventeenth century, in the Southeast, the *bandeirantes*, explorers, cattle men, and slave traders and capturers, were opening up the interior of São Paulo. They started activities as slavers around 1600, seizing and deporting Indians to the coast, especially those from the Jesuit missions in the state of Guayra, which they occupied. The attack of the *bandeirantes* on these missions between 1628 and 1638 was so fierce that the missions were eventually forced to move across the Paraná into Paraguay proper and Argentina. Once having cleared the territory, it was ready for repopulating with gold miners and cattle.

Some of the expeditions were *bona fide* mineral searches, and it became increasingly important for Brazilians to find minerals as the sugar boom declined with European favour given to their own colonies' supply of cane. Gold was found in alluvium on the Rio das Velhas, in 1698, and diamonds in 1728. Further west in Goiás and Cuyabá, gold was found in the early eighteenth century. The effect of the gold rush was in the long term to re-orient economic activity from the old northeast into the southeast, a re-orientation confirmed by the removal of the national capital from Bahia to Rio de Janeiro.

Cotton and coffee

In the late eighteenth century, gold declined in importance and cotton became important, re-

Fig. 39 The Brazilian road system of the 1970s

emphasizing the Nordeste, but the focus in the Southeast was fixed more firmly, from the early nineteenth century, by iron, which replaced gold as a mineral resource, and by coffee. Thus, while in 1700, 70 per cent of the population of 200000 was in the northeast, by 1800 the southern states had over 50 per cent of a 2.5 million population. At the time of independence from Portugal, effectively reached when the Portuguese monarch was forced out to Brazil in 1808, Brazil was a country with substantially single history and culture, despite its mixed population. No region had enough sectional consciousness to separate and the giant nation held together. The kingdom lasted till the 1880s, by which time São Paulo was becoming established with Rio de Janeiro as joint metropolis, at the centre of a core region with both industrial and agricultural strength. The coffee, first planted on a large scale in Rio de Janeiro state, spread out into eastern São Paulo, then westwards to the Paraná river, and into northern Paraná state. Its commercial focus remained in São Paulo where great mansions were built around the old city by the new coffee barons.

The twentieth century
The eighteenth-century *sertão,* the back country, was reached by the tracks of the *bandeirantes.* In the nineteenth century the coffee boom depended on rail-line development, though railways were never flexible enough to meet the demands of a moving coffee frontier. The present century seems likely to be recorded as the century when peripheral areas were first brought into effective occupation, and the key is the new road network, accomplishing linkages never possible before. Figure 39 shows the crossing of the Amazon basin from east to west, linking to Peru and Ecuador and the Carretera Marginal de las Selvas, and at the other end to the poverty-stricken Nordeste. There are also north—south roads, linking the industrial core to the Amazon, especially along the Belém—Brasília road, intended to promote both agricultural colonization and trade. Much has been done in the 1964-72 period, during which period the national highway department tripled the federal highway network in terms of paved roads, while the state and *município* (county) roads grew at almost the same rate.
   Even on the edges of the industrial Southeast,

there are large areas never before reached by real roads. These areas, in western Paraná, eastern Mato Grosso and Goiás, are experiencing sudden upgrading into potential small-farmer land, using the modern roads to truck out goods to market. The roads are not all paved, and most still turn to dust in the dry season, and impassable mud in the wet, but they are all graded from time to time by heavy machines, and are capable of handling heavy traffic under normal circumstances.

CORE AND PERIPHERY

The comments above on the physical integration of distant regions into the national life by road improvements do not mean that economic and social differences have been eliminated. The process of development in the Core Region of the Southeast has been so rapid that peripheral regions have been left behind, indeed southeastern growth has been partly at the expense of the other regions, because of the migration of people, capital and resources to the growing point. Roads may even hasten the movement by allowing a more rapid migration to the big cities, and greater flows of information about the opportunities available in the cities are liable to reach the peripheral areas as a result of the same improvements.
   One measure of the difference in economic levels may be provided in the per capita products of the states, given for 1939 and 1960 in the table below (data for the most recent years have not been published in the statistical year books of Brazil). This table does not show income but production levels, and it is important to note that income trends do not seem to be moving in the same direction as production levels. While differences in production per capita are being narrowed among the states, recent research* suggests that the income disparities have been growing: in 1960 agricultural employees averaged 2.6 new cruzeiros' monthly income against 8 new cruzeiros for non-agricultural. In adjusted values for 1970, the rates were 2.5 new cruzeiros agricultural to 10.5 non-agricultural. Given the concentration of farm workers in certain parts of the country, this widening

* Alfred Stepan (ed), *Authoritarian Brazil* (Yale University Press, 1973), Chapter 3, p. 91.

PER CAPITA DOMESTIC PRODUCT, CR. 1000

State	1940	1960
NORTH		
Amazonas[1]	.86	19.80
Pará[2]	.67	19.40
Maranhão	.41	10.12
NORTHEAST		
Piauí	.43	7.41
Ceará	.41	13.44
Río Grande d.N.	.44	17.53
Paraíba	.37	16.08
Pernambuco	.65	19.20
Alagoas	.37	14.49
Sergipe	.46	14.71
Bahia	.46	16.17
SOUTHEAST		
Minas Gerais	.61	22.90
Espirito Santo	.62	16.86
Rio de Janeiro	.92	33.78
Guanabara[3]	3.90	83.05
São Paulo	1.78	61.17
SOUTH		
Paraná	.96	34.12
Sta. Catarina	.78	27.56
Rio Grande d.S.	1.26	36.83
WEST		
Mato Grosso	.88	25.36
Goiás and		
Fed. District	.58	15.80
Disparity Index	808.7	634.0*

NOTES:

1. *Includes Rondonia, Roraima and Acre territories.*

2. *Includes Amapa territory.*

3. *When Brasília became Federal District in 1960, this state was created out of Rio city. Since 1975, it is amalgamated with Rio de Janeiro state.*

*. The calculation of the Disparity Index is from the following formula:

$$\frac{\sum (y - \bar{y})^2 x}{n}$$

where y = state domestic product per capita

$\bar{y}$ = average for all Brazil

x = weight for each state according to population

n = total number of inhabitants

difference means also an areal increase in disparities. In particular, the figures on wages and production put together mean that while efficient industries are moving to the periphery and increasing output there, their profits are being sent back to Rio and São Paulo or abroad, rather than going to local workers.

The table also shows that there are three types of economic region: first, and covering most of the country, are areas of low per capita output, the poor periphery which includes the whole northeast, north and west; somewhat above these rank the states of the south, in intermediate positions, and the non-industrial parts of the Southeast; and finally there are the high-income industrial areas, the city state of Guanabara (Rio de Janeiro) and São Paulo state. From a comparison of 1940 and 1960 figures, it emerges that the relative position of the periphery has improved through time, though the poor states are still less than half as productive as the rich ones.

Some other significant distinctions between peripheral and central regions may be brought out from the demographic table which shows that the periphery has most of the area but a minority of the population, and that its population is growing at a rapid rate. There is a high level of urbanization in the periphery which suggests lack of agricultural development rather than the high overall development which is usually associated with urbanization.

On the basis of the phenomena hinted at in these two tables, it may be seen that a broad division between the centre and the various peripheral regions is the most important one to be made. In the following pages some analysis of peripheral regions is given, followed by the central region.

DEMOGRAPHIC DATA FOR BRAZILIAN REGIONS (1980 estimates)

Region	Per cent of Area	Per cent of Population 1980	Population 1960	(000s) 1980	Percentage Growth 1960–80	Percentage Urban in 1980
Norte	42	4.0	2 562	4 923	92	49.9
Nordeste	18	29.5	22 182	36 251	63	47.4
Sudeste	11	41.9	30 631	51 574	68	83.8
Sul	7	18.3	11 753	22 495	91	49.0
Centro-Oeste	22	6.3	2 943	7 787	165	54.4
Totals	100	100.0	70 070	123 030	76.5	63.5

Source: Anuario Estatistico do Brasil 1979

14. Brazil: The Peripheral Regions

These are lands of great difficulty, with problem areas of two principal kinds. One of these is the vast population desert occupying the whole of the west and north (fig. 42). Here the problem stems not so much from lack of resources as from a total lack of infrastructure for development. The very size of the area imposes great isolation and resultant lack of progress. The other type of problem is in the Nordeste, where there was once prosperity and wealth, but where the situation has changed, leaving the region with few resources apart from its impoverished people.

THE NORTH

The land

In hydrographic terms the Amazon Basin covers 56 per cent of Brazil, but the north region is confined by the statisticians to the northernmost states (fig. 42), about 42 per cent of total area. This region is still effectively a demographic desert, despite a rapid growth of population since the Second World War, from 1.84 to 4.49 million over 1950-77. Most people live near the watercourses which are both roads and sources of food, and many live in the few Amazon towns, Manaus, Santarém, Belém, leaving the interior empty apart from sparse and dwindling pure Indian groups.

Some of the foreigner's preconceptions regarding the Amazon have a good foundation in facts. The region is one dominated by the action of nature: tree growth is amazingly rapid and strong on the fertile alluvial *varzea*, the floodplain, where forest giants provide a deep shade to lower storeys of vegetation, and sometimes nearly exclude it. Land is named according to its relation to water level, *terra firme,* upland, *varzea,* floodplain, and *igapó,* frequently flooded land, divisions which are strong because of the enormous variation in the river level, ten metres average from high to low season, and sometimes far more. Structurally, the *terras firmes* are low terraces, of which the most widespread is a bench of sands, sometimes silts or clays, of probably Tertiary origin. The *igapós* occupy islands in the rivers, or backswamps, and the *varzeas*, only 1 per cent or 2 per cent of the total but still an area of perhaps 65 000 sq km, are the floodplains over which the rivers are actively working, eroding laterally and depositing a part of their load.

The river itself can only be described in superlatives. Accurate measures of the Amazon's flow date only from the 1960s, and show its discharge, at over 160 000 cubic metres per second, to be far greater than ever thought, and four times greater than its nearest competitor, the Congo.* The depth of channel is maintained at the astonishing depth of about 50 metres over a 2-km width, at the Obidos narrows; at the mouth of the tributary Rio Negro, the water reaches 90 metres depth. The Amazon's suspended particle load, carried out to sea, exceeds 1.3 million tons per

* H. O'Reilly Sternberg, *The Amazon River of Brazil* (Wiesbaden, Steiner, 1975), p.17

diem, serving to clog the Guiana coast for hundreds of kilometres to the northwest with a fine cloying mud.

Most of this huge load, however, does not come from Brazil as might be imagined. One estimate is that 12 per cent of the basin of the Amazon, its Andean section, provides 82 per cent of the solid load, because of an environment of steep slopes and heavy rainfall which favours erosion. The upper Amazon, or Solimões, reaches Manaus yellow—white with its silt load, contrasting with the Rio Negro, a dark-coloured river with little silt or biological activity, running out of plains country. South-bank tributaries like the Xingú and Tapajós, draining the drier sandstone tablelands and metamorphics of the Shield, have a very low sediment load.

Life is everywhere adjusted to the river, the farmer on the *varzea* particularly working to harvest a crop from land that may be underwater during the high stage of the river, or grazing beef cattle on the meadows which are temporarily available, moving his manioc crop, which needs good drainage, to new sites as the river cuts away his field on an old terrace. Fishers and farmers both cling closely to the river banks, leaving the interior a near-desert.

Some parts of the north have a different aspect, like the Rio Branco country in Roraima Territory, a savanna land, its inhabitants living from the rearing of scrub cattle on the flat plains, like their neighbours in Venezuela's Llanos. *Campo cerrado* occupies the south of Pará and Amazonas states, and there are even substantial mountain ranges. the Tumac Humac on the Guiana border and Serra Pacaraima on the Venezuelan front, with an altitude of over 1200 m. On Marajó island in the Amazon estuary, an extensive cattle economy is found in the savanna covering half the island.

Settlement

Historically this region had a distinctive identity, and at one time even the makings of a separate state. Difficulties in reaching the rest of Brazil, because of the long east—west coast of Maranhão along which both wind and current set westwards, allowed a separate state of Maranhão to come into being for a while in the seventeenth century. Isolation of the interior was made complete in the hands of the Jesuits who set up *aldeias* where they protected the Indians from

slavery and encouraged spice production for export. Later, isolation by land was discovered to be a fact, by explorers seeking overland routes between southeast and north; these hardy men, penetrating up the great southern tributaries of the Amazon, the Tocantins, Xingú and Araguaia, found falls and rapids barring their path, forcing portages around them and permitting no access for heavy craft.

After the expulsion of the Jesuits in 1757-60 by civil authorities fearful of their growing power, the Amazon was virtually abandoned till midnineteenth century, for many Indians retired inland away from the rivers to escape slavers. After 1850, the rubber boom revived trade for a while, based on the inefficient collection of wild rubber by the poor *seringueiro,* sent into the forest to collect latex from trees which he had to discover for himself, on company credit he could ill afford. This made him a debt serf, feeding the growth of a new aristocracy of 'rubber barons' at Belém and particularly at Manaus, where rubber wealth built an opera house, theatres, ballrooms and fine stone mansions, 1600 km from the nearest outpost of civilization on the lower river. Belém and Manaus were centres of control from which agents went out to collect new workers by trickery or bribes and take them upstream to the rubber lands; they were also centres to which the cured rubber was brought, via the river.

Manaus thus grew up from an obscure Portuguese slaving trade base at the outlet of the Rio Negro, to boom town and capital of a new state, Amazonas. Vital to its growth was the new steamer service on the river, inaugurated in 1853. The town lost all vitality in the early twentieth century because of a change in the form of rubber production, from wild-tree collection to plantations. The rubber plant, *Hevea brasiliensis,* was smuggled out to London and thus to Malaya, where it flourished as well as in its homeland, and the irregular and wasteful process of tapping, and thereby destroying, a declining number of wild trees was replaced by the much more efficient method of controlled tapping of the growing trees by plantation workers in Malaya.

The latest chapter in Manaus's book is another boom, this time from 1968 with the initiation of a Free Trade Zone. From 1968 to 1975 under the impetus of free trade and special tax concessions to the city, population has grown from 250000 to 390 000 and many industries have emerged. They are all of a particular type — high value/weight ratio industries — including electronics, watchmaking, jewelry, clothing, all of them able to use aeroplane transport to move their product.

Manaus's growth still leaves Belém as main city centre to the North, with 800 000 population in the metropolitan area,* 1975, and an important function as administrative centre and gateway to the region. The city of Our Lady of Bethlehem (Belém), a Portuguese foundation of 1615 on the river Pará, not on the Amazon, is not really well-placed as outlet to the river, and it is possible that the Portuguese founded their city here in mistake. But in any case it attracts most shipping, and ocean-going ships can proceed up the passages connecting it into the Amazon main channel north of Marajó island.

Economic alternatives: minerals

Fuel, power and mineral resources are not currently very large in the North. Most obvious among them is the forest itself, at present little exploited because of a combination of inaccessibility and mixture of species, which make the cost of extraction and transport to consuming centres too high to compete with areas near the coast. Manganese is the only important ore mined to date, coming from the Serra do Navio in Amapá, and sent by rail to Port Santana near Macapá, where freighters can load it. There have been iron ore discoveries in the Serra dos Carajas between Xingú and Tocantins rivers, in large quantities and with 57 per cent iron content, but working must await the decline in high-grade resources elsewhere. Tin ore is also known from the upper basin and may well be exploited if prices remain high. Usable power supplies, despite the great Amazon, seem to be low because of the lack of localized heads of water and basin topography for reservoirs; the tributaries with their concentration of head of water at the rapids are more promising, and the Tocantins is due to be harnessed soon for HEP to make aluminium with bauxite from the Trombetas river area.

* Population figures of cities refer to city *municipios* only unless otherwise noted. Metropolitan areas cover much more land than the cities proper.

Agriculture: a question mark

Farming peoples are already entering the region in fairly large numbers along the fast-advancing Transamazon Highway, and it is expected that agricultural use of the region will soon be very general; but, though shifting agriculture has long been practised, there remain serious difficulties in settling large numbers of colonists in the forest region.

An example of the agricultural problem is presented in Bragantina, an area which is productive and well settled, between Bragança and Belém in the lower basin. In 1848, when H.W. Bates, the naturalist, visited Belém, it was little more than a village, though already with 15 000 inhabitants, and he commented that the forest reached to the very outskirts of the settlement. Intensive land use came after 1900 along the railway line between the two towns. Shifting agriculture has eaten its way through all this land so that no natural, fertile selvas soil remains, only secondary forest and brush and low amounts of humus. The ancient slash-and-burn technique is still practised by shifting farmers who must expend continuous effort on clearing as their staple food crops, manioc, corn and beans, suffer a 50 per cent fall in yield from first year to second. The short dry season from September to November allows complete burning which gives good ash fertilizer for the first crop, but also burns out humus and exposes the soil directly to the burning action of the sun. The loss of soil fertility is a problem for shifting agriculture and thus for the commercial farmer who follows. Forest destruction and resultant soil depletion and erosion are also produced by the *caboclos* who practise wood burning for charcoal to be sold in the towns.

Commercial farming in Bragantina is confined to *malvas* (a vegetable fibre, *Urena lobata,* used as a successful jute substitute), tobacco and black pepper, introduced by Japanese settlers in the 1940s. Below the Bragantina zone, on the flat alluvium near the river, there is also jute grown on a commercial scale. Pepper has become an export crop of some magnitude, though there are some undesirable features. Profits go partly to merchants and middlemen who advance credit to farmers. Prices are so unstable that the smallest farmers must always be dependent on this kind of credit, in the absence of other financial institutions. Tobacco is sometimes grown on plots fertilized by cattle kept for the purpose; this may look like a rare case of mixed farming in the tropics, but it differs in that cattle are quite subordinate in the system, brought in solely for their fertilizing dung.

A third land use is rubber, developed after 1950 when Brazil was suffering acute shortages of this strategic material. In 1927 the Ford Company had attempted rubber plantations in the lower Tapajós, a commercial failure because of disease and labour problems. At last modern technology has succeeded, and Pirelli and Goodyear own large plantations of several thousand ha, where the soil is preserved by ground-cover plantings, and by avoiding burning of the forest as a preliminary to planting, because this destroys soil humus. Disease is controlled by trained agronomists. The problem in this sector is not economic success but ownership; much land, skills and capital are retained in the hands of a trained group which manages the estates, not disseminated among other producers.

These same problems, of soil preservation, financing of farmers, and ownership of land, skills or entrepreneurial ability, are repeated with minor variations throughout the region; such features make the massive agricultural settlement of the area along penetration roads, notably the Transamazon Highway, not entirely a pleasing prospect, and careful watch will be needed to prevent extension of the same problems into new territory.

THE WEST

The two states of Mato Grosso and Goiás, with Brasília, cover nearly 1.9 million sq km. Like the north, this is an empty region with few permanent settlements of any kind, and most people live in the southern part where the vegetation is *campo cerrado* rather than selvas. Northern Mato Grosso, on the middle courses of the Xingú and Tapajós, is still one of the least known parts of the inhabitable world, occupied by a thin population of Indian cultivators and hunters who have never had real contact with white populations.

The dominant land use is cattle rearing, throughout the *chapadas*, the dry flat uplands lying at 1000 m on natural or induced grasslands. There has been a rapid build up of cattle

numbers in the West, which had 10.5 million head in 1960, and 19.5 in 1975. However, the region has a very low carrying capacity, especially in Goiás, where a third of the cattle are maintained on pastures with under 15 head per sq km, compared with Rio Grande do Sul, itself an extensive cattle district, where 50 per sq km is typical. In Mato Grosso there is a higher density because of the Pantanal, the upper Paraguay river flood-plain with a 160-km width of seasonally flooded meadow producing fine natural pastures. In the early maps of South America and up to the eighteenth century this was marked as a great lake, the Lake of the Xarayas, and it was not entirely mythical, for wide stretches of water may be seen at times of flood. Outside the Pantanal, the West has infertile soils, often lateritic, sometimes poorly drained, except for the valleys cut into the surface. These expose fresh minerals which plants may use, and allow agriculture to develop for local markets. Rice, beans and maize are grown.

From the 1940s the federal government has promoted colonization, especially in Southern Goiás, in forest lands of slope and valley bottom which were ignored by the cattle *fazendas*, pre-emptors of the open lands, but even this minor expansion is on uncertain footing, for small lots have been granted, too small because a part of them must be left in forest for rotation because of rapid soil depletion under cultivation.

Regional isolation

The West, incorporated into Brazil in the eighteenth century by the expeditions of *bandeirantes*, had no direct connections with the coast, and communicated with it more via the Paraná—Paraguay system of rivers than overland on the long and difficult trails. Only in the present century was there a rail connection to the east, from Corumbá to São Paulo, effectively bringing the region into the national ambit. The region's isolation and the urge to fill what appeared to be a dangerous void on the borders of Spanish lands led to the *Marcha para o Oeste,* the westwards march, a popular phrase in the government of Getulio Vargas in the 1930s. In order to assist the growth of the West, new federal territories were created out of isolated portions of states, in a Vargas decree of 1943. These included Amapá, Rio Branco (now called

Roraima), Guaporé (now Rondonia), taken out of Mato Grosso and Amazonas, Ponta Porã from Mato Grosso, and Iguaçu, from Paraná and Santa Catarina. The two last were returned to their states in 1946, but the others remained federal districts which received special aids to development. Since the federal lands were mostly peopled by Indians with little knowledge of white men, the Indian Protection Service was utilized to attempt a gradual transition of the life the primitives had known into something compatible with modern farming and to protect their hunting grounds until they could be educated for other employment.

Indians

The treatment of Indians on the farming frontier has become something of an issue for Brazil, because of allegations by foreigners, by the Church and by anthropologists and others within the country, that Indians have been mistreated, even shot at like animals, in order to move them away from estates which have acquired value for their owners with the gradual advance of the farmer frontier; even the Indian Protection Service has been implicated in criticisms of Indian treatment, along with cattlemen, farmers and prospectors. The most useful work, now terminated by the government, was that done by the anthropologist brothers Vilas Boas, in teaching the Indians and preparing them for the cultural shock of Western civilization. This is the most that could be done, for complete isolation in National Reserves, desired by some anthropologists to prevent the irrevocable destruction of their culture, is a hopeless ideal.

Brasília

Part of the urge for westwards movement, to fulfil Brazil's 'continental destiny', expressed itself in the move to locate the capital in the west, an idea dating back to the eighteenth century and the rebellious miners who sought freedom from Europe and a symbolic turning inland away from the coast. Brasília is located on a plot of land symbolically at the headwaters of the three major rivers, Amazon, Paraná and São Francisco, indicating Brazilian dominion over all three. Brasília's interior location symbolizes the conquest of the *sertão,* the backwoods which have been the continuous challenge to Brazilians. At the same time, the idea of an implanted,

created city is scarcely new or original. Belo Horizonte, capital of Minas Gerais, was inaugurated in 1897, a new city to replace the old, picturesque but overcrowded town of Ouro Prêto. In this there is something of a parallel with Brasília and Rio de Janeiro, which it replaced; there is also a parallel in the opposition to the transfer by established interests in the old settlement. Teresina and Aracaju in the northeast are other nineteenth-century created capitals; nearer to Brasília, in Goiás, Goiânia was made state capital in 1937, replacing Goiás city. There are, then, antecedents for a move of the national capital.

A long time lapsed between initial proposals and movement, which only began under the Kubitschek government and, since public programmes have a habit of falling by the wayside if not completed under a single mandate, was to be completed in five years. In fact the basic structure of the capital was laid out in this period, following the superbly monumental design of the architect Lucio Costa. Later additions and modifications, shanty towns and suburbs, have not changed this structure (fig. 40), with the central axes forming an aeroplane design of high blocks for public buildings and functionaries' residences.

The effects of moving the capital have been substantial; the western states have been invigorated to some extent by increased expenditures here, and a new road, the Belém—Brasília, 2276 km long, has been an axis for some settlement of farm population. Some of the pressure of migrants on the resources of São Paulo and Rio cities has been released by the alternative available at Brasília.

QUESTIONS
In spite of being a largely administrative city (itself a potential problem though government is currently a growth industry), Brasília has suffered some of the usual growth problems of Brazilian cities. The *favela* has been a feature here as much as in Rio, for many people have been attracted in by job possibilities. In the mid-1960s, it was estimated that 100 000 people, a third of the population, were in substandard housing, for the most part *favelas*. These were the migrants, hungry for jobs in the construction industry, in service industries, in anything open to uneducated *caboclos*. They occupied land near

Fig. 40 Brasília

the Pilot Plan which centres on lake Paranoá, in areas which became known as the Social Security Invasion, Vila Tenório, Candangolândia and Taguatinga. Blocks of flats had been built in the initial planned areas, but they were too expensive for penniless migrants with absolutely no resources. Towns outside the capital but within the District could also have been used to house the *favelados*, but there was no system of organized public transport to bring them in from these places, nor housing to accommodate them. Brasília's grandiose design, expressive of high aims and excellence, it must be concluded, was not built for the poor who were to constitute a large part of its inhabitants.

Another question which must be asked about the city is whether it has been worthwhile for the nation. It was constructed at enormous expense by a nation with limited public funds, in a region which was not the main problem area of the country; its employment possibilities were not great for the untrained, nor were its industries capable of stimulating much local development. In some ways Brasília is just another expression of a national addiction to great public works programmes, like the Drought Polygon pro-gramme, or the ultra-modern road programme for interior settlement.

THE NORDESTE

This region, a fifth of Brazil, includes the northern marginal state of Maranhão, Piauí, Ceará, Rio Grande do Norte, Pernambuco, Alagoas, Sergipe, and Bahia on the southern margins, with in 1977 an estimated population of 33.6 million, or 30 per cent of the total. If we were to look for a rough parallel to the Nordeste in the developed world, it might be among the old coal-field regions of North Britain or Pennsylvania. In such areas, development has come many years ago, promoted prosperity for a while, and then gone to leave a dense population with a shortage of useful work, with the unemployment that breeds discontent and rebellion. In the Nordeste the sugar cycle brought prosperity to the rich *massapé* black-clay soils of the *mata*, the coastal belt, during the seventeenth century, cotton prolonged it to the nineteenth, but no new resource was found for the twentieth century. Given the social structure of the region, the phenomenon is perhaps predictable: a region with successive agricultural export bases, when these are no longer viable, has no ongoing dynamic source of ideas or entrepreneurs for a new export base, and relapses into poverty.

The culture of rebellion

The Nordeste is defined not only in terms of poverty, but also in its distinctive culture, identified by historians and celebrated in literature. Especially since the decline in regional fortunes in the nineteenth century, various kinds of outburst, functions of the internal stresses in the system, have occurred here.

Early antecedents were the establishment of runaway slave colonies, notably the Republic of Palmares (1630-97) in the backcountry. In Maranhão a peasant revolt took place in 1838-40. In 1896-7 a religious movement under the ascetic Antonio Conselheiro brought together bandits and fanatics in what seemed to some a threat to the new Brazilian Republic, at Canudos in northern Bahia. In fact this was never an organized threat to authority, but it showed the difficulty of governing the *sertão*, for whole brigades had to be sent to take a village of a few thousand determined fighters, and many lives were lost both to these defenders and to the drought and inhospitable environment of the interior.* Throughout the centuries, Robin Hood characters, half-bandit and half idealist, have entered into the folklore and history of the *sertão*. In more recent years, Peasant Leagues, first formed in 1955, among the sugar mills of the coast, have focussed the bitterness and the aspirations of the labourers.

The expression, almost caricature, of the *sertão* type is the *vaqueiro,* the independent cowboy who is no one's master and nobody's servant. He watches the cattle on a share basis with the owner, taking one calf in four, and is trusted to do this without overseers. His clothing, adapted to a hostile environment of spiny bushes, is more like that of a medieval knight than that of a cowboy, with tight leather leggings, leather gloves, shinguards, leather jerkin and vest. Physically he may be a

* The Canudos campaign, and the *sertão* environment, are admirably portrayed in the work of Euclides da Cunha, *Os Sertoes,* first published in 1902, and in shortened form in English as *Revolt in the Backlands,* translated by Samuel Putnam (London, Victor Gollancz, 1947).

mameluco, mixture of white and Indian, or a *cafuso*, Indian—Negro mix.

Coastal society

On the coast, there was a more settled, stable, less nomadic society, allowing harder lines to be drawn in the social stratification.

> The cane culture of the Nordeste aristocratized the white man into a lord, and degraded the Indian and principally the Negro, first into a slave, then into a pariah. It aristocratized the house of stone and cement into a mansion and degraded the straw into mucambo. It inflated the plantation and depreciated the *mata*, the virgin forest.
>
> *Gilberto Freyre,* Nordeste, *edited by J. Olympio, 1951, p. 124*

Tradition centred on the *senhores de engenho*, secure in their rich lands and the leaders of their society, but so conservative that they allowed Cuba to steal the advantage when the age of improvements came for sugar, with the introduction of steam-powered mills in the nineteenth century. Another tradition, more independent like that of the *sertanejo*, is that of the small fisherman on the coast, with his fragile *jangada* which takes him out almost literally in search of tomorrow's food (plate 32).

Racially this is another mixed region, but with a strong current of African blood, some of it from the higher civilizations of West Africa, metalworkers and of Moslem faith, rather than the more primitive Bantu tribesmen. These skilled workers were of use in developing and working the little mines of the interior, and were also experienced herdsmen. African culture, despite the deliberate mixing of tribal groups to avoid formation of communities, has survived in a variety of dances and semi-religious rites, kinds of food and cooking, and clothing, which seem to be of Moslem origin.

Land use

THE SERTÃO

Physically the interior of the Nordeste has enormous difficulties for man. This land of ancient gneiss and schist rocks, or dry sandstones, is cut through by a great river, the São Francisco, running first northeast then cutting southeast to the sea. This northern elbow of the river and the plateaus, hills and mountains to the north, suffer

Fig. 41 Vegetation zones of the Nordeste and the Drought Polygon

from drought, not a continuous lack of water — most of the land has over 600 mm and some 1000 mm annually — but a more dangerous phenomenon, a dry season which sometimes lasts four months, sometimes for twelve, when it causes disaster, famine and emigration of countless thousands of *retirantes*, quitters, leaving the land and going to the coast, to the towns, anywhere in order to survive. The Drought Polygon, as it is called, is roughly defined by the region with seven or more months' drought (fig. 41). It

lies in the interior, reaching the coast only between Fortaleza and Natal. Along the east-facing coast, there is adequate rainfall of 1500 mm or more, and often thicker soils with alluvial material. This is the *zona da mata*, literally the forest zone, which it was when first met by Portuguese explorers. Inland, there is a belt of transitional country with thin forest, the *agreste*, and further in the *sertão* (fig. 41). Both *agreste* and *sertão* may be affected by drought. In the driest country of the *sertão* the vegetation is *caatinga*, the scrub forest dominated by thorn trees, cactus and bromeliads.

Here drought is not easily combated with irrigation schemes; the water of the São Francisco is too far below the northern plateaus to allow simple diversion with dam techniques for irrigation, and in any case the area is isolated and cannot well compete in the provision of irrigation crops to the urban markets of the coast. Thus most of the *sertão* is cattle land, used for tough unimproved beef animals which only reach slaughter weight at six years, and then only achieve a carcass weight half that of a North European animal. In the driest parts sheep and goats are kept on pastures that are virtually useless for other animals and have been progressively degraded by overgrazing and cultivation in the course of the century.

In the northern part of the Drought Polygon, the rivers dry up in the dry season, their floodplains occupied by carnauba palms in gallery forests, feeding on the groundwater and rich soil.

The wax formed on the leaves to prevent evaporation loss of water is an important commercial product, increasing output now coming from Piauí, Ceará and Grande do Norte, where the tree is also used for its edible nut and its strong wood.

AGRESTE AND MATA

The densest population in the Nordeste is in the *agreste* and *mata*, and the coastal belt is still occupied by sugar plantations, especially in Pernambuco and Alagoas, leading sugar states in the region. Cocoa is also an important estate crop on the Bahia coast, and oil palms have become successful in this area. Apart from plantations, there is a large body of subsistence farmers cultivating small plots for beans, rice and maize, and making ends meet by seasonal labour for plantation owners who may indeed own their land, making them completely dependent.

Minerals have also favoured the coastal *mata*,

32 Jangadas, *primitive fishing craft, at Prainha, Ceará, in the Brazilian Nordeste*

where oil has been produced in substantial quantities since 1950. Bahia's Recôncavo basin of Mesozoic rocks accounts for nearly all Brazilian natural gas and 80 per cent of her petroleum. Sergipe, neighbour state to the north, produces most of the rest. A new coast road being built between Rio and Salvador (Bahia), in addition to the existing one which runs inland, should help the coastal developments, especially the potential lumbering and cocoa-producing country of southern Bahia and Espirito Santo state to the south. Fishing is practised along the whole coast, from villages standing in the shade of palm trees behind the long beaches. The fish catch is not enormous, only a third of Brazil's total, but the industry is labour-intensive and takes little capital, points to recommend it to a country where men are less scarce than money. The fishermen work from tiny boats without motors which they re-make themselves every year when the wood begins to crumble away.

Urbanization

Towns now hold the majority of the regional population. There are three major foci: Fortaleza in the north with 1.1 million population in 1975; in the centre Recife 1.2 million in 1975 (2.2 million metropolitan area), capital to the Nordeste in general; and Salvador (1.2 million). Because of waves of immigrants from the countryside in recent years, there is high unemployment in these cities and in the many smaller towns of the interior. Port processing industries are still, as in colonial times, important in Recife and Salvador, but tax concessions have brought a host of unconnected light industries to the Aratu industrial estate at Salvador and to the suburbs of Recife, such as electronics, electrical hardware, synthetic fibres and petrochemicals. Not all of these new industries can use the migrant labour force, with its skills oriented to an earlier stage of industrial development, to weaving, basketry and leather-work, craft industries which are rapidly declining in the country. Many migrants end up in the already overstaffed tertiary sector where wages are minimal.

Maranhão

A fourth region of the Nordeste is the Amazon fringe, mostly in the state of Maranhao, a region which is physically transitional from the dry zone of the *sertão* to the humid environment of the selvas. Some writers have even referred to the Maranhão—Piauí area as a separate region, the Middle North, a distinction that has some justification on economic, physical and cultural grounds. It has an easily cleared selva cover, replaced by secondary growth of the babaçu palm also found to a lesser extent throughout the Nordeste. This region differs in an important aspect from the rest of the Nordeste, in its lack of population. It has been able to act as steamvalve for the Nordeste, accepting over the last century untold thousands of migrants leaving the dry lands during hard times.

Culturally the region was typical plantation country, focussing on the colonial centre of São Luís, and producing rice, sugar and cotton in the seventeenth century. Thereafter it fell into complete decadence so that fossilized townships are to be found scattered throughout the coastal plain. The small population turned in part to a primitive existence, living from hunting and fishing with traditional techniques, and growing only subsistence crops of rice and manioc. To earn money salt, fish and animal skins were sold in small quantity. In the present century the babaçu became a new source of some wealth, because of its valuable vegetable oil; it is collected in nut form by tenants who must sell to the landowners in return for a small payment, and the lack of organization of collection or marketing means poor quality at times and irregular supply.

In recent years the local economy has been stimulated by large numbers of migrants from neighbour states of the Nordeste, coming spontaneously or in government-sponsored schemes which have had varying fortune. Over most of the interior however, cattle are raised with little help from man, on an ultra-extensive basis of zero provision of improvements. The cattle must often migrate great distances because of floods in the low plains of western Maranhão, or droughts in the east.

STRATEGIES FOR THE NORDESTE

Over time there has been a gradual appreciation of the Nordeste problem. Central to it is poverty, which is multiple in its causes and effects. The structure of the entrenched plantation economy of the *zona da mata* never allowed distribution of its substantial wealth, but kept it in the hands of a few owners. In the interior, unimproved land could never support prosperous small farming. National economic evolution has also been unfavourable to the Nordeste, focussing on the southeast over the last century or more and leaching human and physical resources out of the region.

A result of poverty, malnutrition — to the point of causing both physical and mental defects in the population — has been pointed at by nutrition experts working in the area, and is an incontrovertible indication of the problem's reality. Malnutrition causes inefficiency in work, and prevents any initiative coming from the poor people, whose work leaves them exhausted and with no energy to solve their own long-term problems. Poverty also means there are no markets for the new range of industrial goods coming from the Nordeste, and they must be marketed in the southeast, an undesirable arrangement for the stability of industry in the area.

The attack on drought

For a considerable period the drought problem, the *secas*, has been treated as the central one. As early as 1877, Emperor Pedro II was moved to set up an investigating committee after the terrible drought of that year which killed half a million people in Ceará. By 1909 a permanent Inspectorate for Droughts had been created, still in existence today as the National Department for Drought Measures (DNOCS). This federal agency has provided emergency relief in food and work for the *flagelados*, those scourged by the drought, and has built over 250 reservoirs in the Drought Polygon. These were intended to retain water through dry seasons, and feed irrigation canal systems, but lack of funds and poor planning have meant that the canals, except for a very few, have not been built. Reservoirs were often too small and dried out in the dry season, to expose a strip of good soil round their edge for cultivation, sometimes the only useful function of the dam. Since 1964 DNOCS has had more money available and doubled the public reservoir capacity from 6.8 million cu m to 11.7 in 1971, though no growth has occurred since then. Many wells have also been drilled in this decade.

The drought programme of DNOCS has not been totally successful, either in a narrow tech-nical sense or as a broad solution for the Nordeste. Only in terms of employment for workless farmers was it ever of vital importance, and even in this matter, it could be queried whether it would not have been better to let the *flagelados* migrate to better-endowed regions. Corruption and mismanagement have been a constant companion of the planners, and an Indústria das Sêcas grew up, whereby exaggerated claims of drought brought in government money when it was most convenient to local political leaders. Basically, however, the failure is one of specialization, of concentrating on infrastructural measures rather than using a broader approach to social and economic problems.

The regional development authorities

A river-basin approach was first attempted in the São Francisco Valley Authority, created in 1948. The northern quarter of the valley lies within the Drought Polygon as officially defined for the DNOCS measures. However, the hands of this agency were tied from the beginning because hydro power was placed outside its control under a separate and successful federal agency which developed the Paulo Afonso Falls site on the river, producing power for the first time in 1955. Only electric power production, which offended no vested interests, could readily be planned.

Up to this time the policy for the Nordeste could be classified as a *política hidráulica*, a policy based on hydraulic engineering measures. Now a move towards comprehensive development planning was made with the setting up of SUDENE, Superintendency for Development of the Northeast, in 1959, as an autonomous agency for coordination of planning throughout the region. The multiple attack on the problem envisaged a) industrialization to diversify the economy, b) agricultural concentration on foodstuff production as a protection against famine and c) colonization of areas outside the densely peopled Nordeste in transitional Maranhão and Goiás.

After 1964, the SUDENE programme was progressively altered by military governments that have controlled Brazil since that year and which have limited the autonomy of the regional agencies. Private industry has continued to be attracted into the area by substantial tax concessions, which in the most favourable cases meant that an investor only had to contribute 12.5 per cent of the capital cost of a new venture. In 1964-9 this served to double the fixed industrial capital in the region. Some economists have expressed doubts about the effectiveness of this approach. Most investment went to the fine new Aratu industrial estate at Salvador, to main road sites around Recife, or to Fortaleza, in other words to places where a good infrastructure for industry was already present. Elsewhere there was little to attract the industrialist, and the small states of the Nordeste were bypassed, in a process of concentration of economic advance on the big cities. Industrial structure was also less than optimal for the purposes of regional policy, because the links of the new industries in the region were not to other local industries, but out and back to the mother companies which were in the Southeast or overseas, and to market and supply industries in the Southern—Southeastern complex. Little in the form of local, regional multiplier effect from the industries could be discerned.

In agriculture, food-crop production expanded according to plan. Over 1950-69 rice production expanded 8.6 per cent annually, beans 7.2 per cent, maize 6.0 per cent against 3.8 per cent for sugar, 3.2 per cent cotton and 1.4 per cent cocoa. There was however a realization that this did not solve any long-term problems, or even some short-term ones, since food crops could avoid famines only if they were grown successfully in the famine areas, and in any case famine was only one facet of the Nordeste problem.

From 1970, year of a severe drought, the orientation of effort changed again under the military government. Now the central point was to be President Medici's National Integration Programme (PIN), aimed at linking in to the centre all the peripheral regions, and thus bringing development and maximum national security. Two roads were to be of importance, the Transamazonica and the Cuiabá—Santarém (fig. 39), along which colonization by farmers was intended, both to aid the development of the North and to act as a safety valve for the still overpopulated Nordeste. Many other modern highways were to be built, in a programme which seems more concerned with strategic and security interests of the military than with regional economic development. It is true that the Trans-

amazonica now provides a fine paved road-link from the river Madeira near the Bolivian frontier to the east coast 3500 km away, and that the road will link to the head of navigation on many southern tributaries of the Amazon, thus incorporating this river into the transport system. But for the farmers who must use the land a less than optimal choice has been made, following the well-drained but infertile uplands above the *varzea* plain. Possibly only the stretch south of Santarém (fig. 39) will provide a long-term basis for farming.

In particular, the programme would seem to be a poor second choice to putting through a thoroughgoing agrarian reform in the Nordeste. Such a reform has never been carried out because of the effective power of the landlords in areas such as the *mata,* where they control both rural land and industries. Agrarian reform has been made a priority in three northeastern states — Pernambuco, Ceará and Paraíba — but the reform proposed is not complete, for it offers payment in compensation for land lost at commercial rates, an expensive proposition which can scarcely be afforded by the government; there is in addition no enforcement of complete breakup of latifundia, only reduction to half size. Finally, breakup is not to be practised on the productive lands at all, so that large sugar estates, with their high production, escape altogether, and only poor cattle lands of the *sertão*, totally unsuited to new small farmers, are likely to be available.

OVERVIEW OF THE PERIPHERAL REGIONS

The Nordeste is obviously the main problem region in the Brazilian periphery. It has a large, poverty-ridden population with few hopes for improvement. The atmosphere of the region is one of tension; this has even been expressed by such conservative elements as the Church. Dom Helder Cámara, Archbishop of Recife and Olinda, has argued that significant reform of Nordestino society has yet to be achieved, and that more than lip-service to change must be given by the government. Dom Helder's voice has considerable weight among the people and he is supported by his bishops and clergy; his voice has not been silenced, but those of leftwing agitators who sought to rouse sugar workers against their masters have been quieted, leaving the tension bottled up and still seeking an outlet.

The problems for Amazonia and the west are of another character and perhaps less obvious; for these regions there are the questions of conservation. How is it possible to press forward with farmers into the selvas without destruction of much that is useful? Indian cultures and the Indians themselves are being killed by the advancing wave of occupants in the Midwest. At the same time there are the proposals for national roads through the north and west and farmer-colonization of huge areas along them — without the experience of trial and error to guide them. Possibly the colonization will be success-ful, though some reservations about this have been expressed. But there remains the destruc-tion of the forest, a secular process in Brazil but one which is now accelerating and which may constitute not only a Brazilian but a world problem, since this forested region is one of the last biological sinks for the atmosphere, control-ling to an unknown but large extent the carbon dioxide and oxygen content and balancing it naturally. Once the selvas cover is gone, it has been observed that replacement is extremely slow because of the close relation of soil and vegetation; this makes destruction all the more serious.

15. The Core Region of Brazil

The Southeast and South are taken together as a core region (fig. 42), distinguished from the rest of the country primarily on the grounds of their greater wealth, and secondarily because they have a more urban and industrial makeup. The map shows that their trade links make all parts of Brazil, except the Nordeste, tributary directly to the metropolitan southeast, but distance and the differences in economy and society which typify the periphery make it desirable to treat them separately.

The south is distinguished by a more rural population, and by an economy based mainly on mining, minerals and farming; the southeast is threequarters urban already, and is the industrial—commercial centre to the country. The problems of the periphery, outmigration, lack of rural employment and poverty, have their counterpart in the city: immigrants in the city slums and *favelas*, lack of urban employment opportunities for the new arrivals, and consequent poverty for the *marginados,* those living on the edge of society without secure employment, sometimes without secure lodgings for themselves and their families.

THE SOUTHEAST

Physical geography

All southeast Brazil is shield country, forming a series of tablelands or *chapadas* at different levels but sloping generally down to the west. The hydrographic net is thus composed mostly of Paraná tributaries, flowing away from the coast, a factor that long retarded exploration and settlement of the interior. Only short streams flow east, apart from the Paraíba which occupies a longitudinal valley between the Serra do Mar and Serra da Mantiqueira. The first of these ranges is still a forested wall of land rising sharply from the coast, a steamy blue—green in the usual humid atmosphere. Climates are subtropical rather than tropical, modified by altitude on the plateau and on the coast by occasional depressions which bring cooler air from the south. A ride by bus from Santos via the superhighway up the Serra do Mar to São Paulo, taking only half an hour, serves to bring home the differences in temperature; in August this writer has regretted the lack of a jacket in the city on the plateau, having been perfectly comfortable in shirt-sleeves in the port.

Historical background

In early colonial times the capitania of São Vicente was able to develop as a commercial centre because of the active trade of São Vicente island, near the modern port of Santos. The trade products included quinces (*marmelos*, basis of the original marmalade), and sugar from the few plantations; a relative abundance of settled Tupi Indians allowed successful farming of the traditional slave-based type. This was not however Brazil's early core region, that honour falling to the Nordeste. In this latter region there was a much greater development of slaving, of sugar, and of trade with Portugal's Oriental Empire — Bahia became a frequent port of call

Fig. 42 Brazilian regions and trade linkages: each stage is linked to its largest single trading partner, according to internal trade statistics

for the India fleet, absorbing its silks and spices before they had a chance to reach the Portuguese markets.

In the São Paulo region, appropriate to the city's plateau rather than coastal situation, there arose a definite tradition of exploration and exploitation of the interior, under the *bandeirantes*, groups of men who went first to look for gold or slaves. Enslavement of the Indians was illegal, but a pretence was made of going to exchange slaves for captives already taken in war. Other men went on a more permanent basis from São Paulo to open up cattle lands in the *campo cerrado* and savannas of the interior, in western Minas and in the São Francisco valley. Gold was found in the late seventeenth century and formed the basis of eighteenth-century wealth, a wealth to which the old city of Ouro Prêto (plate 33) testifies: this was the capital of the mining kingdom and, with the transfer of its administrative functions to Belo Horizonte in the 1890s, has been fossilized

33 The city of Ouro Prêto, fossilized in its eighteenth-century form, its architecture protected as an ancient monument

in its narrow valley, the purest example of Portuguese Baroque architecture in Brazil.

Gold, and also diamonds from northern Minas Gerais, were the basis for an economic cycle that attracted new settlers, including Nordestinos with their troupe of slaves, to the mines of the Southeast. The decline of mining in the nineteenth century was followed by the coffee cycle, giving rise to a new coffee aristocracy which built its ornate mansions around São Paulo, matching those of the gold and diamond merchants in Rio. Finally, over the last hundred years the rise of industry, using in many cases the capital won in trade from coffee, has confirmed the central position of the Southeast.

The rural economy
Market-oriented commercial farming has long been established in the Southeast. In some remote areas or on difficult sloping land in the Serra do Mar or Serra da Mantiqueira there are semi-subsistence farmers growing more for themselves than for the market, but these are the exception, not the rule. Important commercial crops include coffee, cotton, and sugar, for this area has replaced the Northeast as centre of cane-sugar production. São Paulo produces 40 per cent of Brazilian coffee, and is responsible for the surpluses that have allowed Brazil to diversify her foreign trade. In 1974, coffee accounted for only 12.6 per cent of export value, sugar for 15.8 per cent. Another important export is soya beans. Food crops are maize, rice on the wetter lowlands, and fruit and vegetables of a wide variety in the suburban market gardens.

Mechanization and technification of farming is advanced, as compared to other regions, as the table below suggests. While the North and Northeast have about 1000 workers per tractor, the South and Southeast have 50-70, and produce far more of the national farm product with a smaller labour force.

Part of the secret of the Southeast's agricultural success is in the general background of education and capital availability, part is in the connections of farming to industry through processing. For example, one advantageous factor for cotton growing is a market location, feeding the local textile industry, for most of Brazil's cotton mills are in the São Paulo metropolitan area, and edible cotton seed oil is also processed here. Cotton is also a useful accompaniment to coffee in its ability to occupy the dry sandy soils that coffee will not tolerate. Other products, like rice and milk, may be seen essentially as responses to the vicinity of great urban markets, and to the competition for land near the cities which ensures that only intensive farming may be practised. The once-marshy valley of the Paraíba, between Rio and São Paulo, is spotted with rice fields along its whole alluvial floor. Yields from the well-tended and irrigated fields are higher than in the Nordeste, because of better management and fertilizer use.

NUMBER OF TRACTORS AND LABOUR FORCE, 1970

Major region	Tractors (units)	Labour force (000s)	Workers per tractor
Norte	1 013	982	969
Nordeste	6 033	7 836	1 299
Sudeste	79 564	4 217	53
Sul	60 533	4 256	70
Centro-Oeste	9 499	957	101
All Brazil	156 592	18 249	116

Source: Anuário Estatístico do Brasil, *1975, p. 151*

COFFEE

This crop has long been the great dynamo of Southeastern agriculture, and it is still a lead product, occupying over a million ha. It was introduced commercially in the Paraíba Valley in the early nineteenth century, but the centre of the producing area has gradually shifted west and southwest, into São Paulo state, while Paraná has become the dominant producer since about 1960. This crop has been extended into the interior by small farmers, continually cutting down forest, burning it, planting and waiting for five years, growing subsistence crops of maize and beans among the young trees. After some years of production yields decline and the farmers abandon the clearing and move on in the face of soil exhaustion and erosion. This cycle is reminiscent of that of the shifting farmer, and indeed the coffee farmer in Brazil is similar in many ways to the subsistence cultivator, the main difference being his attachment to commercial markets. Little attention has been given to land ownership by the generality of small farmers, who have advanced spontaneously, on a moving front, to the south and west, without concern for title to land. Those who have sought title have often been forced to pay for it to several different claimants, as the state has never regularized occupation on this frontier.

Hollow frontiers or stable colonization

Soil erosion, soil exhaustion, and ruthless landlords have driven the frontiersman on to the west to produce in his wake a 'Hollow Frontier', as it has been called by the American geographer Preston James, with no useful occupance for the land left behind apart from poor grazing for cattle, since topsoil has largely been lost through cultivation. This frontier will only fill in when farmers are forced to adopt more ecologically satisfactory methods of farming, planting and cultivating less on the steep slopes, using shade trees and mulches to conserve soil moisture, and contour ploughing and cropping. A somewhat more stable environment has been possible in the areas filled in by colonization companies, principally along the rail lines to the west from São Paulo. Here small farms were set up from the 1930s, for immigrants and native Brazilians, and title to land was firmly established. Even in such cases there has been a tendency to reduction of the independent farmer population. On the Paraná Plateau, south of São Paulo and above 1000 m, frost liability is a major difficulty, causing damage or even killing trees in July or August, and reducing the harvest to nothing. Only medium-size farms of over 50 ha can stand this variability in harvest due to frost or cold, and the small farmer has been edged out by his lack of reserves.

Another factor making this frontier a difficult one for the small farmer is the variation in world demand and price for coffee, despite the attempts led by Brazil to control production internationally. Variation in production out of harmony with demand variation is likely to occur anyway because of the five-year lag between planting and production. Thus the government agency which has had the task of protecting farmers by guaranteeing prices has also had to supervise such operations as the mass uprooting of coffee trees and burning of coffee during the 1930s. Coffee beans were even used at one point for fuel on the Brazilian railways, a desperate solution to overproduction problems. Agricultural research stations, promoted under the Vargas government of the 1930s, are finally making coffee-growing much more rational and efficient on the best lands, though conservation methods have yet to penetrate to the frontier.

Industries and cities

THE STEEL INDUSTRY (fig. 43)

The basis of the great Brazilian steel industry is the rich haematite of Minas Gerais, ores of over 65 per cent iron content being worked in the upper Rio Doce valley and around Belo Horizonte, where an industrial complex has grown up unusually far from the Brazilian coast. Mining is carried on mostly by the government owned Vale do Rio Doce company, which ships out much ore by rail either along the one-metre gauge Rio Doce line to Vitória or on a smaller scale through the port of Rio. Total production of ore exceeds 30 million tons annually, 90 per cent of it moving out through Vitória. Half a million tons of manganese are also produced per annum from the Minas deposits. In this state, the attraction of gold and diamonds has created a mining tradition over the centuries. Thousands of *garimpeiros*, single miners with no capital or machinery, wash

Fig. 43 *Iron and steel making capacity in the Industrial Core, 1970*

alluvial gravels in the remote hills of the state, many of them nourished by the hope of striking rich, but few ever rising above a subsistence level of living.

Although textiles are still the main employing group of industries in Brazil, steel is more important in terms of its wages bill and links to other industries. Many of the dynamic growth industries, owned by foreign firms or multinational corporations, are dependent on this steel industry and located in relation to it. The map pattern may be systematized as follows: 1. The non-integrated steel furnaces, rolling and shaping mills, in an aureole around São Paulo city; these were often set up as backward linkages by engineering firms which sought their own supply of steel. For example, one firm set up a steel works to make steel for its sugar-mill machinery industry. Many firms make special steels, requiring electric furnaces and using the abundant hydroelectric power supplied from stations on the escarpment to east of the city. 2. Fifty small blast furnaces making pig iron in the west of Minas province, based on cheap charcoal from the natural forests. 3. The large integrated iron and steel plants, government-owned in part, modern plants gaining economies of scale and through their use of modern technology. The main mills are CSN, at Volta Redonda, COSIPA at Santos, and USIMINAS at Ipatinga on the Doce.* The pull of urban markets has been important for COSIPA and Volta Redonda, charcoal and power for Ipatinga, but the main location factor has been the political pull of each state, São Paulo obtaining the Santos plant, Minas Gerais the Ipatinga one, and Volta Redonda representing an earlier (1940s', rather than 1950s') compromise between Rio and São Paulo, with a special mission in solving unemployment problems of the depression-hit Paraíba valley after 1930.

SÃO PAULO

Figure 42 shows the centrality of the two cities (of São Paulo and Rio de Janeiro) to all Brazil apart from the distinctive Nordeste. Of the two metropolises, São Paulo is the younger, an upstart of only 30000 in 1872 when Rio had

275000 inhabitants, but since about 1955 São Paulo has been the larger, with 7.2 million in 1975 to 4.9 million in Rio (metropolitan areas had 10 million and 8.3 million respectively). São Paulo is a visibly dynamic city, with great concrete skyscrapers in the centre and constant rebuilding on old sites (plate 34). São Paulo has always looked to the interior, as its plateau position suggests, depending on products from a wide hinterland, and producing goods for that hinterland and for itself. Industrially it is complex, but the car industry stands out as one notable concentration: Volkswagen plants here produce over half the Brazilian output of cars. Textiles, electrical goods, chemicals, paper, cement and leather working are all large industries, both in the city and in a number of industrial suburbs.

The city's population is varied in origin: many of the Paulistas are immigrants who came penniless to the coffee fazendas in the nineteenth century from all parts of Europe. These Spaniards, Germans, Jews and other groups from eastern Europe have been joined by an important group of Japanese. All migrants are represented in the city's commercial and industrial middle classes. Apart from this human resource, the city has advantages in its infrastructure for industry, including excellent transport connections to the interior of the state and along the coast to Rio, its own outlet in the port of Santos and a better power supply than any other Brazilian city, soon to be augmented by the plants shared with Paraguay at Ilha Solteira and Itaipú on the Paraná, the latter begun in 1974 and to have a capacity of 12000 MW.

RIO DE JANEIRO

This is a city of greater dignity, with a tradition of culture and the sophisticated society proper to a capital with long links with Europe. Its wealth grew on the sugar mills and naval garrison of the seventeenth century, and was augmented in the eighteenth by trade in gold and diamonds, which were brought out from the hinterland in Minas. It finally came into glory with its designation as capital in 1763, replacing Bahia. It still has some aspects of the traditional colonial city in its social patterns, including a large number of luxury dwellings near the centre rather than in the suburbs.

* CSN is the Companhia Nacional Siderúrgica; COSIPA is the Companhia Siderúrgica Paulista; USIMINAS the Uniao Siderúrgica de Minas Gerais.

34 São Paulo — the city centre, with its many levels of vertical development, a result of its explosively rapid growth

Compared to São Paulo, Rio exhibits only steady growth rates though it is still in second place in absolute population growth. The process of giving way to São Paulo was already begun when it was accelerated from 1956 by the beginning of Brasília, which quickly took away its federal government function, the last ministry to leave, protesting as it did so at relegation to the uncivilized interior, being the Foreign Ministry. Banking and financial operations, as well as the home offices of many large companies, remain in the city, and would seem more likely to move to São Paulo than to the interior.

Rio's industries are widely diversified, with textiles, clothing, printing and publishing, and food industries, employing the largest numbers,

though even in publishing and printing São Paulo exceeds Rio in quantity if not in quality, with a larger circulation volume for her dailies and a larger list of books published every year. Though not comparable with São Paulo's, Rio has a small steel industry, the Cosigua company, which is to be built up to 1.5 million tons per annum in 1981, using seaborne coal as does São Paulo. But Rio's energy base is weaker than that of her sister and this situation will change only marginally with the building of two more nuclear power stations at nearby Angra dos Reis, following Brazil's first such venture which is already in operation there.

As in São Paulo the suburbs, mostly in the area beyond the old federal district, have most of the new industrial growth, which seeks the open space totally unavailable in crowded Rio. Heroic efforts have been made to overcome the awkward geography of Rio's site: swamps near sealevel; *morros*, the sharp steepsided sugar-loaf mountains typical of tropical erosion eating into a long-weathered plateau surface; and connections to offshore islands — all have been conquered by means of tunnels, bridges and pumping systems. The new bridge to Niteroi across Guanabara bay is the latest in a long line of similar feats.

FAVELAS

Rio's shanty towns have an interesting relation to topography, occupying as the map (fig. 44) shows the edges of *morros* throughout the city. In contrast with other South American cities,

favelas are not peripheral, but are scattered through the city, spreading out with it through time, and growing with particular strength from about 1940, so that they now hold over 10 per cent of the urban population, despite clearance programmes. *Favelas* are often grouped near industrial zones, where their occupants may work, near the rail lines on land undesirable for building, and on marshy land, as well as on the *morros*, in fact wherever there has been unused and accessible land in the city. *Favelas* are a symbol of the life of the poor in Rio and in all Brazil; the *cariocas* (Rio dwellers) also have other expressions of their interest and vitality, notably the February carnival, essentially and in origin a feast of the poor of the city, with many African elements in its dances and songs.

Fig. 44 Location and growth of favelas in Rio de Janeiro

THE SOUTH

The southern panhandle of Brazil may be treated alongside the Southeast because of several similarities it has with it, including its high per capita wealth, good resource base, and situation on the important river Plate—São Paulo axis, which ensures its long-term importance for trade and industry.

This is non-tropical Brazil, and because it lies mostly above 200 m altitude, frost and snow are possible as well as changeable middle-latitude weather brought in along the coast from the south. Climatic uniqueness in Brazil, the resource of the south, allows temperate crops, such as wheat, soy beans and potatoes, to be produced, middle-latitude grasslands in Rio Grande do Sul which support large beef herds of cattle, and middle-latitude forests of Paraná pine (*Araucaria angustifolia*) and other species occurring in single species stands. Temperateness of climate no doubt helped in attracting the immigrants who came to the southern states during the nineteenth century and allowing their successful settlement. It must be admitted however that the immediate coastal belt where the immigrants first landed was subtropical in character and more suitable for crops of tobacco and sugar cane, still grown there, than for North European crops.

Landforms are dominated by the great Paraná plateau, with its sharp east-facing scarp and gentle tilt to the west. The coastal plain is tiny in the north but in Rio Grande prograding has built out the plain and forms the Lagoa dos Patos, behind sand bars and dunes, and the Lagoa Mirim which extends south into Uruguay. Behind these shallow lakes, the southern plain is continued as the campanha, an open prairie.

Settlement and agriculture

Original settlement was very thin in this border region. A few trading posts were scattered along the trails used to bring cattle north to the great fair at Sorocaba near São Paulo, from the southern grasslands, including some essentially military settlements, to consolidate claims on this southern territory, which was also claimed by Spain. Colônia do Sacramento in Uruguay was the southernmost of the line of posts marking Brazilian pretensions.

Agricultural colonization dates only from the early nineteenth century, and had a slow start, with a few small settlements in favoured parts of the Rio Grande and Santa Catarina coast, first by Germans, then by Italians, who were forced to take up the nearby areas of the plateau after 1870 when the valleys were filled, followed by Slavic groups who moved still further inland and into Paraná state. Though the numbers of settlers were small, their influence was important, for they established in Brazil for the first time a small-farmer and owner-operator type of farming, on plots of 20-50 ha, an economy quite different from the great cattle *fazendas* of the South.

MIGRANTS

There was something of a mutual exclusion between cattle men and cultivators, for the new settlers chose the woodland, unwanted by the cattle ranchers who relied on natural grasslands for their herds. The new men did more than change land use; they introduced their own types of house construction, as in southern Chile, and built carefully, with fences, windmills, sheds and other buildings designed for permanent occupation, in contrast with the shifting agriculture which was hitherto the only common form of cultivation by small farmers. Crop rotation and the use of animal manure allowed this permanent occupation of a single plot of land. Wandering into the interior, some of the new immigrants eventually gave up their European way of farming and became *caboclos* like the mestizos of the region, using no capital or machinery, but these were a minority and the region as a whole has a high level of productivity and farm organization; farm cooperatives are a good index of farmer education and technical levels, and the South has 500 of them, or 30 per cent of the Brazilian total. Extension agencies also provide a better service in this region than in any other.

RANCHERS

Estancias have remained the dominant land users on the *campanha* of Rio Grande do Sul, great cattle ranches worked like their neighbours on the other side of the Uruguayan border by a few *gauchos* (the term of all the Pampas lands for the cowboy, rather than *vaqueiro* as further north) who herd the animals but provide little in the way of hygiene or care. Some *estancieros* have improved their herds with pedigree stock but the grass quality is low as it is natural cover in a subtropical environment with little attempt at seeding or improvement. Carrying capacity is very low, less than one animal per hectare on many ranches, and the economic size of ranch is thus many thousands of hectares.

FORESTS

A major mineral resource is the southern forest. This is of commercial value because generally composed of large stands of only one species, and the Paraná pine forests, on the cool dry heights above 1000 m, are of particular interest, forming the basis of a useful export trade in timber. All three southern states produce large quantities of wood, though the most valuable, and much of the Paraná pine, is from Rio Grande. Paper mills are most important in Paraná, though new developments are extending this industry into Santa Catarina. All Brazilian forests have a 'collecting' economy, based in the Amazon on Brazil nuts, in the Northeast on carnauba palms or babaçu. In the South it is Indian tea, *erva mate* (in Spanish *yerba mate*), which is still collected from wild trees in Rio Grande do Sul, and to a lesser extent in other southern states, as well as from plantations of the tree in a few places.

Another mineral resource is coal, and all of Brazil's five million tons' annual production comes from the South, mostly from Santa Catarina, secondly from Rio Grande. Production is being encouraged to try to reduce Brazilian dependence on imports of fuel from overseas. More important than the coal is the hydro power, available on the Paraná tributaries such as the Iguacu, soon to be tapped at Salto de Santiago and Salto Osorio on this river.

The cities

Pôrto Alegre, Florianopolis and Curitiba, the three state capitals, are thriving cities, particularly the first, a city whose metropolitan area has 1.8 million (1975), and where construction is proceeding at a rate only exceeded in São Paulo and Rio, much of it being factories for the budding industries. Pôrto Alegre is a town of relatively rich people, compared with the rest of Brazil, with many cars and few shanty towns. Its factories make engineering products such as wires and cables, machine tools, items using special steels, as well as products for a growing

farm sector, such as farm machinery and fertilizers. It has access to the coastal trade via a six-metre channel. Caxias do Sul, a few kilometres north of Pôrto Alegre, Novo Hamburgo and São Leopoldo share in this industrial growth, with engineering works, textile mills, *bodegas* and flour mills. These industries have grown up from the capital investments of the small independent farmers, who have thus proved the advantage of their type of farming over one dominated by large landowners with tenants.

Florianopolis is a more provincial centre, with wooden rather than concrete houses, an administrative rather than industrial centre, and a hinterland which is nearly all plateau, having little of the rich coastal plain. Curitiba, state capital to Paraná state, is well-placed to administer the plateau section, though this position (at 905 m altitude) is a disadvantage for the coastal region, and a separate major urban centre has emerged at Paranagua. This port has recently seen a new burst of activity because of the new trade from Paraguay, which country has free-port facilities at this site. Passengers can also travel by bus from Asunción in one day to this point. Much of Paranagua's trade is now international and the value of trade makes it second only to Santos in Brazil. Other transport links are also being developed in the Panhandle, never formerly well connected to any other area. The rail link Pôrto Alegre—São Paulo is being improved and shortened in length, and the coastal road has been paved over its whole distance to São Paulo. The international road and rail links to Uruguay, Argentina and Paraguay are all being rapidly upgraded.

PROSPECTS FOR THE CORE REGION

A Brazilian megalopolis?

In terms of physical resources, the Core Region, South and Southeast, is better provided than other parts of the country. Even its soil, located in more temperate belts, is less prone to erosion and depletion than further north. These resources, but more the human resource which is conveyed in the names of the great cities, serve to reinforce the centripetal dynamics of socio-economic evolution in the country. Both labour and capital are evidently attracted more readily to the centre than to any peripheral region. The reasons for this dynamism of the centre cannot be investigated in detail here, but they are the same as those noted for other countries in the continent, and some account of them is given in the chapters on population and industrial development.

Looking ahead to predict future population and related patterns is particularly difficult in a country like Brazil, where population growth rate is nearly 3 per cent, where the modal family size is 6-9 persons, and where migration to cities is continuing apace. It is confidently, and by many Brazilians proudly, predicted that the present population of 125 million will reach 210 million by the year 2000. Of these, some 70 million are likely to be in the Rio—São Paulo — Belo Horizonte triangle, the Megalopolis of Brazil, with three of Brazil's millionaire cities. The others are Recife, Salvador and Pôrto Alegre, and one vision of the Brazilian Megalopolis is a 1600-km stretch along the coast including all these cities, but this seems to distort the idea of Megalopolis too much; the urbanized area loses its unity.

On the other hand, to think of this triangle as a single conurbation would be wrong; it is 550 km on the longest leg, São Paulo to Belo Horizonte,

and there will be open ground over large areas for farming, recreation and forest in the Serra do Mar and Serra da Mantiqueira. It may quite definitely be thought of as a unit for considerations such as atmospheric pollution, sewerage disposal, water supply and consumption patterns, and land use competition, like its North American equivalent on the New York to Washington axis, and it will present equal problems in congestion and planning optimal land-use patterns.

It is perhaps disturbing to think of a basically centripetal growth of population and economy when the oecumene of the nation is being stretched out to new frontiers in the west and north. Yet this centrifugal movement is to be viewed as part of the same process of growth which causes massing in the centre; the higher the pyramid being built, the broader must be the base. This metaphor is not the ideal one, for the shape of the curve of population densities, from distant frontiers to metropolitan areas, is likely to be strongly concave; more appropriate then is that of the giant selvas tree, for example the Brazil-nut tree, with a narrow but very high peak, flourishing in the sunlight and nourishing itself from roots spreading over a great area of the forest floor.

16. The Guianas

Perhaps the most obvious examples of colonial economy in Latin America are to be found in the Guianas. In these countries, there was a straight-forward, uncomplicated development of planta-tion economy from the time of earliest European settlement, to feed European mouths with American sugar and other foodstuffs. There was never any need to modify this economy by adjusting to local labour availability or local customs, nor by any orientation to local urban markets or commercial centres. Instead, in the Guianas, European capital and African labour were brought together in a new land where all social and economic options were open to them. Logically, they chose the best land for production and for accessibility from the coast, and established the plantation economy, an efficient means of producing commercial sur-pluses of valuable tropical farm products. The forms and organizations established in the plantations are still responsible today for many patterns in the man-made environment of the Guianas.

SETTLEMENTS: THE COASTAL FOCUS

To the first explorers, Guiana was a name given to all the lands from Orinoco to Amazon, but within this great stretch of country only the three former north European colonies, British, Dutch and French Guiana, are considered here. By their political and cultural attachments to northern Europe, these countries have come to have a distinct identity, and are certainly quite different from neighbouring territories in Brazil or Venezuala.

The principal Spanish base on mainland South America was at Darien, in Panama, far from Guiana, where there were no strong attractions, either in the form of docile Indians or as gold or precious metals. The Darien base was early confirmed by its accessibility to the Pacific and by the discovery of Peru, leaving the Guianas without action till the 1590s, when Sir Walter Raleigh, hearing of gold in the interior, explored the Orinoco in search of a hidden El Dorado; in all probability this mythical source of gold was rumoured by the Spanish to divert Raleigh's attention from more profitable areas such as the Peruvian wealth which they were exploiting themselves in the Andes. In any case, no gold was found, and no further luck was had in English attempts at settlement in the decade from 1600 to 1610, made on the river Oyapok.

Permanent settlements date only from the 1610s, when Dutchmen established themselves on the Mazaruni, incorporating these colonies with others elsewhere in the Indies under the Dutch West India Company, which used the *patroon* system. This social—administrative institution gave feudal rights to any merchant or landowner who would bring in settlers and buy land, and operated as well here as in New York State area within what was to be the United States. Dutch settlement centred first on the island fort of Kijk-over-al, in the Mazaruni river, and produced sugar and tobacco. Settlements grew in 1640s, with the colonists driven out of Brazil, and the Pomeroon and Essequibo rivers were settled and put to sugar. In these lands, the coastal area, a flat and lowlying malarial plain with frequent flooding, was shunned from the beginning. Instead, settlements were made on the edge of the plain or even within the sterile White Sands zone behind it.

In Surinam, attempts were made by the English and French to settle in the 1630s, but permanent colonies date from 1650. Here the success factor seems to have been management by men with experience of the tropics, for the founder was Lord Willoughby, governor of Barbados, who made a start by establishing good relations with the Amerindians.* This had been a major stumbling block in previous settlement attempts. An important contingent of colonists was the Jewish one, coming from Brazil along with the expelled Dutch.

The coastal frontier
By the eighteenth century, flourishing colonies on the rivers, especially those of present-day Guyana, the Essequibo, Pomeroon, Berbice, and Demerara, but also the Surinam, were established under Dutch rule. In the French section no poldering or irrigation was carried out as in the other areas, and agricultural production was slight. In the second half of the century, growing demand for sugar and cotton required good soils and African slave labour was employed on a large scale to extend coastwards the polder and irrigation system. At the same time, the poor soils of the White Sands zone could not support prolonged intensive exploitation and the land here was abandoned and reverted to forest. The centre of economic activity thus moved downstream, Stabroek (Georgetown from 1812) on the lower Demerara becoming capital in 1783, to replace Kijk-over-al, while on the Berbice, settlement moved down eighty km to New Amsterdam in the same period.

Effectively, the move downstream onto the new polders was a colonization towards the coast, the opposite of that conducted towards the interior in most of the other countries of the

continent. It may be regarded as a technical frontier, subject to poldering abilities, rather than a small-farmer spread in search of open lands, and for this reason it had no democratizing influence in terms of land ownership and frontier society. The polders were all taken up by plantations, excluding the small farmer even if he had been present in numbers sufficient to demand more farming land.

Ethnic mixture
Population structure began to change with the large slave influx (over 300000 into Surinam alone) and with additions of European origin. Dutch colonies were open to all nationalities from 1738, in contrast with Spanish and Portuguese areas which excluded foreigners. In the nineteenth century abolition of slavery forced a search for new labour, as the ex-slaves often left the plantations as soon as they were free to do so. This labour crisis was solved by bringing in indentured servants from southeast Asia, poor peasants who were willing to accept tough conditions of work. They came on five-year contracts, passage paid but with no pay until half the contract period was over. Indians, Chinese and Javanese all came to Surinam in great numbers. In French Guiana, few labourers could be attracted because of the evil reputation of the colony, which was used as a penal settlement. A few indentured labourers came to the Guianas from Europe, most notably Portuguese from Madeira; these soon moved from plantations to town, as did the Chinese, becoming shopkeepers and merchants. In all, this influx of migrants pushed the Amerindian population far into the backcountry, where it forms a small and independent minority living a semi-subsistence economic life and enjoying its own non-western culture.

PHYSICAL GEOGRAPHY

The Guianas are formed out of the ancient Guiana Shield, a block once attached to the Brazilian Shield but separated in the Tertiary when the Amazon basin came into being. There is little evidence of tectonic activity, for the most ancient sediments, the sandstones of the Pakaraima mass, have been flatlying since their deposition in Precambrian times. These sandstones are responsible for *mesa* landforms, with sheer rocky

* The term Amerindian, used in Guyana, will be used here to distinguish American Indians from the immigrants from the Indian subcontinent who came into Guiana as indentured servants in the nineteenth century.

Fig. 45 Physical map of the Guianas

cliff edges, overlying a crystalline plateau which forms most of the interior, a hilly, heavily forested land. Fringing the shield is a narrow coastal plain, formed of marine mud, much of it washed along the coast from the Amazon mouth, a belt 15 to 80 km wide (fig. 45). It is in this narrow plain that 80 per cent of the people and practically all agricultural land is located. Locally there are savanna areas, on the White Sands and far into the interior, in the Rupununi.

Climatically, the region is equatorial, with year-round high temperatures and rainfall. Near the coast, the combination of heat and humidity is tolerable while sea breezes blow, which is for most of the time as the trades are fairly consistent here. In the interior, both rainfall and humidity are lower. Whereas 2250 mm annual

rainfall is common on the coast, interior mountains have around 1500 mm and Rupununi 1000 mm per annum.

RESOURCES

Agricultural land is concentrated near the coast because of the problems of erosion on steep slopes inland, and poor lateritic soils on the flatter areas, or unproductive soils of the White Sands region. Isolation and lack of any infrastructure are other obvious drawbacks. Mineral resources of the shield are however substantial. Over much of the interior there are broad surfaces of deep weathering and laterization, forming in some cases bauxite, a laterite with large amounts of aluminium oxide. Currently these ores are mined only on the edge of the plain, but their existence is known from surveys of the interior as well. Apart from bauxite, there has been irregular working of other minerals though generally without any mechanization and thus not tapping major ore bodies.

The mountains harbour another resource, hydroelectric power, already tapped at dams for alumina and aluminium production in Surinam. A major difficulty here is the lack of natural deep basins to contain reservoirs, at least in areas accessible to the coast. Fossil fuels are not found, though there is mounting interest in offshore deposits of petroleum which have already been identified.

GUYANA

The neo-plantation economy

The former colony of British Guiana became a sovereign state in 1966, remaining a member of the British Commonwealth till 1970, since when it has been a republic with a markedly Socialist regime. Like the other Guianas, one obvious characteristic of the nation is its varied population, dominated by Creoles or Africans who make up some 30 per cent of the total, and Asians who form 50 per cent, though exercising less influence in the community than their numbers suggest. Portuguese and other European peoples form small minorities. Amerindians are about 5 per cent of the population, geographically isolated from all other groups in the interior. Guyana is the most important of the three former colonies, in terms of population size and economy, with a fair variety of export products though dominated by bauxite and alumina.

Physically this is the most diversified of the Guianas, sharing with Venezuela the large region of dissected sandstone tablelands which present superb cliff scenery and waterfalls such as the famous Kaietur Falls, and many still little-known ones in the deep interior. There are four principal physical regions, the first being the coastal plain of alluvium and marine mud, with associated backswamps and lakes. Behind this lies the leached White Sands belt, with savanna and scrub forest, at its widest on the Berbice river. Behind this again is the forested shield country, with overlying sandstones of the Pakaraima and other ranges. In the far southwest the Rupununi forms a last region of open savanna plains.

The human landscape

The drama of nature cannot be matched by man's efforts in Guyana, restricted to a narrow strip of land, but making a definite impact in this limited zone. Flat land has suited the plantation economy based on sugar which has proved more stable here than elsewhere in the Guianas. A landscape of ordered, straightline patterns, both for settlement and agriculture, is the norm throughout the plantation area. The city of Georgetown is similarly on an open, rectangular plan of precise lines, though its houses are not for the most part of any great age, as fires have repeatedly destroyed the light wooden buildings on low brick bases. In aspect, the town is like a southern United States county town, with two-storey verandahed houses, spacious treelined streets and a slightly somnolent air.

Economic infrastructure

A principal infrastructural element is the water

COMPARATIVE STATISTICS FOR THE GUIANAS

	Guyana	Surinam	French Guiana
Population 1978	820 000	374 000	66 000
Area in sq km	215 000	163 000	91 000
GNP per capita (1972 US dollars)	550	2 110	2 340
Exports f.o.b. (million US dollars 1977)	178	277	7
Imports c.i.f. (million US dollars 1977)	337	262 (1975)	144
Percent arable land	1.0	0.3	0.0

Sources: United Nations Statistical Yearbook *1979 (New York, 1979)*, and World Bank Atlas 1979 *(Washington, 1979)* system, including sea wall, drainage and irrigation ditches. Flooding by the sea is possible for eight or more kilometres inland, and further inland still, river flooding must be guarded against. The present sea wall was built between 1874 and 1882, its concrete and stone replacing and augmenting earlier earth walls. Through the sea wall, sluices or kokers allow the exit of fresh water from drainage ditches; they open at low tide to allow drainage and close to keep out the sea at high tide. In addition, steam pumps replacing nineteenth-century windmills are used to eliminate excess river water. Behind the sea wall, estates run back in long lines from the sea and river fronts, backed by a second wall to keep out excess river water. Behind the back walls, accumulated river and rain water form shallow lakes, known as conservancies since they are a water reserve for the irrigation of the plantation lands.

Control of all water works comes under a separate government department which coordinates all local systems. This department has recently been active in increasing the reserves available in the conservancies, with the special aim of extending the land area for rice fields. This policy is certainly increasing production, though only absorbing a small part of the excess rural labour force.

Apart from the water works, infrastructure is sadly lacking. Only one decent road is in existence, along the coast, and even this is not completely paved. Inland, transport depends on the rivers, or on state air lines which use light aeroplanes and makeshift airfields. A railway, claiming to be the oldest in South America, runs from Georgetown to a point opposite New Amsterdam, and private lines run short distances between mines and rivers, but these do not add up to a system.

Agriculture

While most agricultural land is in small farms, typically under four hectares and worked by peasant farmers, about 20 per cent belongs to twelve great sugar plantations of over 400 ha; these are the remnants of formerly extensive plantations which occupied nearly all farm land in the colony. They are no longer traditional plantations, but neo-plantations, where few workers are employed and mechanization is well advanced, using modern technology.

Sugar is grown as a monoculture on the great estates. Machinery is used for preparing ditches and ridging the land when too wet and in need of drainage, and fertilizers and pesticides are applied from the air (plate 35). Thus labour requirements are low and irregular, most being needed for cane cutting with the traditional cutlass, when temporary hands are taken on to supplement the small permanent labour force. Sugar-cane is grown continuously for eight to nine years and then put to flood fallow, land being flooded for several months to add new fertile alluvial topsoil. The product, bulky cane, is brought by barge trains along estate canals to the sugar mills within the estate, then coarse unrefined sugar from these mills is taken by coaster to the Sugar Terminal at Georgetown for loading onto ships and export, making a major contribution to national foreign trade earnings.

Most sugar is grown on the plantations of one firm, Booker McConnell, a British company whose interests extend through subsidiary companies into manufacturing and service activities. In sugar, it controls all production from ditch laying and cleaning to the transport overseas in ocean-going ships. Most of its plantations are concentrated around the lower Demerara river, close to Georgetown. Concentration of plantations under a single foreign owner emphasizes the plantation-orientation of the whole economy, and makes it more dependent, like any colonial economy, on market conditions, enterprise and politics in a distant country.*

Rice, a staple of all the coastal peoples and now an export crop as well (though still second to sugar), is produced on 100000 ha by the Indian small farmers who came bringing the grain from East Asia in the nineteenth century and have always grown it as a subsistence crop. Two crops a year are possible if water is available, or alternatively the land may be grazed over by cattle after a single harvest. Besides rice, there is small-scale market gardening and some citrus production around the towns. All these farming patterns are however subordinate to sugar, the leading farm product.

Away from the coastal area there are other patterns. In the deep interior forests, the Amerindians live on shifting cultivation just as they do in neighbouring Venezuela and Brazil, in

---

* Booker's interests in Guyana have now (1977) been taken over by the government.

35 Ditch digging on a sugar estate, Guyana

good ecological adjustment to the land, though the balance is now threatened by the advance of commercial farming from the coast. The only commercial area of production is the Rupununi, where there are large ranches shipping out carcasses of cattle reared on the coarse savanna grasses, nowadays using air freight rather than the long overland trail which still exists between this region and the coast.

Minerals

Guyana has a long history as a source of precious metals, and gold is still panned in the interior and diamonds taken out of the Pakaraima Mountains, though in tiny quantities and by single miners, the pork-knockers as they are called because of their former reliance on salt pork rations. In modern times timber has been a modest contributor to exports and there is a large

untapped resource of good hardwoods. Only the greenheart, still used in dock and harbour works, is important among the timbers. Manganese is an important modern ore, produced in the Matthews Ridge area of the north, but bauxite is the main mineral of value, developed since the First World War by the Aluminium Company of Canada (Alcan), at Mackenzie, now renamed Linden, on the Demerara river. A smaller unit is on the Berbice at Kwakwani. Bauxite is widespread and other less accessible areas will no doubt be exploited in time. In 1961, an alumina plant was set up at Linden, so that bauxite and alumina are now both exported, and rank among the principal export products.

At present Guyana has an agreement with Trinidad to send alumina there to be smelted at a new smelter using natural gas. But longer-term plans would seem to favour smelting within

36 A punt train on a sugar estate, which takes the bulky produce to cane mills along the irrigation canals

Guyana itself, because of its considerable power potential, and there is a plan to utilize a site at Latipu on the upper, mountain course of the Mazaruni river, for a large dam with hydro-electric output eventually at 1500 to 2000 mega-watts. Even with a Guyanese smelter at Linden, about half of this power would be excess to national requirements and other power-hungry industries would presumably be the market, as neighbouring parts of Venezuela are supplied by the Guri dam on the Caroní, and Surinam with a big new complex planned on the Courantyne can scarcely be expected to import electricity.

Gearing to foreign markets, large units of operation, small labour requirements and limited processing of the minerals, make for a mineral 'enclave' economy comparable to plantation agriculture. Although Alcan and Reynolds were nationalized in 1971, refining and smelting have not been expanded for want of capital and inter-national companies have expanded bauxite operations in other parts of the world.

Social structure and the urbanization process

Guyana was thinly peopled by an Amerindian population base, over which have been laid African and Asian elements, while Dutch, British and other Europeans occupied the towns. Much has been made of the diversity in ethnic and racial backgrounds by observers of the Guyana scene, and the topic has had a political aspect because of some polarization of political feeling according to ethnic groupings. Currently the dominant ethnic group is the African, which supports the government of Forbes Burnham. Progressive integration of the different groups is being fostered and it is claimed that the old rivalries are now being eliminated.

GROUP MIGRATION WAVES

Following independence, some Europeans left the country. This has created a vacuum in the top echelons of power in politics and commerce, to be rapidly filled by people of African origin, who have moved up out of lower middle class jobs in offices and small shops in the towns, jobs which they have tended to monopolize during the first half of this century. As these urbanites have moved up the economic and social ladder, they have in turn been replaced by East Indians in the small shops and offices, and by the sons of peasant farmers or labourers on the plantations who have acquired a minimum education and who have insufficient land to support them well in agriculture. On the plantations themselves, the large East Indian group is still dominant, itself somewhat divided between Moslem and Hindu groups. These are the most traditional and least educated groups, holding onto a near peasant existence, and with least experience in the new land of America.

Group migrations may of course be seen as nothing more than the general process of rural to urban migration going on all over Latin America, but in this example we can see that the migration is not a disordered mass movement into towns but one affecting specific groups with greater or lesser intensity according to qualifications and group background. Similar regularities of migration patterns may no doubt be seen in the other countries.

THE AMERINDIANS: THE AKAWAIO CASE

Group migrations form a chain reaction involving all groups except the Amerindians, who have been artificially excluded from social interaction by legislation dating from the early part of this century. This legislation was enacted with the laudable intentions of protecting the group from the exploitation of their labour which was then beginning to emerge, but it served in the long run to isolate them both racially and culturally from the newer occupants of the land.

One major question is land rights. In 1966, when Britain handed over to the rulers of the new country, one condition was that the Amerindians be given legal rights to the land they occupied. A commission was set up to investigate and report on this matter, which it did in 1969,

recommending title grants to many tribes, but little was done because of a reported difficulty in surveying the lands in question. Among the tribes were the 4000 members of the Akawaio tribe in the upper Mazaruni country, the colourful hill country northeast of mount Roraima. This tribe is threatened by the proposed construction of the new dam referred to above, at Latipu, which if built will have a reservoir of 250000 ha, covering almost all the tribal lands, and the central government seems determined to proceed with the project despite powerful reasons for not doing so. One is the fact that the Akawaio will lose their lands. Another is the availability of other sites, notably one on the lower Mazaruni, generating less power but quite sufficient for Guyanese demands over the next decade and causing no disturbance to Amerindians. Yet another reason for leaving the upper Mazaruni alone is that it lies near a frontier disputed with Venezuala, where there is a moratorium signed in 1970 and forbidding any unilateral action to enhance one country's claims on the land.

Questions concerning Guyana's Amerindians must be expected to arise with increasing frequency now as a policy of integration replaces the former quarantine in which the tribes were placed. So far, as in Brazil, humanitarian concerns in this integration have not been conspicuous and land greed on the part of modern farmers and even central governments must be feared by the defenceless tribes.

SURINAM

A plantation socio-economic structure was established in the mid-seventeenth century in the lower valleys of the Surinam and Cottica rivers. It developed principally after 1667, when the territory was given to Holland as recompense for New York, which the British had captured three years earlier. Today, Surinam shows the hand of Dutch architects and engineers in its tiny settled strip, which has never expanded since the eighteenth century and has even retreated coastwards from the interior edge of the plain.

Paramaribo, the capital, has Dutch eighteenth-century styles in some public buildings, copied faithfully in wood. Dutch influence is also present in the straight lines of villages in the plain, though only the newer properties have truly rectangular outlines, and old plantation lands have been subdivided along irregular division lines.

As in Guyana, a narrow coastal plain is backed by slightly rolling or flat countryside of dissected old terraces, the White Sands zone, with a savanna or scrub cover (fig. 46). The back-country is the gneiss and granite of the shield, thickly forested with hardwoods. Southwards the land is higher and reaches over 500 metres in the Tumac Humac mountains on the Brazilian border. Main rivers in the dense stream network are the Courantyne or Corantijn on the Guyana boundary, the Coppename, Saramacca, Suriname, and on the French Guiana border the Marowijne (Maroni).

Settlement and population

The Dutch plantation colony enjoyed relative prosperity until 1712, when French corsairs raided along the coast and started a negative trend in the colony's fortunes. Negroes were taken from the plantations by their masters to hide from the pirates, and some escaped from slavery at this time, never to return, but forming instead an independent group which raised the plantations and liberated more slaves, thus swelling the ranks of a Bush Negro group which survives to this day. After slavery, indentured labour from India and Java came in, but planta-tions were unable to progress because of Dutch refocussing on a commercially more interesting area, Java, with its rich soils that could readily be put to sugar. Settlement in Surinam declined, plantations were abandoned in inland parts, and the country came into this century with few prospects, eventually to be resuscitated by a new economic colonialism, that of bauxite.

Population patterns today are somewhat distinct from those of Guyana, for sand and shell ridges break up the settled area of the coastal plain; in addition, settlement tends to penetrate farther up the rivers than in Guyana, for these rivers give quite good access to the interior. In Guyana, they are obstructed at the inner edge of the plain by rapids impeding navigation such as that of the river steamers used in Surinam. Sixty per cent of the population lives in and around Paramaribo, and in a few small towns linked to it by the coast road. Paramaribo's population is very mixed, including Europeans of all kinds, as well as Chinese, Indians and Javanese. As in Guyana, a selective migration process has taken some groups into the city, leaving others, later comers, in the rural areas, most notably the Javanese, but also many Indian small farmers.

GOVERNMENT POLICY AND RACIAL MIXTURES

In the remoter inland areas there are definite racial groupings, partly because of a government policy which allowed these groups to form villages and take over estate lands when aban-doned, in order not to let them revert to forest. Thus, for example, there are villages on the middle Suriname, Saramacca and Tapanahony rivers, inhabited solely by Bush Negroes; in the far interior there are many purely Amerindian villages.

Bush Negroes however make up only 8 per cent of the population and Amerindians only 2 per cent. In general, a broad cultural unity is being imposed on the diverse ethnic groups by modern education and compulsory instruction in the Dutch language for all young people. The melting-pot effect is particularly strong in the urban areas. National costumes and the old slave tongue which was commonly used in the seven-teenth and eighteenth centuries have disappeared in the standardization of modern life.

The mineral-exporting economy

Surinam, far more than Guyana, is a one-product economic unit. 80 per cent of its exports are made up of bauxite and alumina, compared to 45 per cent in Guyana. If Guyana may be cate-gorized as a neo-plantation economy, Surinam has a mining economy organized in plantation manner, that is, production by largely foreign firms, for foreign markets, with heavy invest-ment of foreign capital and relatively little labour. Investment in mining is of course the more striking because in the country generally there is very little capital investment, and the economic infrastructure is tiny. Roads, railways, ports and power from electricity or whatever source are poorly provided. One major hydro-power development has been made on the Suriname river above Paramaribo, but it is in connection with industrial needs for aluminium production and would scarcely have been developed for urban consumer needs. Paramaribo has the only modern port, with improved facilities in recent years, financed largely from Europe because of Surinam's links to the EEC through Holland.

MINING

Bauxite is the lifeblood of the modern economy, providing 35 per cent of GDP but 80 per cent of exports in recent years. Surinam has advanced from being a mere bauxite shipper to aluminium and alumina manufacturer, which serves to bring some diversification, but still within a framework dependent on one basic product.

Bauxite was first developed at Moengo, near the French Guiana border, after the First World War. In 1941, Paranam (fig. 46) became the principal mining site on the Suriname river, using coastal bauxites as at Moengo. In both areas production is at low cost because the ores are rich, containing over 50 per cent usable oxide,

Fig. 46 Bauxite and aluminium industries of Surinam

with only moderate overburden. A major change in the bauxite economy came in 1959, when the big Brokopondo project was put into action. This involved a dam on the Suriname river, generation of hydroelectricity for refining and smelting nearby at Paranam, and the production of alumina and aluminium for export, so that these products now far exceed bauxite in value of exports.

The Bakhuis Mountains development

Most recently, there have been important developments in the Bakhuis Mountains, in western Surinam, where a large lateritic cap of 45 per cent aluminium oxide is known and has been surveyed. This is to be developed by the Reynolds Metal Company of the United States, in partnership with the Surinam government. Ore will be sent by rail to Apoera on the Corantijn river and smelted there using hydro power from the Kabalebo, a tributary of the Corantijn.

This project, like the existing Brokopondo one, has a major potential ecological and economic effect, for the associated dams cause flooding of huge stretches of forest country, in the absence of deep basin-shaped valleys suited for storing water in a small space. A general impoverishment of wildlife in the area takes place, while in economic terms the huge lakes could have the effect of sterilizing the whole interior by putting a neutral or negative belt across the middle country, flooding land of little current value and with only a thin population, but possibly important to future generations. It is a symbol of the power of the bauxite kingdom that pre-emption of vast areas has been permitted and even encouraged by the authorities, and it is all too typical of countries at this modest level of development, that organized public opinion against the developments in mining has scarcely been voiced.

Possibly even more important in the case of Bakhuis is the fact that the Corantijn river borders with Guyana, and this latter country has threatened to take retaliatory action if the river's flow is affected, as it must be by any major scheme such as that planned.

Agriculture

Agricultural production is confined strictly to the coastal strip, and most land is in small farms,

principally for rice. The old plantation economy has disappeared. Paddy rice is grown along the whole coast, but most intensively around Paramaribo and in the Wageningen estate in the west, established in 1949 with Dutch assistance as a mechanized unit producing high-quality rice for export. Small farmers operating around Paramaribo for the town markets usually own less than 4 hectares of rice-land. Sugar, once the principal crop, is today grown only by two plantations. Coffee and cocoa, other former cash crops, are now also unimportant, though some commercial production is beginning to reappear, in banana and other fruit production for export to Europe.

FRENCH GUIANA

Beside Guyana and Surinam the French effort in their segment of the Guianas seems slight. Physical reasons for the lack of progress are not at once apparent, since the country continues the same zones found to the west in Surinam, though the coastal plain, the all-important lowland, becomes narrow and somewhat discontinuous. In the interior, the shield country is heavily forested for the most part though with savanna breaks, and access is made difficult by the rapids sections on the rivers.

In the early seventeenth century when British and Dutch Guiana were first settled, this section of the coast seems to have attracted no settlers. From the time the French acquired it in 1667, little was done until the nineteenth century and there are records of poor relations with the Amerindian population. From the mid-nineteenth century the French, in tacit admission of their failure to achieve civil settlement, set up penal colonies, both along the Maroni river near St Laurent and on the Iles du Salut, notorious for their harsh life and the difficulty of escape. The ill fame of the penal colonies was enough to sterilize the land for all further colonization for a hundred years. Some stories about the camps are doubtless inventions,* but it is true that the mainland camps on the Maroni where the

---

* The best-seller adventure story *Papillon* by Henri Charrière (translated by Patrick O'Brian, Rupert Hart-Davis, 1970) provides a fine picture of the islands in the 1930s as seen by a deportee who successfully escaped, and a picture which is accurate in all major respects.

workers were forced to cut hardwoods under terrible conditions, had very high death rates from infectious and deficiency diseases acquired from their poor diet. The islands, high-standing and dry and some ten kilometres offshore, were relatively healthy. In the Second World War it was agreed to close the penal settlements and the last prisoners were repatriated to France in 1946 and 1947. This left only the tiny population of 'Creoles', a Negro—White mix, plus some relatively pure Bush Negro blood originating in escapees from Surinam plantations during past centuries.

Economically the country, now elevated to the status of overseas *département* of France, is weak. Some immediate needs in food products are met, including sugar, manioc, maize and bananas. Fishing, especially shrimp fishing and packing for the United States market, is a relatively healthy industry. Minerals have little economic attraction as yet; gold prospectors have always gone off into the interior to find small amounts by panning, and there is untapped bauxite. In 1969 an agreement was reached between ALCOA, owner of the Surinamese Paranam workings, and a French company, for exploiting bauxite in French Guiana and smelting it in Surinam, a project which should boost the economies of both countries.

Another mineral resource with long-term possibilities is the hardwood forest; since the departure of the prisoners in the camps of the Maroni, little is done with the valuable rosewood and other cabinet woods of this zone. Finally, a substantial break away from the traditional exploitative economy has been made by the French in introducing a space centre, constructed at Kourou following closure of their facilities in Algeria in 1967. Kourou, a village-port, has grown up to be a town of nearly 10000 inhabitants.

OUTLOOK FOR THE GUIANAS

It might be expected that the Guianas, only recently promoted from effectively colonial status, would stand at considerable disadvantage in relation to countries with a longer history of independence. In fact, western colonialism has itself changed in the course of the last century and a half, and the Guianas, benefiting from more liberal and comprehending attitudes

towards colonial territories everywhere, have relatively little leeway to make up. Some educational, cultural and economic advances have been possible in the Dutch and British sectors.

It is obvious that the economy suffers from a heavy one-sidedness, especially in Surinam, and the most urgent current needs are to find new markets, new alliances, and new products to sell. Without them, these little states stand open to all the cold winds of market change in international preference.

On the external front the Guianas would appear to be disadvantaged as non-members of LAFTA. As in the case of internal affairs though, prospects are probably better than they seem for there are links to Europe which may preserve a special position for these countries in European markets. Surinam has had access to the EEC's regional development funds as an overseas territory of Holland and, although she became an independent republic in November 1975, may continue to reap some advantage of her special relationship. French Guiana is similarly provided for as an overseas *département* of France. As for Guyana, the British commitment remains important. Following the end of the Commonwealth Sugar Agreement in 1974, Britain negotiated guarantees of the EEC's intention to continue drawing substantial sugar supplies from Guyana and the Caribbean Commonwealth countries.

It is to the Caribbean that Guyana is now increasingly turning, and she has found an alternative to LAFTA through her membership of the Caribbean Community, CARICOM, which she joined together with the other Commonwealth states of the Caribbean under the Treaty of Chaguaramas of July 1973. Surinam, along with Haiti, has indicated her intention to join CARICOM. This community is far-reaching in its aims, including both a coordination of external and internal tariff levels in Common Market fashion, a regional industrialization plan combining, for example, Guyana bauxite with Trinidad natural gas to make aluminium, and a common foreign policy. This new alignment emphasizes the elements of common culture and economy of the Caribbean and the Guianas, and must be looked on as a promising development, though a doubt remains over Guyana's willingness to accept common cause with island territories whose aims could clash with her own. Her large land area and relatively low density of population must attract migrants from overcrowded Jamaica or Trinidad in the face of immigration restrictions in Britain and Europe. Indeed, the present African-dominated government has suggested bringing West Indians into Guyana, people who with their African background might be expected to support the present regime. But Guyana is numerically dominated by Asians, and this must cause friction if and when the Asian populace achieves political maturity.

17. Ecuador

To the north of Peru, Ecuador shares some of the heartland characteristics, though in modified form, and introduces others which are distinctive. Like Peru and Bolivia, it has a core area in the highlands where pre-Columbian civilisations were strongest, though the Inca domination was only for one generation before the arrival of the Spaniards, and Inca remains are few. The Quechua language was extended through the country mostly after the Conquest. This core area in the Sierra is also limited in extent because the two parallel cordilleras are here close together, leaving only a narrow, disconnected upland valley area between them. Like Peru and Bolivia, it has some human groups which are fairly pure Indian, while most of the *serranos* are mestizo, mixed White-Indian. The Sierra economy is like that to the south, one of small subsistence peasant farms mixed with large *haciendas*, though the latter are disappearing through subdivision. Industrial development is slight and artisan industries remain important, most of the Sierra towns operating more as service centres to a limited regional hinterland.

West of the Sierra there is a large lowland which has no counterpart to the south, occupied by the Guayas basin and coastal hills; this region has had an increasingly important role in the Ecuadorian economy since independence, producing a variety of tropical export crops. Some of it is still little developed and is the object of modern colonization schemes. The duality Costa–Sierra is expressed in the rivalry between Guayaquil, largest city of Ecuador, and the capital Quito in the Sierra.

The Sierran landscapes recall some elements of those of Peru, with bare landscapes, eroded soils, eucalyptus plantations and hedgerows, towns with open-air markets made colourful by the red, brown, white and black of traditional woven goods and numerous different vegetables and fruits on sale, in squares surrounded by long, low, broad-eaved houses with red-tiled roofs. Costa landscapes bring in a new tropical lowland element — lush tree-weeds invading fields wherever they have been allowed to flourish, zebu cattle feeding on tall grasses, houses of bamboo built on stilts above the poorly draine flat lands, coffee, cocoa, banana and manila hemp plantations. To the east of the mountains there is an equally tropical and less developed Oriente. Throughout there is however, as to the south, continual evidence of extreme poverty, both in rural and urban areas.

PHYSICAL BACKGROUND (Fig. 47)

The Andes form two major cordilleras in Ecuador, Eastern or Oriental, and Occidental. To the east there are low hills adjacent to the eastern Cordillera at 2 000–2 500 m, and to the west along the Pacific fringe there are low hills which curve back eastwards to die out at Guayaquil.

The Eastern Cordillera is a high and fairly continuous line of mountains, a massive wall of sedimentary and metamorphic rocks crowned by Tertiary and Recent volcanoes such as Cayambe

Fig. 47 Ecuador: geological structure

Legend:

Eastern and Western hills of Laramide orogeny (Mesozoic)

Western Cordillera volcanic rocks of Laramide

Metamorphics of Cordillera Real (Central) palaeozoic

and Cotopaxi, Antisana and Sangay. These are classic cone-shaped volcanoes which have been active in the recent past and have filled the narrow Sierra valleys to a depth of several hundred metres in places, with grey-white volcanic ash that produces Loess-like landscapes of cliffy slopes and arid tablelands where it is cut through by the rivers. The peaks rise to over 5 000 m (Chimborazo to 6 300 m) and thus are permanently snow-crowned. Their activity represents a constant threat to human activity. Cotopaxi erupted violently in 1877, forming a burning gas cloud which melted snow and ice and set off mudflows that reached the town of Latacunga and destroyed large areas of fertile valley land. Earthquakes have also caused disaster; in Riobamba, the 1797 earthquake set off a landslide which killed 4 900 people, over half the population at that time. Other major earthquakes of this city occured in 1645 and 1698. Ibarra, north of Quito, was wiped out by an earthquake in 1868. The giant volcanoes, located on the edge of the inter-montane north–south valley, help divide it up into separate basins, *hoyas*, partially isolated from one another by mountain knots, the *nudos*.

To the west, the Western Cordillera is slightly lower, formed mostly of sedimentary rocks and cut into by innumerable rivers running in narrow canyon valleys to the west. Below it, the Costa lies generally at under 200 m elevation, though the break with the Western Cordillera and its steep slopes is reached at 600 m or more in some places. Much of it is a fertile plains land of soft Tertiary sediments covered locally by river alluvium. North of the Guayas valley estuary, there is a tectonic swell near the coast and a belt of higher, drier and poorer land, marked by a flat upper surface probably representing marine-eroded terraces, *tablazos*, and cut into by steep-sided and intricate river valley patterns. The lower Guayas basin around Guayaquil is a flat broad floodplain, poorly drained and without topographic accidents. The Oriente, east of the mountains, is an ever-flatter plain towards the east, formed by the many strongly-flowing tributaries of the Marañon or upper Amazon river.

Climate and vegetation patterns

The typical altitude-controlled variety of climatic and biotic belts characteristic of Andean countries is found, from lowland semi-desert and scrub through palm savannas to rainforest in the lowlands, followed by cloudforest at 2 000–3 000 m and at higher levels, open grasslands becoming poorer in the *páramos* which lead up to the snowline.

There is a variation not only between Costa, Sierra and Oriente, but also within the regions. On the southern Costa, near the Peruvian border, and again at Manabí northwest of Guayaquil, the climate is dry, coming under the influence of the Humboldt current and the south Pacific high pressure cell, and in these regions the natural vegetation seems to be a scrub forest dominated by the kapok tree, the *ceibo*. In the northernmost Costa, there is rainforest and 1 500 mm annual rainfall. Similarly within the Sierra, there are many dry pockets in rainshadow positions, causing sudden transition from well watered to dry zones where there is under 500 mm of annual rainfall and a semi-desert aspect with acacia scrub, cactus and coarse grass. For example, a few miles north of Quito which has 1 200 mm rainfall, it is under 400 mm on the equatorial line and crops are only possible with

irrigation. Throughout the Sierra the natural vegetation has long been removed, and tree cover is absent, except for planted eucalyptus and Monterrey pine. Seasonal variations in temperature are slight in the Sierra, where day–night differences of 20°C are of far greater importance. There are rainy and dry seasons however, the wet season on Costa and Sierra corresponding to the Northern Hemisphere winter, when the influence of the Pacific cell wanes and moves further south, allowing unstable equatorial westerlies to enter both these regions. The Oriente does not have an important dry season, but the Cordillera Oriental prevents its humid air from affecting the Sierra at any season.

THE EMERGENCE OF COSTA-SIERRA DUALITY

Colonial development

Ecuadorian civilization seems to date from about 2 700 BC, when settled agriculture and pottery are known from the Costa. Ecuador was probably tributary to the Peruvian coast, or at least developed through the diffusion of technology and culture from the Peruvian centre. A strong social and political organization may be dated to about AD 500, with the emergence of regional states on Costa and Sierra. Inca settlement was delayed by the strong defence of the regional kingdoms of the Sierra, until the fifteenth century, and few Inca remains are found. However, the racial mix was probably modified by some Quechua-speaking people brought in as a conscious policy by the Incas.

Quito was burnt by the Incas to keep it from the Spanish, but was thereafter rebuilt as a colonial city and important centre within the Lima viceroyality. Other cities followed in the sixteenth century occupying the Sierra, where Spanish overlords could settle in the towns and live from a dependent Indian population. Up to 1640, mining was the most important economic activity relating the land to the exterior, and also accounting for some of the new town settlements. But the mineral wealth was never great, and from 1640 to 1740 textiles were central, and *obrajes*, large woollen mills based on primitive technology and Indian serf labour, were important in the Sierra between Ibarra and Riobamba;

they took advantage of the lack of textiles from Spain and the existence of a pre-Colombian tradition in weaving. Compared with this intensive development, the Costa had only great *haciendas* with cattle, cocoa and sugar cane, some worked by slave labour. A mulatto and pure negro population emerged on the Costa, distinct from the mestizo blood of the Sierra. These differences remain in the racial mix today, as the census figures show (they relate to 1950 as later censuses did not ascertain race).

ETHNIC COMPOSITION 1950

Race	Sierra	Costa	Total
White	29.0	28.0	28.5
Indian	28.0	7.0	17.5
Mestizo	42.0	28.0	35.0
Mulatto	0.5	28.5	14.5
Negro	0.5	8.5	4.5
	100.0	100.0	100.0

The Costa focus

After 1740 textiles became less important to the national economy than cocoa, produced in the Guayas basin and elsewhere in the Costa, and this latter region now asserted its dominant role in the Ecuadorean economy as well as a leading political and social role. Freedom from Spain was achieved in 1822, Quito Presidency forming part of Gran Colombia with Venezuela and Colombia, but almost immediately, in 1830 Ecuador separated from Colombia and became the Republic of Ecuador. The origin of this name, in a French geodetic expedition sent in the 18th century to measure an arc of meridian at the equator, symbolizes Ecuador's lack of a strong political identity. In spite of having a respectable name, that of the ancient pre-Columbian kingdom and colonial province of Quito, a mathematical, geodetic interest of external powers was made into the patriotic inspiration.

In the nineteenth century, the existing polarization of interest between Costa and Sierra was reinforced by politicians and parties, the Guayaquileños representing the interest in trade and commerce and the exterior, the Quiteños representing conservative, traditional landowners of the Sierra. Guayaquil was export focus for not only cocoa, but also coffee, tagua nuts, hides and natural rubber. Although Quito was the largest Andean city, it did not benefit from any

boom in the later century comparable to the guano and nitrates of Peru and Chile, nor yet the industrial surge of Antioquia in Colombia. Cocoa and the other exports of the Costa became competitive in Europe, especially with the opening of the Panama canal in 1915. However, after 1925, cocoa declined because of soil depletion and fungus disease, and was followed by other crops, coffee, rice, and more recently in the 1960s, bananas, to be followed in the 1970s by African palm and *abacá*, manila hemp. During the first half of the century, Quito had become a sleepy regional centre to the Sierra. A narrow-gauge railway was finished from Durán opposite Guayaquil to Quito in 1909, but did not radically alter the way of life in the Sierra. There was no drive from the Sierra to occupy the Oriente, and large areas were lost to Brazil and then, in 1941, to Peru, to form *terra irredenta* for present-day politicians to argue over.

Today's population has changed its focus to the coastlands. In 1780, it was estimated that 81% of the population were in the Sierra, 19% in the Costa. For 1972, of Ecuador's 6 million people, 52.2% were on the Costa, 45.3% in the Sierra and 2.5% in the Oriente. (The 1500 m altitude line is used as demarcator of these zones.) The balance is still moving in favour of the Costa, with a vegetative growth which exceeds that in the highlands, compounded by out-migration from Sierra to the lowlands. Within the Sierra, Quito has been growing rapidly in recent years due to oil-related activity and the growth of central government. The overall population growth in Ecuador at 3.4% annually (1975–1978) the highest in South America, is an important problem because this increase is focussed in two cities.

MODERN ECONOMY

Ecuador has an economic structure typical of underdeveloped countries, with a concentration of all export effort on one or two commodities. Thus its development areas on both eastern and western peripheries have an inherent tendency to 'boom and bust' conditions. On the west side there is the costeño agricultural resource, varying from one decade to the next, and currently shared between cocoa (14% of exports in 1979), coffee (13%) and bananas (10%). On the east, febrile expansion in the oilfield regions of the northern Oriente (oil provided nearly 46% of exports in 1979) is also a phenomenon which may or may not bring long-term expansion of the regional economy. Between the two, the Sierra is a region not geared to any export activity and with large pockets of subsistence agriculture, its principal resource being its population, a resource which is scarcely tapped and presents formidable obstacles to change.

Oil: a key sector

In the 1970s Ecuador's fuel and power position was dramatically changed by major finds of oil in the northern Oriente near Lago Agrio (Fig. 48) after many years of fruitless exploration. Four major international consortia drilling here struck rich low-sulphur fields in 1970, and produced 75 000 barrels per diem in 1973, compared to the mere 5 000 barrels per diem in the previous sole area of production, on the Santa Elena peninsula 140 km west of Guayaquil.

While the Santa Elena fields, developed and worked by Anglo-Ecuadorean Oilfields Co., a British company, had supplied domestic needs fairly well up to 1960, they could not do so thereafter and oil imports began to drain the country's foreign exchange reserves. Today, domestic supplies plus an exportable surplus of 150 000 barrels a day daily is available, and a pipeline has been built from Lago Agrio to Esmeraldas on the Pacific where there is a tanker terminal, and a major refinery. It is possible that the most important oil and gas region will be not the Oriente but the Costa; in the Gulf of Guayaquil substantial natural gas structures have been known for some time but not exploited. Now they are to be used in a project to use gas for making chemical fertilizers, and as fuel for a coastal steel-making plant. In addition, the oil potential of the Costa is now being explored and it is likely that important oil fields will be opened within the coastal hills and the Guayas basin.

The Sierra benefits of course from the oil

37 Otavalo, a traditional Sierra centre of handicraft industries such as spinning

development. The national oil company CEPE shares in oil production, and the national government which is centred in Quito relies directly and indirectly on oil for large revenues. Quito is thus experiencing in mild form the oil-based boom of capital cities experienced in the 1920s in Caracas. Oil combines with hydro-electric power to form the basis for electric power generation in Ecuador. At Guayaquil, major oil-fired plant supplies that city and a surplus which can now be transferred to Quito by an interconnecting line opened in 1980. Quito and the Sierra, in turn, may be able to supply the lowlands with a surplus at least during the wet season, when some major hydro-electric installations are completed in the 1980s. It must be said that a national grid network is still very far from completion, and that many rural areas and small towns rely on high-cost diesel generators.

The rural economy

Agriculture's longstanding central importance has had some impact on government thinking, and a colonization agency was founded in 1957, aimed at settling the eastern selvas. The Agrarian Reform Law was passed in 1964, with the purpose of correcting the unbalanced structure in which a third of sierran farms were under 1 hectare, and another half between 1 and 5 hectares. On the Costa the situation was less crucial, for this region had been colonized in large measure spontaneously, by Sierra emigrants who selected for themselves adequately-sized plots of land. In this region, the obstacles to farmer progress were such matters as access to markets, to credit, to technical advice, and to all kinds of service.

The main criticism of IERAC, the Ecuadorean Agricultural Colonization and Reform agency, must be that much of its attention has been to colonization and not to reform; and that within the set of reform measures, it has chosen the easier ones related to outlawing old forms of tenure such as the *huasipungo* and payment of

38 Outside Otavalo, one of the town centres of the little Sierra basins. Horses and mules for transport, unmade roads, eucalyptus trees and agave to right, small fields of minifundia on the bare eroded hillsides, are all typical of the Sierra landscape

39 *A village market in Ecuador, typical scene in the Andean countries*

non-money rents, but has not changed the farm size structure and the monopolization of good farm land by the great estates.

Agricultural regions

THE COSTA

In 1950 most of the Costa was still non-agricultural land, and of that land classified as agricultural, half was occupied by forest and wasteland. Much of the landscape was one of old, abandoned plantations, now turned to savanna-like grasslands with interspersed palm trees, the coarse grass being used to feed tough *criollo* cattle for beef. In the Esmeraldas region of the north-west, it was a forest landscape. The population was thin, and in all regions lived dominantly in single houses on stilts constructed of split bamboo cane.

This landscape has been altered locally in the recent decades by population pressure on the Sierra and new opportunities on the Costa. The Guayas basin has become a region of more intensive use, with migrants from both west (Manabí suffered intense droughts in the 1950s) and east, from the Sierra. Bananas became the dominant crop in the 1960s and remain important today, wherever good transport is available, their optimum physical environment being one of very high rainfall, over 2 000 mm annually, and a short dry season, plus reasonable soil fertility. These conditions are best met, not in the poorly drained lowlands of the central Guayas valley nor on the dry western edge, but on much of the eastern fringe of the Costa, and in El Oro province south of Guayaquil. Bananas are not grown on estates as in Central America, where foreign control has been typical, but on medium size farms of 50 ha, privately owned and often family farms. Successful marketing is important and depends on co-operatives of farmers or merchants with packing stations for washing, dividing and packing the crop. Successful marketing, plus Ecuador's relative freedon from Sigatoka disease compared to Central America, permitted Ecuador to become the world's largest banana exporter in the 1960s, feeding the USA and Japan. However, banana cultivation as a long-term monoculture has exhausted some soils, as around Santo Domingo which has been colonized since about 1950, and bananas are replaced in such areas by grassland and African oilpalm.

Coffee and cocoa are other export crops. Coffee comes from the banana lands and also from the drier margins to which it is better suited. Cocoa is grown in the Guayas Basin, the main concentration being in Los Rios province about 100 km northeast of Guayaquil. Cocoa is of increasing importance, expanding from 155 000 ha in 1950 to 287 000 ha in 1980. There has been some yield improvement as well as a real expansion, though there is still room for further increases, and often up to 40% of the crop may be lost through disease.

Sugar cane is another commercial crop, mostly for domestic consumption, its location determined largely by that of the sugar mills which own most of the sugar land. There was an expansion of cane land from 78 000 ha in 1960–65 to 110 000 ha in 1975. Production centres around Milagro, a few miles east of Guayaquil, where the largest *ingenios* are found. Alternative commercial crops are *abacá* or manila hemp, cotton, especially in dry Manabí, and African oilpalm, this latter a successful replacement of banana and requiring similarly sized properties for successful management.

Cattle are traditional occupants of the Costa, and improvements have taken place in nearly all herds, with the use of resistant crosses of Zebu Indian cattle with the *criollo* or European breeds that have good beef producing potential. Cattle and grass may be regarded as the dominants wherever there are large estates with little labour available, and also as a follow-on after intensive land use has depleted soil fertility.

Ecuador's dry coasts, in the south and in the westernmost province, Manabí, offer less to the farmer, and more to the fishermen. Ecuador lies on the northernmost coastal section of the Humboldt current, which only sweeps out to sea at the equator itself, at least in the northern hemisphere summer when the South Pacific high pressure cell, and the ocean currents which follow it, are furthest north. This current is notably rich in fish resources. Ecuador also has a very large offshore claim, up to 200 miles (320 km) from the continent, plus a 200-mile radius circle around the tiny Galapagos Islands, which belong to Ecuador and lie 600 miles (960 km) west of the continent. At present the richest fishing grounds are in the Gulf of Guayaquil and near the Peruvian border, and the principal fish resources are tunny and shrimp which latter is fish-farmed in the mangrove swamp areas of the Gulf. Deep-sea fishing is little developed to date, as the fleet is mostly composed of small vessels limited to coastal fishing. In addition, freezing and canning facilities, at Manta and Guayaquil, are inadequate.

THE SIERRA

This region provides the foreigner's usual stereotype of Ecuador: small fields, steep mountain slopes, rows of eucalyptus or agave as field boundaries and larger blocks of eucalyptus planted on estates, poorly surfaced roads, and small market towns (plate 38). The pressure of farm population on the land around the towns often produces a half-bleached fringe effect, in the aureole of fields nearest to the houses from which the topsoil has been totally eroded to show the bare grey-white volcanic ash subsoil. Many farms are tiny, unable to support families without other employment, and rural poverty does not pemit education in better farming techniques or mechanization. Much of the produce of the farms under 5 ha is for subsistence, and marketing is in any case difficult because of the lack of farm-market roads and the long chains of intermediaries between farmer and consumer, chains which account for low farm prices and high market prices.

Outdated land tenure is another old feature of sierra backwardness, typified in the *huasipungo*, whereby the Indian farmer had merely the right to use a small plot of land on the estate, in return for several days labour each week from him or a member of his family. This system is officially outlawed though there are recrudescences of it from time to time in various disguises.

Maize, potatoes and barley are the twin staffs of life for the poor and are supplemented by pro-

Fig. 48 Ecuador: road and rail transport

tein from beans, lentils, peas, and only a very limited amount of meat or fish. Lack of iodine from seafish or any other source has meant there is endemic goitre in much of the central Sierra, which in alliance with malnutrition produces physical stunting and sometimes mental deficiencies, all affecting the poorest segment of the population. Quinoa, oca, lupin seeds and arracacha are other mior minor crops of the uplands. On the tiny plots of the *minifundio*, intercropping of beans, lupins and maize is often to be seen, an ecologically good choice because the plant variety gives some protection against insects and disease, and because the nitrogen from the leguminous crops helps feed the maize. It would be a more successful system were it not for the lack of sufficient land and consequent overcultivation.

Physical factors account for some differences in farming within the Sierra. On the *páramos* above 3 500 m the temperatures are too low for grain, and grazing is found with occasional potato crops; in areas not exposed to moist air currents from the west, drought forces seasonal grazing where irrigation cannot be applied.

THE ORIENTE

Development of the eastern territories is still hindered by their relative inaccessibility. The Eastern Cordillera provides a topographic obstacle which makes road building costly and tedious. Road building has not been organized by central government but begun here and there by Sierra municipalities aiming at expand their influence and area eastwards, only for the work to be abandoned when interest declines after some years of work. A few links have been made,

Fig. 49 Guayaquil: site and situation

notably linking Ambato, Loja and Cuenca to the Oriente, but in no case reaching further than the marginal area of piedmont alluvial slopes and relatively fertile soils. Population pressure has however continued to send an important stream of landless farmworkers into the zone, most notably colonizing along the road accompanying the oil pipeline to Lago Agrio in the northeast, completed in 1971.

Agricultural colonization, whether spontaneous or official, has had only limited success in the east, and only in the piedmont zone. For most commodities which it might be possible to export from the region to the Sierra, transport problems have been an insuperable barrier, favouring only beef cattle, with their own means of locomotion to market areas, or such high value/weight articles as *naranjilla*, a tomato-like fruit used in drinks, or *panela*, crudely refined sugar. The national government is interested in colonizing the far east on the Peruvian border, but this project stems more from strategic, frontier occupation motives, than economic or social ones. The frontier areas have no adequate linkages to the Sierra and their soils are generally infertile and have poor drainage.

The government is also interested in pressing forward with the Carretera Marginal de las Selvas, a north–south road through the piedmont zone from the Peruvian frontier to that of Colombia. This kind of transport development seems unwarranted, in that it links, not the complementary zones of Sierra and Oriente, but similar regions within the Oriente, so that the possibilities for trade use of the road are slight.

URBAN STRUCTURE

Like many other countries of Latin America, Ecuador has a markedly primate urban hierarchy, i.e. one that is dominated by its largest city, except that in this case it is two cities that dominate: Guayaquil and Quito.

QUITO (807,665 projected population 1980)
The differences between Quito and Guayaquil symbolize and are part of the more general differences between the Costa and the Sierra. Quito retains, at least in its centre, a somewhat more traditional and refined atmosphere, as centre of government and historical capital. It attracts most of the tourists from abroad, for the city is rich in colonial Baroque architecture, with some

priceless art treasures decorating the interiors of the many churches and monastries.

The site of Quito is on the western edge of its *hoya* or basin, on a shelf above the main valley floor, and at an altitude of 2 800 m, which gives it a remarkably equable and enjoyable climate with temperatures ranging commonly between 12°C and 20°C from day to night, throughout the year. The western fringe of the city climbs the lower slopes of Mount Pichincha, and the east is cut off by a river gorge, making expansion a dominantly north–south affair. Colonial Quito is still largely intact, a compact town of whitewashed three-storey buildings with red-tiled roofs at the south end of the shelf. Expansion has been an expansion of middle class villas over the north half of the shelf during the last 50 years, dragging out some commercial development with it, and recently flowing right round the airport site which must now be removed to the main valley floor well away from the city.

The urban poor live either in the old town in old mansions converted to tenements, or in shanty towns, the *barrios marginales*, particularly along the western mountain edge of the city. They are less apparent than in other large cities of Latin America as their construction is generally good, of locally hand-made bricks or composition blocks, and they are hidden in the ravine-like valleys cut into the slope of Pichincha. But they may account for 10–15% of the city's population. Municipal policy of maintaining a green belt of eucalyptus along this front, and of not providing water above the level of 2 850 metres, has failed to hold back barrio growth in the 1970s.

GUAYAQUIL (1 116 000 1980)
Guayaquil is a bustling city combining the functions of national port and manufacturing centre to the nation. It has a nodal situation within the Costa, not in mathematical terms but by virtue of its good access to the most important part of the lowlands. Its hinterland is reached over relatively flat country, and it has good sea links to the exterior; both of these factors constitute advantages over interior, isolated Quito. Roads connect it to all parts of the rich Guayas Basin, and it has both road and rail links to Quito, though the railway is antiquated and inefficient, and its terminal is at Durán on the east side of the Guayas river. The main road crosses this river on

a good modern bridge. The city has grown from an original site at the tip of the ridge where the coastal hills curve in from the west and die out at the river's edge. The site is high and well above the marshy plains on either side. From here the city has grown downstream, the main business centre occupying land just south of the hill ridge. In the last ten years growth has taken the city on far to the south towards the New Port, built on the Estero Salado which is much more silt-free than the Guayas and has a 10 m deep-water channel maintained to it from the open sea some 70 km out. (Fig. 49).

Heat, humidity and occasional floods gave Guayaquil an evil reputation for malaria, yellow fever and other diseases in the last century. Even in 1910 it could be said that:

The lower parts of the town are partially flooded in the rainy season . . . . the old town is in the upper or northern part and is inhabited by the poorer classes, its streets being badly paved, crooked, un-drained, dirty and pestilential . . . . malarial and bilious fevers are common, the latter being known as 'Guayaquil fever', and epidemics of yellow fever are frequent.

Encyclopaedia Britannica, *11th edn., Vol. XII, Cambridge University Press, 1910, p.665*

Now the city is relatively healthy, and has become the largest city in Ecuador, having over-taken Quito in population in about 1950. Its commercial hinterland is more extensive than that of Quito, reaching over nearly all the Costa and into the southern part of the Sierra. Its in-dustrial makeup is diversified, including vege-table oil and flourmilling, sawmills and related woodworking industries, cement manufacturing and other heavy industries, but also light in-dustry such as textiles and electrical goods, and a massive construction and construction-related industry. Guayaquil has a very smart modern centre, where concrete blocks, and some high-rise buildings, have replaced nearly all the old-fashioned wood and bamboo buildings that were typical and were regularly destroyed by fires in previous generations. Much of the city's economic activity is associated with the port, which is the principal port for imports and ex-ports, and has a large part of the new port de-voted to container traffic, with specialized cranes and warehouses, to replace the older and much slower system still used at smaller ports, of con-tainer ships using their deck cranes to unload cargo.

Guayaquil is not without its shanty area. The *suburbio* as it is called, has grown out in all direc-tions but most notably to the west of the old city over the swamps around the Estero Salado and onto the Estero itself. The process involves first the building of traditional stilt-houses of bamboo over the water, connected by catwalks to dry land; next there is pressure put on the municipality to improve the area, by filling in the swamps with material from the narrow neck of hill-land mentioned previously. The original owners can then sell their improved houses at a good price to new incomers, who in turn may make their own improvements by replacing the bamboo with bricks and blocks. Unfortunately the first areas filled in are the streets, which leaves the house-backs as unhealthy stagnant morasses until they are filled. Drinking water supplies, sewage provision and storm drainage are only provided later. It is calculated that 40% of the population live either in these shanties, or in central slums.

Other cities: the Sierra
Quito and Guayaquil dominate the urban hierarchy as other cities do elsewhere in South America. After these two, Cuenca is number three with a population of only 139 000 (1980). Each basin in the Sierra has however its own urban centre from Loja in the south, through Cuenca, Riobamba, Latacunga to Quito and further north Ibarra, Otavalo and Tulcan. These towns of roughly 50–100 000 act as administra-tive centres to their provinces, and centres for most of the trade of their basin, wholesale and retail. Traditional open-air markets are a con-spicuous and colourful visual aspect of this trade, sometimes handling all trade together, elsewhere having two or three separate markets for farm products, for manufactured goods brought in for sale from other regions, and for artisan goods.

Cuenca as the largest, has many representative features of this group of towns. It is a town of two-storey buildings, many in local stone, with a few new ten-storey blocks for offices and hotels to accommodate a respectable tourist trade. It is laid in strict chessboard fashion with a large central square, and is flanked on one side by a river forming a cliff front of the city towards the south. It has a number of modern factories on an industrial estate which represents the efforts of the regional development agency to attract light industry, but in addition a sizeable artisan industry making panama hats (very finely woven straw hats), wood-working and leather working, and jewellery making. Some of these industries are organised on an urban–rural basis, with most of the work being done in the villages around the city, while finishing and marketing are carried out by merchants who visit the villages and take up the production from a large number of families. Cuenca has a small airport linking it to other cities, but otherwise relies on road servies which gave regular and frequent links north, south and west. The railway service here is virtually defunct; the only passenger train leaves Cuenca at 4 a.m. for Quito.

REGIONAL DEVELOPMENT

A country as small as Ecuador might be thought to have insufficient regional differences to warrant special attention. But its relatively small population of 8.08 million (1980) has very varied conditions and levels of living.

The are no accurate measures of the distribution of poverty and wealth in Ecuador, but it may safely be said that the twin metropolises are areas of relatively high average incomes and the other regions are poor. Because of the powerful focussing of manufacturing industries, migration, and capital investment in the two cities, there are great disparities between conditions of life in them and in the rest of the country. It may be asked if regional development agencies have not been able to reduce these differences, or if the central government cannot at least focus some of its sectoral policies on the poorer areas.

One problem is that only a few regions have any kind of regional development organization, notably the area around Cuenca, the province of Manabí, the Guayas river basin and the southern frontier zone bordering on Peru. These regional agencies have come into being not because of a national policy for the regions, but as a reaction to specific crises — in Azuay, the province of Cuenca, it was drought in the 1950s, plus a decline in the Panama hat industry; in Manabí, it was successive major droughts; in the south, it was the delicate nature of relations with Peru and the need to guide carefully the joint river basin development of the Puyango and Tumbes valleys.

With the oustanding exception of CREA, the agency for the Cuenca area, the regional agencies have not been concerned with a broad-based development of their whole region, but with a narrow focus on a few projects within one sector. Thus in Manabí, the focus has been on the small river valley of Portoviejo, only 3% of the provincial area. In the southern frontier area the focus has been on a river basin project, the Puyango–Tumbes scheme for hydro-electricity and irrigation, with little spent on other areas although most of the population lives outside this dry coastal frontier zone.

For the Guayas River agency, the potential regional scope is much greater, covering the whole physical river basin, and thus parts of nine provinces, but the sectoral concentration is equally narrow, with the emphasis firmly on water projects, especially at Babahoyo and Daule Peripa, which latter will provide some water for the dry western Costa, as well as reducing floods within the main valley. Only in CREA, centred in Cuenca, where there were no funds initially for giant river basin projects, has there been a useful focus on small projects which provide work for local labour, not only in construction phases but on a permanent basis. These projects have wide sectoral cover from agriculture through commerce and trade to artisan industries, and infrastructure such as rural electrification.

The civilian government brought to power in 1980 after a decade of military rule has promised a strong regional planning function, covering the whole country. This will obviously be an improvement over the present state of affairs, though it will still require strong and clever administration to ensure that the present polarization does not continue to build up. The record of governments to date in controlling the growth of Guayaquil and Quito has been poor, and there has never been any serious effort at removing industries or building up new ones in the regions. On the other hand, agriculture, the backbone of the regions, has always been taxed heavily, as one of the easier types of tax to collect is that on exports of primary commodities. Export taxes on coffee for example, have worked against the farmers and thus against all rural areas of the country.

Economic planning, whether for regions or on

a sectoral basis, is not sufficient in Ecuador. It is necessary to begin with social reforms, in order to integrate in some way the poorest rural groups into the life of the country. As these groups are commonly the pure Indian stock of the Sierra, social policy becomes a policy for racial groups. Criteria for such policies have scarcely been examined, but the problem should not been seen as one of simply getting the Indians to adopt western ways and organizations. In Ecuador as throughout the Andes there are remnants of traditional communal organization not based on monetary exchange but simply on mutual aid among members of a community. These pre-Columbian *comunidades indígenas* may well form the basis for co-operative action to develop the rural community, as well as help in slowing the outmigration from rural areas. Outside the Sierra, modern co-operatives may be used to promote the rural areas, though their organization needs some improvement over that commonly found today.

18. Colombia

In the two seas which bathe her, in the three cordilleras which cross her territory, in her forests and tropical selvas, in her enormous rivers, in her abundant fauna, in her snowy *páramos* and volcanoes, in the strange world of the Eastern Llanos and Amazonia all will find in Colombia those remarkable contrasts of a land which offers all climates, all landscapes.

JAIME PAREDES PARDO

Colombia is an Andean country like her neighbours, and shares with them a variety of environments from tropical vegetation through temperate environments up to the high *páramos* and snow peaks. Colombia resembles its neighbours also in its backward economic structure, for it is dependent on agriculture for the production of export commodities to sell in exchange for other manufactures. Like its neighbours, a single crop, coffee in the case of Colombia, provides most of the export earnings, and Colombian fortunes rise and fall with the price of coffee on Northern Hemisphere exchanges.

Beyond these broad similarities, differences from the other Andean states are more apparent. Colombia's physical geography tends to divide its people. The country is large (1.14 million sq km), and thinly populated, with over 20 million inhabitants (23.4 million in 1975). More important, the populated highlands do not comprise a united mass as they do further south, but three separate ranges, so that groups of people live in areas more or less isolated from each other by hot swampy lowlands or high mountains. Most

of Colombia's efforts must therefore be devoted to integrating the various regions into a whole, efforts which are fortunately aided by a comparative lack of racial divisiveness.

PHYSICAL GEOGRAPHY

Colombia has an equatorial situation which, combined with her adjacency to both Pacific and Atlantic, would seem to ensure constant high temperatures and humidity. Topography, however, and the nature of the northeast trades in this zone, make this not entirely true. The basic relief features, the three mountain ranges named somewhat unimaginatively Cordillera Occidental, Central and Oriental, open out fanwise from the Pasto knot in the south, leaving two major structural valleys between, occupied by the Magdalena and Cauca rivers. West of the mountains is the Atrato river in another structural low between coast hills, the Serranía de Baudó, and the Cordillera Occidental.

Of the three ranges, the Central is the highest, with volcanic peaks of over 5000 m in its central section. The Oriental, east of the Magdalena, is broader, with high-level plateaus created by the infilling of old lake basins. Little lakes and flat grassy plains framed by surrounding mountains, with scattered eucalyptus trees, provide a beautiful landscape where man has been active for many centuries without spoiling the scene. The Sabana de Bogotá, home of the national capital, is one of these upland basins. To the west, the Cordillera Occidental has slopes as steep as the

Fig. 50 Coffee zones of Colombia

others but is lower and cuts into Mesozoic sediments rather than igneous rocks. West of the mountains, the Pacific lowlands are low hills rather than plains, a difficult and rugged country. The Caribbean coast is flatter but has the great mass of the Santa Marta mountains and the upland area of Goajira in the northeast.

Colombia's section of the Oriente, like those of Peru and Bolivia, is inhabited only by a scanty Indian population and by cattle men. There are two distinct sections, in the south a true selvas of the upper Amazon, in the north the Llanos, open grasslands which suffer alternately from flood and drought.

Climate

Altitudinal differences are the most noteworthy, with *tierra caliente* extending up to 1000 m, *tierra templada* between 1000 and 2000 m, *tierra fría* between 2000 and 3000 m, and *páramos* above this. The *templada*, with temperatures of 17°C to 24°C and annual rainfall of over 2500 mm, is the coffee belt par excellence, usually a narrow strip of land on the steep slopes above the main river valleys (fig. 50).

Rainfall produced by airmasses coming either from the Pacific or from the Amazon valley gives plenty of moisture to the eastern and western flanks of the mountains, but leaves the deep valley floors of main rivers such as the Magdalena and Cauca in a rainshadow with totals around 1500 mm, making supplementary irrigation desirable. On the Caribbean coast there is substantial drought in the tradewind zone, especially in Goajira, where Uribia, on the north coast, has 330 mm rainfall annually, allowing only scrub vegetation.

HISTORICAL ASPECTS

This region lies on the highway between Central American and Peruvian centres of civilization, and while not occupied itself by high cultures such as the Inca or Aztec states, it did boast chiefdoms of several thousand persons and a considerable social organization, appropriate to an area which must have been strongly influenced by its neighbours. Evidence of contact is present for example in the San Agustín culture in the south, which has many stone-carved monuments, art motifs and ceramic decorations comparable to the Central Andes and to Mesoamerica, dating from pre-Christian times to the Conquest. The fine metallurgy of Colombian prehistory also seems to derive from the Central Andes.

Settled Indians were concentrated at the time of conquest in the mountain basins above 2000 m, notably in the Cordillera Oriental, occupied by the Chibcha. Physical remains of the Chibcha culture have been little preserved, for they used daub and wattle rather than stone, and occupied open country where grave looting was easy and profitable in colonial times. They cultivated the potato and other tubers, used irrigation and drainage of the flat plains, and organized commerce in metals, textiles and farm products at town centres such as Bogotá and Tunja, later to become important Spanish settlements. The Chibcha were conquered with ease and absorbed very completely into the mestizo race which forms modern Colombia, more so than in Peru where the Indian element isolated itself and remained a separate race.

El Dorado

Santa Fé de Bogotá, the capital, was founded by Jimenez de Quesada in 1538, as the culmination of his journey up the Magdalena valley in search of gold, no doubt urged on by the rumours he must have heard of El Dorado, the prince who regularly covered himself in gold dust, and who lived in this region. He reached the Indian centre of Bogotá a little ahead of another party of Spaniards under the leadership of Belalcazar, governor of Quito and lieutenant of Pizarro, moving in from the south, and finally a third force under Nicolas Federmann, a German expeditionary from the colony of Coro in Venezuela which at that time was held by the Welser financier family from Germany, in recognition of their aid to Charles V during his campaign for election as Holy Roman Emperor. The Germans had made many expeditions in search of gold and it must have come as a cruel blow to them to arrive just after another group had found the source.

In the event, the Chibcha gold was found to be small in quantity and not even derived locally but from alluvial deposits in streams to the west. Emeralds were the only valuable local mineral. El Dorado was a real person, a tribal chief from near Bogotá, but the ceremony of coating him in gold dust and dipping him in the holy Lake of Guatavita had died out some seventy years before the Spaniards arrived, leaving no easily accessible gold. To the chagrin of the other claimants, Quesada was confirmed as commander of Bogotá and the region, and the land became part of the Peruvian Viceroyalty, to split off under the Bourbon reforms of the eighteenth century and become the Viceroyalty of New Granada, including Colombia, Venezuela and Ecuador.

Fig. 51 Colonial foci of settlement and cultural identity in Colombia

COLONIAL AND NINETEENTH-CENTURY DIFFERENTIATION OF REGIONS (fig. 51)

Cundinamarca and Santander
Availability of Indians to some extent determined the colonial economy. In the centre where there had been a dense Chibcha populace a typical semi-feudal society, similar to that of much of Latin America, grew up with Spaniards occupying positions of power and mestizos operating a near-subsistence farming economy. Bogotá grew as the hub of this regional economy, with a more shadowy role as administrative centre to the whole of the northern Andes.

A quite distinctive set of conditions prevailed to the north of traditional Bogotá and Cundinamarca: in the region called Oriente by Colombians, the present departments of Santander and Norte de Santander, there were few Indians to rely on for farm work and an industrious colonizing spirit developed among the people. Eighteenth-century Spanish immigrants were attracted to the farmlands being opened up at this time, and to the little towns of the region where an artisan cotton industry flourished. Eventually the identity of this region was lost, through colonial taxation, which hindered the development of tobacco farming and removed it gradually in the nineteenth century to the middle Magdalena valley. Competition to the artisan industry from large modern mills in Europe and in Antioquia also caused decline, so that regional identity was almost totally lost, in economic terms, by the twentieth century.

Antioquia

As in Santander, in the Central Cordillera there was a lack of settled Indians and flat land, and enterprising mestizos became responsible for the growth of independent small farming and mining for gold on a small scale. There is something of a myth surrounding the role of Antioqueños in Colombian development; according to some writers there was a peculiarly distinctive Antioqueño character, forceful and hardworking, which made the region a leader, especially in industrial growth during the last hundred years. Another opinion, which seems more acceptable in view of its simplicity, is that straightforward economic factors helped the region's emergence to prosperity. In any case there is little need for special explanations since the Antioqueños were only a little ahead of other regions, such as the capital, and differed from the rest more in the kind of industry than in timing.

The factors that seem to have importance are the old development of mining, which brought some entrepreneurial skills to industry, and, more important, the development of coffee farming on small owner-operator units. Coffee may indeed be seen as the main motor to industrialization from within the region. Introduced quite late into the country, after 1850, production was still small in 1870 and concentrated in Santander on poor soils and marginal climatic regions. A dramatic shift of coffee growing occurred by 1914 as the crop took up the best zones of Antioquia, and already by this time 35 per cent of the crop was grown there, on the well-drained land and fertile volcanically-derived soils. Coffee was grown by small farmers

generally with under 10 ha, among other crops on the same farm.

In the period between 1900 and 1914 profits from coffee-growing went directly and indirectly into manufacturing, through the expansion of railways for coffee exports, the development of urban labour forces, and investment in cotton mills by the merchants and farmers of coffee.

The Antioqueños also expanded their influence by colonization movements in the nineteenth century, reaching south into the middle Cauca valley in search of gold and finding instead good farm land for coffee, so that the Middle Valley acquired something of the Antioqueño identity. Large land holdings on the fertile valley floor prevented a total modernization of this region, leaving this to the present day and the efforts of the CVC (see pp. 225-28).

The Pacific coast

To the west of the mountains the isolated hills had few Indians, and these could not be brought readily into mining ventures. The rich colonial mining of old gravels for gold on the upper Atrato and San Juan rivers was thus manned by imports of slaves through Cartagena, and a regional identity was imparted by the Negro slave, forming the dominant element in a racial mix of Europeans, Indians and Negroes. When freed from slavery these people, becoming small farmers, moved out along the coast and, from Panama into northern Ecuador, made it a Negro coast with a primitive subsistence economy.

MODERN ECONOMY

Transportation (fig. 52)

A central factor in any discussion of the Colombian economy is the transport network, for the long high cordilleras and deep valleys present formidable obstacles to interregional relationships and movement. As late as 1889, the British consul in Colombia reported that travel from Bogotá to the Magdalena took as long as from Europe to Colombia. Many routes were only possible for *tercios*, human baggage carriers who could go where even mules might have difficulty.

Transport difficulties were reduced a little by river steamers in the 1850s, but major improvements depended on railways, introduced on a big

Fig. 52 Roads and railways in Colombia

scale only from the last decade of the last century. Even these were built only as special-purpose lines and never comprised a complete network. In more recent time, there has been a drift away from rail and onto road, as the table shows, while air traffic was of considerable importance only in the 1950s before road traffic extended into the northern and eastern lowlands.

FREIGHT TRAFFIC IN COLOMBIA

Year	Percentage moved by				
	Rail	Road	Air	River	Sea
1938	28.8	16.9	0.3	39.6	14.4
1946	34.9	21.1	1.1	34.8	8.1
1954	21.2	40.3	2.2	30.9	5.3
1966	17.6	56.4	1.4	11.7	12.9

Source: OECEI, Colombia, Buenos Aires, 1967, p. 117

Railways and rivers remain vital to some regions, such centres as Barrancabermeja depending heavily on the Magdalena for their trade, and Cali relying on rail connections to Buenaventura and Bogotá. Transport modes here are complementary rather than competitive, road and river filling in the transport gaps where rails are not possible or justifiable.

The most important river for navigation is the Magdalena, carrying more than 90 per cent of all river traffic. On its lower 500 km, navigation is possible at all times for 1.5 m draught vessels. Above this point up to Barrancabermeja, this level is maintained except for two months' lower water, but problems of silting, aggravated by the erosion caused by farmers occupying and clearing the valley slopes indiscriminately, are constantly present. Barranquilla and Cartagena share the Magdalena traffic, the first lying on the river itself 18 km inland from the mouth, the second connected by a 130 km canal to Calamar on the river.

The Cauca is navigable for river steamers for 200 km inland from its junction with the Magdalena, and the Atrato would also be a useful river if its valley were to experience any commercial development. There is a plan of far-reaching significance, to cut an ocean canal through Colombia, using the Atrato and the San Juan on the Pacific side, converting their upper courses into inland reservoirs or lakes, and

replacing in function the Panama canal. On the Pacific coast, Buenaventura is Colombia's largest port, handling 40 per cent of all foreign trade, with a protected bay site and 10 m of water at high tide on the entrance bar.

The railways were all constructed to the one-yard gauge, which could make their integration easy in one respect; however, they have never been turned into a national network, despite much infilling, including the major line run down the Magdalena valley during the 1950s. Even this line did not connect to the ports of Cartagena and Barranquilla, but only to the banana port of Santa Marta, and only now is construction being extended to Barranquilla. Significantly, the most heavily travelled rail links are the east—west ones between the valleys, where river traffic is not possible, and the Medellín—Puerto Berrío line is the most heavily used of all. Long north—south lines such as the Magdalena valley line have not proved a great success as they follow the same lines as road and river. Throughout, apart from the Magdalena line, the equipment and lines are in a poor state of repair and generally single-track.

The road network is also limited, despite rapid recent improvements. Only a few thousand kilometres of paved roads are in use, and the roads, like the railways, suffer from constant landslides and floods in the mountains and must continually undergo repair. Apart from north—south routes, there are some useful transverse roads cutting across mountains and linking outlying settlements. Such are the roads to Tumaco and Pasto in the south, from Bogotá through Medellín to Turbo and Quibdó, and the Rio Meta road in the east. The most noticeable gaps are the whole Pacific coast and the link to Central America, the last connection to be made in the Panamerican highway. The Panama road must cross the Tapón de Darién or Darien plug as it is aptly called in Colombia, consisting of the difficult swamp country of the lower Atrato river valley. The completion of this road will no doubt help the Medellín, and through it the Colombian economy, though long-distance traffic is likely to be slight.

Agriculture
Colombia remains a strongly agricultural country despite modern industrialization, whether we measure the fact according to

employment, output or export value of farm products. Half the population is rural, far more than in most South American countries, and most rural people are on farms. Besides being strongly agricultural, Colombia has the added emphasis on one product, coffee, which together with bananas generates three-fourths of foreign exchange. Despite the importance of farming, only a quarter of the land is used for production, and of this, 5.1 million ha or 5 per cent (1974) of the land total is for crops, the rest being natural and improved pastures; these figures suggest an enormous potential for future expansion of production, but much unused land is either in the east on acid leached soil or in the mountains where soil erosion is a limiting factor. For much of the unused land heavy infrastructure investment in roads, forest cutting, flood control and drainage would be a necessity. Something of a movement onto lower lands has taken place already, into the Magdalena valley, into the northern lowlands, and into the near Oriente, but this is minor compared to the land remaining unused.

Farm tenure and structure of farm holdings are important problems; two-thirds of the properties are registered as owner-operator, but in fact many are run by administrators rather than by their owners. Owner-operator farms are most common in Antioquia and Boyacá. Tenancy, accounting for 7.4 per cent of land but 23.4 per cent of farms in 1960, is often of backward form, including much sharecropping on coffee farms and tobacco farms in Santander. Cash tenancies are common on the lower river plains. On hill lands public domain has been occupied by squatters, who move off to new homes when their crops decline through soil erosion on the steep slopes.

The distribution of farm sizes is lopsided; a quarter of all farms in 1960 were under 1 ha, while 786 farms, 0.1 per cent of the total, were over 2500 ha and occupied 20 per cent of the farmland. This situation has not been affected by land reform, for the reform agency has only managed to settle some 50 000 new farmers and give proper titles to some squatter farmers.

Farm production

SUBSISTENCE

In the highlands traditional farming is practised without the help of government price guarantees and without machines, either by small owner-operator or tenant farmers. Maize for domestic consumption is common, and on the cooler lands potatoes and beans. In the *tierra fría* such edible tubers as arracacha, oca and ulluco are still common mestizo-grown crops, along with temperate grains. No fertilizers other than animal or human dung are used.

On the Pacific coastlands an interesting variant of the slash—burn system of farming is practised, which has been called slash—mulch farming. Secondary forest is sown with maize seed or rootstocks of banana or manioc, then the rest merely cut down with machetes to form a mulch through which the crops grow. This system is employed rather than slash—burn because of the lack of any dry season on this extremely well-watered coast, while the rapid breakdown of vegetation provides nutrition to the new plants.

Commercial agriculture

COFFEE

The key role of coffee in promoting industrial and commercial development in Antioquia has been noted. Coffee is still a key product for Colombia; for the last forty years it has been the leading crop and, to judge from the renown of Colombian mild coffees which command premium prices on the markets, it might be imagined that coffee covers a large part of Colombia. In fact the *cafetales* are a narrow belt of land (fig. 50) along the slopes of the river valleys, at 1000-2000 m. The crop is grown on small farms of under 50 ha, for steep slopes and difficult terrain do not lend themselves to large properties and mechanization. Much of the crop must be carried on mule back to the mills. Coffee is commonly grown here under shade trees, usually plantains. These give a longer ripening period to the tree, so that berries may be gathered by selecting only the red ones over a period of time — again a process favouring family farm operators — rather than all at once as in Brazil, and the result is the fine mild coffee of the country, without the bitterness induced by green berries which are inevitable in the Brazilian stripping of the tree. Shade trees also help to preserve soil with their leaf litter and shade, and their roots protect against erosion.

OTHER CROPS

Overdependence on coffee is recognized as undesirable and other crops have been given some official encouragement. One is cacao, though poor cultivation and low-yield varieties have hindered interest in expansion in the producing areas, principally the Cauca valley and Antioquia. Government encouragement is being given to increase the plantings from the present level (1975) of 62 000 ha. Cotton has also been of interest because of local demand in the textile industry; cotton lands are widely dispersed, but most comes from the Caribbean coastlands, and production has increased substantially since the 1950s on medium and large farms with mechanization. Sugar-cane is also in good demand, and production has increased, but most still goes to the production of simple *panela* cakes of brown sugar, a major element of diet among the Colombian poor. Cane is grown all over the *tierra templada* and Atlantic coast, but the best, used in mills in Cali and Manizales for white sugar, is grown in the Cauca valley on mechanized farms. Bananas are another commercial crop and have been a major export, from the Santa Marta region which developed under the United Fruit Company, no longer an owner of land in the country; the Atrato valley and the area around Turbo also has modern banana plantations on good alluvial soils, developed since the 1950s.

Livestock is an important element of farming, raised either on the poor natural grasses of the tropical north or the Llanos, or on rather better pastures in the highlands. On the Llanos cattle are produced only for beef, of relatively low quality, on plains where they must wander far in search of pasture in the dry season, and must migrate out of some regions altogether when the rains bring floods. In the eastern and central sierras small cattle farms are found sometimes occupying deserted coffee lands when erosion has set in, with a stock of local white cattle, together with some European breeds for milk as well as beef. In the *tierra fría* a fair proportion of pure dairy cattle is found. Compared to cattle,

40 Fishing is little developed in Colombia. These are fishermen's huts at Tumaco, on the Pacific coast

sheep have minor importance with a stock of 1.9 million head against 2.3 million horned cattle in 1975. Fish are yet another animal resource, little tapped to date, as most of the catch comes from the rivers rather than the ocean (plate 40).

MINERAL INDUSTRIES

Minerals as yet contribute relatively little to the economy. A little gold and silver is still extracted as in colonial times from mines and placer gravels in Antioquia, and from the Pacific coast-lands where platinum is also worked.

Emeralds, for which Colombia has long been noted, still come from mines in Boyacá, but are not important. More significant are the iron-ore deposits of the Cordillera Oriental, used for the steel mills of Paz del Río in the industrial valley of the Chicamocha, in conjunction with local limestone and coal.

Coal is found mostly in Tertiary basins within the Cordillera Oriental, where the massive reserves give Colombia pre-eminence in all of Latin America. As geological survey is incomplete there is substantial difference between the 400 million tons proved and the 10000 to 40000 million tons estimated reserves in Colombia. Some coals have been discovered only recently in the far southeast, in Amazon country. Most of the coal is high-grade bituminous, large amounts of it suitable for coking, a vital factor in a continent where all coal is in short supply, and coking coal is precious; there is also some anthracite, a commodity which is eminently suited to long-distance transport. Within the highlands the greatest concentration of estimated reserves, 50-60 per cent, is in Cundinamarca and Boyacá, north of Bogotá. Another important area is the El Cerrejon field in the Goajira peninsula with 400 million tons estimated reserves, now to be developed jointly by Colombian and North American (Peabody Company) interests.

Colombia is the only Latin American country with a major potential for coal exporting, though there are substantial problems in taking coal out to the coast. Goajira is best sited for ocean movement, but has no transport infrastructure at all at present. The port of Riohacha would need improvement for this field to be developed. Interior fields present greater difficulties and improvement of the Rio Magdalena railway or of the river navigation facilities would be necessary

to expand from the present negligible export levels. Internal markets are however likely to take much more coal than they now do (3-4 million tons annually) as declining petroleum reserves are exhausted. Colombia is already importing petroleum.

Salt, another little-used resource, is to be developed in Goajira too, at Manaure, and at Cerromatoso in Córdoba, south of Cartagena, a major new development in mining nickel and cobalt is being pressed with North American participation. It is of long-term significance that Colombia looks much more favourably on foreign participation in minerals extraction than do most of her neighbours, and the growth of the minerals sector may be more rapid because of this factor.

POWER INDUSTRIES

The geography of electric power production is distinctive, for there are two major producing regions with different power bases. In the Andes, a major power source is the river flow, already tapped in part in the Cauca valley and at the new Chivor dam north of Bogotá. This contrasts with the northern plains where power comes from oil and coal, and in recent years from natural gas. Dependence on one kind of supply has its disadvantages in the different levels of response possible to demands which themselves fluctuate through time. Obviously it is desirable to have a national grid to iron out supply and demand irregularities by switching supply from one region to another, but to date the systems are not integrated. The industrial triangle of Medellín—Cali—Bogotá has connections, with 230V lines, but is not connected to the north.

Some 30 per cent of Colombian electricity is still generated by private producers, mostly for their own consumption, a good index of the lack of public provision. For future improvements, the main potential is the middle Cauca, with its canyon section north of the open valley, and the San Juan—Atrato canal project, which would also be a major generator of power. Further power resources from oil and gas are possible in the oil-fields of the Oriente, northeast of Bogotá, where a number of promising finds have been made.

INDUSTRIALIZATION: URBAN AND REGIONAL DEVELOPMENT

Origins of the multiple-centre urban network

In most developed countries an urban network of cities of varying size, where rank in the urban hierarchy is matched to city size in a rank—size relationship, is expected and found. In less developed countries the relationship does not generally hold, and is replaced by a city system dominated by one or two major cities. For Colombia the rank—size theory does hold good however, for a variety of reasons. In colonial time, placing the capital city at an inland site meant a need for other cities to act as ports, and Cartagena, Santa Marta and Barranquilla grew up on the Atlantic front. Other cities were important because of regional isolation, Cali, Medellín and Popayán in the highlands, Barrancabermeja as a river port, Bucaramanga as centre to Santander.

A separate cultural and economic identity was possible for each of these towns because of the inordinate cost of transport between them. Nineteenth-century growth modified this scheme of things, but did not overthrow it, and the period of rapid growth after 1850 helped the port cities as much as it did Bogotá and the regional centres of the highlands. Coffee and tobacco exports helped first the Atlantic ports, Santa Marta and Cartagena with its fine natural harbour, then Barranquilla, after construction of a short railway to an outport on the ocean. After 1914 the Panama Canal and a railway from Cali led to rapid growth at Buenaventura on the Pacific. Medellín had its own source of growth, first as coffee emporium, then also as cotton-textile manufacturer to the nation. Only Cartagena lost status during the century, through the disappearance of its special function as port of call for the Spanish fleet. Its population, 18000 in 1825, was in 1905 only 9700.

Recent trends

More recently, the very largest cities, Bogotá, Medellín and Cali, have asserted a tendency to dominate over all others, with more rapid growth of population and industry. Bogotá, with about 2.9 million in 1973, had had a growth rate of 7.5 per cent per annum in its postwar population.

Bogotá's function as administrative and political nerve centre to an increasingly centralized state accounts for much of its importance; administrative centrality has meant growth in employment areas such as printing and publishing, the head offices of private industries, retailing and wholesaling, metals and electrical engineering industries, foreign-owned chemicals, pharmaceuticals, food and drink and car assembly industries, as well as in central government itself and governmental agencies and public bodies.

Bogotá's potential for growth remains large, with improvements in transport making it more accessible to the Magdalena Valley, while it is the largest centre in the vicinity of the integrated iron and steel works of Belencito, where a state enterprise, Paz del Río, was set up in 1955 to use ore and coal in the Chicamocha valley, now becoming something of an industrial valley within the Eastern Cordillera. Hydroelectric power is now being tapped at small dams and the new Chivor dam with a 1000 mW capacity north of Bogotá. Efforts are being made by the government to contain Bogotá's growth by credits to industrialists moving out and positive restrictions on new construction in the city, but the impetus of migration to the capital, demonstrated in the mushrooming shanty towns, is difficult to check.

Cali and the Cauca valley

The Cauca river flows in its upper course through the mountains of the southern end of the Central Cordillera; it breaks out in its middle section into a long structural trough, from the town of Santander above Cali, to Cartago, beyond which there is a small further island of flat land (plate 41) before a gorge section through the mountains to the lowland course.

Centre to the fertile flat lands of the Middle Valley is Cali (923000 in 1973), its industries based in part on the valley's products, on sugar-milling, papermaking using *bagazo* cane fibre, and local forests. Local coffee is milled and made into instant coffee in the city.

The CVC

Apart from a natural identity conferred by the enclosed valley, a separate identity has been sought through an autonomous public body, the Cauca Valley Corporation (CVC). This body provides a good example of the possible role of

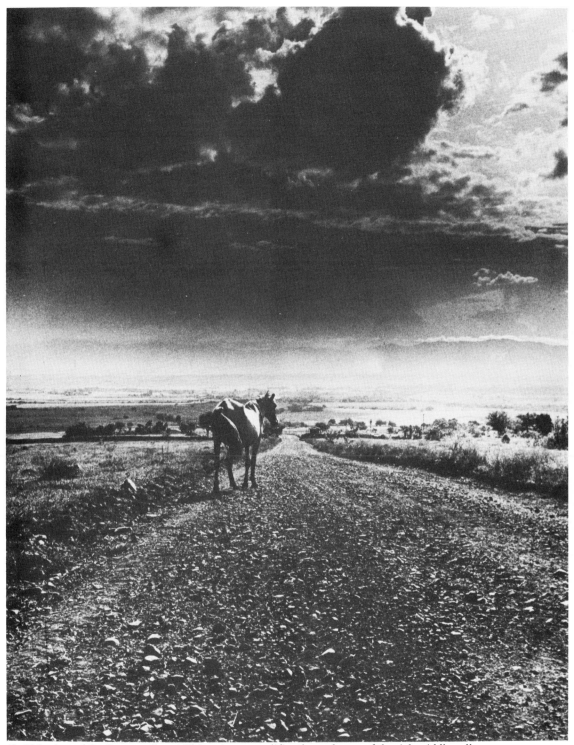

41 This view of the Cauca valley at El Paraiso exemplifies the underuse of the rich middle valley

Fig. 53 The CVC: main power projects and the floodable area of the Cauca valley

multi-purpose river-basin bodies though it has not been successful in many of its stated aims (fig. 53).

It was created in 1954 on the instigation of the local populace, especially Cali interests, who saw a set of interrelated barriers to development which should be solved jointly. A South American TVA was envisaged, covering not only the Department of Valle Del Cauca but also other departments on the river.

The problem was that the river was subject to damaging floods over a quarter of the 400 000 ha of flat land in the Middle Valley, where the best soils and irrigation water were available. Flood damage was increasing over time with the depredation of forest cover on the steep slopes surrounding the valley by small farmers. The intensity of small-farmer cultivation was itself in part a consequence of the monopolization of the lower flat land by big farmers, ranchers with great herds of cattle feeding on natural pastures, or by sugar planters; the land was concentrated in the hands of a few owners. Cattle ranching was in turn a natural result of the flood liability of the flat lands.

To improve matters, the CVC was to place high dams on the Cauca river in its upper course above Cali, which would both generate power and moderate river flow. In addition they would straighten the river course with cuts by some 30 per cent, and place levees as further protection. Other dams on the Anchicayá and Calima rivers of the Pacific drainage would raise further power. Irrigation of farmlands and drainage of lowlying land would help to make the land suitable for mechanized arable farming. The mountainous slopes would be relieved of cultivation pressure and be subject to conservation measures. The human resources of the valley would be mobilized by education and improved social services.

The CVC encountered opposition in its plans from other departments, which refused to join it, from central government which saw a challenge to authority, and from local landowners who would have to pay a tax to finance the new corporation. Over the long term the CVC was defused by uncooperative attitudes and limited to its central functions of power generation and river control, like the Magdalena Valley Corporation, set up with similar aims.

The criticism has been made that the CVC

concentrated developmental attack on a relatively rich and advanced part of the country, while other areas remained backward, though this is in fact in complete accordance with the standard growth pole theory of concentration of effort on viable centres from which growth might be expected to spread.

THE ATLANTIC COAST CITIES

The Atlantic or Caribbean coast is another area where growth industries are beginning to emerge. There are several sources of this growth. First, the push into lowlands by farmers is taking up more of the north coast hinterlands, with tropical fruits, sugar and beef cattle; secondly, there are the thriving power and fuel industries, located in the north and bringing processing to the port cities; finally, there is a nascent tourist industry.

Cartagena profits from all these elements. As an old colonial city with its walls and many buildings intact from the eighteenth century and earlier, it has many attractions for tourists, which will be amplified by the new coast road being built from the Venezuelan frontier through Santa Marta. Its location on the Caribbean should also bring Northern Hemisphere tourists, and Santa Marta is building a new international airport to receive them. Cartagena also has the usual gamut of port processing industries and there is a large oil refinery and petrochemical works at Mamonal nearby, making fertilizers for domestic and export markets.

Barranquilla (727000 in 1973) has the advantage of ready access to the Magdalena river valley, though rail access has never been direct. It has large chemical factories and cement works, and a new integrated pulp and paper industry making cardboard packaging for new delicate varieties of banana which must be packed on the farm rather than shipped direct to ports. A new bridge over the Magdalena will link this city more closely to the Santa Marta and Goajira tourist coast and to Venezuela.

DIRECTIONS FOR DEVELOPMENT

The territorial development question for Colombia is not, as in Brazil or Peru, whether to concentrate efforts on a core area with its better endowment of infrastructure, and to hope for spread effects, or to try to help the poorer lowland regions by encouraging settlement and making investments in infrastructure. The distinctive Colombian feature is multiple nuclei of relatively advanced economy and wealth: Medellín, Cali—Valle del Cauca, Bogotá, Santa Marta—Barranquilla-Cartagena. Between these there are large negative areas or areas of lesser development. Thus the Colombian strategy must be the integration of the developed areas, with new power lines, roads and railways, to aid mutually in the growth and development process, and maintain an already strong unity of political and social orientation in the country.

In the process of this linking of the major centres, the intervening regions may be helped; the example of the railway along the Magdalena Valley, linking Bogotá to the Caribbean cities, is apposite. While assisting in the process of linking the capital to the coast, it has been perhaps still more successful in bringing colonists to the *tierra caliente* along the valley floor. Colonization of new lands in Colombia thus does not necessarily mean movement out to the difficult Chocó or to the Llanos, though there has been a trickle of settlers in these directions. Lands closer to hand are available, in the Magdalena and Cauca valleys, and in the northern plains.

It is perhaps fortunate that ready outlets are available for some of the surplus farm labour force; Bogotá already suffers from immigration of landless peasants at a rate exceeding the expansion rate of her industries. Rural malaise, in terms of labour needs, more than matches the urban economic euphoria.

19. Venezuela

This country occupies 916 000 sq km, not including 150 000 sq km which it disputes with Guyana, making it one of the region's larger countries, but it has the small population of 13.5 million (1980), mostly concentrated in and around the urban centres of the north and leaving a huge region of minimal density population in the Llanos and Guayana. The republic is divided into twenty states, two federal territories, the federal district of Caracas, and some seventy tiny islands in the Caribbean which are federal dependencies. Effective power is however heavily concentrated in the national capital.

Venezuela is outstanding in the continent for its contrasts and contradictions in economic and social life: on the one hand, a slow-changing, traditional rural economy based on semi-subsistence farming and primitive ranching; on the other, the oil industry providing the impetus for urban and industrial growth in the present century and source of wealth for a small minority of Venezuelans, many of them city-dwelling executives who live not far from the *barrios*, slums that house people with infinitely lower standards of living.

HISTORY OF SETTLEMENT

Indian cultures
There are still Indian groups living in little modified native communities in Venezuela. For example, the Guaraunos live in parts of the Orinoco Delta region liable to periodic river or tidal flooding, and depend on fish for their livelihood, isolated by a semi-amphibious way of life. Primitive tribal communities are to be found in the remote Andes too, especially in the Sierra de Perijá, where the Yukpa shifting cultivators are protected by an Indian reserve since the 1940s, though their way of life is gradually being changed by contact with outsiders. On the plains below them live the once-feared Motilones, primitive gatherers of the Maracaibo lowlands. There is evidence of more advanced cultures, notably the Timoto-cuicas, in the Andean region of Mérida, who once lived a life more comparable to the Incas or Chibchas than their neighbours. They constructed terraces, knew how to build in stone, how to establish irrigation systems, and store water in reservoirs, against occasional drought. Their farm products, manioc, potatoes, maize, tobacco and cotton, could be stored in great underground warehouses. Manufactures included cotton goods, basketry and metal work, and they had a form of money. They made settlements of up to 800 stonewalled houses. Their relations to the Inca and Chibcha peoples are uncertain, but they seem to provide further evidence of ancient links throughout the whole Andean oecumene from northern Argentina to Venezuela.

Spanish conquest and rule
Spanish interest first focussed in the eastern island of Cubagua, in 1507. In the glassy Caribbean waters of this little island pearls were brought up by native divers, though this resource could

Fig. 54 Locations map of Venezuela

never be longlasting and Cubagua was soon overshadowed by other areas. In the sixteenth century, the island of Margarita replaced Cubagua as pearl centre and it is now a deserted island, while the whole industry has declined with the competition from cultured pearls.

Around 1520, the Spaniards moved inland to found Cumaná (1520), Coro (1527) and other towns, but then Charles V of Spain leased out the Coro colony to his German bankers Welser, whose material interests led them both to try colonization and hunt for gold. In both attempts they failed and as the Coro colony had become a financial drain on Welser resources, Spanish direct rule returned, with a capital at El Tocuyo

from 1545 (fig. 54). By the end of the century there were 26 towns, including Caracas (1569) which replaced El Tocuyo as capital in 1577, Maracaibo, Barquisimeto and Valencia, all founded on the sites of old Indian settlements, mostly in upland valleys where native labour and fertile soil could supply them with life's necessities.

The process of occupation was slow and difficult compared to that in Peru, because in this zone there were many small tribal groups each fighting for survival in a difficult terrain, rather than a great empire whose nerve centre had only to be attacked in order to disorganize the whole nation. Movement far into Venezuela had to await the seventeenth century, when Salesian and other missionaries entered and effectively pacified parts of the Maracaibo Basin and the Llanos and Guayana regions, paving the way for a trickle of settlers.

Colonial economy and society
Cocoa and tobacco were early plantation crops and Negro slaves came in quite large numbers to work on plantations as in the Barlovento region, the lower Tuy valley where elements of their language, costumes and music survive. In many places they went as supervisors of Indian serf-workers, though themselves remaining as slaves. Today, a strong admixture of Negro is found in the coastal mestizo blood. On the Llanos a few cattle drovers herded lean steers to the north to sun-dry or salt their meat for *charqui*, and sent out hides and tallow. The colonial trade centre was Cartagena in Colombia, but smugglers also took out an unmeasured but large volume of goods.

Independence and modern settlement
There was very little successful nineteenth-century immigration, and no great advance of agriculture or industry in what was a sleepy cul-de-sac of the continent. Venezuela's emergence still awaited the arrival of oil. Oil brought new focuses, principally in the Maracaibo Basin, but itself could scarcely bring major changes in the distribution of population, except for a growing tide of rural—urban migration. Twentieth-century farming frontiers have been extended a little to the Llanos piedmonts, but this migratory movement, like the recent one into the Maracaibo Basin lowlands, has had relatively little strength. Venezuela's very high modern population growth of 4.9 per cent over 1950-66 and its more modest recent rates of growth (2.9 per cent 1970-5) have been absorbed by city mushrooming, in old areas of settlement.

Eighty per cent of today's population is thus, like the pre-Conquest Indian populace, concentrated in the Andean and Coastal Ranges, leaving the Llanos and Guayana regions with a few urban settlements resulting from recent oil and iron-ore exploitation.

PHYSICAL GEOGRAPHY

A number of well-defined physical regions may

be distinguished. To the north there are two groups of mountain ranges, the Andes, enclosing the Maracaibo Basin, and the Coastal Ranges. In the centre are the Llanos, to the south again Guayana.

The Andes
The Western Cordillera or Andes loses height from Peru northward, and in Venezuela lies at around 3000 m, with peaks to 4000 m. This is mainly a region of vertiginous slopes covered in dense rainforest, deep-gashed valleys and silt-laden rivers. Intense folding has exposed old rocks in the mountain core, and Tertiary folding has made the landscape one of fault blocks rather than fold mountains.

The main topographic features are the narrow Cordillera de Perijá on the Colombian frontier, and the Cordillera de Mérida, a broader mountain mass of several ranges. While Perijá has little flat land, Mérida has many wide alluvial terraces at different levels, the result of recent uplifting, and these flat *mesas,* as they are called, provide good farm land. Mérida and Trujillo are sited on such terraces within the *tierra templada.*

In the north the Andes fade into a transitional zone of low hills and drought, in the states of Lara and Falcón, east of Maracaibo. Drought affects the whole coast, especially the west-facing or lee shores and those projecting far north. To the northwest lies the Maracaibo tectonic depression, partly occupied by the lake, a largely fresh-water lake though open to the sea, for it is fed by abundant river water. Poldering may assist in the rapid infilling of the lake which is now occurring naturally by sedimentation.

Northern Cordilleras
These differ from the Andes in their geological history, structure and appearance; they run east—west like the West Indies, breaking away from the Andean directions beyond the divisory depression east of Barquisimeto. Two broad groups of mountains may be discerned, the Cordillera de la Costa (fig. 55) and the Serranía del Interior, separated by the Valencia Basin, the Tuy Valley and the Gulfs of Paria and Cariaco. Behind the coastal ranges there are some of the most important economic zones of Venezuela. Valencia and El Tuy are old colonial lands of tropical farming and they have additional roles today. The coastal landscapes differ from those

Fig. 55 Flooded area of Apure and Orinoco rivers in June–August 1976. A discussion of this flood and Venezuelan policy is given in the last section of Chapter 1

of the interior hills by their increasing drought to the north, with 400-800 mm of rainfall and scrub vegetation.

Llanos

This plain extends 1000 km east—west and has a regional slope to the southeast and the Orinoco. In the northern and western margins there are broad alluvial fans with coarser and more fertile material than the south, where during the April-October season of maximum rainfall, there is flooding over huge areas of the savanna. Cattle are driven onto slightly higher ground, the old levees of the west and *mesas*, ancient alluvial terraces of the east, during this period. On the

southern edge of the plain, the Orinoco is broad and shallow, skirting the mass of hard rock which is Guayana. River flooding and seasonal rainfall give an alternation of drought and moisture which makes tree growth difficult, and coarse grasses are the usual cover except for the *galería* forests of Mauritia palm along the water courses. (Fig. 55)

The Orinoco Delta region is a somewhat different part of the Llanos, under constant threat of flooding from river or sea. Active building out of the delta has been going on in recent years and added about 900 sq km to the delta in the period 1875-1950.

Guayana highlands

This section of the Shield is of metamorphic rock, including useful iron ores, the itabirites, in the north. In the south there are tabular forms, the *tepuis,* pre-Cambrian quartzites which form remarkable vertical cliffs. The south is subject to heavy rainfall, reaching over 3000 mm per annum; this allows a dense selva and powerful rivers which make dramatic leaps as they leave the *tepuis*, including the Angel Falls, 972 m high, at the edge of Auyan Tepui. The Caroní, draining the high southeast of Guayana, is second only to the Orinoco in flow. In the north, lower rainfall gives a chaparral vegetation of low open tree cover and coarse grasses comparable to the Brazilian *campo cerrado*, with under 2000 mm rainfall.

Southern Guayana and Mount Roraima (2800 m) were the inspiration for *The Lost World* of Conan Doyle, a reasonable choice for the tops of the *tepuis*, including Roraima, are ecologically isolated areas, islands surrounded by cliffs up to 1000 m high. Such mountain fastnesses do in fact hold many rare and hitherto unknown flowers, orchids and other epiphytes, and species of birds not known elsewhere, as has been documented by recent expeditions to Roraima.

> The mystery of the tepuis was more a matter of man's romanticism though it must be admitted that situation, structure, impenetrability of adjacent regions, the primitive Indian groups which live on the riverbanks and look with awe on the heights where they place, as did the ancient Hellenes, the god—demons of their primitive theogony, all this has contributed and still contributes to create round the tepuis an atmosphere of legend and mystery difficult to dissipate.
>
> *Alfonso Vinci*, Los Andes de Venezuela, Caracas, 1953

AGRICULTURE: THE DUAL ECONOMY

The problem

Within the long-occupied mountain regions of the Andes and Northern Cordilleras, there are the features common to most Latin American countries, an excessive concentration of land-holdings and of commercial production, contrasting with the great majority of farms which are *minifundios* that can produce little for the

market and often cannot even support their owners with food. Many of these tiny farms are sedentary, fixed in location, but in Venezuela an important part of the problem is that of the *conuco*, the shifting farm, and the *conuquero*, its owner. As practised in the Venezuelan Andes, the *conuco* differs little from its relatives in neighbouring countries, such as the *roça* of Brazil, and in its basic form consists of the age-old processes of selecting and cutting a plot of forest during the dry season, burning it at the end of this drought (February-April) so as to clear the land and feed it with the valuable wood ash, then sowing seeds of maize, beans and a variety of other seeds, as well as bananas, plantains, manioc and taro, plants that are reproduced vegetatively without seeds, using simple wooden digging sticks, and harvesting the crop after a few months in which there may be little weeding, especially in new plots. After a year or two the yield may have declined so much that the plot is abandoned and the farmer cuts out another *conuco*. Such farms are found throughout the humid subtropical forest lands at levels below 1600 m and in difficult country with very steep slopes.

This traditional system was perhaps the optimum for low density Indian populations. Ecologically it was well adjusted to the environment because it represented a modification rather than a destruction of the natural conditions. Shade was preserved, an important factor, by leaving shade trees and by planting other trees within the *conuco*. A storied cover and balance of demands on the soil was achieved by inter-cropping of different crops and use of tiny plots when a single crop was grown. A long forest fallow after abandonment was typical. Now the system is breaking down, with increased pressures on the land. Although population densities are low — in the area of traditional pure Indian tribal lands in the Perijá mountains, there are some 2200 Yukpa and Yuko Indians, giving an overall density of 1.5 persons per square kilometre* — the plots of land chosen for the *conuco* must be of adequate quality, and if possible come from the best alluvial or terrace lands; other lands which they are being forced to use in Perijá are of much lower farming poten-

---

* Kenneth Ruddle, 'The Yukpa cultivation system', *Ibero-Americana*, No. 52, University of California (1974), p. 28.

tial. Furthermore, the forest fallow period is being continually reduced, and the soil is thereby depleted and opened to erosion for longer and longer periods, reducing its productivity.

Other kinds of *conuco* may pose even more of a threat through soil depletion, though as they are on lesser slopes they do not lead to rapid erosion. On the north coast in the Barlovento zone shifting cultivation is practised by small farmers whose primary interest is growing cacao trees, and *conuco* is followed by planting of cacao and shade trees. Here commercial production replaces subsistence cropping, and monoculture replaces the ecologically sounder polyculture of the Indians. Another variety of *conuco* is that of the northern Llanos, practised by employees or tenants of land on the big ranches known as *hatos*. Here the land used for the clearing is the gallery forest along the streams. In such cases, the problem is perhaps less an ecological one and more one of tenurial relations, for the *conuquero* is a minifundista who must pay for his land in labour or cash that he can ill afford from his earnings.

Solutions

Taking these problems in hand has been a major concern of governments since the liberal Acción Democrática party came to power in 1959. This party has always sought rural support and injected capital into schemes for farm betterment. An agrarian reform law was enacted in 1960 and has since then allowed the legalizing of hundreds of thousands of squatter farms, some of them *conucos*, by granting title to land. Also, though only with modest success, private latifundia have been expropriated and divided among small farmers after payment of compensation to owners.

These two measures have had the effect of reducing migratory or shifting cultivation, but have not eliminated minifundia. Census statistics show that in 1971 43 per cent of farms were still under 5 ha, compared to 52 per cent in 1956 and 49 per cent in 1961. It should also be obvious from the preceding discussion that change from shifting to sedentary cultivation is not ecologically or economically sound unless radical changes are made in techniques of cultivation, changes which many farmers have been unwilling or unable to make. Surveys have shown a continuation of patch cultivation on post-reform

farms leaving most of the land as an uncultivated reserve. At the other end of the scale, the 1.7 per cent of farms over 1000 ha still have 67 per cent (1971) of all land (71.7 per cent in 1961). Land tenure also remains a problem. Eighty per cent of the 120 000 families (1975) settled by the agrarian reform institute are not legal occupants since they have taken plots given to others but then abandoned, or have become tenants on their own plots. Such statistics reflect a lack of social infrastructure and support for the new farm owners, a policy over-concentrated on the simple handing over of land.

Irrigation

Another approach to the small-farmer problem has been via expansion of the irrigated area along with electrification, roadbuilding and education. Enthusiasm for the irrigation approach was enough to double the 240 000 ha of irrigated land between 1950 and 1970, though most was still private schemes.

One major government project, the Guárico, involving over 100 000 ha on a northern tributary of the Orinoco and begun in 1954, illustrates the problems in the main region of irrigation expansion, the Llanos. Construction of the works meant very heavy capital expenditure before any returns were possible, including excavation of a reservoir for water because the river runs over the Llanos where no natural basins are available; canals had also to be dug. Soils, apart from small areas of alluvium, are poor compared to those in parts of the highlands, lateritic and infertile with poor drainage. This has allowed large-scale rice and now foragegrass production, but is of little use for other crops. Rice and irrigated grassland crops are suited to fairly large farms, and small farmers have not had much access to the Guárico. Indeed, from the beginning, land was given to *empresarios*, managers of 150-200 ha farms, rather than to *campesinos*. After some years campesino families came in but only 845 families were settled by 1971. Nor is the size of irrigated area satisfactory, with only 40 000 ha achieved.

In recent years and continuing under present plans, vast areas of the northern Llanos, including Guárico and similar schemes, are being reclaimed for irrigation to provide fodder for cattle, an enterprise that fits in well with the traditional ranching economy of the area as it economizes on the need for sending cattle north to the mountains for fattening, but does not do much to slake the campesino thirst for land. It may be asked whether too much has not been invested in vast schemes, rather than in improvement and extension of small schemes which are working well in the highlands. Irrigation schemes sponsored by government in the highlands have proved inexpensive and highly productive, and government favour seems to be finally turning more to these smaller schemes. It must be emphasized that the primary failure of the big schemes is not in their poor level of production, however, but in lack of settlement. Only 3715 families under government projects for irrigation were settled by 1971, though there are perhaps 200 000 farmers in need of land.

Land pressure is being relieved at present by spontaneous colonization in some areas such as the Maracaibo lowlands, moving out ahead of roads, public service or extension agency aid. Again, with relatively little expenditure such schemes of colonization could become commercially productive and serve many more farmers with a redirection of governmental interest, especially by bringing technical assistance to change subsistence farmers into commercial agriculturalists.

FARMING POTENTIAL OF THE REGIONS

The mountains

In the Andes of northwest Venezuela, commercial farming is restricted mostly to patches of slope land at lower angles than the average. Old river terraces provide the best sites. The region is very productive, yielding some 20 per cent of national farm goods from only 3 per cent of farm area, mostly minifundia holdings. Commercial crops of coffee and sugar-cane dominate the lower altitudes, wheat and maize compete with them in the *tierra templada*, and potatoes and cattle, dairy and beef, are important in the *tierra fría*, at 2200-3000 m. Fattening of cattle is traditional in Táchira and Aragua states.

In the northern Cordilleras agriculture is more concentrated, in the intermediate longitudinal depression between the coastal ranges and the Serranía del Interior. Within this depression, the Valencia Basin, lying at 400-500 m, has a fine subtropical climate and alluvial soils, with rainwater supplemented by irrigation sources. Immediate access to markets in the industrial cities of Maracay and Valencia, within the basin, has allowed development of market gardening along with field crops in an intensive commercial system. Sugar and coffee are processed in modern mills in the basin. The lower Tuy valley, Barlovento, is predominant in cocoa production and irrigation has extended the growing zone upstream into the dry middle Tuy south of Caracas.

To the northwest of the mountains are two zones of distinct potential. The Maracaibo Basin, little settled to date, has good potential farm land in its southern half, and with irrigation this could extend to the north. In the 1960s tropical dairying made some impact here, but much infrastructural work such as drainage and roads needs completion first. The other zone is Falcón—Lara—Yaracuy, the dry limestone hills which have long been deforested with their soil often eroded to rock surfaces, the preserve of wandering goats. Only deep valleys between the hills have intensive sugar-cane or maize cultivation.

The south

Traditionally, Llanos land use has been the pasturing of cattle; the Llanero is a cowboy as tough as his rangy cattle, which are the descendants of Spanish longhorns introduced to the plains in mid-sixteenth century, spreading rapidly in the wild. In recent years these hardy animals have been given still greater resistance to tropical conditions by crossing with the zebu. State irrigation schemes in the northwest Llanos, mentioned above, are now radically altering this way of life. The state of Portuguesa has most cultivated land in the Llanos, centred on the piedmont urban site of Acarigua. The rice-growing area under this stimulus has grown from 41 000 ha in 1948-52 to 120 000 ha in 1975.

Beyond the Llanos, Guayana promises little for farmers, for it is remote, with poor soils. Possibly cattle raising may be extended into the northern chaparral belt, but its grazing capacity is very low.

THE PETROLEUM INDUSTRY

As recently as 1920 Venezuela was tiny in the world's oil league, producing 0.1 per cent of the

Fig. 56 Coal, oil and heavy petroleum fields, oil refineries and pipelines

total: in 1957 it supplied a massive 15%, only to decline again in relative terms through the rise of Russia and the Middle East. Oil is still central to the economy, as may be seen from the fact that 90% of exports are oil and oil products. The geography of the industry is indicated in Fig. 56. Oil is found in large Tertiary structures in the Maracaibo Basin, both inshore south of Cabimas and offshore under the lake, and to a lesser extent west of the lake. Maracaibo state accounts for 80% of Venezuelan production. Oil also comes from numerous small fields in the eastern Llanos, developed in the 1930s and now declining in production.

Oil movement is generally by pipeline to coastal refineries at Barcelona, Puerto Cabello, and especially to the large refineries on the Paraguaná peninsula where most refining capacity is located. In addition, the Dutch Antilles, Aruba and Curaçao, have refineries catering largely to Venezuelan oil. Refineries were mostly built with a view to demand from the east coast USA, largely for heavy fuel oil for industry. Now Venezuela has deliberately sought new markets worldwide, and the demands are for lighter oil products, so that the refineries have

been substantially modified in recent years.

Natural gas is associated with the oil in many fields, but was not used by the companies before the 1950s, being burned off or simply allowed to escape from the wellhead. Now some gas is piped to starage tanks and liquified for transport in liquid gas carrier ships to overseas markets, though millions of cubic metres are still flared off in a dramatic waste of precious resources.

Alternative oil sources

There are other potential areas for oil development, notably the Gulf of Venezuela, within the reach of modern offshore techniques, though here a dispute over territorial rights has been simmering for a long time between Venezuela which claims the whole gulf and Colombia which claims part of the west side. Other offshore areas of promise are the Caribbean coastal seas — oil has been found near Margarita — and the huge deposits of the Heavy Petroleum Belt of the Orinoco. This latter was discovered in the 1930s but no way of extracting it economically was known. It lies south of the worked fields around Tigre in the Llanos, and extends as a band 40–60 km wide adjacent to the Orinoco and the hard rocks of the Guayana Shield, from the Orinoco delta at least as far west as San Fernando de Apure. Venezuelans prefer the name Heavy Petroleum Belt to the older Tar Belt, emphasizing the new possibilities for these oils using new secondary recovery techniques. The most promising technique, already used successfully in extracting more oil from the old fields of Lake Maracaibo, is of injecting steam at regular spaced intervals into the oil-bearing stratum. This is found to increase the yield from 5% to over 30% of total oil in the deposit, and make the potential reseve in the Belt 840 billion barrels, which may be compared to a present 18 billion barrels of proven reserves from conventional sources in Venezuela. There are other problems with the heavy oils, notably their high content of sulphur, vanadium and some other metals, which must be separated out before the oil is passed to the consumer.

More important as an obstacle to immediate massive use is the availability of oil from the older exploited areas. Since the private companies were granted no new concessions after 1959, and under a threat of nationalization, they made no new investments and let their installations gradually run down in the 1960s and 1970s. But since nationalization in 1976, new exploration by the state firm, Petroven, which has assumed responsibility for the whole industry, has discovered deposits in deeper beds of older Tertiary and Cretaceous age underneath the presently worked fields. Secondary recovery also maintains some of the older structures in operation, and in any case, Venezuela has reduced her output of oil in a more conservationalist attitude towards the leading resource of the country. It is however still planned to have large-scale production from the Heavy Petroleum Belt from about 1985.

Foreign control

Though a national oil company was first in production in the 1880s, a Venezuelan president, Castro, granted concessions which were sold in 1907 to British and North American firms. Reaction against this loss of national control only asserted itself after 1945, when further concessions were withheld, and an increasing share of profits insisted on by the government. Since then, the great increase in oil prices of 1973 allowed Venezuela to anticipate her stated inten-

tion to take over oil in 1983, and establish a state oil firm, Petroven, to replace all the foreign firms from 1 January 1976. This has been accomplished peacefully because the firms have been paid large amounts in compensation, and indeed continue to provide technological knowhow. Dependence on foreigners, it might be claimed, has not been reduced by nationalization, since Petroven has no control over the marketing of its product, in foreign countries.

Diversification or oil?

Income from oil royalties, from income tax and company tax on oil companies, local taxes and special exchange rates, have all contributed to sustain the Venezuelan economy in recent decades, and oil is inevitably still strong with profits going directly to the central government, déspite a firm control on the physical level of production today. There is a movement away from oil towards diversified production, spoken of since the 1930s as 'sowing the oil' but not really embarked on until after the Second World War.

Arguments supporting diversification can be summarized as follows. First, the ruling party, Acción Democrática, has traditionally had much of its support in the rural areas, and must spend money on farming if only to maintain farmers' support. On an economic level, it is necessary to diversify to avoid dependence on one commodity and its uncertain prices. This argument has always been present though it looks dubious in the present age of high oil prices. Finally, the unassisted expansion of manufacturing industry in the country has been small, so that only some light consumer goods manufacturing and assembly have become established. This means that the state should take a hand through setting up state agencies as in the case of steel, aluminium, petrochemicals and refining.

Against diversification, it can be said that petroleum has in fact proved a very stable and rising source of income especially under the aegis of OPEC with no sign of any future period with low oil prices to come. It is also possible to develop petrochemicals and refining, as Venezuela is trying to do, without moving outside the oil sector. In addition, within South America, and especially within the Andean Pact of which she is a member, Venezuela's forte is not in agriculture or industry generally, but in oil, which she could sell in refined or crude form throughout the continent.

STEEL IN VENEZUELA

Venezuela's first small private steel plant was built in 1950 and used scrap steel. The much larger state-owned SIDOR plant was finished in 1962, as a part of the Guayana investment scheme under CVG the Guayana Regional Corporation, and located just to the west of Ciudad Guayana. It grew out of the massive iron-ore export industries which has been built up from 1950 by Bethlehem Steel and United States Steel corporations, and out of a political promise to make Venezuela more than a raw-material exporting country.

The ore is present in massive deposits at El Pao and Cerro Bolivar within the Guayana massif (see the physical regions map), totalling 1.8 billion tonnes of high grade ore, with still larger deposits of lower-grade ore. In 1975 the iron ore industry was nationalized and made into another state agency under CVG. Other physical resources are also abundant — hydroelectric power, first from the Macagua dam on the Caroni river (Fig. 58) adjacent to the city and more recently from the giant Guri Dam further upstream, which is being built in stages and will have an ultimate capacity of 9 million kW.

SIDOR, the state steel firm, is rapidly increasing production to 5 million tonnes, using the direct reduction process, which eliminates the need for coke but does need large amounts of heat. This was efficient in Venezuela because of her abundant oil and natural gas, and lack of coke. The sponge iron which is produced goes directly to an electric arc furnace rather than the standard steel converter, again favouring Venezuela's abundant hydroelectric power at Ciudad Guayana. This is a unique case of the direct reduction process being used on a very large scale, and relates to the unusual Venezuelan resource combination. The principal limitation has in fact been the lack of suitably skilled labour. A completely separate new steel plant is now being planned at a site near Maracaibo, to be based on conventional steel-making techniques using coal from the nearby Guasare coalfield, and iron ore from the northern hills (Serranía del Interior) near Barcelona. A coastal site makes alternative ore sources possbile for this plant which will have a 5 million tonne capacity. It also makes transport of the product easier than at the present Ciudad Guayana site, from which huge 60 tonne lorries are currently used on inadequate roads to transport the steel to Caracas region. A projected east-west railway through the Llanos from Ciudad Guayana will alleviate this problem.

URBAN AND REGIONAL DEVELOPMENT

Caracas

The central element of Venezuelan urbanization is Caracas. This city, whose metropolitan area holds 2 480 000 people (1975), dates back to 1569 as a Spanish settlement, and as capital to 1577, and the historical inertia of a long colonial dominance of a region stretching from the Guiana coasts to lake Maracaibo has given it an unchallenged position. It grew up and remained largely an administrative centre for its region until the present century, in a small fertile valley with the climate of an English summer day, 1000 metres above the hot Caribbean coastlands. Despite the growth of a new industrial focus on oil in the distant Maracaibo Basin, Caracas remained the hub of all economic and political activity. Maracaibo's oil made that town a point of ultra-rapid expansion in the period from the first commercially successful oil well, in 1914, to about 1925, but thereafter the offices of oil companies, which had no pressing need or desire to stay in an isolated provincial town, moved away to Caracas, principal link to the outside world.

Symbolic of the links to foreign markets and capital sources was the fine new motorway built after the Second World War as a four-lane toll-road across the coastal hills to Maiquetia, Caracas's international airport, and to La Guaira, its principal port. This was a great improvement over the old narrow-gauge railway, built 1883, which had been the first modern link to the exterior. La Guaira, despite its poor open roadstead site for a port, has been maintained in its historic role as chief port for the city, handling in particular its substantial imports.

Most city growth has occurred since 1950, and Caracas, receiving huge numbers of migrants from rural areas, has had acute housing problems in its long but narrow and steep-sided valley. It spread out from the confining colonial chessboard pattern of the early city only after 1920 (fig. 57), expanding both east and west along the valley floor, absorbing fertile farmland and by 1966 occupying all accessible land (plate 42). Future growth of population will inevitably be accommodated by higher densities in the existing city, already an urban jungle of motorways and high residence or office blocks — 30 per cent of the populace are flat-dwellers — that is known as the Los Angeles of Latin America (plate 43). Oil revenues and the pressure of land scarcity are obvious factors in the surge of high-rise developments, but they still appear remarkable monuments to wealth in a land where most people are very poor. Some further growth can be taken up on the sharp slopes surrounding the valley, where the *barrios* or shanty towns are found, but the city's plans are to reduce suburban densities, concentrating population in the city centre and at the same time making movement easier there by introducing an underground rail system linking together all inner areas.

The Metro, as this system is called, will, however, consist when opened in 1984, solely of an east–west line through the valley, confirming the already elongated shape of the city, and will not reach most of the southern suburbs which contribute heavily to the traffic moving into the centre, as there are no important employment centres in these suburbs. The inconveniences of urban pollution by noise, air and water pollutants, and the difficulties of living in a city built essentially for a population of cars, with few areas for walking and with its retailing structure already in the North American mould of shopping centres designed for a car-borne clientele, are likely to persist. Designing a city for car users is perhaps thinkable in North America, but in Latin America a substantial segment of the population is dependent solely on public transportation.

42 *Rapid growth produces the incongruities of massive skyscrapers and old public buildings in central Caracas. Here the Municipal Theatre and Bolivar Centre, built under the last dictator, Perez Jimenez, in the 1950s, stand side by side*

Original nucleus of Caracas

Urbanized area in 1930

Urbanized area in 1963

Urbanized area in 1966

Ranchos

Main streets and roads

Hills above 1000m

Fig. 57 Caracas city

The barrio problem

Exploding city populations have led to shanty-town development everywhere. Seventy per cent of Maracay's population, 50 per cent of Maracaibo's and 35 per cent of Caracas's is housed in *barrios*, the growth of which engenders a variety of problems. Municipal services are often initally unable to cope with demand for new roads, sewers, drains, electricity, gas and water, especially as the *barrios* are usually in areas distant from the city centre. *Barrios* supply some of these services themselves, but they have not the capital to make permanent provision. Economically, the inhabitants suffer from their own lack of education and training, and high rates of unemployment are common.

In one view, the *barrios* are a dynamic feature demonstrating the drive in the economy, and their less desirable features are temporary maladjustments, in process of elimination. They represent the attraction of growing cities, of new aspirations and possibilities. The opposing viewpoint is that the *barrios* are collections of the poorest parts of society in one place, a bad form of urban zoning of natural occurrence, and also that they represent a migration of misery from an intolerable rural environment.

Something of both views is acceptable; *barrios* are certainly in part the result of lack of farming opportunity, but they also attract people because of positive long-term job and social prospects in the city. They are useful in a laissez-faire economy, where housing and infrastructure are difficult or expensive for a city to provide. Made of old oil drums, adobe with canes, corrugated iron and packing cases, they cost nothing to the authorities and, for want of funds, have been institutionalized — Caracas has included them in her official plans for housing over the rest of the century.

Cities and regions

Massive population growth in Caracas with its 3 million inhabitants, and to a lesser extent in the second line cities – Maracaibo is second with 920 000 – is both an index of the regional imbalance in the country and the origin of some of the problems associated with imbalance. In the cities there is a lack of housing and urban infrastructure such as roads and sewers, and pollution and traffic congestion are increasingly severe. In the rural regions there is the reverse problem of out-migration. The argument might be made that since 80% of the population is in one third of the area, the northern mountain fringe of the country, regional balance is undesirable – the Llanos and Guayana must remain thinly-peopled resource regions and their intensive development is impossible.

This may be accepted but even within the north fringe there are large differences in welfare. The Andes of Mérida, Trujillo and San Cristóbal are poor, as is the northern Oriente east of Barcelona. They have little part in the industrialization that is going on in the central region. In 1977, 58.6% of value added in manufacturing was in the Central-North Coast region, i.e. the Valencia-Maracay-Caracas axis. In the poor Southern Andes, Mérida, Táchira, and Trujillo had 50%, 53% and 43% of the national

average per capita regional product, of 2865 Bs in 1961.* In the north east Sucre and Nueva Esparta (the island of Margarita) had 50% and 36%. At the same time, the Federal District of Caracas, and neighbouring Miranda state, had 160% and 143%.

John Friedmann, concerned with Venezuelan regional planning in the 1960s, advocated regional concentrations of an urban-industrial nature, a kind of growth pole policy, to solve Venezuela's overwhelming economic concentration and the continuing centripetal movement of men, physical resources and capital to the Caracas region. His main poles were at:

1 Valencia-Maracay (population 450 000 and 320 000, respectively), using the agricultural wealth of the Lake Valencia basin to support

*J. Chi-Yi Chen, *Estrategia del Desarrollo Regional*, Caracas 1971.

43 *A Caracas motorway. Such roads have not solved Caracas's urban traffic problems, for there is no effective public transport system*

food-processing industries, and well connected to Caracas so that assembly-type industries such as car manufacturing could be developed here;

2 Barquisimeto (504 000), route nexus between the Andes and the Northern Cordillera;

3 Barcelona-Puerto La Cruz-Guanta (284 000 total), an urbanized 20 km long strip of coast with a coal port at Guanta, an oil-refining and general port at Puerto La Cruz, and an administrative and manufacturing centre at Barcelona;

4 El Tablazo, Tuy Medio, and Ciudad Guayana (new growth points). These latter three differ in function among themselves.

El Tablazo was designated a new city in 1967, on Lake Marcaibo opposite Maracaibo city, and intended first as a petrochemical town. Because this was realized as too narrow a base, other manufacturing industries have been sought to help growth. Some of El Tablazo's growth may

be seen simply as overspill from Maracaibo across the lake, and it is well linked to the city by a giant road bridge built in 1963.

Tuy Medio is being developed with a comparable role, as overspill receiver for Caracas, providing both jobs and housing and thus becoming more than a commuter suburb. This town is in the middle Tuy valley, 10 km south of Caracas, well linked by road, and in the future by rail, to other regions. But if brought into being as planned, with a population of 500 000 by 1990, it will represent an enormous urban sprawl as it will inevitably link to Caracas to form a single mass. Problems of pollution of air and water are likely to become increasingly severe.

Ciudad Guayana

The third growth centre, Ciudad Guayana, is different in function and in scale from the other

Fig. 58 Ciudad Guayana

two. It dates back to 1960, and has had the bene-fit of vast financial resources poured into it and a specially created government agency, the Corp-oración Venezolana de Guayana (CVG) which watched over it and which had the advantage of considerable autonomy of action. Though a regional effort, the developments were concen-trated at the junction of the Caroní River with the Orinoco (Fig. 58), where a few small villages had existed, including the iron ore exporting terminal. A new town was built and a bridge crossing the Caroní, economic development be-coming based on the steel industry, hydro-electricity for the Caroní, and water transport for ore carriers up to 60 000 tonnes out to the sea by way of a dredged canal. The population of Ciudad Guayana has reached about 210 000 (1981) while 100 km upstream, Ciudad Bolívar, (once known as Angostura because of the nar-rows on the Orinoco here) has 150 000 popula-tion, and is growing almost as rapidly as the industrial city below it.

Steel manufacturing at Ciudad Guayana has already been mentioned. Unfortunately the steel industry has been unable to attract many linked engineering industries, as the principal markets and skilled labour are in the north and industries such as shipbuilding are tied to the coast. Cheap hydroelectric power has attracted some industry, notably pulp and paper manufacture, and it is to supply this industry that a large area north of the river in the infertile acid sands of southern Monagas, has been planted with Monterrey pine (*Pinus insignis*), which may help to bring this whole region into the industrial hinterland of Ciudad Guayana. Another industry using local resources is alumina and aluminium. This is being built up rapidly on the basis of first, the cheap electricity, and secondly, discoveries in 1976 of up to 500 million tonnes of bauxite with-in Northern Guayana, at Los Pijiguaos. A re-finery to produce alumina with one million tonnes ore capacity annually is being built at Puerto Ordaz. This will feed into existing smelters to produce aluminium, and replace imports from Caribbean countries.

Industrial growth at Ciudad Guayana may be seen as a success story, in terms of production; whether it is so in regional terms is less clear. The growth-pole effect of the key industries (steel, paper, energy, aluminium) is very slight, after the construction phase which employs large numbers of men for a short time. Forward link-ages to consumer and intermediate industries have been particularly slight, and the multiplier effects of the major investments are thus felt not in the region but in Caracas. Power is exported via hightension lines, and aluminium, paper and steel go to markets in the core region. Ciudad Guayana still has something of an enclave economy, more so than the older and smaller centre at Ciudad Bolívar, which ironically enough was never intended to form the growth pole of the region.

Rather than a regional development, Guayana may be seen as a national development project which happens to be sited in one of the periph-eral regions, but whose function is still primarily national. It could well be argued that the focus of effort should have been placed in the Andean highlands, where the greatest combination of large population and great poverty is to be found, or in the poor area of the northern Oriente, once a land of cocoa plantations, but without any modern economic base. If the aim is to reduce the flows of migrants, capital and resources from these regions to the centre, some investment must be made in them. The Guayana region was poor but not densely peopled, and it has proved no solution to the problems of the poor regions on the other national peripheries.

20. Economic Development and International Relations

Latin America, together with Africa and parts of the Middle and Far East, forms part of the 'underdeveloped', 'less developed', or 'developing' world, terms that imply poverty, lack of education and lack of opportunity for social and economic advance for the individual. Underdevelopment is a relative term, and so any consideration of the situation must compare the countries concerned with the most developed ones; the question of which indices to use in the comparison is raised in this chapter.

Another name for the underdeveloped countries is the 'Third World', placing these countries between the West, and the Soviet bloc. This term has political as well as economic implications, making Latin America part of an unaligned, neutral bloc between the great powers, and with a separate weight in international assemblies. There is some truth in this picture of a third region; in international affairs, the Third World countries tend to play off East against West, seeking to obtain maximum aid for their own development, while preserving political neutrality.

DEFINITIONS AND MEASUREMENT

Definitions

It is valid to ask of the experts how and why they define countries as 'developed' or 'under-developed', for the criteria are open to some question, and the definitions vary according to the criterion chosen. In Venezuela, for example, it might be difficult to accept a definition of the country as underdeveloped if this were to be based solely on the per capita GNP. This figure is an average, but an average made up of two extremes, a large body of low wage earners and peasant farmers, and a tiny minority of high salary executives, landowners and merchants. Few people earn the average wage. Other indices, such as the birth rate, death rate and rate of infant mortality, portray a quite different picture of Venezuelan life, and one that is perhaps just as valid as GNP for measuring overall national advance. It is generally accepted that the term 'development' applies not only to strictly economic phenomena, such as GNP, income or production levels, but also to a cluster of related features: education, birth and death rates, communication and transportation efficiency and extent, even the structure of government. None of these measures the total socio-economic complex but each contributes to the pattern.

Measurement

Obviously, given the complexity of the concept of development, any measurement should also be complex and use a variety of indices. One simple measure is per capita GNP, the measure of total

ECONOMIC INDICES

Country	1	2	3	4	5	6	7	8
Argentina	980	37.0	58.3	17.9	63.1	81.6	—	92.0
Bolivia	170	1.0	77.3	52.0	49.7	47.3	74.6	42.4
Brazil	350	43.7	107.6	52.5	60.7	66.3	69.7	54.7
Chile	569	11.6	92.6	27.5	54.4	77.2	47.2	84.8
Colombia	345	12.1	74.9	47.4	44.2	49.3	62.4	74.8
Ecuador	229	1.6	86.1	55.4	51.0	48.5	67.9	68.4
Guyana	298	0.7	38.3	32.3	59.0	—	—	90.9
Paraguay	229	0.3	51.8	54.5	59.4	64.0	37.3	80.8
Peru	291	8.2	60.2	49.1	52.6	58.6	66.0	74.4
Uruguay	651	2.6	53.9	17.6	65.5	94.5	55.1	91.0
Venezuela	944	21.6	46.2	32.4	66.4	58.7	39.2	68.0
U.S.A.	4379	2189.5	20.8	4.0	66.6	91.2	57.6	—

Source: Statistical Abstract of Latin America,
1971, *and* Statistical Abstract of the United
States, 1970

Headings:
1. Per capita GNP in dollars (U.S.), 1968
*2. Energy consumption, millions of tonnes coal
equivalent, 1969*
3. Infant mortality rate, 1968 or latest date
*4. Percentage economically active in agriculture
and other primary industry (latest date)*

5. Male life expectancy (various dates)
6. Total protein intake, (1961-3)
*7. Owner-operator farms as percentage of all
holdings (various dates)*
*8. Male adult literacy rate in percentage (various
years)*

output of goods and services per person, a good overall measure but failing in some respects, as for example in the inaccuracies of recording a farmer's production for his own family, or in the lack of any possibility of recording utility of production. Less housing, clothing and food are needed in hot countries than in cold, and much 'production' in the developed countries is of articles or services with a very dubious value.

Other measures are more easily obtainable, but are less all-embracing than GNP. Output and consumption of steel, power and paper are fairly easily calculated, but none gives a complete picture. Demographic rates, literacy and education statistics are measures of social advance but may be only marginally related to economic progress. In some countries, such as Cuba or Chile, social advance may outrun economic advance and the people may be literate, well educated and organized into western social communities, without achieving much economic dynamism. This imbalanced situation is in fact close to the root of political extremism, an expression of the frustration and lack of outlet

for the creative capacity of educated individuals in poor societies, in Cuba, Chile or Uruguay. Uruguay's Tupamaros, the Chilean Marxists and the breeding of Castroism under the Batista government of the 1950s are all symptoms of an imbalance between knowledge and education on the one hand, and opportunity and rewards on the other.

The tree diagram shows the result of correlation processes at different levels. First, basic pairs were formed of countries whose strongest correlation was with each other, based on the various indices given above as well as birth rates, number of radios and per capita newsprint consumption, and some other similar measures. The level of correlation of **r** value for these basic pairs was 0.95 or over, where **r** can reach a maximum of 1.0 in the Pearsonian correlation formula used. Next, clusters were formed by adding other countries to the basic pairs according to their highest **r** value. This gave the clusters which are to be seen in the diagram. Finally, grouping of the clusters was made on the basis of mean correlation between members of different

TREE DIAGRAM OF CORRELATION

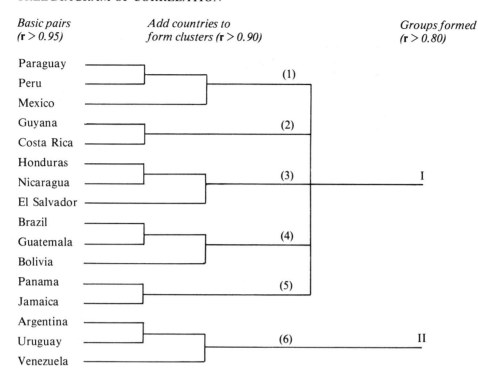

clusters, and this separated the Argentina—Uruguay—Venezuela group from all others, emphasizing the relatively higher status enjoyed by these three countries and their differences from the rest of Latin America.

THEORIES OF UNDERDEVELOPMENT

Why do some countries become rich, and others poor? This question to which Adam Smith addressed himself in *The Wealth of Nations*, remains a major problem and one which the economist's techniques have not been able to resolve satisfactorily to this date. We may group the explanations of the growth/development process into two broad kinds, which are termed here endogenous and exogenous, according to whether internal or external origins are seen as most important.

Some economists have treated development as a self-contained endogenous process. W.W. Rostow's picture of development* was of a con-

stant forward movement, which he likened to the take-off of an aeroplane, slow at first, then accelerating and gaining height until cruising altitude is reached and the climb levels off at the state of full development. This change is induced by an internal change towards a modest level of saving which makes money available for capital investment in new tools and machinery and starts a snowball effect which results in development. No outside impulse is necessary to set the movement going and once started, it continues in the same direction because successful investment produces money profits which may be re-invested in further improvements such as more efficient motors and other machines.

Another writer who regarded development as endogenous was Esther Boserup† who for agricultural societies saw a change from extensive 'primitive' methods such as slash-and-burn

*W.W. Rostow, *The Stages of Economic Development*, Cambridge University Press, 1960
†E. Boserup, *The Conditions of Agricultural Growth*, Allen & Unwin, London, 1965

Fig. 59 Economic systems in South America

farming through forest fallow and bush fallow (systems using ever shorter fallow periods, and thus ever more intensive farming) to permanently cultivated fields, which we would call development because this evolution produces more per hectare, has higher inputs of fertilizers and human labour per hectare, requires the installation of roads, drains and other infrastructure such as irrigation works, and is associated with urbanization. These changes she attributed to a gradually rising population pressure on a fixed land area, and endogenous change, though perhaps ultimately due to outside medical influence which lowered the regional death rates.

Other writers have described development merely as a change from predominance of primary activity (farming and fishing) to secondary (manufacturing) and then to tertiary (services and retailing). As the most developed countries today have a large proportion of their workforce in services, and at a previous stage had a dominance of manufacturing employment, while the early stages of development were associated with high employment in agriculture, development may be viewed, or at least measured, as a change of dominant employment. Following such theories, it would not be necessary to have development policies, because the endogenous processes would automatically, internally, produce change and evolutionary development.

Exogenous theories

Counter to such ideas are the now more popular theories which stress external agents of change. It is acknowledged by writers such as Harold Brookfield* that development is an inter-dependent process, whether we view it at the scale of interaction between cities, between regions of one country, or between countries, at the international level.

The export base concept, widely applied to explain the development of cities and regions, is of this kind. It treats development as due to a leading sector which provides a surplus that is exported to the rest of the world, and is able to induce development in the rest of the region or country because it stimulates the growth of other industries and activities. Thus Sao Paulo's growth in the nineteenth century is explained as a function of its coffee trade, and Peru's 1960's development on the basis of fishmeal and copper exports.

Another exogenous view, which has been widely applied in planning, is the growth pole concept. This was first thought of as a dynamic industry or sector which induced development through its own growth but also through its many links to other industries. Applied to regions the theory refers to growth poles as places, such as cities, which will also have growth pole industries and will draw forward all the region around the city. It is an exogenous theory because development of all areas around the central growth pole requires outside effects – i.e. those of the pole itself – to advance. A growth pole might be a city with an industry such as petrochemicals; it has regional links to user industries (e.g. manufacturers of fertilizers or synthetic textiles) and to suppliers, the refineries, as well as links to the local population which supplies labour, or services to the industry, such as financial or management advice, marketing, warehousing or advertising. As the pole industry grows, so too does its region.

This theory is related to the more basic spatial concept of centre and periphery. Development was seen by writers such as Friedmann† as basically unbalanced, the centres or metropolises receiving a large part of the national flows of

*H.C. Brookfield, *Interdependent Development*, Methuen, London, 1975
†J. Friedman, *Regional Development: a case study of Venezuela*, M.I.T. Press, Cambridge, Massachusetts, 1966

capital, goods and persons, while outer areas lose all these elements through outmovement. Friedmann's scheme referred to a national structure, but the pattern may be observed on an international scale too (Fig. 59). Migration of labour forms a huge system focussing on a few centres in South America, notably Buenos Aires, Sao Paulo – Rio and Caracas, and draining the hinterlands of these centres, both rural and urban, of their best human resources, the most educated and most ambitious, and much of the young adult population.

Dependency

A viewpoint which has been particularly developed by writers from Latin America is a kind of centre-periphery structure in which the centre, the industrial-urban heartland, is also a political dominant which forces the dependent periphery into a particular kind of economy, producing raw materials, and is actively respons-ible for repressing urban-industrial development and diversification. This idea goes on from the centre-periphery model to ascribe the basic causes of difference in development not to economic forces but political ones. It has been most forcefully applied to Latin America by A.G. Frank, in an interpretation of colonial history, showing that Chile, for example, was forced into a position of raw material producer – of wheat, wool, meat and gold – at the other end of a continuous chain of capitalist exploitation originating in Spain or ultimately in Northern Europe which provided Spain and Portugal with exportable manufactures.

This is another exogenous theory, relying on the influence of outside forces to control, not development in this case but the *lack* of develop-ment or even active negative development, a worsening position among peripheral countries and regions. The theory may obviously be applied at various scales.

It is not possible to choose one theory amongst these that provides a total explanation of Latin American development. The growth of the Argentine Pampas region, for example, might be viewed as an export-based type of process, rely-ing on the export of hides and salt meat, then of wool, wheat and frozen beef to ever-growing European markets in the nineteenth century. This region was the most dynamic and pros-perous in Argentina because it was the one best able to contribute to the export trade. By contrast, Chile's national development might be a case more in the dependency mould, because Spanish and Peruvian restrictions made Chile a contributor of raw materials under a system in which the profits from this activity went only to merchants and great landowners, not being widely spread in the regions of wheat and cattle production. This was followed in the nineteenth century by economic domination from first, Britain in the age of nitrates extraction from the northern deserts, then the United States during the present century. Conditions of unequal exchange, whereby Chile and especially her producing population, never received adequate compensation for the valuable resources they exported, meant the preservation of an underdeveloped state.

The social factor

Yet another line of reasoning which is essentially exogenous insofar as it attempts to explain development, refers to the social organization of mankind. The viewpoint of Karl Polanyi* was that economic institutions are all dependent on social or cultural ones, especially the non-market societies which use reciprocity (sharing of work and benefits) or redistribution (gathering of surpluses and their redistribution by a central authority, as in the ancient empires) as their basis. According to this view, in such old societies as those of the Andean-Inca civilization, there is no necessary adoption of a more 'modernized' type of economy once it is introduced, and in fact there may be rejection of the market economy by these people who see no need for it.

For such societies, any attempt at modern development must reckon with the power of social structure and, because changes in this structure are only likely to come from the outside, development is an exogeneous process, though not primarily economic.

DEVELOPMENT POLICIES — REGIONAL AND NATIONAL

The following section reviews some attempts to apply particular development strategies to individual regions within a country. This is

*K. Polanyi, *The Livelihood of Man*, ed. H.W. Pearson, New York, Academic Press, 1977

followed by a review of development at the national level.

Regional development

Four types of regional development strategy are commonly mentioned with respect to South America:
1 river-basin development
2 problem area development
3 colonization of new lands
4 growth pole policies.
Of these, the problem area approach is so individual to each problem area that few generalizations can be made. Colonization of new lands is a policy which lacks a strong theoretical base, except the temporary alleviation of excess population in some areas of the occupation of new lands. Here we will comment on the other two types, plus a more recent approach which tries to achieve more rounded development.

River basins have comprised attractive areas for defining the scope of development programmes, ever since the successful action of the Tennessee Valley Authority in the United States, begun in the 1930s. The idea was that action centres on improvement of the river itself, for irrigation, navigation, flood control and power production, will eventually branch out into a variety of other related activities and affect the whole region. Such a policy implies a centre-periphery view of development and the need to overcome centralization through improvements on peripheries. It requires a powerful unitary body in charge of the programme, able to impose its will over a wide variety of decision areas. It also presupposes that the main problem of the region is in its infrastructure, and makes its task the improvement of this infrastructure through massive programmes of dam construction, laying out of power lines, canals, roads, extending into afforestation and headwater erosion control through advice to farmers.

River basin programmes have been tried in various places in Latin America. Within South America, the CVC, Cauca Valley Corporation of Colombia, is perhaps best known and its particular failures (see also Chapter 18), throw some light on the kind of problem that may occur. Lack of autonomy for the agency, its subjection to pressures from both national and local governments, led to conflict and the total emasculation of CVC, which remains only as a body co-ordinating the generation of electric power and directly-related activities. Apart from such political problems, there may be some more fundamental misgivings about the possibility for success with a CVC type of programme. It was addressed very largely to the installation of infrastructure of a physical nature, whereas it may be claimed that the primary need was for social infrastructure, for the reallocation of farm land between the big farmers, holding the fertile bottom lands, and the small farmers, with tiny over-cultivated patches on the hill slopes around about.

Ecuador's regional development agencies illustrate some other dangers of a river-basin approach. In the province of Manabí, CRM, the provincial development agency concentrates its efforts in a tiny part of the west of the province, and on water provision alone. It is aware of the narrowness of this approach, but because of the massive and fixed nature of investments already made or committed to by the agency, in dams, irrigation and domestic water systems, etc., it cannot do much to broaden its scope, either in the sense of moving from water control to such matters as agricultural credit or land use planning, or in the sense of a geographical expansion from the small area of the Portoviejo valley to the remainder of the province.

In another river basin, that of the Guayas, the concentration has been on flood control and water transfers to drier regions. Again there has been no real attempt at a comprehensive, integrated approach. Similarly, the effort in the southern frontier area by PREDESUR has been concentrated very largely on a river-basin project, Puyango-Tumbes, with irrigation and power production the main achievements to be obtained. One is led to view these efforts as useful contributors to national production of power or of agricultural goods through the improvements in irrigation, but only occasionally and by coincidence helping the poorest areas and most needy human groups. River basin development could only be endorsed if it acted as a pole, spreading out its effect to all localities and groups in its region, and even then there would be many regions which did not coincide with river basins and would not fit the framework.

Growth poles

River basin policy was seen as related to centre-periphery concepts, but, as we have noted, this investment tends to become sectorally and regionally concentrated and thus a kind of growth pole policy. This latter policy is itself used more for manufacturing industry development, and applied to urban places in particular. Growth poles have been popular in a number of South American countries as a development formula. Chile, during the late 1960s before Allende, had a series of 12 development poles, one in each of the planning regions which spread from south to north over the whole length of the country. It was hoped with this policy to achieve a better balance and in particular to reduce the overcentralization of economy of Santiago. Poles were designated at various levels, with Santiago seen as national pole, Concepción, Valparaiso and Antofagasta as second level poles and 'counter-magnets' to Santiago, and most of the provincial capitals were a third level of development poles. In Chile, however, as elsewhere, the designation of poles was much easier than making them work. Few industries could be persuaded to move out to remote country towns and those that did required legislation to keep them in place. Within each planning region, the new industries came only to the pole itself, and other parts of the region suffered. In Antofagasta city, for example, development was primarily of copper-related industry and of cement manufacture, linked to single mining sites, especially Chuquicamata, but with no spread effects through the province of Antofagasta.

Growth pole policies were publicly abandoned by the Allende government of 1970–73, not for reasons of their economic inoperability, but because they were considered to reproduce the urban hierarchy exactly and thus merely to reinforce the dominance of town over country, failing to attack the question of poverty which was concentrated in the rural areas, not in the towns at all. Allende hoped instead to sponsor a deconcentrated development corridor, strung out over a 1600 km line through the Central Valley, from Coquimbo on the Elqui river south to Puerto Montt where the valley ends. Development would, according to the plans, be evenly spread along this line because of the ease of moving raw materials, power products in either direction along it; thus no region would be particularly favoured, and the earlier aim of deconcentration from Santiago would also be served. This policy was not tried for a period sufficient to say whether it would have been more effective than its predecessors, but it appears a less radical change than was claimed at the time.

Like Chile, with variations in accordance with local conditions, Colombia, Ecuador, Peru, Venezuela, Brazil and Argentina have endorsed the growth pole idea. In most such cases, the policy has not been continued long enough to show much in results, as the effects to be felt would be possible only over a long period of building up linkages. In any case, the implementation has been defective, because the pole industries chosen were not such as to allow linkages to be strong with other local activities. Even on theoretical grounds, the idea may be challenged in its application to Latin America because the linkages are generally likely to be absent – the most dynamic industries are likely to be foreign-owned and thus have their links to industries in a foreign country, while for industries which are truly home-owned, the structure of ownership is not likely to favour linkage. Great entrepreneurs in Latin America are likely to own firms in widely different industries, not in a single group related by vertical ties of consumer-supplier or through use of similar processes.

Integrated development
In the last few years, the vogue for strong concentration on specific industries or sectors, and on specific regions, has given way to a broader concept of integrated regional development, especially for rural areas. Economic measures have been found to be insufficient and sometimes irrelevant in the countryside where the central problems of agrarian structure must be tackled, and constitute a social and political rather than an economic problem.

We may distinguish three important threads in this movement towards integrated development, local organization, alternative technology and agrarian reform. There is a need for local organizations to begin planning from the grass-roots level, rather than have it handed down from above. Planning from above means centralization and impersonal relations, resulting at best in local apathy in the region, at worst in active opposition. It also means lack of adapta-

tion of standard plans to the vagaries of local conditions. An example of the emphasis on local-level organization is in the Cañar province project of CREA, the development agency of the Cuenca region in southern Ecuador. Here importance is being laid during the initial period of development, on the reinforcement and re-creation where necessary, of Indian communities which were formerly the strongest social organization of the local population. Modern co-operatives created with agrarian reform from 1964, but which had since ceased to function properly, are also being strengthened. Only after this phase is complete will the emphasis be laid on economic measures. This follows the theoretical basis outlined above in which social factors are seen as all-important in any explanation of underdevelopment and development. It is also intended that the local communities should be the initiators of projects, and actively participate in planning and executing them. Such a revolutionary change from the traditional administration from above has no previous parallels in Latin America; the nearest similar structure is perhaps the Ujamaa policy applied in Tanzania, Africa.

Another concept is the use of what is termed either intermediate, appropriate or alternative technology. The reasons for this focus are evident from the names given. Use of labour-intensive small-scale simple technology is intermediate between the traditional total lack of machines, it is appropriate to the capital poverty of the countries concerned, and it represents an alternative to the western standard. At CREA, the focus is not on giant hydro-electric projects, but on the development of craft industries such as pottery, jewellery, leatherwork and weaving, industries using little machinery or capital, but much labour skill, which is the factor in good supply in the region. In agriculture, the emphasis is on traditional crops with the aid of small irrigation schemes to intensify production, and small processing industries (vegetable oils, jams, spices) to use the product.

Finally, agrarian reform is intimately bound in with such schemes because it provides the structural changes, of farm size, land tenure, access to markets, that make technological change possible, and because it serves to break down, if properly carried through, the class divisions between great landowner and small farmer, thus making viable the local social organizations such as co-operatives.

Regional development and sectoral development

For many parts of Latin America the power and political will of governments to enact directly regional measures is limited; help for one region is a cause for resentment by other regions; help to all regions may be looked on with disfavour by the governing elite which lives largely in the metropolitan centres; or the personnel skills of the regions may be too weak to administer a regional programme.

In such cases, existing national programmes for various economic sectors, such as for energy, for manufacturing, or for agriculture, may be of greater significance to regions than any specifically regional programme. A national policy of taxing agricultural exports, long practised in countries such as Argentina, Uruguay and Ecuador, makes a definite negative impact on agricultural regions, and especially on those regions where the export crops are important. Such a policy is applied in order to raise revenue rather than damage the regions, but it may restrain development.

Conversely, Argentina has also had a policy of maximum development of energy resources. This has helped peripheral regions somewhat because hydroelectric power (in the Andes and on the Middle Paraná) and oil and gas (in Patagonia, Tierra del Fuego, Bolivian borderlands) are concentrated in the peripheries. Urban policies may also be important to regions. Much of the attraction and meteoric growth of the metropolitan centres has been due to the policy of 'conspicuous investment' in them by central governments. These governments have been anxious to emulate advanced countries by having their own underground railway systems, skyscrapers, great airports, and have consciously focussed all their attention on their most important city.

Tax policies are very important given the high level of some tariffs, of well over 100% of value at port of entry. Policies of import substitution, through tariff barriers, have helped industries grow, but very largely in one region, the metropolitan market centre. This kind of policy is now less favoured and some countries (Chile, Colombia, Argentina) are beginning to use export-subsidy policies instead. This changes regional development prospects altogether, because peripheral, resource regions are now favoured over the metropolitan one. In general, we may conclude that the financial resources used or implied in all these 'non-regional' government policies are greater than those used directly in regional aid, and their effect, though somewhat indirect, is stronger.

NATIONAL LEVEL DEVELOPMENT

Prior to World War II, Latin America could be regarded as part of the West's economic empire, particularly that of the United States. As long ago as 1820 the Monroe Doctrine enunciated a theory of US hegemony in the western hemisphere. President Monroe's statement was made in military-strategic terms, but it became, at least after the gradual decline of British dominance in the region in the late nineteenth century, an economic reality.

For the United States, the area was of interest as a raw material producer and it was this which was aided by private investments from the USA in the region. For some countries the weight of US dominance was suffocating — in Venezuela, where 23% of US investment in Latin America was concentrated in 1969, North American firms had the following proportions of total investment in publicly-quoted firms:

Sector	Percentage US of Crude investment
Petroleum	71.41
Iron Ore	99.89
Commerce	64.93
Industry	67.31
Services	65.53
Financial Institutions	68.82
Construction	19.72

Source: F. Brito Figueroa, *Historia Económica y Social de Venezuela*, Tomo III. 9.743, Univ. Central de Venezuela, Caracas, 1975.

This picture has of course changed in more recent years; in the Venezuelan case, petroleum and iron ore have both been taken over by the state. The structure of trade, previously dominated by the investment partners, the USA and Western Europe, has been made somewhat more open, so as to include now a wide variety of trading relationships (see table below).

LAFTA TOTAL AND INTRAZONAL EXPORTS (Million dollars)

Country	Average 1962–4			1978		
	Total	Intrazonal	Percentage intrazonal	Total	Intrazonal	Percentage intrazonal
Argentina	1 330	196	14.7	6 350	1 513	23.16
Bolivia	92	3	3.3	649	194	29.89
Brazil	1 350	99	7.3	12 659	1 619	12.79
Chile	567	50	8.8	2 408	606	25.17
Colombia	486	9	1.9	3.221	1 435	44.55
Ecuador	125	8	6.4	1 494	229	15.33
Mexico	835	33	4.0	5 438	406	7.47
Paraguay	41	12	29.3	257	67	26.07
Peru	583	58	9.9	1 941	235	12.11
Uruguay	166	13	7.8	686	192	27.99
Venezuela	2 678	143	5.3	9 174	449	4.89
Total	8 253	624	7.6	43 998	6 943	15.68

Source: Inter-American Development Bank, Economic and Social Progress in Latin America, *Annual Reports* 1973, 1978 and 1979 *Washington D.C.*

In other countries the state has also been the agent of change away from foreign ownership. In Brazil the state has taken an increasing role since 1964, and dominates the oil, steel, electric and nuclear power, railways, shipping, banking, telecommunications and iron ore industries. It is responsible for over 60% of fixed capital investment in Brazil, It is still possible to argue that these countries are wholly dependent on the exterior because their technology is imported designs, formulae and processes, and a major concern for development is thus now the transfer of technology.

International agencies
Aid from the international agencies such as the World Bank and the Interamerican Development Bank (IDB) to development has not formally followed any theory of development, but with the failure of aid to industry as the main thrust of aid in the 1960s, more aid has gone to social welfare and especially to agriculture. In 1961–65,

the Agency for International Development, World Bank, Eximbank of the USA, IDA and IDB, placed only 10.7% of its loans in agriculture. In 1979, 21.45% of them went to agriculture. This is a welcome change reflecting a realization that industrialization has not worked entirely satisfactorily, but it remains true that the greater part of the aid given has been highly biased regionally and sectorally. Three of the biases may be listed:
1. Large schemes, involving standardized modern techniques for which calculation can be made by a team of experts in advance construction, have been favoured, which has meant priority to large scale industry or investment in infrastructure such as dams on rivers. Schemes for school provision, education, urban planning and agriculture are less amenable to cost-benefit analysis and have been less favoured on that account.
2. Schemes which are primarily sectoral have been favoured, for the same kind of reasons.

Broad regional schemes involving agriculture, social change, education etc, have too many interlinkages to be able to make precise assessments of their impact.

3. Aid has often gone to the more developed countries, which have been able to present better drawn up plans and projects because they either have more competent professional engineers and planners, or can afford to hire them. There is thus a tendency to invest in and reinforce success. The World Bank in the 1960s loaned 46.6 US dollars per capita to Uruguay, its highest per capita rate, while poor Bolivia received only 5.4 dollars per capita.

Broadly speaking, both foreign aid and domestic national planning has been towards the aim of import substitution. The United Nations Economic Commission for Latin America (ECLA), especially under Raul Prebisch in the 1960s, endorsed a view of development as exogenously controlled, in a centre-periphery model in which the central countries produced manufactured goods which they sold to the peripheral ones in exchange for raw materials. However, in the exchange the periphery lost because its raw materials were sold cheaply, while manufactured exports from the developed world were sold expensively. This 'Prebisch thesis' thus concerns what the economist calls the *terms of trade*. Adverse terms of trade hold back the peripheral countries.

Import substitution

A solution is thus the diversification of the peripheral economies to make them manufacturing as well as raw material producing. Most international loans have helped this industrial growth which substitutes local products for former imports, but most substitution has been because of the protection of high tariffs on imported goods. The results have not however been altogether desirable. First, and perhaps foremost, industrial growth has mostly been by the transnational companies, which have been able to take up offers of loans and tax remissions at short notice, but whose factories have not helped the regions they settle in because they act only as 'enclaves', island economies within a region to which they are attached only for use of its labour. Such firms are often concerned to make their overseas branches as self-contained as possible, not relying on local firms for services of

any kind nor for inputs or outputs from their factories.

Another disadvantage noted in the section on regional development, is that the industrial growth tends to be concentrated at one or two cities causing greater regional imbalance; this is because it is often light, consumer-oriented industry and chooses a market location, and because of less obvious but equally real factors, such as greater information about the metropolis on the part of the firm, better government agency contacts there, and the better living environment in the metropolis for executives of the firm who must manage the factory.

All manufacturing industry built up behind the protection of tariff barriers and with the aid of special credits, as has happened in the process of important substitution, is likely to be inefficient because it grows up in artificial circumstances and is not forced into competitiveness. The consequence is commonly lower-quality goods and higher prices than might have been the case with an open market. Tariff barriers are also a blunt tool as far as industrial development is concerned, because they tend to encourage indiscriminate growth of industries, mostly of consumer type because these are easier to set up initially, and leave industries without the vertical linkages to their imputs of semi-manufactured goods which must still be imported.

Finally, industries such as steel, car manufacture and others which thrive on increasing size, which achieve what are called 'economies of scale', cannot find a sufficient market within the confines of one country, and either have to export or produce very inefficiently.

INTEGRATION OF LATIN AMERICA

One solution for the problem of small size national markets, which may also help in controlling the activities of the transnational firms, and also allow a more balanced and vertically integrated industrial development, is an international grouping of Latin American countries. Integration movements thus may be seen as following through the Prebisch argument to is logical conclusions. Ideally, they allow import substitution to take place without the problems enumerated in the previous section.

LAFTA — Latin American Free Trade Association

LAFTA was created by the Treaty of Montevideo in 1960, a first attempt at integration and embracing most countries of the region. Since the entry of Venezuela in 1966 and Bolivia in 1967, LAFTA has managed to incorporate all of South America apart from the Guianas, and also includes Mexico. As a functioning entity it has had less success. Proposals and timetables for total freeing of trade in the group were constantly delayed and finally abandoned as agreement was not reached for each deadline. The approach, based not on the freeing of major sectors of trade at a blow, but on the cautious agreement on each individual item for which tariffs were to be reduced, was too slow and led to too many blockages. Although over 11 000 concessions were negotiated among members, only 30% are actually in use and these cover less than 20% of trade among members. A common list of free trade items was intended, but never achieved, so that each country has a different set of concessions. Common-market type measures, notably the introduction of a common external tariff, were not introduced. Now it is hoped to replace the LAFTA structure with a stronger and more comprehensive measure, a regional margin of preference, looking towards a regional common market. In trade terms, it might be said that some improvement has taken place, though it is uncertain to what extent this is due to LAFTA's efforts. The table shows that intrazonal exports have increased from 7.6% of all trade in 1962–64, to 15.7% in 1978 or to 18.7% if we exclude Venezuela from the calculation as a country whose petroleum links to the outside world make her a special case. Other countries with powerful links to the outside are obviously Peru, as a raw material exporter, Brazil, and Mexico.

The Andean Pact

Dissatisfaction with LAFTA over the rate of progress, and fears for their own position as poorer members, lay behind the decision to form a new smaller group within LAFTA, the Andean Group, under the Cartagena Agreement of 1969; the countries involved were Bolivia, Colombia, Chile, Ecuador and Peru, joined by Venezuela in 1973. In addition to a free-trade zone, the group is setting up its own common external tariff, and will become a full customs union, the rate of progress being standardized by articles in the agreement which require members to reach the same level of tariffs at the same time, regardless of momentary setbacks. Bolivia and Ecuador are given special treatment as poorer countries but this grouping of countries is less significant than in the case of LAFTA, and the higher homogeneity of the group will help it towards integration.

One distinctive feature of the Pact is the international planning of economic activity, especially industry, but also power and transportation, so as to achieve maximum economies for the Group. There have been two major agreements, to allocate branches of engineering and of petrochemicals manufacture to individual countries, so that, for example, Bolivia is to monopolize pneumatic tool making, Colombia light aircraft, Chile was to make railway equipment, and Ecuador clocks.

One cloud that has gathered over the Andean Pact is Chile's withdrawal in 1976, under a government whose economic policy is not compatible with many clauses of the Pact, for Chile seeks industrialization through a Brazilian approach, using heavy and free foreign investment and hoping to avoid the distortions inevitable in a protectionist policy, even when it is practised at a group level. Chile's departure makes the Pact look more fragile, and other countries could leave it in the future. Another difficulty is that the regional industrial programmes of allocation proceed very slowly, only two having been enacted in six years. For the remaining five countries, the future seems uncertain.

The river Plate basin

Another grouping is that of the Paraná—Paraguay river basin countries, Brazil and Argentina being the major partners, with Bolivia, Paraguay and Uruguay, and the possible addition of Chile. Under a 1969 treaty, these countries are to cooperate in physical integration schemes, especially those concerning the river basin itself, and allowing agreements between any two members or other subgroup of the whole to be made. This is a more limited approach to integration than that of a free-trade zone or customs union, and in addition runs into the problems facing any multipurpose river-basin project in Latin America. A major difficulty is that the members are excessively unbalanced in political and economical power. Up to the present, only limited progress has been made, and discord between the two major nations has been a stumbling block. In 1973, Argentina revoked an agreement with Brazil on the use of the Paraná in the vicinity of the international frontier, because of conflicting desires for power production and water use by these two countries.

The Caribbean

The Guianas, because of their recent colonial status and association with North Europe rather than Iberia, have not been involved in LAFTA or other Latin groupings. Instead, Guyana has since 1968 been included with the other British Commonwealth countries of the Caribbean, in the Caribbean Free Trade Association, CARIFTA. Its members are Barbados, Guyana, Jamaica and Trinidad—Tobago, four relatively more developed members, and Antigua, Belize (formerly British Honduras), Dominica, Grenada, Montserrat, St Lucia, St Vincent and St Kitts—Nevis—Anguilla, the less-developed members. Between 1968 and 1974, a tripling of intra-zone trade has taken place. In 1973, a Caribbean Community and Common Market (CARICOM) was created to supersede CARIFTA and to aim for both political and economic integration of its members. (For Guyana, 35.8 per cent of exports and 59.8 per cent of imports were within CARICOM in 1974.) This will in the middle term align Guyana further away from the rest of the continent and towards its island neighbours to the north. An international grouping can be isolating as well as integrating, and it remains to be seen where the advantage will eventually lie in this case.

THE ROOTS OF SEPARATENESS

As the above may suggest, the process of international integration is not a smooth one for South American countries, and has a long course to run. There are long historical roots for some of the observed difficulties and problems, reaching back in some cases to colonial times. From the sixteenth to the eighteenth century, most trade was with Iberia and very little with neighbour countries, under the prevailing mercantilist system of management. In politics, a policy of divide and rule was effectively practised and no doubt delayed the emergence of any force capable of challenging the mother countries. An attitude of mistrust of their neighbours, as competing suppliers to Europe, was carried over into the first century of independence, when the dominant trading partner became Britain, and then the United States. This old attitude of mistrust is taking a long time to overcome and to be replaced by a common front.

In the case of industrial development the problem is also old, in the beginning a matter of colonial manufacturing prohibitions, to reduce competition with the homeland; while these prohibitions have long gone, a similar effect was created in the twentieth century by the high tariffs of the 1930s and later. High tariffs came in with the collapse of free trade at that time, and were especially favoured in Latin America as a means to promote new industry. In the early 1960s, tariffs averaged over 100 per cent for the imports of some countries, an awesome level from which it was a major operation to reduce to zero levels, much more difficult than for the countries of the European Common Market. High tariffs also created the problem of inefficient industries which needed the tariff shelter, and moves to reduce them were opposed by local industrialists with force and skill.

SOME IMPLICATIONS

There is no easy solution to the problem of underdevelopment in Latin America any more than for any other part of the Third World. Neither aid, on the present scale and in present forms, nor trade, if controlled by the West, seems to be the key to the problems of these countries. Looking for the factors in underdevelopment, it is apparent that not all the blame for the situation can be laid at the door of the countries concerned. Internal faults exist in the socio-economic structure of most of the region's countries, but they are only part of the story; the rest must be told by the industrial countries of the Northern Hemisphere, holding the reins of economic and political power throughout the subcontinent.

There is a wind of change blowing over the South American land, just as there is over other parts of the Underdeveloped World, a wind whose political expression is to be found in increasingly successful attempts to obtain a better hearing in international parliaments. Without the strength conferred by military force, various countries or groups have been able to demand and obtain substantial concessions on the part of the West. The nationalization of Chilean copper and the virtual expropriation of oil resources in Venezuela and elsewhere may not yet be permanent, but they give cause for thought among industrialists and governments in the West, as does the emergence of political power on the extreme left, polarized out in opposition to military dictatorships in several countries. The very fact that Chile, Peru or Bolivia can obtain aid and trade with the Eastern Bloc can be used as a lever for these and neighbour countries to obtain better terms in their dealings with the West.

What may still paralyse the continent's efforts to change its status and to break out of a structure imposed by the world economy, is the polarization of political thought into two camps, a revolutionary, radical Left wing, and a Right represented currently by the Army and repressive rule. Conflicts between these two forces are still sapping the energies of otherwise vital and expanding nations.

Appendix I
GLOSSARY OF PORTUGUESE AND SPANISH TERMS

Portuguese

aldeia	Jesuit mission village
bandeirante	member of slave-catching, exploring, or cattle droving party: the *bandeira* was the flag carried at the head of the party; especially in São Paulo in the colonial period
caboclo	backwoodsman, farm labourer, peasant
cafuso	Indian—Negro racial mixture (Brazil)
capoeira	secondary growth, brush forest
cerrado	wooded savanna
chapada	upland surface, plateau; *chapadão* refers to a larger plateau
donatária	grant of land and rights by the Portuguese king, including powers of tax raising and slave dealing, to its recipient, a *donatário*
engenho	sugar mill, usually with plantation land
favela	slum, shanty town; especially Rio de Janeiro
fazenda	ranch, large farm, estate; cf. *hacienda* in Spanish
mameluco	white—Indian cross
mata	forest. More specifically the coastlands of the Nordeste, originally densely forested.
morro	an isolated hill or small mountain
roça	cleared land; the field used in shifting cultivation
seringueiro	rubber collector
sertão	wilderness, backcountry; plural — *sertões*
tugurio	central city slum
vaqueiro	cowboy, especially in the Nordeste; cf. Spanish *vaquero*
varzea	lowland, usually alluvial floodplain, providing the best soil

Spanish

andén	terrace, especially the Inca and other Indian artificial terraces for agriculture
barriada	shanty town
barrio	suburb; shanty town (Venezuela)
cabildo	municipal authorities; town hall
callampa	shanty town (literally a mushroom) in Chile
charqui	dried or jerked beef
cimarrón	wild cattle; the descendants of escaped domestic cattle
comunidad	community, especially the Peruvian communities set up after agrarian reform and replacing older communities
conuco	shifting cultivation of forest areas, or plot of land under such cultivation. The *conuquero* is farmer of the *conuco*
criollo	local, native; more specifically, persons of Spanish extract but born in the New World. Sometimes translated into English as *creole*

estancia	a ranch or cattle farm of the Pampas region, owned by an *estanciero*
feria	a fair or market
frigorífico	meat freezing and chilling plant or factory
fundo	large farm, especially in Chile
gaucho	cowboy in Argentina, Uruguay, Rio Grande do Sul. Elsewhere the term *vaquero* (Portuguese *vaqueiro*) is used
hacendado	owner of *hacienda*
hacienda	large farm or estate
hato	large farm or ranch, Venezuelan Llanos
hoya	enclosed basin among hills
ingenio	sugar mill and plantation attached; cf. *engenho*, Portuguese
inquilino	tenant; more specifically in Chile, landless small farmer with rights of usufruct of a small plot
latifundio	large and underused estate
merced	grant of land by Spanish crown
minga	*voluntary collective work of village (quechua)*
mestizo	European—Indian racial mixture
minifundio	excessively small and intensively used farm
mita	forced labour service to landlord (Quechua, Peru)
mulato	white—negro mixture
nudo	mountain knot
oficina	nitrate works (Chile)
pampero	strong, dry, south wind of Argentine Pampas
páramo	high-level bunch-grass region above forest line. More generally, a deserted or desert area
rancho	*hut or precarious urban dwelling*
reducción	Jesuit mission village
salar	salt flat
selva	tropical rain forest
sindicato	trade union, union
templada	temperate, as in *tierra templada;* above it lies the *tierra fría* and *páramos*, below is the *tierra caliente*
tugurio	shanty town (Colombia)
yerba mate	mate tea

ABBREVIATIONS

C	temperature, degrees Centigrade
ECLA	United Nations Economic Commission for Latin America
EEC	The European Economic Community
GDP	Gross Domestic Product; the total value of all goods produced ignoring foreign trade
GNP	Gross National Product, value of all goods produced including foreign trade
ha	hectare
HEP	hydroelectric power
km	kilometres (m metre, cm centimetre, mm millimetre)
LAFTA	Latin American Free Trade Association

Note
Foreign words are generally italicized and given accentuation marks, which provide an indication of which syllable is stressed in pronunciation in Portuguese and Spanish. Town populations are given in some cases; these refer to the latest available figures where the date is not given. Measurements are in metric units.

Appendix II
BIBLIOGRAPHY

The following list tries to do several things. It covers most of the topics treated in any detail within the book, and is indeed often the basis for that treatment; it cites a few Spanish and Portuguese language sources, especially where English language writing is scarce; and it tries to be eclectic, using old as well as new sources, and varied viewpoints. The journals of most value will be apparent from the bibliographic entries, but apart from those regularly cited, some periodicals with special concern for the Latin American region are: *Americas*, published in English, Portuguese and Spanish by the Pan American Union, Washington, D.C. (monthly); *America Latina*, mostly in Spanish and Portuguese, from the Latin American Centre for Research in Social Sciences, Rio de Janerio (quarterly); *Bolsa Review* from Lloyds Bank International, London (monthly); *Economic Development and Cultural Change*, quarterly from the University of Chicago Press; the *Journal of Latin American Studies*, Cambridge, England (biannual); and *Revista Geografica*, mostly in English, from the Geography Commission of the Panamerican Institute of Geography and History, Mexico City, (triannual).

Useful annuals are the *South American Handbook*, edited by John Brooks and published by Trade and Travel Publications, Bath, England (a travellers' guide but with much background information), the *Economic Survey of Latin America*, from the UN Economic Commission for Latin America, and *Economic and Social Progress in Latin America*, from the Inter-American Development Bank, Washington, D.C. A unique publication is the annual series of Proceedings of the Conference of Latin American Geographers (CLAG), published since 1971 and available from the Department of Geography, Ball State University, Muncie, Indiana. A statistical source, apart from the regular United Nations yearbooks,

with coverage of the whole region, is *Statistical Abstract of Latin America*, from the University of California, Los Angeles, Latin American Center Publications, edited by J.W. Wilkie.

Place of publication is London unless indicated.

General Works

Blakemore, H. and Smith, C.T., (eds.), *Latin America: Geographical Perspectives*, Methuen, 1971

Cole, J.P., *Latin America, an Economic and Social Geography*, 3rd. edn., Butterworths, 1976

Cunill, P., *L'Amérique Andine*, translated from the Spanish by H. Lecomte de Martonne, Paris, Presses Universitaires, 1966

James, P.E., *Latin America*, New York, Odyssey Press, 5th edn., 1975

Niedergang, M., *The Twenty Latin Americas*, 2 vols., Penguin 1971

Odell, P.R. and Preston, D.A., *Economies and Societies in Latin America*, Wiley, 2nd. edn., 1978

Schmieder, O., *Geografía de América Latina*, Buenos Aires, Fondo de Cultura Económica (Spanish edn.) 1965

Veliz, C. (ed.), *Latin America and the Caribbean: A Handbook*, Blond, 1968

Webb, K.E., *Geography of Latin America*, Englewood Cliffs, N.J., Prentice-Hall, 1972

Physical

Barker, Mary L., 'National parks, conservation and agrarian reform in Peru', *Geog. Review, 70* (1980), pp. 1–18

Cole, M.M., 'Cerrado, Caatinga and Pantanal: the distribution and origin of the savanna vegetation of

Brazil', *Geog. Journal,* **126** (1960), pp. 168–79

Eden, Michael J., 'Ecology and land development: the case of the Amazonian rainforest', *Transactions Inst. Brit. Geog.*, N.S. 3/4 (1978), pp. 444–64

Fittkau, E.J., Illies, J, *et al.*, *Biogeography and Ecology in South America*, The Hague, W. Junk, 1968, 2 volumes

Goodland, R., *The Savanna Controversy: Background Information on the Brazilian Cerrado Vegetation*, Savanna Research Series No. 15, Montreal, McGill University, 1970

Goodland, R.J.A. and Irwin, H.S., *Amazon Jungle: Green Hell to Red Desert?* Amsterdam, Elsevier, (1975)

Harris, D.R. Human Ecology in Savanna Environments, Academic Press (1980), 'Europeanization of the savanna lands of North South America', pp. 267–289

Nelson, J.G., Needham, R.D., and Mann, D.L., *International Experience with National Parks and Related Reserves.* Department of Geography, Publication Series No. 12, University of Waterloo, Waterloo, Ontario, (1978). *Paper 7* — 'Colombian National Parks and Related Reserves: research needs and management', Wetterberg, G.B., and Meganek, R.A., pp. 175–232

Rudolph, W.E., *Vanishing Trails of Atacama*, New York, Amer. Geog. Society, 1963

Schwerdtfeger, W. (ed.), 'Climates of Central and South America', in: *World Survey of Climatology*, Vol. 12, Oxford, Elsevier Scientific Publishing Co. 1976

Trewartha, G.L., *The World's Problem Climates*, Ch. 1, Madison, Wisconsin, University of Wisconsin Press, 1962

Tricart, J., *Landforms of the Humid Tropics, Savannas and Forests*, (translated C.J.K. de Yonge), Longmans,1972

History

Borah, W., *Early Colonial Trade and Navigation between Mexico and Peru*, Los Angeles, Univ. of California, Ibero-American Series, 1954

Camacho, G., *Latin America*, Penguin, 1973

Cobb, G., 'Supply and transportation for the Potosi mines 1545–1640', *Hispanic American Historical Review*, 29 (1949), pp. 25–45

Conde, R. Cortes, *The First Stages of Modernization in Spanish America*, translated by Tony Talbot, New York, Harpe and Row, 1974

Denevan, William M., *The native population of the Americas in 1492*, Madison, Univ. of Wisconsin, 1976.

Hanke, L., *History of Latin American Civilization*, Vol. 1, *The Colonial Experience*, Methuen, 1969

Hennessy, Alistair, *The Frontier in Latin American History*, Edward Arnold, 1978

MacNeish, R.S., 'The origins of New World civilization', Ch. 16, pp. 155–63 in *New World Archaeology*, readings from *Scientific American*, San Francisco, W.H. Freeman, 1974

Pendle, G.A., *A History of Latin America*, Penguin, 1963

Sanders, W.T. and Marino, J., *New World Prehistory*, Englewood Cliffs, N.J., Prentice-Hall, 1970

Sauer, C.O., *The Early Spanish Main*, Berkeley, Univ. of California, 1966

Agriculture

Augelli, J.P., 'The Latvians of Varpa: a foreign colony on the Brazilian pioneer fringe', *Geog. Review, 48* (1958), pp. 365–87

Burke, M., 'Land reform and its effects upon production and productivity in the Lake Titicaca region', *Econ. Devt. and Cultural Change, 18* (1970), pp. 410–50

Clark, R.J., 'Land reform and peasant participation on the northern highlands of Bolivia', *Land Economics, 44* (1968), pp. 153–72

Dorner, P., *Land Reform and Economic Development*, Penguin, 1972

Dozier, C.L., *Land Development and Colonization in Latin America*, New York, Praeger, 1969

Eidt, R.D., 'Pioneer settlement in eastern Peru', *Annals A.A.G., 52* (1962), pp. 255–78

Hiraoka, M. and Yamamoto, S. *'Agricultural development in the upper Amazon of Ecuador'*, *Geog. Review, 70/4*, (1980) pp. 423–45

Jones, David M., 'The Green Revolution in Latin America; success or failure', *C.L.A.G. Publications* Vol. 6, pp. 55–64, Ball State Univ. Muncie, Indiana (1977)

Nelson, Michael, *The Development of Tropical Lands: Policy Issues in Latin America*, Baltimore, Johns Hopkins Press, 1973

Ruddle, K., *The Yukpa Cultivation System: a study of shifting cultivation in Colombia and Venezuela*, Los Angeles, Univ. of California Press, Ibero-Americana Series No. 52, 1974

Smith, C.T., 'Aspects of agriculture and settlement in Peru', *Geog. Journal,* **126** (1960), pp. 397–412

Industrial infrastructure and manufacturing

Benham, F. and Holley, H.A., *A Short Introduction to the Economy of Latin America*, Oxford Univ. Press, 1960

Brown, R.T., *Transport and the Economic Integration of South America*, Washington D.C., Brookings Inst., 1966

Cunningham, Susan, 'Brazil: recent trends in industrial development', *BOLSA Review*, **13/4** (1979), pp. 212–20

Dickenson, J., 'Electric power development in Minas Gerais, Brazil', *Revista Geográfica*, **70** (1969), pp. 213–21

Fox, D.J., *Tin and the Bolivian Economy*, Latin American Publications Fund, 1970

Gilbert, Alan, 'Industrial location theory: its relevance to an industrializing nation', Ch. 14, pp. 271–89, in B.S. Hoyle, (ed.), *Spatial Aspects of Development*, Wiley, 1974

Niering, F., *et al.*, *Latin American and Caribbean Oil Report*, Petroleum Economist, London, 1979

Odell, P.R., 'The oil industry in Latin America', in Penrose, E., *The Large International Firm in Developing Countries*, Cass, 1968

Stokes, C.J., *Transportation and Economic Development in Latin America*, New York, Praeger, 1968

Inter-American Development Bank, *Economic and Social Progress in Latin America*, (annual report), Inter-American Development Bank, Washington D.C.

Social and demographic patterns and processes

Amato, P.W., 'Elitism and settlement patterns in the Latin American city', *Journal Amer. Inst. of Planners*, **36** (1970), pp. 96–105

Breton, F., 'Working and living conditions of migrant workers in S. America', *International Labour Review*, **144**/3 (1976), pp. 339–54

Bromley, Rosemary, and Bromley, R.D.F., 'Defining central place systems through the analysis of bus services: the case of Ecuador', *Geog. Journal*, **145**/3 (1979), pp. 416–36

Cahiers des Ameriques Latines: Numéro Special, *Villes et regions en Amérique Latine*, ed. O. Dollfus, Paris, CNRS, 1973, p. 446

Geisse, G. and Hardoy, J.E. (eds.), Latin American Urban Research Vol. 2, *Regional and urban development policies*, Beverley Hills, Calif., Sage, 1972

Graham, D.H., 'Divergent and convergent regional economic growth and internal migration in Brazil 1940–60', *Econ. Devt. and Cultural Change*, **18** (1970), pp. 362–82

Hall, M. Françoise, 'Population growth: U.S. and Latin American views', *Population Studies*, **27** (1973), pp. 415–29

Hardoy, J.E., *Urbanization in Latin America: approaches and issues*, New York, Anchor-Doubleday, 1975

Havens A.E. and Flinn, W.L., *Internal Colonialism and Structure Change in Colombia*, New York, Praeger, 1970

Morris, A.S., 'Urban growth patterns in Latin America, with illustrations from Caracas', *Urban Studies*, **15** (1978), pp. 299–312

Portes, A. and Browning, H.L., *Current Perspectives in Latin American Urban Research*, Austin, Univ, of Texas, 1976

Rabinowitz F.F., and Trueblood, F.M. (eds.), *Latin American Urban Research*, Vol. 1, Beverley Hills, Calif, Sage, 1971

Sanchez-Albornoz, Nicolás, *The population of Latin America; a history*, Berkeley, Univ. of California, 1974

Steward, J.H. and Faron, L.C., *Native Peoples of South America*, New York, McGraw-Hill, 1959

Peru

Cole, J.P., and Mather, P.M., 'Peru province level factor analysis', *Revista Geográfica*, **77** (1972), pp. 7-37

Collin Delavaud, Claude, 'Agrarian reform in Peru', Ch. 2, pp. 37–52 in Preston, D.A. (ed.), *Environment, Society and rural change in Latin America*, Chichester, Wiley, 1980

Coull, J.R., 'The development of the fishing industry in Peru', *Geography*, **39** (1974), pp. 322–32

Dickinson, J.C., 'The Eucalypt in the Sierra of Southern Peru', *Annals A.A.G.*, **59**/2 (1969), pp. 294–307

Hemming, J., *The Conquest of the Incas*, Macmillan, 1970

Horna, H., 'The fish industry of Peru', *Journal of Developing Areas,* **2** (1968), pp. 393–406

Lowenthal, A.F., *The Peruvian Experiment*, Princeton, Princeton Univ. Press, 1975

Reparaz, G., 'La zone aride du Perou', *Geografiska Annaler* (1958), pp. 1–61

Rowe, J.H., 'The distribution of Indians and Indian languages in Peru', *Geog. Review*, **37** (1947), pp. 202–15

Smith, C.T., 'Problems of regional development in Peru', *Geography*, **53** (1968), pp. 260–81

Winterhalder, Bruce P. and Brooks, T.R., *Geoecology of Southern Highland Peru*, Boulder, Inst. of Arctic and Alpine Research, Univ. of Colorado, Occasional Paper No. 27, 1978

Bolivia

Crossley, J.C., 'Santa Cruz at the cross-roads; a study of development in eastern Bolivia', *Tijdschrift voor Econ. en Soc. Geografie*, **52** (1971), pp. 197–296 and 230–41

Denevan, W.M., *The aboriginal cultural geography of the Llanos de Mojos of Bolivia*, Berkeley, Univ. of California, Ibero-Americana Series, 1966

Fifer, J.V., *Bolivia: Land, Location and Politics since 1825*, Cambridge Univ. Press, 1972

Hanke, L., *The Imperial City of Potosí*, The Hague, Martinus Nijhoff, 1956

Heath, D.B. *et al.*, *Land Reform and Social Revolution in Bolivia*, New York, Pall Mall Press, 1969

Osborne, H., *Bolivia, a Land Divided*, Oxford Univ. Press, 3rd edn., 1964

Preston, D.A., 'New towns: a major change in the settlement pattern of highland Bolivia', *Journal Lat. Amer. Studies*, **2** (1970), pp. 1–27

Preston, D.A., 'Land tenure and agricultural development in the central Altiplano, Bolivia', Ch. 12, pp. 231–51 in B.S. Hoyle (ed.), *Spatial Aspects of Development*, Chichester, Wiley, 1974

Argentina

Eidt, R.C., 'Japanese agricultural colonization; a new attempt at land opening in Argentina', *Econ. Geog.*, **44** (1968), pp. 1–20

Eidt, R.C., *Pioneer Settlement in Northeast Argentina*, Madison, Univ. of Wisconsin Press, 1971

Ferns, H.S., *Argentina*, Benn, 1969

Jefferson, M., *Peopling the Argentine Pampa*, New York, Amer. Geog. Society, 1926

Morris, A.S., 'The irrigation economy of Mendoza, Argentina', *Annals, A.A.G.*, **59** (1969), pp. 97–115

Morris, A.S., 'The regional problem in Argentine economic development', *Geography*, **57** (1972), pp. 289–306

Morris, A.S., 'The failure of small farmer settlement in Buenos Aires province', *Revista Geográfica*, **85** (1977), pp. 63–77

Scobie, J.R., *Revolution on the Pampas*, Austin, Texas, Univ. of Texas Press

Scobie, J.R., *Argentina: a City and a Nation*, Oxford Univ. Press, 1964

Sternberg, Rolf, 'Occupance of the humid Pampa: 1856–1914', *Revista Geográfica*, **76** (1972), pp. 61–102

Taylor, C.C., *Rural Life in Argentina*, Baton Rouge, La., Louisiana State Univ. Press, 1948

Uruguay

Alisky, M., *Uruguay*, New York, Praeger, 1969

Brannon, R.H., *Uruguay: Portrait of a Democracy*, Allen and Unwin, 1956

Griffin, E., 'Testing the von Thünen theory in Uruguay', *Geog. Review*, **63** (1973), pp. 500–16

Lamas, J. Martinez, *Riqueza y Pobreza del Uruguay*, Montevideo, Palacio del Libro, 1930

Snyder, D.E., 'The metropolitan nodality of Montevideo', *Econ. Geography*, **38** (1962), pp. 95–112

Paraguay

Hopkins, E.A., Crist, R.E. and Snow, W.P., *Paraguay*, New York, American Geographical Society, Occasional Publication No. 2, 1968

Service, Elman R. and Service, Helen S., *Tobati, Paraguayan Town*, Chicago, Univ. of Chicago Press, 1954

Wilhelmy, H. and Rohmeder, W., *Die La Plata-Länder: Argentinien, Paraguay, Uruguay*, Braunschweig, Westermann, 1963

Chile

Butland, G.J., *The Human Geography of Southern Chile*, Inst. Brit. Geographers, Publication No. 24, 1957

CORFO, *Geografía Económica de Chile*, Santiago, Editorial Universitaria, 1965

Cunill, P., *Geografía de Chile*, Santiago, Editorial Universitaria, 2nd edn., 1976

Fried, J. and Bianchi, J., 'Small-scale forestry enterprise in three zones of southern Chile', *Tijdschrift voor Econ. en Soc. Geografie*, **61** (1970), pp. 223–31

Gwynne, R.N., 'Government planning and the location of the motor vehicle industry in Chile', *Tijdschrift voor Econ. en Soc. Geografie*, **69** (1978), pp. 130–40

Jefferies, A., 'Agrarian reform in Chile', *Geography*, **56** (1971), pp. 221–30

Johnson, L.J., 'Problems of import substitution: the Chilean auto industry', *Econ. Devt. and Cult. Change*, **15** (1967), pp. 202–16

Larrain, M.A., 'A Chilean regional development policy', *Latin American Urban Research*, **5** (1975), pp. 143–50

MacBride, G.M., *Chile: Land and Society*, New York, Amer. Geog. Society, 1936

Brazil

Baer, W., *The Development of the Brazilian Steel Industry*, Nashville, Tenn., Vanderbilt Univ. Press, 1969

Bourne, *Assault on the Amazon*, London, Gollancz (1978)

Brooks, R.H., 'Human response to recurrent drought in northeast Brazil', *Professional Geographer*, **23** (1971), pp. 40–44

Brooks, R.H., 'Drought and public policy in Northeast Brazil: alternatives to starvation', *Professional Geographer*, **25** (1973), pp. 338–46

Campbell, G., *Brazil Struggles for Development*, Charles Knight, 1972

Castro, J. de, *Death in the Northeast*, New York, Vintage Books, 1969

Cunha, Euclides de, *Rebellion in the Backlands*, Chicago, Univ. of Chicago Press, 1944

Dickenson, John P., *Brazil: Studies in Industrial Geography*, Folkestone, Dawson, 1978

Dickenson, John P., 'Innovations for regional development in north east Brazil', *Third World Planning Review*, **2**/1 (1980), pp. 57–74

Epstein, D.G., *Brasília, Plan and Reality*, Berkeley, Univ. of California Press, 1973

Freyre, G., *The Masters and the Slaves*, translated by

S. Putnam, New York, Alfred Knopf, 1956

Furneaux, R., *The Amazon*, Hamish Hamilton, 1969

Henshall, J.D., and Momsen, R.P., *A Geography of Brazilian Development*, Bell, 1974

Johnson, A.W., *Sharecroppers of the Sertao*, Stanford, Calif., Stanford Univ. Press, 1971

Katzmann, 'Regional development policy in Brazil: the role of growth poles and development highways in Goias', *Econ. Devt. and Cult. Change*, **24** (1975–76), pp. 75–107

Kleinpenning, J.M.C., 'Objectives and results of the development policy in Northeast Brazil', *Tijdschrift voor Econ. en Soc. Geografie*, **62** (1971), pp. 271–84

Kleinpenning, J.M.G., 'A further evaluation of the policy for the integration of the Amazon Region', *Tijdschrift voor Econ. en Soc. Geografie*, **69** (1978), pp. 78–85

Momsen, R.P., *Brazil, A Giant Stirs*, New York, Van Nostrand, 1968

Sanders, J.H., and Bain, F.L., 'Agricultural development on the Brazilian frontier; southern Mato Grosso', *Econ. Devt. and Cultural Change*, **24** (1975), pp. 593–610

Simonsen, R.C., *História Económica do Brasil 1500–1810*, Sao Paulo, Editôra Nacional, 4th edn., 1962

The Guianas

Auty, R.M., 'Transforming mineral enclaves; Caribbean bauxite in the nineteen-seventies', *Tijdschrift voor Econ. en Soc. Geografie*, **71** (1980), pp. 169–79

Dudler, H.J., Hurst, E., Hardon, M., and Lambert, M.H., 'The economy of Surinam', *International Monetary Fund Staff Papers* Nov. 1971, pp. 668–705

Goslinga, C. Ch., *A short history of the Netherlands Antilles and Surinam*, Martinus Nijhoff, The Hague, 1979

Smith, R.T., *British Guiana*, New York, Oxford University Press, 1962

Strachan, A.J., 'Water control in Guyana', *Geography*, **65**/4 (1980), pp. 297–304

Ecuador

Bromley, R.J., 'Agricultural colonization in the upper Amazon Basin', *Tijdschrift voor Econ. en Soc. Geografie*, **63** (1972), pp. 278–94

Bromley, R.J., *Development and Planning in Ecuador*, Latin Amer. Publications Fund 1977

Collin Delavaud, Anne, 'From colonization to agricultural development: the case of coastal Ecuador', Ch. 5, pp. 67–81, in Preston, D.A., (ed.), *Environment, Society and Rural Change in Latin America*, Chichester, Wiley, 1980

Preston, D.A., 'Negro, Mestizo and Indian in an Andean environment', *Geog. Journal*, **131** (1965), pp. 220–34

Redclift, M.R., and Preston, D.A., 'Agrarian reform and rural change in Ecuador', Ch. 4, pp. 53–63, in Preston, D.A. (ed.), *Environment, Society and Rural Change in Latin America*, Chichester, Wiley, 1980

Zuvekas, C., 'Agrarian reform in Ecuador's Guayas River Basin', *Land Economics*, **52**/3 (1976), pp. 314–29

Colombia

Eidt., R.C., 'Aboriginal Chibcha settlement in Colombia', *Annals A.A.G.*, **49** (1959), pp. 374–92

Hagen, V.W. von, *The Golden Man: the quest for El Dorado*, Farnborough, Saxon House, 1974

McGreevey, W.P., *An Economic History of Colombia, 1845–1930*, Cambridge Univ. Press, 1971

Parsons, J.J., *Antioqueño Colonization in Western Colombia*, Berkeley, Univ. of California Press, Ibero-Americana Series, revised edn. 1968

Posada, A.J., and Posada, J. de, *The C.V.C.; challenge to underdevelopment and traditionalism*, Bogotá, Ediciones Tercer Mundo, 1966

Ridler, Neil B., 'Development through urbanization: a partial evaluation of the Colombian experiment', *International Journal of Urban and Regional Research*, **3**/1 (1979), pp. 49–59

Stokes, C.J., 'The freight transport system of Colombia, 1959', *Econ. Geography*, **43** (1967), pp. 71–90

West, R.C., *The Pacific Lowlands of Colombia*, Baton Rouge, La., Louisiana State Univ. Press, 1957

Venezuela

Eden, M.J., 'Irrigation systems and the development of peasant agriculture in Venezuela', *Tijdschrift voor Econ. en Soc. Geografie*, **65** (1974), pp. 48–54

Eidt, Robert C., 'Agrarian reform and the growth of new rural settlements in Venezuela', *Erdkunde*, **29**/2 (1975), pp. 118–33

Friedmann, J., *Regional Development Policy: a Case study of Venezuela*, Cambridge, Mass, MIT, 1966

Levy, D.F., *Economic Planning in Venezuela*, New York, Praeger, 1968

Lynch, E., 'Propositions for planning new towns in Venezuela', *Journal of Developing Areas*, **7** (1973)

Penfold, A., 'Caracas: urban growth and transportation', *Town Planning Review*, **41** (1970), pp. 103–20

Rodwin, L. and associates, *Planning urban growth and regional development: the experience of the Guayana program of Venezuela*, Cambridge, Mass., MIT, 1969

Turner, A. and Smulian J., 'New cities in Venezuela', *Town Planning Review*, **42** (1971), pp. 3–27

National and regional development

Brookfield, H., *Interdependent Development*, Methuen, 1975

Conroy, M.E., 'Rejection of growth center strategy in Latin American regional development planning', *Land Economics*, **49**/4 (1973), pp. 371–80

Frank, A.G., *Latin America: Underdevelopment or Revolution*, New York, Monthly Review Press, 1969

Friedmann, J. and Weaver, C., *Territory and Function: the Evolution of Regional Planning*, Edward Arnold, London 1979

Furtado, C., *Economic Development of Latin America*, Cambridge, Cambridge Univ. Press, 1970

Gilbert, A., *Latin American Development: a Geographical Perspective*, Penguin, 1974

Gilbert, A., 'The state and regional income disparity in Latin America', *Bulletin, Society for Latin American Sutdies*, No. 29 (1978), pp. 5–30

Griffin, K., *Underdevelopment in Spanish America*, Allen and Unwin, 1969

Hill, A. David, *Latin American Development Issues*, C.L.A.G., No. 3, Muncie, Ind., Ball State Univ., 1971

Holland, S., *The Regional Problem*, Macmillan, London 1976

Morris, A.S., 'The Argentine Colorado — Inter-provincial rivalries over water resources', *Scottish Geog. Magazine*, **94** (1978), pp. 169–80

Morris, A.S., *Regional Development and Differentiation in Latin America*, Hutchinson, 1981

Nisbet, C. (ed.), *Latin America: Problems in Economic Development*, New York, Free Press, 1969

Pedersen, P.O., *Urban-Regional Development in South America: a Process of Diffusion and Integration*, UNRISD Regional Planning Series Vol 10, The Hague, Mouton, 1975

Prebisch, R., *Change and Development: Latin America's Great Task*, New York, Praeger, 1971

Richardson, H.W. 'The relevance of growth centre strategies to Latin America', *Econ. Geography*, **51** (1975), pp. 163–78

Slater, D., 'Underdevelopment and spatial inequality; approaches to the problems of regional planning in the Third World', *Progress in Planning*, **4**/2 (1975), pp. 97–167

Urquidi, V.L. and Thorp, R. (eds.), *Latin America in the International Economy*, Macmillan, 1973

Wionczek, M.S. (ed.), *Latin American Economic Integration*, New York, Praeger, 1966

Index